History's Erratics

THE WORKING CLASS
IN AMERICAN HISTORY

Editorial Advisors
James R. Barrett, Thavolia Glymph, Julie Greene,
William P. Jones, and Nelson Lichtenstein

*For a list of books in the series, please see
our website at www.press.uillinois.edu.*

History's Erratics

Irish Catholic Dissidents
and the Transformation of
American Capitalism, 1870–1930

DAVID M. EMMONS

UNIVERSITY OF
ILLINOIS PRESS
Urbana, Chicago, and Springfield

© 2024 by the Board of Trustees
of the University of Illinois
All rights reserved
1 2 3 4 5 C P 5 4 3 2 1
∞ This book is printed on acid-free paper.

Library of Congress Cataloging-in-Publication Data

Names: Emmons, David M., author.
Title: History's erratics : Irish Catholic dissidents and the
  transformation of American capitalism, 1870–1930 / David
  M. Emmons.
Other titles: Irish Catholic dissidents and the transformation of
  American capitalism, 1870–1930
Description: Urbana : University of Illinois Press, [2024] |
  Series: The working class in American history | Includes
  bibliographical references and index.
Identifiers: LCCN 2024008359 (print) | LCCN 2024008360
  (ebook) | ISBN 9780252046094 (cloth) | ISBN
  9780252088193 (paperback) | ISBN 9780252047312 (ebook)
Subjects: LCSH: Irish Americans—Economic conditions. |
  Irish—United States—History. | Catholics—United States—
  History. | Working class—United States—History. | Labor
  movement—United States—History. | Capitalism—United
  States—History. | Radicalism—Religious aspects—Catholic
  Church. | United States—Economic conditions—1865–1918. |
  United States—Economic conditions—1918–1945.
Classification: LCC E184.I6 E46 2024 (print) | LCC E184.I6
  (ebook) | DDC 973.04916/2—dc23/eng/20240314
LC record available at https://lccn.loc.gov/2024008359
LC ebook record available at https://lccn.loc.gov/2024008360

For Ann and Mari, Ireland 1977

Contents

Acknowledgments ix

Introduction: The Characteristics of an
Erratic Culture 1

1 "Ancestral Sorrows": The Making of an
Irish Catholic Culture 21

2 "And a Fourth There Is Who Wants Me to Dig":
Patsy Caliban and the Limits of American Liberalism 53

3 A Transnational "Freemasonry of the Disinherited":
The Premaking of an Oppositional Irish American
Working Class 85

4 An Irish Catholic Working Class:
The Butte "Rising" of 1917 115

5 Celtic Communists: "The Irish Contingent"
among America's Radicals 147

6 A "People Very Unlike Any Other People":
The Irish Catholic Challenge to
American Capitalism 177

7 "The Irish Movement Has Forgotten to
Be American": Woodrow Wilson and the
Transatlantic Great Red Green Scare 211

Epilogue. The Durability of Culture:
The Erratic '20s..245
Notes 271
Bibliography...309
Index 327

Acknowledgments

This book is an extension of work begun in the 1980s. It is the concluding chapter in a trilogy. I acknowledge again the help I received from hundreds of people and institutions in the preparation of the first two books to appear in it. I hope that all of those many hundreds know my gratitude to them.

There are, however, a few who were involved only in this third volume, as well as some whose contribution to it or to the whole trilogy was especially meaningful.

I want first to thank Alison Syring, my editor at the University of Illinois Press. She answered what must have been a confusing voice message from me that set this whole project in motion. From that first contact, she has been a model of professionalism, patience, and good humor. I cannot imagine having a better editor.

Alan Noonan, an Irishman in America, and a fine young historian of others in that same category, shared with me his ideas about his misplaced countrymen. He also, out of respect for my age, allowed me to beat him occasionally in handball. Ken Egan, a University of Montana colleague and historian, read an early draft of the manuscript. His comments made it and all the drafts that followed it better. I would like also to thank the two anonymous referees, particularly the mysterious R1 who brought Raymond Williams and Dorothy Thompson back to my attention.

No one did more to jump-start this three-part project than Kerby Miller. He's also a major player in my finishing it. My reference is not just to his splendid scholarship but to his remarkable generosity. He has shared with me hundreds of the Irish letters he gathered, not to mention selected items of his research notes in which he knew I'd have an interest. The academic world in general is a sharing one. Kerby has established a new and very high bar.

The last time I was with Kerby was at a wonderful conference hosted by the Canadian Association of Irish Studies. He had invited me to join a panel consisting of himself, Brendán Mac Suibhne, and David Wilson, then told me not to miss the conference's final dinner. He's a wise man. Let me here thank Brendán and David and the entire CAIS for their company and for their good ideas about how to deal with erratics—of sundry sorts.

Speaking of goods hosts, I must also thank Joe Lee and Cormac O'Malley and the Glucksman Ireland House at NYU for two invitations to come to New York, first to give the Ernie O'Malley Lecture, then, a few years later, to participate in the conference on Modern Ireland and Revolution.

I had other kind invitations to speak that I wish to acknowledge: To Tony Bucher, Pat and Ute Goggins, and Maureen Barry of the Irish Literary and Historical Society of San Francisco for the gracious hosts they were during my visit and talk before the society. Caleb Richardson invited me to give the annual Mary Power Lecture at the University of New Mexico; it was a wonderful opportunity to talk with Caleb and others about the fissiparous Irish. I had another chance to do the same when Ryan Dye asked me to give the Larry McCaffrey Lecture at St. Ambrose and then served as tour guide along the Mississippi River.

My very special thanks go out to Aideen Doherty and the Donegal County Council for their invitation to speak before the Donegal Diaspora Project in Letterkenny. While I was there, Joe Gallagher provided fine company and took me and my wife to parts of Donegal known only to the lucky ones who live there. It was also during my time in Letterkenny that I met Anthony Doogan, who shared with me the immigrant letters of his grandfather and great uncles.

I have also some debts only indirectly academic. My thanks to Sam and Julie Baldridge for being great friends, and for a grant from the University of Montana's Baldridge Fund in support of this book. I wish also to express my appreciation to the Butte/Silver Bow Archives and the people of that wondrous city; to handball players everywhere, a crowd that includes Sam, Alan the Noonan, and—as I was to learn—Frank Walsh. Knowing that about Walsh made me like him even more than I already did.

Finally, there is no way for me to give adequate thanks to my dear wife Caroline and to our children. They put up with me and my erratic friends longer than they should have had to. Neighborhoods out of place and out of time are hard places to visit. I took them with me anyway. I'm pleased, however, to be able to report that Caroline, Mike, Mari, Ann, and John share my gratitude to those erratic sorts for all that they did to soften the harder edges of American capitalism and make it more just.

History's Erratics

INTRODUCTION

The Characteristics of an Erratic Culture

> [In] "the Irish understanding of actuality. . . . The dead are almost closer to us . . . than the living and things like 'miracles' seem to fit into life like toast and cream"
> —Ernie O'Malley, letter, 1935

This is a book about cultural divergence, specifically, the mismatch of values between Protestant Americans and working-class Catholic Irish, two self-identified collections of people who, more by accident than intent, found themselves sharing the national home of the first named of them. They did not share it equally. Culturally and politically, the place belonged to those who got to it first and claimed it for themselves. They were the Natives. The Catholic Irish were the Strangers in this historical set piece, admitted to America only on the sufferance of the Natives who owned it. Of course, the American "natives" were themselves once invading and colonizing "strangers." They appropriated the title of Native. No matter; the Irish were just visitors.

The first Anglo Protestants who came to this New World did not just claim it for themselves; they imprinted it with their culture. They claimed it in the name of Protestantism and of the God who had led them to this sanctuary, an ocean distant from the Old World's maledictions. Popery was the first among them. The American views of Irish Catholics were an inheritance from the English, leftovers of the Cromwellian Reformation and the Cromwellian conquest. Americans conflated the two—as Cromwell had: The Irish were a flawed people of a false faith. The one reenforced and confirmed the other. There was no reason to distinguish between them, and Americans seldom did. I will signal that close association by a neologism: In America, they were IrishCatholics, political fifth-columnists as well as social, moral, and racial outcasts. The doctrines of their church, as Americans understood them—which was at best imperfectly—were antithetical to Americans' self-identity, to freedom and democracy, to political stability, even to personal salvation. Anti-Catholicism is implied in nearly everything that follows; its presence may be presumed.[1]

The Catholic Irish relationship with their new American world was not a proprietary one. They were citizens, to be sure, but citizens of a different race and of alien, even culturally seditious, ideas and habits. In 1857, the New Englander George Templeton Strong commented that Irish Catholics were "as remote from us in temperament and constitution as the Chinese." The Irish writer Luke Gibbons wrote of the "otherness of Irish Catholicism" and of its "ineradicable ethnic component." The Irish-Australian historian Oliver MacDonagh used the same theoretically appropriate language: The Irish were America's Occidental Orientals—a term clearly used in the context of cultural and racial "Otherness." Irish Catholic "values," MacDonagh went on, the standards they used in "judging men and things," were "altogether alien to the Yankee." Divergence can be stretched no further than that.[2]

I needed a shorthand title for these cultural outsiders, a way to make the cultural divide between Catholic Irish and America literally memorable. If that title could also indicate the origins of their cultural heterodoxy, so very much the better. IrishCatholic serves a variety of purposes—but not this one. John Lewis Gaddis in his *The Landscape of History* didn't provide me with a label, but he told me where to look for one. He writes that "science, history, and art have something in common: they all depend on metaphor." Metaphors, Gaddis goes on, "help historians think ... and [they] have every reason to rely on them and use them unashamedly." After all, "they need all the help [they] can get."[3]

And so, without shame and because it helps, I offer a metaphor of my own. Like many in immigration history, I take it from the sciences, not botany as is common, but geology—petrology, to be exact. Petrologists study the makeup of rocks; they know the rocks' characteristics—their culture, if you will. Petrologists develop taxonomies of rocks; they study where those of each sort are found in nature; they know what external forces can relocate and transform them over time. Principal among those external forces are glaciers. They move rocks from their native ground to places both distant and different. When the glaciers retreat, the rocks—many of them quite huge, others scarcely more than pebbles—stay where they were tumbled and left.

These abandoned and orphaned ones are called *glacial erratics*. Petrologists are to be praised; that itself is an inspired metaphor. A few of these erratics sit alone, the only ones of their kind in the vicinity. Far more often, there's a collection of them, all from the same point of origin. They stand out because, though they are still demonstrably rocks, they're rocks of a different order and unlike the rocks all around them. They don't belong where they are; they are strangers, not native to the place. I could have called IrishCatholics America's contrarians, dissidents, dissenters, a people ill-fitted, mismatched, and misaligned. Now I have a better name for them, one that can be made cultural or political or both. They were erratics—a people out of time and out of place. Even the Latin root of erratic applies; the word comes from *errare*, to wander, from which also comes *errant*, as in rowdy and badly behaved. That too sounded about right.

Divergence, however, and by definition, is two-sided. What of American values and American standards for judging men and things? We know what American Natives thought of Irish Catholic Strangers. Their negative feelings on that topic were made abundantly clear. Strong intended no compliment to either the Irish or the Chinese when he said that there was a vast cultural divide between Americans and both of those sets of Orientals. The story of American nativism and anti-Catholicism is a testament to cultural and racial division. We know what Americans thought of Irish Catholics. There was no effort, however, at the time or later by historians, to ask what Irish Catholics thought of America. This book is an effort to reverse that usual order of things and ask.

But first, this partial and unenthusiastic defense of American anti-Catholicism, Strong's included, is in order: It can be too easy to dismiss the attacks on Catholicism, and on the Irish whose faith it was, as nothing more than blind and unreasoning prejudice. In fact, there were good, or at least not bad, reasons why Protestant American Natives distrusted and feared Catholic Irish Strangers. Pope Pius IX's 1864 Syllabus of Errors cannot be reconciled with Lincoln's 1863 Gettysburg Address. But, viewed as Irish Catholics did—and that is the perspective here—nothing that Lincoln said at Gettysburg, or Jefferson in the Declaration of Independence, or in the Americans' definition of democracy generally, addressed the communal values of Irish Catholics. The values of each confronted and contradicted those of the other.

My focus, as just noted, is less on the disfavor in which Americans held Irish Catholics and more on what Irish Catholics thought of America. Which leads to another and related reversal of the usual order: We know that coming to America changed Irish Catholics; how much it changed them can be debated—and I will—but more important is the largely unexamined issue of how Irish Catholics changed America. There were a great many Catholic Irish who did not, or could not, fully assimilate to America. That includes those who—*as Irish*—didn't even like America very much. I'll also have room for the indeterminant number of them who—again, *as Irish*—didn't like it at all. I have assigned them to three categories, ranked by degrees of divergence: the uncomprehending, the vaguely adversarial, and the rebellious. Regardless of where placed on that sliding scale, dissent always involves a challenge to prevailing values. In this instance, that meant to translate American society into Irish and render it fair.

Given the imbalance of power between Catholic Irish strangers and Protestant American natives, that translation would be halting, selective, and incomplete. It would also, however, over time, be perceptible. Its effects were felt in every aspect of American life, political, social, and economic. I chose the word *capitalism* for my subtitle because capitalism was—and is—more than simply a description of an economic system. It arises out of and comes finally to comprise a set of moral principles; capitalism is a psychology, a philosophy, a culture. I mean it in all those ways. "Capitalist system" is my ultimate catch-all phrase. I could have chosen *democracy* for that purpose, but capitalism takes in far more ground—including democracy. In fact, by IrishCatholic accounting, its values contradicted democracy's. That was a major reason for their challenge to it.

The Catholic Irish did not undo capitalism, but they were witnesses to the many expressed disapprovals of it and of the fundamental moral values that underlay it. And there were a great many times when the disapproval came from IrishCatholics and in the name of Irish Catholicism. It's worth listening to their nonconforming voices. There is more to be learned about America from those who didn't share and defied—or didn't understand and ignored—America's beliefs about itself, both its Protestant creation story and the triumphalist Protestant narratives that followed from it. What the Catholic Irish thought about America transformed America. That needs to be added to my previously identified reversals of the usual narrative. Call it a reinterpretation by accretion.

I will refer to these dissident Irish by religion and by race/ethnicity; religion because theirs was noteworthy if not notorious, ethnicity because their Irishness, as Gibbons said, was inextricable from their Catholicism. But I've added a third category, a third marker identifying the men and women whom I have chosen as my topic. The vast majority were not just Catholic by religion and Irish by race. They were also overwhelmingly part of America's working class and as aware of that as they were of the other two interdependent variables that went into their identities. I do place working class slightly to the side of race and religion; for most Irish immigrants, it had to be learned; they were not born to it. Their daughters and sons were, but even they joined Irish and Catholic to it, harmoniously for the most part.[4]

Here's another point when reinterpretation by accretion applies: The congruence of their ethnic and social-class identities did not arise solely because working for wages was what Irish Catholics did in America. That's an argument from correlation and coincidence. A major part of this reinterpretation by addition is my contention that the factors that produced that association of identities went deeper than the fact that most of the Catholic Irish in America were in or on the side of the working class. As the distinguished Irish literary critic Declan Kiberd wrote in his *Inventing Ireland*, there was an "old truism that in Ireland 'socialism' never stood for much more than a fundamental goodness of heart." Socialism was not, of course, the only available working-class challenge to capitalism but, for present purposes, it may be allowed to stand for all the rest.[5]

In that context, socialism may also have stood for a well-developed survival skill; favors done were favors returned and the Irish had few other than themselves doing them any favors. I prefer to think that goodness of heart takes in both. There are a lot of truisms in Ireland, but the one Kiberd recalled captures perfectly the point I'm trying to make. Goodness of heart was an *old* truism; survival was an *old* issue. They antedated the Irish immigration to America by centuries. Accretion will also include giving far more attention to Ireland and the Irish *before* they left it for America than is commonly the case in immigration history. Becoming part of the American working class brought out their goodness of heart, but it did not create it. The Catholic Irish were the friends of labor before they were laborers. They were born to the role.

Irish and working-class issues and identities were sewn together as on a seam. They were separate but tightly joined. The Irish saw themselves as a subject people, the collateral damage of imperialism. That was a political issue. Workers, Irish Catholics prominently among them, saw themselves as a subject class, the collateral damage of capitalism. That was a social and economic issue. Americans divided the two. IrishCatholics did not, for the ones who are the focus here, Ireland Free meant Ireland Fair—fair to labor was part of that. Let the two causes be pursued simultaneously. Indeed, let them be the same cause.

• • •

All of the preceding presupposes the existence of an IrishCatholic culture, a set of beliefs and principles that gave order to their lives. Taking this cultural turn obliges me to discuss what, as a general category, is meant by culture. I begin with Raymond Williams. Like many, I consulted on Irish topics, Williams does not deal with Irish Catholics specifically; they are present in his account only by inference and on my assignment. In his influential *Culture and Society*, Williams writes that "culture" is "one of the two or three most complicated words in the English language." It is "a thing in itself," which gives it a kind of strand-alone and elevated status.[6]

But what kind of a complicated thing? For this, I enlist the help of Terry Eagleton and his recent *Culture*, a book he hopes "perspicacious readers will note . . . has an Irish motif." The Irish are only briefly present—but this time they are on the author's assignment. With a bow to Williams, Eagleton lists the four senses in which the word *culture* is used. The first is to indicate a "body of artistic or intellectual work"; the second is to signify a "process of spiritual and intellectual development"; the third is to enumerate and define the "values, customs, beliefs, and symbolic practices by which men and women live"; the fourth is to describe "a whole way of life," to which Williams had added, "material, intellectual, and spiritual."[7]

Cultural values are well and deeply entrenched; they "exist in a semi-inchoate form ... the vast repository of instincts, prejudices, pieties, sentiments, half-formed opinions and spontaneous assumptions." Emotions, almost without number, must be added to that repository: love, hate, envy, bitterness, resentment, anger, fear. Taken together, they form what Eagleton calls the "the untotalisable content in which our speech and behaviour acquire their sense." Cultures provide a "model of how to live, a form of self-fashioning or self-realisation, ... the life form of a whole people." They are the "social unconscious" of a people. ... too close to the eyeball to be fully objectified." Cultures contain multitudes.[8]

"Social unconscious" is a wonderfully description phrase. It establishes that culture is a part of social reality. It then detaches it from the day-to-day aspects of that reality by pointing out that even those whose culture it is are unaware of what's in it until something external to them brings it to consciousness. A people may be unconscious, even oblivious, of the operation of their culture, but they are intensely engaged in the operation of their society and politics; the Irish, British, and American people certainly were. So are historians of Ireland and the Irish people wherever found. Eagleton accommodates us by joining the two: Culture, "is not [only] a medium of power. It can also be a "critique of the present," even a "medium of resistance." Cultural values and "symbolic practices" provide the ultimate test of what is politically acceptable, even politically righteous. "Not everything in culture is ideological, though everything in it *might become so*." It would definitely become so in Ireland and in Irish America.[9]

Cultures distinguished one "nation, region, social class or ethnic group" from all the others. Cultural differences were duly noted by each of those self-identified assemblages of people and in Eagleton's masterful understatement, a "degree of suspicion" of those not of the group set in. Often, so did a warlike spirit. The loaded language of otherness arose from those suspicions, words like *foreign, alien, stranger, outlander*. It distinguished the Irish nation from the English nation, the Irish people from the American people, Catholics from Protestants, the working classes from the middle and upper classes. Cultural divergence can have a sharp ideological edge to it. There are Irish—and American—notes strung out through all of that.[10]

As there are, or can be made to be, Irish and American notes when Eagleton quotes Edmund Burke—approvingly, I should add: "To make us love our country, our country ought to be loveable." To make the Irish love being in the British Empire, the Empire had to be lovable. It wasn't; in no small part because the ostensibly *United* Kingdom was not that. The Irish didn't fit it. For Irish Americans to love America, America had to be lovable. It wasn't, and for the same reason of Irish cultural otherness. Eagleton makes the general point: "Politics," to be effective, "must be embedded in . . . culture." A wise government must not traduce, ignore, or allow itself to be totally separated from and intensely hostile toward the "spiritual foundation" of those it presumes to govern. That's an inherently historical thing to say, largely because it brings power relationships and politics back into the discussion. It is at this point that Eagleton turns his Irish motif into something Irish-specific. "It is thus that a history of injustice and inequality, of Protestant supremacy and Catholic subjugation, [was] converted into a . . . question of alternative cultural identities."[11]

• • •

Kevin Kenny, in a 2003 article, said that Irish immigrants who came to America brought with them "diasporic sensibilities" that arose, I think he would agree, from the immigrants' culture. Those cultural sensibilities then confronted the "power of the American national-state" and became the basis of the "transnational" Irish-Americans, a people whose culture was unlike that of either of the two component parts of their hybridized identity. I will occasionally follow Kenny's lead and use the nonaligned word *sensibilities*. It's succinct. It is also, however, imprecise—as Kenny may have intended.[12]

A people's self-identity, however, cannot be summed up by something as scanty and unsubstantial as sensibilities. In that interest, I offer this definition; its synonymity with sensibilities I take as a given. I found it in a 1913 dictionary: Sensibilities are "the inner, non-rational receptors that filter experiences"; they are the "receptivity of [the] soul." I like every part of that definition. The allusions to "non-rational" and the "soul" are crucial, almost prescient. They are a perfect fit for Catholic Irish, a people for whom the nonrational was central to reality, and who soul-filtered experiences more than most. Terry Eagleton called those filtering receptors "obligations written in the heart." R. H. Tawney went further: "Culture is not an assortment of aesthetic sugar-plums for fastidious palates, but an energy of the soul." Perhaps they had the same dictionary I do.[13]

But what made Irish culture? Not the differences between it and the American but the simple fact of it? Let me begin with a short aside on what did not. Irish Catholic culture—or Irish Catholic anything else—was not a racial, as in a "blooded," inheritance. To say that it was—and many between 1870 and 1930 did—was to defer to what the social economist Karl Polanyi called "zoological determinism." Being of the Irish race doesn't explain anything. Being thought inferior because of being of the Irish race was a different matter. So was the strongly held English and American belief that

Catholicism was an inferior, an inauthentic, religious faith. Facing the racial and religious prejudice of the English and American people was a part of the Irish's history. And that explains a great deal.[14]

Their past as lived and as recorded—historicism without the theoretical trappings that sometimes accompany it—accounted for that vast repository of semi-inchoate Irish cultural forms. When History is made up, I will capitalize the word; I will do the same for the invented Past. When the words are meant to convey a reality, I will leave them in lowercase, but always with this appended truth: The Past is part of the past; History is part of history. The ethnologist Greg Dening wrote this: "History . . . is "our past . . . transformed, translated, interpreted, encapsulated. . . . [It] *suffuses our presents*." Raymond Williams said that he "could hope to understand . . . [culture and] society . . . [only] through . . . history which had *delivered* this strange, unsettling . . . world to us." Conrad Arensberg, who wrote most about the Irish Catholic peasantry, said that "cultural patterns . . . emerge as historical events." Eagleton offers this drumbeat of agreement: "The unconscious of a culture is . . . an effect of its historicity"; culture is "organic, not of our own making." It is of history's making. "It is history . . . that converts politics into that second nature we call culture." Cultures "are free standing . . . resting on . . . [among other things] the march of history." And finally this: "culture . . . is an experiential affair."[15]

All that happened to them, as remembered, misremembered, and passed down, was imprinted in the Irish's collective memory. It is important here to recall Dening's words just quoted: History is our past "transformed and translated." The inaccuracy of much of that transformation and translation may be assumed. The Past is created. Myths arise. But they are as much a part of the past that suffused the Irish Catholic present as objective truths. There is nothing uniquely Irish about that. The same can be said of all cultures; they emerge out of and take their "untotalizable content" from what a people remember of their past. W. B. Yeats once wrote of Ireland's "ancestral sorrows." He didn't say what they were or if the memories of them were true. He didn't have to. The Irish knew what had happened to them—or thought they did. What else but history could account for the "receptivity of the Irish soul"?

History, as interpreted, made the Irish what they were; then, as if it had not done mischief enough, it put them on the road toward America, a place run by people who had no liking for them and no interest in their ancestral sorrows—which included having to leave Ireland. Americans were avowed mind-filterers; *enlightened* would have been their word for it. The nonrational for them was very nearly the same thing as the irrational. They had only truths arising out of reason. That was an invention, one of the foundational myths Americans told themselves about themselves. It was also a part of their cultural inheritance from Anglo-Saxon and Protestant England.[16]

When the occasion calls for it—and it frequently will—I'll append "Anglo-" to America and Americans. I do not use the "Anglo-" modifier to express an official bilateral alliance between two former rivals; "Anglo-America" refers to something far more basic. It signifies a family reunion, a racial and sectarian lovefest. It began at the time of the first colonial settlements and—notwithstanding the Revolution and other various fallings-out after that—it never ended. Anglo-America is meant to signify a collectively held set of religious and racial ideas and values, a hybrid transatlantic nation of same-believers complete with Protestant Anglo-Saxon "race patriots"— with religion as race's implied coefficient—who were the guardians of those beliefs. It is expressive of shared principles, not shared interests.[17]

Philip Bagenal, a Protestant Anglo-Irish barrister of some distinction, was one of those race patriots. In 1882, he wrote a book about the Irish in America. In it he said that rebel Ireland had been exported intact to America. That could not end well. Americans "had inherited from their ancestors the national English contempt" for the Catholic Irish. Like the Occidental Orientals they were, the Irish response to the contempt in which Anglo-Americans held them was to "persist . . . in keeping up their distinctiveness of race and religion in a manner antagonistic to the great mass of the American people." It doesn't excuse his prejudices, but Bagenal was right on both counts.[18]

Bagenal's conflation of British and American racial attitudes is why I do not deal with the Protestant immigrants from Ireland, the self-styled Scotch-Irish, their Anglo-Saxon and Protestant bona fides intact. As Sean Connolly put it in his recent *On Every Tide*, Protestant Irish "were far more likely . . . to be quietly absorbed into the mainstream [American] culture." I find it fascinating that David Hackett Fischer, in his *Albion's Seed: Four British Folkways in America*, includes the "northeast of Ireland," but no other part of the island, among the four sources of America's inherited folkways. Albion was Protestant. Religious ways were folkways, so the Ulster Protestants had to be counted. Ireland outside the northeast was Hibernian; it along with its seed, was papist. The folkways were as divergent as the cultures.[19]

I hasten to add that I am not arguing that the only real Irish were the Catholic ones; I do not deny the Irishness of the Protestants; I do not dispute the importance of their immigration. But this is an American story, and in America the "No Irish Need Apply" notices contained an implied denominational adjective. The Protestant Irish were for the most part right at home in America, never more so than when they were among its anti-Catholic nativists. All of which is to say, I didn't pick this fight. I have left the Protestants out because my historical actors, the English, Irish, and American people, did. I have no choice but to take what they have given me, a historical reality in which there were large differences between how Irish of diverse and rival faiths were perceived and treated in America. From large differences in history come large differences in sensibilities.

I need at this point to situate myself as observer with those I am observing. Recall George Templeton Strong's comment that Irish Catholics were "as remote from us in temperament and constitution as the Chinese." I'm not sure what Strong meant by "constitution," but it certainly sounds racialized. Being temperamentally remote is easier to decrypt. I take it to mean culturally divergent. Eliminate his bigotry and I agree with Strong: the Irish were different, as in culturally distant from Anglo-Americans. Strong's racism led him to think that. But what led me to think the same?[20]

I have been studying the history of Irish Catholics in America for more than thirty years; the history of Americans generally for more than that. My focus was always on the immigrants and ethnics in the American working class, with particular attention to the striking cultural differences that I found between Catholic workers, particularly the Irish, and everyone else. I was in the History Department at the University of Montana in Missoula. Butte, Montana, the world's greatest hard rock mining city, was 120 miles away. It called itself the "richest hill on earth." I was next door to it. For a historian from a working-class background interested in immigration, labor, and cultural differences, finding—or being found by—the Irish Catholic miners of Butte was like stumbling into Aladdin's Cave.

In his great book, *The Making of the English Working Class*, E. P. Thompson said there was a specific "structure of feeling to working-class neighborhoods." He took that idea in part from Raymond Williams, another British (Welsh) historian whose distinctly leftist politics matched Thompson's own. Both meant far more by "neighborhood" than a geographically bounded area of a city or town. A neighborhood is a social organism, a human community held together by shared cultural values, people living what Williams called "common lives." It was where "friends" were, even those one didn't like. I will use the words *friends* and *neighborhood* in that much wider context.[21]

Butte, the entirety of the place, was essentially a gigantic working-class neighborhood, and its culture reflected that. It *felt* working-class. Butte was also, however, a gigantic Irish Catholic neighborhood and its culture reflected that too. It *felt* Irish and Catholic—and IrishCatholic. The two cultures, one social class, the other ethnic[/religious], suffused and determined the culture of the whole. I've been trying to figure out the relationship between those two structures of feeling for the entire thirty-five years I've been studying working-class Irish Catholics in America. Which was the privileged allegiance and did there have to be one? Which of those two presumably independent variables, was the "false consciousness"? Was the relationship between class and ethnicity dialectical or conflictive? Aladdin's Cave, I was learning, had some unexpected things in it.

The wonderful Irish writer Seamus Deane helped me sort them out. In his book *Strange Country*, Deane wrote that "competing loyalties," local, political, ideological, confirm "the . . . unity of Irishness by the fissiparous nature" of being Irish. "For what could be more Irish than the tendency to split into factions? Factions . . . confirm the unity they appear to deny." To agree on what being Irish meant was to cease to be Irish. Strange country, indeed. But the same could be—and has been—said of labor movements, America's included. Were working classes not at least as "fissiparous" as the Irish? Conflicts internal to Irishness and internal to the working class often matched in recrimination and fervor the fights with those outside and hostile to either or both. Trying to decide which was the dominant allegiance of Irish Catholic workers foundered on the fact that the "true" nature of ethnic and working-class identities were themselves indeterminate.[22]

One thing, however, remained constant: Irish Catholics were out of time and out of place in the modern world, of which America and Britain were the lodestars. That was less true in a place like Butte, but speaking generally now, modernity did not fit them. Deane mentions modernity's "lack of historical sense, its refusal of habitual practices, its disabling tendency to abstraction, its aesthetic of distance, and its global pretensions." If that's too Irish a reading, here is Jackson Lears's: He spoke of modernity's "evasive banality, . . . spiritual sterility, . . . self-absorption, . . . its crackpot obsession with efficiency, its humanist hubris, its complacent creed of progress." The erratic Irish were both uncomprehending and critical of that modern world and of the capitalist values that guided it. Moderns looked forward; the Irish looked backward. But, as Jackson Lears has shown, "the most powerful critics of capitalism have often looked backward not forward."[23]

That does not make oracles of Irish Catholics. Neither does it make political insurgents of them. They were critics, not bomb-throwers. They wished to see the system transformed, not dismantled and replaced by something even more alien to them. It was enough just to translate it into Irish and made a place of fundamental goodness of heart. Had my topic been Irish radicals—the Irish equivalent of, say, Tony Michaels's edited volume, *Jewish Radicals* or Alain Brossat's *Revolutionary Yiddishland*—I would have left the petrologists at peace and called it "Catholic Irish Radicals in America." It was Irish erraticism, not Irish radicalism, that made up the composite culture, the structure of feeling, of Irish Catholic working-class worlds.

There is another phrase that signifies what I mean by composite culture. Once again, I conscript the service of another historian—this one without even a hint of an Irish motif. John Lewis Gaddis not only urged historians to find metaphors to "help them think," he provided them with thoughtful counsel about how to deal with something as complicated as culture. "There is a balance," Gaddis writes, "between [the] universal . . . and [the] particular"—between what Eagleton called a "spurious universalism" and specific historical experiences and the cultures that derive from them. Gaddis goes on: "There's little room here for the belief in independent variables or in the superiority of reductionism as a mode of inquiry." I would cite pitting class against ethnicity as an example. "Rather, everything is interdependent: a peoples' collective *"personality becomes ecology."* (The italics are Gaddis's and entirely warranted.) That is an ideal addition to my word pantry of synonyms for cultural sensibilities.[24]

What better metaphor than ecology to define human cultures? Setting aside the ideological context of his remarks, Friedrich Engels stated clearly what Gaddis meant: "there is an *interaction* of ... elements ... an endless *host* of ... things ... whose *inner connection* is remote." The inner connectedness of cultural elements is definitional. There is no culture without it. Finding how the untotalizable connect, the balance and ecological oneness of specific cultural ecosystems, writes Gaddis, is "what [historians] mean by being well-rounded. It's what keeps us sane." In the complicated world of "mapping the [landscapes of the] past,"—the metaphorical subtitle for Gaddis's wonderful book—sanity is greatly to be prized.[25]

• • •

Which leads to the historical context in which the divergent cultures played out. Between 1870 and 1930, most of America would have said that the Irish-Catholics were not purposefully wayward; purpose required agency, and they didn't possess any. They couldn't help themselves; their race/religion made them what they were. That certainly uncomplicated things. We give different and more complex answers now. Using Gaddis's perfect metaphor, IrishCatholics and Anglo-Americans had different and incompatible cultural ecologies; their collective personalities were ill matched. But why and in what ways?

As Herbert Gutman and other American labor historians after him have shown, many of the immigrants to an industrializing and industrial America came from preindustrial cultures. They had to be taught the pace and rhythm of industrial life. IrishCatholics were conspicuous among them. So were their American-born children. But to be preindustrial was to be premodern as well. Of all the explanations for their erraticism, being socially unprepared is the simplest and the most common. They had not had the opportunity to rehearse. Catholic Irish were social and cultural recidivists doing the bidding of their dead. They were what they had long been, out of time and out of place. Nostalgia was their dominant outlook. They would have to be taught what the modern world required of them. The lessons would be painful.[26]

From that perspective, premodern is not a bad description of them. I have a problem only with the way the word was used. Modernity, in its neutral guise, can mean contemporaneity, the present moment. That wasn't the context in capitalist America. It didn't just mean "now"; it was evaluative. It meant civilized. Premodern was a word of reproach. Premodern, however, doesn't exist in a morally neutral state; it describes a people in the process of becoming. Let *traditional* replace it. Traditional was an active state of being. It defined what a people were, not what they were not, but one remote and lucky day, might be. Traditionalism is not about people in the process of becoming; it is about people as they were and preferred to remain. From an Irish Catholic perspective—which is the one in play here—they weren't premodern; Anglo-Americans were antitraditional. From such discrepancies come cultural divergence.

Both pre-modern and traditional, however, are descriptive rather than analytical; they raise more questions than they answer. What did it mean to be a traditionalist Irish Catholic working for an American wage? Karl Polanyi's 1944 book *The Great Transformation*, without really intending to, provides answers that significantly advance Gutman's use of *preindustrial*. Like others of my conscripted allies, Polanyi had nothing to say about the Irish. He was speaking generally; the subtitle of his book was *The Political and Economic Origins of Our Time*, and by "our" he meant all humanity. To oversimplify a complex argument, the "great transformation" was occasioned by a slow-motion Industrial Revolution and the development and emergence in the nineteenth century of modern national, even global, market economies. For centuries, if not millennia, economies had been nonmarket-driven and local. The economic exchanges that took place within geographically isolated social worlds were not determined by markets; they were embedded in and subordinate to the moral ecosystems by which local societies governed themselves. As Polanyi put it, "the economic system [is] a mere function of social organization."[27]

Polanyi's work is having something of a revival lately among the newest iteration of a New Left. I was drawn to his ideas for different reasons: Polanyi gave me another explanation for why cultures diverge. The more I read of Polanyi's writings the more convinced I became that he had a great deal to say on the question of what explained Irish Catholic erraticism. Modern market economies were capitalist economies; the Irish were not simply traditionalists, they were antimodern and, if not anticapitalists, unlikely converts to any modern form of capitalism.

What else made me think that the Irish could fairly be made a part of his argument—and he a part of mine—was Polanyi's close association with Conrad Arensberg, a faculty colleague of his at Columbia. In 1957 the two coedited and contributed to a collection of essays titled *Trade and Market in the Early Empires*. Arensberg was one of the first academic anthropologists to study the culture of a mostly literate people living in the modern world. For reasons he never really explained, he chose the peasants of the west of Ireland as his study group. His two best-known books were *The Irish Countryman* (1937) and *Family and Community in Ireland* (1940), two ethnographic accounts of the lives of Irish men and women as they had been for centuries, and as they were when millions of them, including those of the post-Famine generation, left Ireland for America.

Both of Arensberg's books appeared before *The Great Transformation*, and I'm convinced they influenced Polanyi's work. Arensberg's Irish were on the wrong side of the "great transformational" divide. His descriptions of the Irish economy perfectly match Polanyi's discussion of nonmarket economies. It seems highly unlikely—were I less cautious, I would say impossible—that the two men did not influence one another. Arensberg wrote Polanyi's "Irish chapters." To use Eagleton's words, he inserted into *The Great Transformation* an "Irish motif."[28]

Arensberg's Irish lived in economies "enmeshed in . . . non-economic institutions . . . religion, magic, fealty." Sacred obligations, long observed, were as important for the structure and functioning of nonmarket economies as banks, stock exchanges, land offices, and employment bureaus were for modern capitalist ones. The social systems of the west of Ireland were communal and organic; they were based on production for use not for gain. What was produced was allocated on the basis of need, distributed and redistributed on the basis of reciprocal obligations. Balance sheets tracking profit and loss had nothing to do with it.[29]

Borrowing from and often citing Aristotle (he could have added Aquinas), Polanyi summarized that in nonmarket economies—like those described by Arensberg—"labor was not a commodity to be purchased in the market, . . . the idea of profit is barred; . . . giving freely is acclaimed as a virtue." The giving extended to both land and labor; neither was commodified. Both were shared. The continuance of the group, said Polanyi, "required it." So did justice. And finally this: "on the face of it, . . . primitive man, far from having a capitalistic psychology, had, in effect, a communistic one." He meant communistic in a generic not an ideological context. According to Arensberg, the nonmarket economies of Ireland fully qualified.[30]

Modern market economies—England's and America's were Polanyi's principal cases in point—presented an entirely different social ecology. Market economies were said by those who favored them—the "formal" economists, as Polanyi called them—to be "self-regulating" and thus "autonomous," "disembedded" from society. That was a "stark utopian" dream according to Polanyi, but that's less important here than the fact that free-market economists wanted social and political considerations to be kept separate from economics, and that governmental institutions and laws should reflect that separation. Had they gotten what they wanted, the results would have "annihilate[ed] the human and natural substance of society . . . [and] physically destroyed man."[31]

Self-annihilation had little appeal. But to that add, as Fred Block did in his excellent introduction to Polanyi's book, the "moral argument that it is simply wrong to treat . . . human beings as objects whose price will be determined entirely by the market." Human lives have a "sacred dimension" that is "impossible to reconcile . . . with the subordination of labor." For both reasons, societies—and the "substantive" economists who took society and moral arguments seriously—took measures to counter the effects of the market revolution; there was what Polanyi called a "double movement"; one disembedded the economy from society, the other worked to reembed it. That lingering quarrel between formal and substantive economics and economists is the core of Polanyi's complex argument. It needs to be introduced and then left to the economists. What matters here is much simpler: Traditional markets are local; modern capitalist markets—labor, commodity, consumer, credit, and more—are national, even global. Traditional societies are based on reciprocity; modern ones on contracts. In Eagleton's words, traditional societies are "organic"; modern are "mechanical." These terms are analytical. For descriptive ones, I would cite to Brad Gregory, a historian of the late medieval and Reformation eras, who wrote that traditionalists— read Irish—left a "good society" and entered a modernist—read American— "goods society."[32]

Capitalist market economies owe society nothing. Nonmarket economies, on the other hand, are beholden to society. The cultural divergence was obvious, even flagrant. Friedrich Engels once commented on how Irish tenants were "under obligation to help [their] poorer neighbours whenever they are in distress." That tradition explained "why political economists and jurists complain of the impossibility of inculcating the modern idea of bourgeois property into the minds of the Irish peasants. Property that has only rights, but no duties, is absolutely beyond the ken of the Irishman." Engels then wrote that when "suddenly cast into the modern great cities of England and America," Irishmen found themselves "among a population with entirely different moral and legal standards."[33]

Here's Polanyi on the topic: I assume Arensberg would have applied each of its lessons to the Irish, and with conclusions similar to Engels's; there's even a decent chance that Arensberg had something to do with the way Polanyi framed the issues. The italicized emphases are mine: Bringing people from the west of Ireland to America and trying to "*integrate* the same with contemporary culture is to [try] to harmonize two *incompatible* institutional systems." "The *distinction* between the principle of [production for] use and that [for] gain was the key to *utterly different civilization[s]* . . . gift-giving . . . [and] the market [are] both . . . mechanism of distribution and survival.

"But they are *different* mechanisms, based on *very different* social arrangements, . . . *opposite* cultural and institutional elaborations. Presumably as well they have *very different* antecedents, . . . *very different* distributions among the world's times, places, and peoples." The "salient fact is that the new economic institutions *fail to be assimilated*. . . . by those from nonmarket cultures." Taking Irish Catholic people from traditional nonmarket economies and putting them into the modern market-driven economies of America was to invite erratic behavior. The key words in this accounting for divergence have been *modern* and—by various labels—the opposite of it. The divide between traditional/premodern and modern is cultural as well as social. And it has to do with more than just one having experienced modern capitalist and industrial work routines—premodernity as a function of chronology.[34]

• • •

Robert Orsi's splendid new book, *History and Presence*, widens the divide even further. *History and Presence* is about Catholicism and Catholics. Ethnic/tribal distinctions are not part of it. But, as Orsi puts it, in the modern world, "religious distinctions and racial taxonomies went hand in hand; as much as religion was racialized, race was religionized." I respectfully offer in evidence "IrishCatholic." And I impute to them, as surely as to all of their co-religionists, Orsi's basic argument.[35]

For Catholics, a trinitarian God—creator, son, and spirit—is present in the world. God was joined in this real presence by God's surrogates, included prominently the virgin mother of God's son. Also present in the world were various of the saints of the Church, along with the dead and such technically unauthorized sorts as spectral creatures, necromancers, changelings, and fairies, all summarized under the general heading of "gods." The belief in the "real presence" ran through everything Catholics did. I include the Irish prominently in that. The real presence was like an omnibus index of the sources of Catholic ecological sensibilities. The "transcendent," Orsi writes, had "broken into [Catholic] time." A case could be made that the transcendent had taken over IrishCatholic time.[36]

They had not, however, taken over Protestant time; they were not present in American worlds. The Americans had expelled the transcendent and the sacred. Presence was a relic of medievalism. As such, it was as much a casualty of the Reformation as modernity and capitalism were products of it. The American world in which Irish Catholics found themselves was based on God's and the gods' absence. Orsi devised a simple formula: "Protestant=Absence; Catholic=Presence." I revise the formula somewhat to make it more applicable to the cultural divergence with which I am dealing: Irish=Presence; Anglo-Americans=Absence.[37]

Orsi calls this division an "ontological fault line" (another metaphor from geology). It was deeper and more unbridgeable than Polanyi's fault line between nonmarket and market societies. It had also been around far longer. Polanyi's "great transformation" began in England in the early nineteenth century with the Industrial Revolution. The history with which presence is linked in Orsi's title, began in the fifteenth century; it had gone on through "all of modernity." Irish Catholic sensibilities were in place long before immigration to America transnationalized them. The cultural divergence of Catholic Irish from Protestant Anglo-Americans was collateral damage of the Reformation, particularly the English one, even more particularly the Cromwellian. It is in that context that "presence versus absence" was played out in modern, which is to say, capitalist, America.[38]

Here's Orsi: "Modernity and secularism were ... utterly Protestant in character ... secular moderns were as much the bearers of anti-Catholicism in the United States as Protestants and Protestantism." He singles out for special attention "American liberalism," which he said "was deeply Protestant." And this—than which nothing more on the point of modernism need be said: *"Modernity exists under the sign of absence."* As a result, "in the modern world," there was something "almost inherently *subversive*" about the idea of presence. Absence versus presence was "the metric for mapping the religious worlds of the planet."[39]

In Eamon Duffy's words, Catholicism was what it had been since the Reformation: "a religion of the living in the service of the dead." G. K. Chesterton called it a "traditional" faith; it gave a "vote to ... [the] ancestors. It was the democracy of the dead." Chapter 5 of Orsi's book carries the interesting title of "the dead in the company of the living." It's hard to imagine an idea more non-, pre-, or antimodern. More to the point, there can have been very little more "inherently subversive" to the self-identification of the race patriots of Anglo-America, they who were the quintessence of modernity, than having the dead counsel them. The Irish might claim that their idea of nationhood came from their "dead generations"; the Americans' source was from "self-evident truths." The American "earth belonged to the living." I need hardly add that "subversive" vastly exceeds "divergent" on the cultural dissent metric.[40]

In a 2012 article, Orsi recalled a conversation he had had as a graduate student with Sydney Ahlstrom, the dean of historians of American religion. Orsi asked Ahlstrom whether he "thought there would ever be another anti-Catholic movement in America." The senior historian's response is a classic: Young man, I can imagine him saying, "America *is* an anti-Catholic movement." I don't know when that conversation took place, likely sometime in the late 1970s. Orsi doesn't repeat the story in *History and Presence*, but I can't help wondering how much the "Ahlstrom thesis" had to do with writing the book.[41]

How could IrishCatholics have been other than nonconforming, dissident, ill fitted, and erratic in America? If America at its core and for the whole of its history was an anti-Catholic movement, were not Catholics by definition cultural "subversives"? Here's more from Orsi: The Real Presence was "out of step with modernity." The ontological divide between absence and presence "defines the modern temperament." Absence "evolved into one of the normative categories of modernity." The modern "intellectual culture was premised on absence." "*All* of the dominant cultural forms of modernity were premised on Protestantism." All of modernity takes in quite a lot. The ontological conflict between Catholic=Presence, Protestantism=Absence affected everything, politics, ideas of justice, democracy, and, most of all, capitalism.[42]

Consider what Orsi's argument means in light of the religious makeup of the American industrial working class. There were sections of it that were overwhelmingly Catholic, some were overwhelmingly Irish. Capitalists were overwhelmingly neither. Anything that divided Catholics from Protestants in the United States divided workers and capitalists. There was a clear social-class aspect to the presence versus absence divide, as there was to IrishCatholic erraticism generally. In a modern and forward-looking world, backward-looking traditionists were not just harmless if sometimes annoying eccentrics. They contradicted, even subverted, the fundamental premises of modern industrial and capitalist America. They didn't have to take the battle to the streets to be menacing.

• • •

Orsi's close association between Protestantism and modernity, including its capitalist economies, along with Lears's reference to backward-looking critics of capitalism, allow me to enter into the erraticism record the 1891 encyclical letter of Pope Leo XIII, *Rerum Novarum: On the Condition of Labor*. The letter, I need hardly add, was written "under the sign of presence," which meant the modern world either didn't understand it or had no use for and didn't read it. The Pope sternly judged both socialism and capitalism. On balance, however, I think his scolding of capitalism was more harshly condemnatory than his rejection of socialism. He wrote of the "misery and wretchedness pressing so heavily and unjustly on the vast majority of the working classes"; of the "yoke little better than that of slavery itself laid on the teeming masses of the laboring poor." It was, he said, "shameful and inhuman to treat men like chattels to make money by or to look upon them merely as so much muscle or physical power." He didn't say that that's not the way it was done in nonmarket economies like Ireland's, but that's what he meant. So I'll say it for him.[43]

Leo's solution was medievalism, or, at the very least, a return to the world before the Protestant Reformation. His admonition to capitalist employers is an example. He told them that their "great and principal duty [was] to give everyone"—including in wages—"what was just." Don Quixote could have written that sentence. Great and principal duties in the interest of justice were what were assigned to medieval knights-errant. The only duty of modern capitalists was to make money for themselves and their investors. Behaving justly had no part in it; justice generally defined had no part in it. In one section of his letter, Leo wrote that both laissez-faire capitalism and socialism were "dissentient." By that he meant they were modern and materialistic, two of the signal features of absence and market-driven economies. Their dissent was from the traditional and the sacred.

The Pope had it backward. To modern Americans, both liberal reformers and reactionary capitalists, *Rerum Novarum* was dissentient, a relic from a premodern era. Capitalists didn't live there; neither did socialists. The worship of the Virgin had been replaced by the worship of the Dynamo. The socialists and the capitalists weren't the dissenters; Pope Leo was—joined by all of the other erratics for and to whom he wrote. Dissentient modernists had stripped God of sovereignty and transferred it to the state, which modern America turned over to the individual. Modernity had atomized society and enshrined individualism. It had freed capitalism of all ethical restraints. For IrishCatholic workers, this was its most afflicting—and unfathomable—legacy.[44]

• • •

Kevin Kenny argues that over time even the most stubbornly Irish assimilated and became American. They did so, however, by the circuitous route of becoming Irish-Americans. "Irish-American" is a hybrid, something akin to a creole. Are the two identities combined into one or are they separate parts of the hybridized whole, each operating independently of the other? Was the prototypical Irish-American sometimes Irish and sometimes American as the occasion demanded? Which is the dominant identity and what percentage of each is required to attain the status of Irish-American? If even some of the ingredients in a melting pot separate out, is it still a melting pot; is it still amalgamation? Becoming American by becoming *Irish*-American is assimilation, but of a partial and incomplete sort. Is it, then, still assimilation, or do we need another word?

I have proffered articulation. What happened on one side of the line where Irish Strangers met American Natives influenced what happened on the opposite side. Each side responded to the other. Neither became the other. The IrishCatholics who are the topic here adapted to America; they did not assimilate to it. Their lives were connected to Americans', but they were not the same lives. Their tracks paralleled the Americans', but they were not the same tracks. The Irish could not be cut and tailored to style. Theirs was already the final form, and, by their reckoning, an altogether lovely form it was. The deal between Irish and America was transactional and based on a tradeoff. Their contribution to modernity and capitalism was weighed against the risk they posed to both. I like what John V. Kelleher wrote on this issue: "What [Irish Catholics] wanted and got was a mutual standoff with the Yankees." I can think of no better definition of articulation than "mutual standoff."[45]

There were, of course, Irish immigrants and ethnics who discarded their Irishness. They serve my interests best by defining erraticism by not being erratic. Irish-born Fr. Peter Yorke, chieftain of San Francisco's Catholic Irish, said that the Irish "who pose as Americans" reminded him of a "hippopotamus which, at a fancy dress ball, got itself up like a swallow...." The Irish had a word for the posers, the hippos dressed like swallows: they were shoneens (*seoínini*), little John Bulls—or little Uncle Sams (*Uncailiní Somhair*) perhaps. In Anglo-America, the differences were slight. Shoneen Irish didn't have a mutual standoff with the Yankees. They were the Yankees.[46]

As for those erratic Irish others, the ones who retained a large share of Irishness, they were, in the order presented here, traditionalists, pre- or antimodern; they came from nonmarket worlds with economies, in Polanyi's italicized language, "*embedded in social relations*; [where the] *distribution of material goods . . .* [was] *ensured by noneconomic motives.*" They retained the psychological and cultural values—the social ecology—of those worlds and brought them with them to an America that found them erratic at best, subversive at their more frequent worst. Orsi's compelling argument that modernity lived "under the sign of [Protestant] absence" could even be used to make counterreformationists of them.[47]

There is a brief passage in Brad Gregory's superb *Unintended Reformation: How a Religious Revolution Secularized Society* that directly addresses these points. In some ways, it sanctions much of what I've tried to do in making my case for Irish Catholic erraticism. Gregory said this: "[t]he distant past is assumed to have been left behind, . . . important to what immediately succeeded it but not to the present. . . . Reformation historians obviously need to understand the late Middle Ages . . . in order to understand the sixteenth-century . . . but twentieth-century American historians supposedly do not." That supposition is entirely wrong. The "distant past" matters greatly—to none more than to historians of American immigration and labor.[48]

CHAPTER ONE

"Ancestral Sorrows"
The Making of an Irish Catholic Culture

> "They were the most simple people I had ever seen.
> . . . They bring all of Ireland's miseries with them."
> —Herman Melville, *Redburn* (1850)

In 1897, the historian Arnold Toynbee, in one of his frequent bursts of imperialistic Anglo-Saxonism, proclaimed that the English and the Americans—except for those in the old Confederacy—had avoided history's more disagreeable features. Anglo-Americans were history-proof. "History," Toynbee said, was "something unpleasant that happens to other people." What the English working class might have thought of that—had they heard or read it—may be guessed at. Among the not-English other people were the Irish. That idea seemed to have come easily to the English; twenty years after Toynbee's comment, Lord Herbert Asquith remarked on England's "unique success" historically in maintaining "imperial unity," and followed it with a reference to "the malignant genius who has hovered over the whole path of Irish history." Toynbee said nothing about a possible connection between the English being history-proof and the Irish being history-cursed. Nor did Asquith ever wonder if England's "imperial unity" had anything to do with Ireland's "malignant genius."[1]

Toynbee's and Asquith's comments formed a kind of Anglo-Saxon colonialists' anthem. But the sentiments contained within them align perfectly with what a pair of Irish said. William Butler Yeats spoke of Ireland's "ancestral sorrows"—most of them, by the Irish accounting of it, the consequences of the acts of the agents of that history-inoculated empire. James Joyce's Stephen Dedalus was considerably more introspective. The British and their empire were not responsible for all of Ireland's sorrows. History, that "nightmare" from which Dedalus was "trying to awake," as Joyce makes painfully clear, was mostly self-inflicted. At that, Haines, Dedalus's English roommate, admitted that the Irish had reason to feel aggrieved; "we feel in England that we have treated you rather unfairly." He offered no apology, saying only that "It seems history is to blame."[2]

For the Irish, history was a thing, a disagreeable thing that had happened to them. It was not, however, an impersonal force. No "hovering malignant genius" brought it. Somebody made the Irish Past, somebody owned it, and somebody had to own up to it. The Irish said and believed that in the case of the worst of their history, that somebody was England. The sensibilities that came out of this were still Irish but they did not arise out of an Ireland responding only to itself. This Irish historical consciousness bordering on obsession was one of the sensibilities that set them apart from the English and the Americans, and from the Anglo-American hybrid nation they had formed. Later in his poem about sorrowing ancestors, Yeats wrote of the "Exiles wandering over lands and seas / And planning, plotting always that some morrow / May set a stone upon ancestral Sorrow."

I said earlier that this account is about what IrishCatholics thought of Americans and Anglo-America. That discussion properly starts with what they thought of Anglo-Saxons and England. Yeats never identified what Ireland's ancestral sorrows were, but in another poem he said that Ireland's "history began / Before God made the angelic clans." That's a long line of sorrowing ancestors. It's more reasonable to go with Eagleton's previously cited list of "a history of injustice and inequality, of Protestant supremacy and Catholic subjugation." However long the historical record, the British and their American racial kindred had "ancestral glories"; the Irish had Dedalus's nightmare and Yeats's "ancestral sorrows." From such come cultural divergence.[3]

What complicated the matter immeasurably was that the Irish believed that the two were connected as cause and effect. Ireland was made poor that England could be made rich. Irish immigrants did brutally hard labor for inadequate pay that America might prosper. Anger and extreme bitterness arose from those beliefs. Whether Ireland's and the Irish's nightmares should have been so attributed is less important than that they were. The Anglophobia arising from Irish history—real and invented—was an entrenched part of the "untotalizable" content of Catholic Irish culture. So was its obverse, the glorification of Ireland and the Irish, Celticism as Anglophobia's partner in self-indulgence. The Irish had a word for the rhetorical excess that was always a part of nationalist speech-making; they called it "sunburstery," Ireland and the Irish rising and avenging their sorrows, both bursting forth like the sun.

・・・

All nations invent a national community around their history. That may be particularly true of subject colonial nations as they proceed toward nationhood. Breaking out of another's empire and becoming one's own nation involves dealing with a colonial past and a postcolonial future. That is a very tricky business. What was a colonial leftover and what was the indigenous and true self? In the instance of Ireland, it led the Irish to define themselves by what they were not; Ireland as the "not-England," the Irish as the "not-English." That's a hard road to national distinction. There's one other issue that arose partly out of the Irish being a subject nation; blaming foreign oppressors for their troubles deflected attention and blame from troubles self-inflicted, including those brought upon poor Catholics by prosperous Catholics, strong farmers, bourgeois capitalists, and assorted other *shoneens*— invented history and sunburstery could also be hegemonic devices.[4]

Thomas O'Flaherty, an Irish speaker born on the Aran Islands, once wrote that there were two kinds of history: that which was "true" and that which was "honest." The Irish could only afford the latter. As O'Flaherty explained, "[we] had no money to bribe the historians." Some of them only wanted the latter. Thomas was the older brother of the better known Irish writer, Liam. Both O'Flahertys were fervent left-wing Irish nationalists; both were also members of the Irish Communist Party. It's hard to know whether the "we" who could not afford the bribes had more to do with Karl Marx and history as written by capitalists or with the "bold Fenian men" and history as written by the imperialists. It's doubtful Thomas O'Flaherty distinguished the two; there was only one "we." Either way, for Irish erratics, history was an applied art. It was put to service.[5]

"Honest" History contains a great deal that is not "true." "Getting its history wrong," as Ernst Renan put it, was "a part of being a nation." That was true of all of them, even those that started from scratch. When the nation abuilding had been a colony of another nation previously built, the history of both was routinely got wrong. Constructing "Ireland the nation" involved deconstructing "Ireland the colony." I leave it to an Irishman to summarize it: "There are elements *in* history," writes Seamus Deane, "that are not 'history.'" In the case of the Irish, however, none of the "not history," the parts of the past that were remembered imperfectly, was allowed to be forgotten. The empire was not just deconstructed; it was pilloried along with all those, however ancient, responsible for Ireland's subject place within it.[6]

Blaming England for Ireland's "sorrows" has been roundly, loudly, often angrily condemned by contemporary revisionist historians. As one of them put it, "serious historical writing eschews blame-casting." (I cannot help asking "since when?"). That same serious historian also referred to the more graphic descriptions of the starving times of the mid-nineteenth century as "famine porn." The revisionists demand a history that is "value free," sternly objective and scientific, almost austere. I prefer Jackson Lears's take on historiography: history "without a moral dimension is pedantry." Seamus Deane, as he so often does, comes directly to the point: For the revisionists, "Britain was not to blame, the landlords were not to blame; indeed, blame itself is not to be attributed—except to those who attribute blame." I would add John Gaddis to that: There is in history an "ubiquitous spectrum that separates the admirable from the abhorrent." It would be hard for historians to make the case that the British administration of Irish affairs was always or even occasionally admirable. Which leaves them to ponder the sometimes abhorrent. That's as far down the rabbit hole of Irish revisionist historiography as I wish to dive.[7]

• • •

Over the years, there have been many hundreds of descriptive histories of the "sorrowful" episodes in the Irish past. Tim Healy, when asked in 1916 when the "rising" in Dublin had begun and when it would end said it began when "Strongbow invaded Ireland"; that was in 1169. It would end when "Cromwell got out of hell," a date he left open. That's a lot of historical ground. John Gaddis called doing history "mapping the past"; Healy left his map empty. There was no need for him to provide the details of what happened between the start and the end—assuming there would be one—of the Irish resistance to English colonial rule. The Irish knew what had happened to them during the eight hundred years he left blank. They also knew that Cromwell deserved his indeterminate sentence. And Healy, it must be noted, was one of Ireland's more moderate nationalists.[8]

Here is a proper place to fill in some of Tim Healy's blank spaces with historical events. My emphasis will be on the cultural and psychological effects of some of Ireland's misfortunes. I'll not describe the events; that's already been done by countless others. In place of description, I offer up my comments in the historical context of interdependent—and untotalizable—variables, of "personality becoming ecology." Call them the map legends on this cartographic representation of Irish history.

The first one is obvious. Between 1846 and 1849, *An Gorta Mór*, the Great Irish Hunger, took the lives of more than a million of Ireland's people through starvation and attendant disease. Between 1845 and 1851, another two million Irish emigrated. Taking one and a half million as the number of deaths yields a death rate of 22 percent. On average, almost nine hundred people died per day every day for four consecutive years. Another two million Irish ran away. It is difficult to call it anything else. It was nearer a jail break than an emigration. Most of those runaways and escapees went to America. They didn't really choose it; they scarcely had choices. Some didn't know where America was. That's the historical description marked on the map.

I will take the language for the map legend from others: The historian Emmet Larkin called the Great Famine "truly a gigantic psychological shock." Terry Eagleton was even more graphic: The famine was "the greatest social disaster of nineteenth-century Europe—an event with something of the characteristics of a low-level nuclear attack." The great Irish poet Seamus Heaney wrote of digging potatoes as ritualistic, an expression of "Fear and homage to the famine god." Neither Larkin's description nor Eagleton's seems exaggerated, and that the Irish would still be genuflecting to Heaney's "famine god" a century after the Famine is entirely credible. Robert Orsi wasn't talking about Ireland's starving time, but his words clearly apply: "there are experiences and events in history and culture that are in excess of available languages, that even undermine the capacity to speak in the old tongue, but instead require new languages."[9]

Let "collective posttraumatic stress disorder" and the collective insecurity that accompanies it be part of that new language. I offer without comment the following from a recent article on collective trauma that appeared in the journal *Frontiers in Psychology*. It was written by Gilad Hirschberger, an Israeli social and political psychologist. The holocaust and Germany are his principal subjects. There is no mention of Ireland or the Irish anywhere in it, but it is clearly relevant to an Gorta Mór and the British governmental response to Irish hunger. "Collective trauma," Hirschberger writes, results from "a crisis of meaning." It affects a "collective memory," culminating finally "in a system of meaning" in which "groups . . . redefine who they are and where they are going." It did that for and to the sorrowing Irish. As for the English "perpetrators" of the event—assuming for purposes of argument that they at least had something to do with it—Hirschberger writes that "the memory of the trauma [they inflicted] may be addressed by denying history . . . transforming the memory of the event, closing the door on history."[10]

In 1863, the Irish radical and exile to America John Mitchel told an American audience that God may have brought the potato blight, but the English brought the Famine. Thomas O'Flaherty would call that an honest historical summary. Revisionist historians call it a libel. I am more concerned with the effect that believing it and other tales of the Irish Past had on Irish Catholics, specifically, those working for wages in Anglo-America. An Gorta Mór was a human catastrophe, a mass and quite unnatural die-off. It is unimaginable that those who witnessed and survived it were unchanged by the experience. Let the map legend also indicate that. That it qualifies as a collective posttraumatic stress disorder is untested and, for present purposes, unimportant. An Gorta Mór was traumatic and it was stressful. It is enough simply to go back to Eagleton's definition of culture's role: It affected their "speech and behaviour [and how] they acquire[d] their sense." Whether it left Irish lives clinically disordered is beside the historical point.

Robin Cohen's book *Global Diasporas* introduces another issue for revisionist historians to ponder. Cohen identifies five types of diasporas: trade, cultural, imperial, labor, and victim. He placed the Irish emigration from 1845 to 1852 along with the Jewish, African, and Armenian in that last category and writes of the "collective trauma" suffered by those who fell into this category. Indeed, citing Christine Kinealy's book on the Famine, *The Great Calamity*, he writes that there was a "hidden agenda" in the English government's response to the Famine. "Land reform" was on it; so was "population control." That latter item is a more polite way of saying ethnic cleansing. There are more heavily loaded terms than that, but not many. It was purposeful. An Gorta Mór was ethnic cleansing by means of ethnic annihilation. That is a hard charge, one filled with blame.[11]

An Gorta Mór was the most conspicuous of Ireland's afflictions because it was the most visible. Other of Ireland's "misfortunes" were less visible. In the early 1830s, having misappropriated Ireland, the English turned to translating and converting the Irish, domesticating them in a sense. Call it ethnic cleansing by means of ethnic remodeling. It was a project centuries in the making: in 1596, Edmund Spenser, in his *View of the Present State of Ireland*, laid out his blueprint for a scorched-earth policy for the conquest of Ireland. It included this bit of advice: The peoples' "speech being Irish, the hart must needs be Irish; for out of the aboundance of the hart, the tonge speaketh." Change the tongue, change the abounding heart.[12]

They waited 250 years, but eventually the British acted on Spenser's suggestion. They began by renaming Ireland and everything in it, the entire natural and built environment. The Irish were a people fixed in place. They named—baptized, really, and thus made sacred—everything in that place. There is a scene in Brian Friel's brilliant play, *Translations*, that speaks directly about their profound sense of place, of where they were and where they belonged in the world. *Translations* is set in the fictional Donegal townland of *Baile Beag* (little settlement or townland; soon to be Ballybeg). Its main character, a hedge teacher named Hugh, sees a copy of "the new English language *Name-Book*," the lexicon for Ballybeg. "He picks it up and leafs through it, pronouncing the strange names as he does.... We must learn those new names. *We must learn where we live.* We must learn to make them our own. *We must make them our new home.*"[13]

That was not simply a matter of adapting to new words, grammar, and syntax. English words did not mean what the Irish words they replaced had meant. To a very great extent, they didn't mean anything. The Irish language, said Hugh, was "full of the mythologies of fantasy and hope and self-deception." It was the Irish "response to mud cabins and a diet of potatoes"—a language expressive of Irish "privacies" and Irish traditions. The "King's good English," on the other hand, was "particularly suited to the purposes of commerce." It could never "really express us." Later, in the 1840s, the Young Irelander Thomas Davis wrote that "to impose another language on... a people is to send their history adrift among the accidents of translation—'tis to tear their identity from all places... 'tis to... separate the people from their forefathers by a deep gulf." As Spenser had indicated, that was the idea. One of the English "translators" in Friel's play said there was a "sinister quality" to what they were doing. "It's an eviction of sorts." It was that.[14]

About this time and to the same colonializing purpose, the British imposed on Ireland their system of National Schools. It was a totally revamped curriculum, all of it taught in English, and designed—as the jingle that opened each school day put it—to make "a happy English child" of every Irish girl and boy in attendance. They were taught English history; they read English literature; they sang English songs and recited English rhymes. Ireland, in the words of Seamus Deane, was being taken from the "territory of tradition" and placed in the "territory of modernity." English was a modern language, a "language of calculation"; Irish was a "language of sensibilities." Deane summed all of it up: "Can [an] . . . account in English represent the history that lives in the mouths of the Irish?"[15]

Translation, whether of Irish place names or of Irish history, was an act of erasure. Its purpose was to Anglicize the Irish. The loss of their native language and their honest history transformed—or deformed—them. As Emmet Larkin points out, translating history, even that which was "got wrong," reshapes "the national identity . . . by . . . remodeling the national memory." In revising the "centering myths[,] . . . the historian is actually touching on the realm of the sacred." Deane wrote similarly: "exile is most profound when it is experienced at home." In this instance, home had been lost in translation. To use a now fashionable phrase, Irish Catholics had become "internal exiles." A "happily English" Irish child was a contradiction in terms.[16]

Their language had once differentiated them from the English. Spenser was right: their "speech being Irish, the hart must needs be Irish." They needed to find something else that could express the "aboundance of [their] harts." They turned to Catholicism. In hindsight, the choice was predictable. The English had made it for them: The Irish spoke an eccentric tongue, one the English thought primitive and which imperial officials made little effort to learn. But it was not *Gaeilge* that really set the Irish apart from the English; it was popery. The Irish agreed and determined to increase their quotient of it. Under the leadership of Archbishop Paul Cullen, they purged the vernacular and festive Catholicism they had known and replaced it with a model that was ceremonial, highly censorious and cheerless—"devotional" in the language of Emmet Larkin. The Irish became conspicuously pious; holier than thou, holier, indeed, than they themselves had ever been.

This devotional model was the Catholicism that came to define them and separate them from the English. Larkin makes the point directly: "The devotional revolution . . . provided the Irish with a substitute symbolic language and offered them a new cultural heritage with which they could identify and be identified and through which they could identify with one another." That's as close to a description of a diasporic sensibility as can be imagined. Larkin quoted an Irish Dominican priest, Father Thomas Burke, whose 1872 *Lectures on Faith and Fatherland* was widely read by the Irish in the United States. Burke made the logical argument: "Take an average Irishman—I don't care where you find him—and you will find that the very first principle in his mind is, '*I am not an Englishman.... I am a Catholic.*'" There was no need for Burke to add that that meant "and in no respect anything like you."[17]

The loss of the language, the Devotional Revolution, an Gorta Mór, and the mass emigration that accompanied and followed it, literally undid the Catholic Irish world. It would be difficult to find any other nation or people whose assorted misfortunes compared in type or number, and whose lives were more fundamentally changed. The Great Hunger was only the most important part of that. These words are Larkin's: The Irish had "been gradually losing their language, their culture, and their way of life for ... years before the famine." Nearly all of them had become cultural emigrants. ... [T]hey had ... moved in their minds before [they] had actually to move in space."[18]

• • •

In important ways, that mental shifting was as true of the Irish who were born after the worst of the bad times as of those who had lived through them. The sufferings of the years of translation, death, and exodus were not theirs directly, but the Irish born after midcentury were nonetheless profoundly affected by what had happened. Black '47 was a part of the lives of their mothers and their fathers and so a felt part of their own. Transnationalism had a temporal as well as a spatial aspect. Hirschberger's account of collective PTSD concludes that from a "cataclysmic event that shatters the basic fabric of society"—and an Gorta Mór was assuredly that—emerges a "*transgenerational collective self.*" To argue that what the erratics of the post-1870 Irish American generation knew of those years was only from illusionists and other conjurers of History ignores the fact that they were raised in and a part of a transgenerational culture. Their "personality as ecology" was suffused with ancestral sorrows. They brought them with them when they immigrated; then they passed them down to their children.[19]

This unconscious component of their culture manifested itself in different and uncountable ways—meaning that the list that follows must be an incomplete one. I preface it with two of Kerby Miller's frequently cited comments from his masterful *Emigrants and Exiles*: There is "much evidence" that the "Catholic Irish [in America] were ... communal, ... dependent, ... fatalistic, ... passive, ... tradition[al], ... and pre-modern." It is not surprising that even those who fared well economically "remained ... remarkably estranged from

W. A. Rogers, "Poor House from Galway," 1883. This cartoon of a badly listing immigrant "ship" appeared in *Harper's Weekly* in 1883, almost forty years after *an Gorta Mór*. Ireland was still sending its poor and crippled (see the crutches on the deck) to the United States. Notice the small boat from New York coming to meet the immigrants and carrying dynamite. Courtesy HarpWeek.

the dominant cultural values of the United States." I agree with all of that, which obliges me to give a few more specific examples of how both sides of that cultural estrangement—John Kelleher's "mutual standoff" between Irish and Yankees—viewed the other.[20]

I'll begin with the Yankees. My emphasis will not be on the more zealous of the nativists, and what the historian Linda Colley's calls their "thuggish paranoia." Maria Monk's "awful disclosures," the Know-Nothings before and their heirs after the Civil War, Thomas Nast's puerile cartoons, the xenophobic howling of the antipapists, have been thoroughly related. What has not is the everyday, systemic prejudice against Irish Catholics. Much of it was polite, almost decorous. It was part of the Yankee's social unconscious. It, too, was transgenerational and transnational, an inheritance from the English, carefully tended by Anglo-American race patriots.[21]

Examples of the routine everydayness of the shared Anglo-American sense that the IrishCatholics were culturally different and racially defective are not as easy to find as cartoons showing the Irish as hairless apes and Catholic clergy as vipers. Examples of the quotidian seldom are. That's what makes Massachusetts senator George Hoar's comments of particular interest. Hoar's political career stretched from the 1850s until the early years of the twentieth century, in the context of American nativism, the years from the Know-Nothings to the American Protective Association (APA). He was intensely hostile to both groups; he thought them bigoted and unnecessarily alarmist.

He also thought they had badly underestimated America's assimilative power. Hoar was convinced that the Irish "Catholic boy who has grown up in our common schools" and gotten to know Protestants would become Americanized. He would be no longer different, no longer apart, and, by Irish Catholic reckoning, no longer Catholic or Irish. Hoar was greatly cheered by that prospect; Catholicism had left the Irish ill equipped to deal with either America's demands or America's promises. Hoar even quoted with approval Lord Macaulay on how the Irish "were doomed to be what the Helots were in Sparta . . . what the blacks now are at New York." Better by far that the "Catholic boy" go to school and become a "happy American child."[22]

The other thing that makes Hoar's reminiscences of those years so relevant here was his understanding that American nativism, though "absolutely unjustified," was also "quite natural." New England's "bitter and almost superstitious dread of the Catholics . . . came to us by lawful inheritance from our English and Puritan ancestors." The "us" in question were the "worthy people . . . [who] had learned from their fathers the stories of Catholic persecution" of Protestants. Foxe's "'Book of Martyrs' . . . was . . . reverently preserved and read in the New England farmhouses" by people who hated no one but were "afraid of the Pope and the influence of Catholicism in this country." As for the Know-Nothings and later the APA, they drew their membership from the "knave-power and the donkey-power." Both sides, the worthies as well as the knaves and donkeys, behaved toward Irish Catholics as their Protestant forebears had taught them. Hoar noted specifically "the eight hundred years during which Ireland had been under the heel of England." It was now Americans who wore the boot.[23]

The anti–Irish Catholic prejudice in Harold Frederic's 1896 novel, *The Damnation of Theron Ware*, was more homegrown than that described by George Hoar, but it was expressed in language almost as courtly as Hoar's. A fair amount has been written about the book, about Theron Ware, the young

Methodist minister in a small New York town in the 1880s who develops a strange fascination for the lovely and quite Irish Celia Madden and for the Catholicism she literally embodied. As a priest told Ware, Celia was "a sort of atavistic idealization of the old Kelt at his finest and best." It would be impossible to call Ware an "idealization" of the "finest and best" of the Anglo-American, but he was certainly a representative one. Which makes the divergence between his sensibilities and those of Celia and the other "Kelts" important.[24]

His preconceptions, his "notions about the Irish," were mean-spirited at best, but it was their banality, the routine matter-of-factness of them, that was most affecting. Ware quoted from hateful nativist speech, but the clear inference is that he himself never used it. Racial prejudice was never given a calmer or less threatening expression than when the book's narrator revealed Theron Ware's feelings and revealed as well the sources of those feelings. Ware admitted that he had known very few of his small town's Irish. Most were either "among the nomadic portion of the hired help in the farm country . . . or lived "on the outskirts" of town, "among the brickyards." But he had "scarcely ever spoken to a person of this curiously alien race." He had never given "their existence even a passing thought. The Irish had been to him only a name."[25]

"But what a sinister and repellent name!" it was among Ware's friends and in his congregation. He had been told stories of Irish "ignorance, squalor, brutality, and vice," that "pigs wallowed in the mire of their cabins," that their neighborhoods were filled with "rows of lowering, ape-like faces." Combine that with the "baleful influence of [their] false and idolatrous religion" and their apparently unshakable "habit of voting the Democratic Party ticket." Ware admitted that he "could not feel sure that he had ever known a Democrat." These, he added, were the views" *common to his communion and his environment.*" Common enough, it would seem, to stand as revealed truths. Ware admitted that he had never thought about "this tacit race and religious aversion in which he had been bred"—and note how easily he combined race and religion, and that his aversion was one to which he had been born.[26]

Toward the end of the book, Ware happens on a Catholic parish picnic, complete with dancing, ball playing, a great deal of beer drinking, and, by all appearances, people who were enjoying themselves. It was a scene that Ware contrasted sadly with the abstemious social gatherings of Methodists. His attraction to a papist picnic confused him. As did the way he felt when he heard Celia Madden play the piano and sing her very Catholic songs. His fascination with Celia Madden was "illuminating." (*The Illumination* was the title of Ware's book in England.) It was the dying Michael Madden, Celia's brother, who brings Ware back to his senses. Madden tells Ware something of these Irish Catholics, "my people," as he calls them. Ware's attraction to

Celia had "altered his direction. It was a great misfortune... that you did not keep among your own people. And so be said by me, Mr. Ware! Go back to the way you were brought up in, and leave alone the people whose ways are different from yours." "Mix yourself up no more with [these] *outside people and outside notions* that only do you mischief."[27]

Hoar's and Fredric's refined nativism was matched by that of Henry Childs Merwin. Merwin was born in Pittsfield, Massachusetts, in 1853, a self-professed "Anglo-Saxon, American, Protestant," Harvard-educated lawyer and writer. He was, in short, a recognizable American social type, a New England Brahmin, "trained, refined, and educated," as he described them and himself. There is no mention of him in any of the standard histories of American nativism. Nor should there be. I bring him into this discussion because of what I consider the sheer ordinariness—and occasional mindlessness—of his ideas.[28]

In 1896, he wrote an article for the *Atlantic Monthly*, "The Irish in American Life." In it he emphasized that "Patrick" and "Bridget," his stand-ins for the whole of American Irishry, were his opposites, racially, nationally, and religiously: They were "Celtic, Irish, Catholic." Most of them were from one of Ireland's western counties, the home ground of "the most Irish of the Irish." Merwin singled out Clare, Kerry, Leitrim, Galway, and Sligo as the counties most "Catholic" in religion and "Celtic" in race. He likened them to America's native Indians; both were a "conquered people" who had "suffered a long and cruel subjugation." That wasn't all they had in common. Both were also distinctly premodern people; they were "passing from a [seminomadic] agricultural community based life"; to what, he didn't say, though he did note that they would have limited options; these most Irish of the Irish were "fundamentally different intellectually from the Anglo-Saxon."[29]

That difference showed itself in various ways. The Irish were confined to America's cities. More accurately, they confined themselves. The "Celt," Merwin said, "is ... a social creature"; he made that point often and with emphasis. They "loved society"; in fact, they could not live without it. They "hated solitude" and resisted anything that would disconnect them from what were essentially ethnic or tribal ghettos. To a person, they wanted to be where they "can be lively and sociable." These were the race's defining characteristics. Clannishness was the trait that "has determined ... the Irish's career as a citizen of the U.S." "Career as a citizen" is an odd construction. He might profitably have asked whether they really were careerists.

Merwin lamented that their gathering instincts were why the Catholic Irish missed out on America's great landed inheritance. "Land in unlimited quantities, rich farm land, was lying idle at the West, and could [the Irish] immigrants have been transported thither ... their prosperity would have been assured." Note first the passive voice; the Irish should have "been transported," perhaps "with some aid . . . from the government." The benefits would have been many, including this unexpected one: Clustering in cities, among people like themselves, "deprived [the Irish] of that brooding, meditative spirit which is nursed in solitude." That comment has to stand as one of the silliest things any American race patriot ever said about the Irish.[30]

So must this one: Irish clannishness was not just a hindrance to their advance, it was *"a source of great danger to our Eastern cities."* The United States was facing what Merwin called an "emergency." He meant a labor war brought on by the unwillingness of working-class Irish Catholics to break out of their neighborhoods, and go west, take the land that was offered them, and grow up—"with the country" was optional. Instead, they stayed in their eastern purlieus and warrens, took over the American labor movement, and agitated. The historian Barbara Solomon writes that some "conservatives . . . interpreted the instability of labor relations . . . as another form of Irish subversion." Merwin didn't call it subversion; that would have required that the Irish had a purpose. They didn't; they had only sociability. Whatever the explanation, it was clear to him "that, in the ways of thinking, in their ideals and mental habits," the Irish "belonged to a different world." They were, he concluded, "so *outré*."[31]

In one sense, he appears to have been of two minds about what explained that advanced case of Irish outsideness. At one point in his essay he said that it was the "difference in religion more than of . . . race or of temperament" that explained why they "still form a distinct . . . part of the [American national] community." Toward the end of his piece, he made a clear judgment from race. "Patrick and Bridget" were lacking in the virtues of the "Anglo-Saxon"; they had "no solidity . . . no balance, . . . no judgment, . . . no moral staying power." There was no disputing the truth of that assessment; even the Irish were "conscious of their inferiority to Anglo-Saxons." Merwin came to the only conclusion he could: The "Catholic Celt . . . and the Protestant Anglo-Saxon . . . stand at the very opposite poles of nationality." In other words, he wasn't of two minds on the issue: Race and religion were intertwined. The Catholic Irish were doubly *outré*.[32]

Other than his reference to their being a "subjugated" and "conquered" people, the malignant genius of Irish history seemed to have had nothing to do with making the Irish the misfits they were. Seven years after his *Atlantic* article, Merwin wrote in *Harper's Magazine* of his "recent impressions of the English." He had been in London, which he described as Toynbee might have; it was "the very core and centre of the greatest empire the world has ever seen." The city fairly "throbs with the sense of imperial power." As for the English people, he was happy to report that they were as robust in "character [and] energy" as they'd ever been. The antimodernists were wrong; the English showed no "signs of moral or physical decadence." He then played his proper role as Anglo-American race patriot, reminding American readers that the English were "our . . . cousins"; they were "of our own blood . . . and 'blood is thicker than water.'"[33]

Merwin's essays were patronizing, pretentious, and singularly lacking in curiosity. In comparison, however, with what Madison Grant had to say on the matter of the inextricable link between race and religion, Merwin's race patriotism was restrained, almost genteel. Early in his book *The Passing of the Great Race; or, The Racial Basis of European History*, Grant made a clear distinction between the Protestant and the Catholic Irish in America. The first, the "Scotch-Irish," as Grant called them, were of "pure Scotch and English blood." They had "resided in Ireland" but they hadn't really lived there and they remained "quite free" of racial "admixture with the older Irish and . . . [were] not to be considered 'Irish' in any sense." Which was a very good thing, for among these "older Irish" were to be found "ancient and primitive racial remnants, ferocious gorilla-like living specimens of the Neanderthal," people of "wild and savage aspect." Unfortunately, the United States had "admitted large numbers of these Irish." Then came the association: They have "impaired . . . our *religious* system and introduced certain undesirable *racial* elements."[34]

In 1911, a few years before Grant's book, the US Congress released the forty-one volumes of the Dillingham *Reports of the Immigration Commission*. Volume 5 bore the interesting title of *Dictionary of Races or Peoples*. The *or* was not there to give the reader a choice; it was there to connote equivalency. I cite it because in its own innocuous way it provided statistical evidence of what this meant in Ireland where there lived "people" of three different "races": Irish, English, and Scots—all "Irish" in terms of nationhood and on census forms and records of immigration but of strikingly different racial characteristics. Fortunately, there was an easy way to tell the three apart. One had only to watch where they went to church. "The Roman Catholics represent approximately the Irish element; the Presbyterians, the Scotch or so-called Scotch-Irish; the Episcopalians, the English or Anglo-Irish." The correlations were exact enough to be quantified: "In 1901," the *Dictionary* reported, "the Roman Catholics numbered 3,308,661, that is, 74 percent . . .; and there were 443,276 Presbyterians . . . and 581,089 Episcopalians." Find the Catholics, find the Irish. The others in Ireland were only "residents."[35]

The point those church-counters were trying to make matters greatly. The Dillingham Commission had been charged with investigating America's "immigration problem." That immigration was a problem was the premise, not the conclusion. That problem was both racial and religious, but in the case of those from Ireland, the one determined the other. The historian James Turner calls that formula a "synecdoche for the intellectual history of orthodox Christianity" in nineteenth-century America. The Catholic Irish, writes Luke Gibbons, were "condemned as much for their degenerate savagery as for their Popish superstitions." Indeed, there existed the real possibility that they were savage because Popish, Popish because savage. Their deformities reinforced one another.[36]

• • •

But what of the Irish side of the mutual standoff with Yankeedom? Michael Madden told Theron Ware that the Catholic Irish were "odd people with odd notions that only do you mischief." He said nothing more on the subject, nothing about traditionalism and modernity, nothing about society and solitude, and certainly nothing about God's absence and God's presence. And what did he mean by "mischief"? Was that an intentional—and mischievous—understatement or was it really the worst that Irish erraticism could do? If IrishCatholic "oddness" is to be understood, Madden's simple declaration needs more detail. That Anglo-Americans would be totally unaware of—and uninterested in—the historical reasons for the behavior of these outside people is taken for granted.

The four-hundred-year-old conflict—summed up by Orsi as Catholic (Irish) = presence versus Protestant (Anglo-American) = absence, by the team of Polanyi and Arensberg as nonmarket versus market economies—needs to show itself. What about them was so outside, so *outré*, as Merwin had it? Since we're back again in the realm of the untotalizable, the list that follows is necessarily partial and subjective. One of the items on it, Irish-Catholic mindlessness when it came to timekeeping, is important enough that I have reserved sections of a subsequent chapter to deal with it.

I begin with beginnings: Terry Eagleton says that, other than their being "cute . . . , in modern civilization, it is hard to say what children are for." The Catholic Irish knew; children "grow up . . . they work . . . take care of you in your old age." They provide "labour power and a welfare system." History had taught the Irish that. By the standards of modernity, it had taught them entirely too well. They had an inordinate number of children. The structure of feeling of their neighborhoods should include their resemblance to rookeries.[37]

It should also include the defensive, almost fortresslike nature of them. Which is a polite way of saying the near-xenophobic clannishness of them. Their neighborhoods were like ethnically closed secret societies. Ancestral and current sorrows were one reason. Who in English-ruled Ireland or in Anglo-America could they count on other than their friends from the neighborhoods? Raymond Williams's contention that "solidarity" was built into the structure of feeling of working-class neighborhoods applies to the Irish Catholic workers within them. Williams followed with a history lesson: The working-class feeling of solidarity was "basically, a defensive attitude, the natural mentality of the long siege" that capitalists had brought against them. That sounded an Irish note. If Tim Healy intended to be taken even half-seriously, the Catholic Irish had been under siege for more than seven hundred years. But consider too what else Williams had to say and apply it to IrishCatholics: the fortress mentality arising from the long siege can produce "the wider and more positive practice of neighbourhood," those small but cooperative Irish commonwealths.[38]

Anglo-Americans didn't need them; they had never been under siege, even short ones. They told themselves that they were self-made and self-reliant. To go back to Merwin's description of Irish Catholics, Americans were not "social creatures"; they did not cluster. Nor did they "hate solitude." Like Daniel Boone, they ran to solitude when they could see the smoke of a nearby cabin. Solitude restored them. Merwin said it was where they went to "nurse" their "meditative spirit." The contrasts with Irish Catholics could not have been more obvious. They were "neighbor"-made, and "neighbor"-reliant. Their self-identities were relational. To separate the composite for a moment: For Catholics, being "in community" is a matter of doctrine, a part of the creedal faith. For working people, being in community was a matter of working-class consciousness and solidarity. For Irish, it was a matter of survival, of self-identity, and, in Gaddis's phrase, "staying sane."

Josiah Strong, celebrated Protestant writer, preacher, and venomous anti-Catholic, included in his 1893 book, *The New Era*, a story of a "poor Irishwoman" found "half starved" in New York City. Kind benefactors found her a job in the country. She stayed a few months, then returned to New York and poverty. When asked whether she had found work in the country and if she had had enough to eat, Strong said that she answered "Yis" to both questions. Why, then, had she returned to the slums—"putrefying sores," Strong called them—of New York? The poor, presumably again half-starved Irishwoman's response should be memorized. I have: "Paples," she said, "is more coompany than sthumps."[39]

Strong may very well have made up that story; there's no good evidence that he even knew any Irish people. He certainly made up the accent. The old woman's comment, Strong went on, "contained whole chapters of [Irish Catholic] philosophy." The condescension is obvious, but that aside for the moment, Strong was right on a key point: That paples were better coompany than sthumps was, indeed, a whole and important chapter of Irish Catholic philosophy. It was also expressive of a far more humane and coherent philosophy than anything that Strong articulated in the eight-hundred-plus pages of his two books on the "Irish Catholic peril." People really are better company than stumps. That was and is a strange and defective philosophy only to stump-lovers.[40]

If living in community was erratic, the idea of Irish exile was a profanation. The idea or motif of exile is, of course, central to Kerby Miller's justly praised *Emigrants and Exiles*. I will take up that issue later. For now, it is enough to return to Thomas O'Flaherty's fine framing of the issue: exile was part of the Irish's honest History. So was the distrust of the English—the Sassenach—who stole their lands, translated them, presided over the starving times, and set them to wandering. Anglophobia, however, was not entirely phobic. A true history can follow from that. But consider Merwin's comment that the Anglos at issue were "America's . . . cousins,"—as Patsy Caliban was the Irish's—the English were "of our own blood . . . and 'blood is thicker than water.'" The exile motif made explicit that IrishCatholics did not want to be in America. Irish Anglophobia made equally explicit that they didn't like Anglo-Americans. Both were entirely outside notions.

I'll here offer a shorthand assessment of my own regarding exile: A case could be made that those who left during the Great Famine were without options, but the vast majority over time were not banished or exiled as those words are usually meant. They chose to leave. *Choosing* to leave, however, is not the same as *wanting* to leave. Anglo-Americans had a different perspective. They presumed that all over the entire globe, sentient and rational people wanted more than anything in the world to leave their homes and come to the heaven-favored land of the free. That was a part of the American secular faith. IrishCatholics were aware of it, but a great many did not share it. Ireland was not just where they were from; it was where they wanted to be. It was where their friends and neighborhoods were. They hadn't come to America because they were yearning to be free. They had come to get something to eat.

Add to this catalog of erratic habits a rather cavalier attitude toward the law. The Irish picnic that Ware happened on was not on a Sunday, but it could have been. It was not in a city park either, but had it been, the Irish would doubtless have broken the law and walked on the grass. Sabbatarianism, middle-class manners, and blue laws generally did not count for much among them. Leo Ward in *Holding Up the Hills*, his wonderful book about the Irish Catholic farm community outside Melrose, Iowa, summed it up perfectly: Sunday mornings "we spent at Mass"; the rest of the day they spent at play. "We are Irish after all," Ward explained, "and we know that it is right—in the sense of not wrong—to play ball on Sundays." Defining "right" as "not wrong," and arrogating to the neighborhood the sole right to decide the matter, was not the Anglo-American way to build a law-abiding and well-ordered society. Michael Madden would have called it mischievous.[41]

Anglo-Americans never asked whether there were reasons from Irish history that might explain the IrishCatholic tendency to be criminally wayward.

Eagleton writes of "the perversity of the colonial, who has only to spot a norm in order to feel the itch to violate it." For norm, read law; for colonial, read Irish. The itch to break norms is one way to say that colonials living on the peripheries generally have no great respect for the legal codes of the imperial metropolis. The historical question is whether they had reason to be respectful. Eagleton was being semisatirical when he called violating the imperial law a perversity. Only imperialists would have found it that. Without dragging colonial and postcolonial theory too deeply into the discussion, for colonials within British-ruled Ireland, violating laws was instinct, something close to an Irish privilege. For IrishCatholic targets of nativist prejudice in America, it was easy to view the laws, as well as other codes of proper conduct, as instruments of Anglo-Americans' meddlesomeness. There was no perversity—and a significant amount of neighborhood honor—in resisting them. Eagleton even adds this: "The strife between colonialists and colonials was imported from the colonial margins to the metropolitan centre."[42]

In his book *Albion's Seed*, David Hackett Fischer cataloged twenty-four varieties of culturally determinative "folkways." They were the component parts of the culture of Albion, as Britain was once known. These folkways were not just quaint, ancestral ways of behaving. They were the standards that determined social conduct and cultural mores. In Fischer's word, they were "normative." These British folkways—"time ways" was one of them—were brought by the first immigrants from Britain to America; they were the seeds from which grew the culture of Anglo-America. As mentioned earlier, the Protestants of northern Ireland were counted among Albion's seed-bearers; the Catholics of the rest of Ireland were not, which suggests—to me, at least—that Albion's seeds were Wesley's and Cromwell's as well.[43]

• • •

The above are not inconsequential examples of the outward expressions of IrishCatholic erraticism. But they provide only hints of the depth of the IrishCatholic challenge to American capitalism. Sean O'Faolain said that Irish history was a "psychological" portrait. I can change *psychological* to *cultural* without affecting O'Faolain's meaning. The four-hundred-year-old ontological divide summed up by Orsi as Catholic (Irish) = presence versus Protestant (Anglo-American) = absence, was involved. It also needs to show itself. So does the one-hundred-year-old clash between nonmarket and market economies identified by the team of Polanyi and Arensberg. The issues in those centuries-long conflicts went deeper than just walking on the grass in city parks, not taking oaths seriously, and the rest of the items on my list of erratics behaving badly.

I begin with Kerby Miller's *Emigrants and Exiles*, the book that defines the field of Irish studies in America. Miller writes that there was a "distinctive

Irish worldview—the impact of a series of interactions among culture, class, and historical circumstance." That worldview was the lens through which Irish Catholics "interpet[ed] experience and adapt[ed] to American life," a statement that recalls my dictionary's definition of cultural sensibilities as "nonrational receptors that filter experience." Miller goes on to state—rather famously by now—that there is "much evidence that in comparison to the Protestants they encountered . . . the Catholic Irish were more communal than individualistic, more dependent than independent, more fatalistic than optimistic." They were also "more passive" than enterprising and more traditional, that is more backward- and downward-looking, than modern, progressive, and forward- and outward-looking. In sum, the Irish view of the American world was "often alienating and dysfunctional"—close enough to erratic to qualify; maybe even close enough to subversive to qualify for it.[44]

I find Miller's arguments entirely persuasive. Not all do. Kevin Kenny, for example, questions some aspects of it and quotes approvingly Donald Harman Akenson, Miller's principal critic, who questions almost all of it. Akenson refers to the descriptive passage above as Miller's "Gaelic Catholic Disability variable." The first problem with Akenson's too-clever-by-half dismissal is his use of the singular "variable." John Lewis Gaddis insists that there is no place in serious history for a singular, hence independent, variable. Only reductionists would argue that such a thing as a variable even exists in history. And Miller is not given to reductionist argument. Akenson's second problem is even more basic: The Irish "worldview" was "disabling" only if the rules by which "ability" and "success" were judged were the rules by which the Irish played. Akenson got only part of it only partly right: There were Irish or "Gaelic Catholic . . . variables," lots of them, all interdependent. To call them "disabilities," however, as in socially and economically disabling, is like calling them premodern while privileging the modern. The Irish could prosper economically without aspiring to, or even caring very much about, economic prosperity. In fact, there had to have been times—possibly many of them—when they prospered *because* of their "Gaelic Catholic variables."[45]

Akenson's argument that Irish Catholics were as socially and economically "successful" in America as Irish Protestants, even if true, misses the point. It's not that their variables enabled or disabled them that's at issue; it's that they differentiated them from Anglo-American Protestant variables, and left many of the Catholic Irish to wonder "if full assimilation" to American values—included those that governed a capitalist economy—"was possible or even desirable." Those are Miller's words. I agree with them, too; I'd even consider dropping the modifying adjective "full." Small acts of defiance—playing Sunday baseball, for example—can reveal matters of consequence—defining right as not wrong, in this instance. The apparently trivial can say a very great deal about the weighty—IrishCatholics' ontological fault lines and their culturally wrenching transition from the traditional to the modern come to mind. That is the methodological assumption behind what follows: the "trivial" as explicative.[46]

Let me begin this discussion of fault lines with Finley Peter Dunne's Chicago Irish barkeep, Martin Dooley. Hennessy, one of his regular customers, told Mr. Dooley that he was thinking about going to Alaska to find a fortune in gold. "Alaska . . . they tell me 'tis fairly smothered in goold'. . . . I'd like to kick up th' sod, an' find a ton iv goold undher me fut," Mr. Dooley posed a simple question: "'What wud ye do if ye found it? . . . I-I dinnaw,' said Hennessey. And he didn't. He'd not been properly brought up. 'I tell ye what ye'd do,' Mr. Dooley said. "Ye'd come back here an' sthrut up and down th' sthreet with ye'er thrumbs in ye'er armpits. . . . ye'd hire a coachman that'd laugh at ye. Ye'er boys'd be . . . ashamed iv ye. . . . Ye'd rack rent ye'er tinants and lie about ye'er taxes. . . . Ye'd go back to Ireland . . . an' put on airs with ye'er cousin Mike . . . an' whin ye'd die, it'd take half ye'er fortune f'r rayqueems to put ye r-right. I don't want ye iver to speak to me whin ye get rich Hinnissy."[47]

In 1948, Mary Doyle Curran wrote a short semiautobiographical novel, *The Parish and the Hill*, about the Irish Catholics of a small unnamed town just outside Boston. The story is set in the late teens and early 1920s. The town was divided by neighborhood. "Irish Parish" was where the "shanty Irish" could be found; "Money Hole Hill" belonged to the "lace curtain" Irish. The Irish of the Parish did not envy those of Money Hole Hill; neither did they fawn before them or want to be like them. The protagonist of Curran's story is John O'Sullivan, a native of County Kerry. He was one of the best of the Kerry storytellers in the parish, largely because he had "the longest memory. . . . [H]e could tell visions that were none of his own, but belonged to those dead ones whose names were forgotten."[48]

One of his stories was about an "Irishman" in Ireland "who had a fire in his head." He "was fatted with riches" and certain that his money and the fire that got it for him made him special and gave him power. He would use that power to intimidate people. He did not stay in the neighborhood; nor did he share his money or use his power to the benefit of it. He wasn't just rich, he was tightfisted. The Irish in the Parish knew a lot of men like that, "English landlords" and "Yankee mill owners," for example. They also knew that those sorts would have a proper reckoning; being rich and stingy came at a heavy price.[49]

"Neither by threats nor violence" could the Irishman with a fire in his head "get a soul who would follow him." Women "shun[ed] him. If he went to have a drink, the place would empty and leave none to serve him. When he became head of a town, he soon found it empty. . . . he was left completely alone, and it was no comfort to sit in a big house with even the dogs shivering at your approach. The walls echoed with his own voice talking to itself and not even a cat would purr within.... [T]here was no one who would walk with him or give him shelter." He was being boycotted and left severely alone, a fitting punishment for a *shoneen*.[50]

Would Anglo-Americans have understood either Mr. Dooley's or John O'Sullivan's story? The seven requiems necessary to redeem Hennessey's soul would have been dismissed as a small price to pay, not to mention a popish superstition. As for the Irishman of O'Sullivan's story, he was rich; he lived in a big house, and he was the head of the town. What matter that the dog shivered and the cat wouldn't purr? Or that he didn't have someone to walk with him and provide shelter? He needed no one to walk with; he liked to walk alone and he was more than adequately sheltered. As for drinking alone, having no one to "go rounds" with, Americans would not know what that meant. O'Sullivan's Irish tragedy would have been an American comedy, in the old-fashioned sense of comedy as a tale of good fortune.

Mr. Dooley and John O'Sullivan were two fictional characters drawn by two Irish writers, neither of them especially distinguished. I chose them because their small stories addressed large themes: absence versus presence, Orsi's "ontological fault line," may have been one of them, but only very indirectly—and unintentionally. Where a tighter connection can be made is with Karl Polanyi's "great transformation. Polanyi addressed the same issues that Dunne and Curran did, though in academic language and in a global context. His discussion lends some theoretical heft to Mr. Dooley's advice to Hennessey and John O'Sullivan's tragic tale of Irishmen turned Yankee.[51]

"In archaic societies," Polanyi wrote, "the maintenance of social ties, ... the accepted code of honor ... exert a continuous pressure on the individual to eliminate economic self-interest ... to the point of making him unable ... even to comprehend" self-interest. "The premium set on generosity is so great ... as to make ... utter self-forgetfulness normative." In such "communit[ies], ... the accumulation of goods is regarded as anti-social ... and ... gainful motives are under a shadow." By archaic, Polanyi meant nonmarket. But the word also means behind the times; it's an antonym of modern. Martin Dooley and John O'Sullivan would not have objected to Polanyi's word choice.[52]

Neither would James Tully, another obscure Irish American author who wrote on the erraticism approaching irrationality of IrishCatholic neighborhoods. He described the Irish who carried with them to America the "inherited burdens"—the ancestral sorrows—"of a thousand dead Irish peasants." There was "a deep mystical strain" in that inheritance, a holdover from "archaic" (that word again) times and places. "They believed in ghosts, in fairies and in witches." Then came a comment that I must italicize: The Irish, he said, "*act the way they do because of Irish history, not American life.*"[53]

One does not have to be in total agreement with Tully to pay special attention to that last remark. The cultural foundations of their erraticism were in place long before they got to America. They were born ill suited to the place and the time. It is also important to note that Tully, like Mary Curran and Finley Peter Dunne, wasn't describing Famine-era immigrants. The cultural "holdovers" that Tully was talking about may have been archaic but their sensibilities obviously aged well. The Irish American writer William Kennedy called them traits and said "they endure." They were "handed down with families from generation to generation," a people of enduring outsideness bequeathing outside notions.[54]

Consider only how Theron Ware would have responded to the cultural values of Dooley and O'Sullivan. In Frederic's book, the "illuminated" Ware left the Methodist ministry and headed to the American West. He intended to go into real estate, make a lot of money, and maybe run for the Senate. That's a kind of extended American cliché. Jackson Lears might well have included it among the other "evasive banalities" of modernity. In the context of the modern and capitalist Anglo-America in which they lived, Mr. Dooley's and John O'Sullivan's ancient and obsolete moral code didn't just diverge from those of their time and place, they subverted them, as Orsi means the word. Americans were meant to go to Alaska and kick up gold—or to places west of New York City and live with the stumps.

Social and economic mobility—getting out of the neighborhood—was in the American grain; so was the social isolation that went with it. Moving up meant moving out and translating oneself. It was also, however, a measure by which a person was evaluated, often to the exclusion of any other standard. The problem was that social mobility was a very unreliable measure of a person's worth, and a very unfair one. That was never more true than when it was used as a yardstick for judging the Catholic Irish in America's working class. The social mobility test was based on a hopelessly flawed assumption: It presumed that in America no one wanted to be in the working class any longer than was absolutely necessary, in other words, any longer than it took to make enough money to escape it and move up into the middle class. This was rational choice and "utility maximization" theory run amok. Wanting to get out of the working class thus becomes a definitional part of being in it. The American labor force consisted solely of strivers and failures.

In 1977, the historian James Henretta wrote an article on the "ideological assumptions and conceptual bias" in the use of "social mobility" as the standard of judgment on how well and how quickly immigrants moved toward remaking themselves and becoming more American-like. It was Henretta's task to demolish the bias that inhered in the social mobility test. He went about his work with a relish. "Is it true," Henretta asked, "that all cultural or racial or class groups 'want' above all else to improve their economic position, to attain a higher standard of living, or to surpass the achievements of their parents or of other groups? If not, if these are *not* their prime aspirations, then to evaluate their lives in such terms . . . is misleading if not completely absurd." I make the same charge against Akenson.[55]

Absurd, but useful to the employing class. Making mobility the test of immigrant successes and failures served a vital purpose. In Henretta's words, it was a spur to "exertion, striving, enterprise, individual achievement as the key to [and the test of] 'the advance of a society.'" He meant by that the whole of the society. Individual advancement was in the nation's interest. It was patriotic. Henretta gives it its proper name: It was a *"new* ideology, . . . acquisitive, and change-oriented . . . the product of the historical convergence of Protestant socio-economic values and the material possibilities of an emergent industrial capitalism." Brad Gregory used similar language: "a capitalist *society* required an *ideological* about-face." That new ideology was a major part of Polanyi's reference to the ideological "transformation" affected by the market revolution of the nineteenth century. The "'hegemonic' Protestant ruling class employed [it] as a . . . weapon in order to perpetuate its power." Perpetuating power is what ruling classes do. Making individual social mobility the benchmark of achievement took the working class's eyes off other prizes; progress, achieved through bootstrapping self-reliance, had become the opiate of the working class.[56]

Henretta needed a test case, a working-class ethnic group whose value system was not based on the primacy of individualism and moving up in social rank. A group, in other words, that would help him make the commonsense case that "the point of departure for the study of any cultural group must be its own values and aspirations." That he selected the Catholic Irish is almost as important as the general arguments the Irish example helped him make. Judging Irish Catholics by how rapidly and far they advanced economically is value-laden and culturally biased, not to mention singularly lacking in subtlety and imagination. It is scorekeeping by imperial decree. Irish Catholics were not the only group judged on the basis of alien values, but they were an important one of them, as Henretta's selection of them to make the point would attest.[57]

Henretta's language was direct and unequivocal: "Among the Irish laboring population itself, there is little evidence that either behavior or goals were shaped by the ideology of individual social mobility." Raymond Williams called it "climbing the ladder" and said it was "the perfect symbol of bourgeois society." A person could climb one "only individually: you go up the ladder alone." It "weakens the principle of common betterment . . . and sweetens the poison of [a social] hierarchy." Henretta applied that bourgeois symbol to Irish laborers, and argued that they were not "atomistic individualists with an intense and overriding goal of self-advancement, but responsible participants in a transatlantic kinship network with strong family ties and communal values. Like their peasant relations in Ireland," these erratic Irish wanted steady work that didn't kill them and at a just wage; in Henretta's words, "security in their old age, a rent-free house to which they could retire." Social mobility for them was intraclass, not interclass; it involved movement from unskilled labor to skilled—or from working class to shop- or bar-owning class. It left them more comfortable and secure, but still in the neighborhood.[58]

This was not just an economic issue. It was more expansive than that. Making a good living has myriad meanings; this one was social. It involved the companionship of neighbors, not the opportunity to move up and away from them. Irish Catholic lives were not determined by the rules of modern capitalism, Henretta's "new ideology." As Henretta puts it, "participation in a capitalist [system] did not necessarily imply an acceptance of [its] ruling ideology." Regardless of their bank accounts, they separated—or exempted—themselves from the new ideology. That's the nature of erratic working-class ethnics in a mutual standoff with a host society that did not love them.[59]

• • •

I want here to return to something Terry Eagleton said: "Ideology denotes those values and symbolic practices which . . . are caught up in the business of politics." Culture is "a more capacious concept . . . much of what it contains may be ideologically innocent." By 1870, the culture, the structure of feeling of Irish Catholic workers, was beginning to lose its ideological innocence, which is to say its political irrelevancy. The excesses of modern Anglo-American capitalism were such by then that for erratic Irish, cultural divergence was being transformed to reformist politics. From this point forward there would be an obvious—and felt—Irish Catholic structure of feeling to their growing resistance and challenge to both the policies of modern American capitalism and the moral principles underlying it.

Kevin Kenny, in his 2003 article "Diaspora and Comparison," includes reference to some Irish Catholic radicals. Two of them mentioned by name were James Connolly and Jim Larkin, Irish labor radicals, both of whom spent considerable time in America, both of whom were Catholic, and both of whom were committed physical-force Irish nationalists. Kenny wrote that the "careers of these men, the movements they led, and the ideologies they *embodied, unite* the study of labor and ethnic nationalism." I'm glad he used the words *embodied* and *unite*. They make clear that Larkin and Connolly were not one-offs but standard-issue Catholic Irish. Few Irish Americans were as radical as they, but it's the "unity" of labor and ethnic nationalism that they "embodied" that counts, not the militancy with which the two causes were pursued. Imperialism and capitalism were joined. So would be the challenge to both. That joining of causes might be the single most erratic thing they did.[60]

Herbert Gutman provided an example—without meaning to. Gutman wrote that he wanted to show that the "dominant view of Gilded Age America" was not the only one. There were alternative views; "conscience and moral purpose" had not "entirely wilted" in what Gutman called the "American Dark Age." Of all the dissident voices, organized labor's was foremost. I'm in only partial agreement. It was of great interest to me that Gutman made that case by tracing the career of Joseph McDonnell. McDonnell was a prominent American labor radical; it was that that drew Gutman's attention.[61]

McDonnell, however, like Connolly and Larkin, was also a militant Irish nationalist and a Catholic. Kenny, interestingly, included his name along with Connolly's and Larkin's in his article. Gutman mentioned McDonnell's Fenianism and devotion to an independent Ireland of distinctly leftist leanings; he mentioned McDonnell's Catholicism; he even cited the statement by Samuel Gompers that McDonnell had studied to be a priest. He did not, however, make McDonnell's Irish nationalism or his Catholicism a part of his portrait of a Gilded Age dissenter. Gutman was looking for someone who embodied radical alternatives to the values of Gilded Age America; he did not look to see whether there was anything joined to McDonnell's militancy in the cause of labor. He did not ask whether the Irishman's "conscience and moral purpose" had sources besides the obvious—hence easy—one of social class.[62]

I agree with Gutman that there were many in the America labor movement who challenged and defied the regnant values of modern American capitalism; I agree that Joe McDonnell was one of those. But I also contend that McDonnell's Irishness and Catholicism were more than just addenda, offered up to fill out his biography. They were as central to what made his an alternative voice as his labor advocacy. Even his membership in Marx's International Working Man's Association did not just arise from his social class. He fought, for example, to persuade the association to separate its Irish members from the British and allow the formation of an Irish branch of the IWMA. He thought the Irish deserved to be identified by what they were—not English was a start. But consider what that meant: not Protestant, not modern, not capitalist. Their composite personality was never more ecological, the variables within it never more interdependent.

Gutman didn't make those connections. His was a one-dimensional portrait of Joseph McDonnell and his critique of capitalism. It's not that Gutman didn't recognize the importance of religion; he wrote a splendid and extremely important article on Protestantism in the Gilded Age. He also, however, admitted that he had "failed to explore the Catholic question," not just in the McDonnell piece but in others. He wasn't alone in that. I'd love to know what exactly he meant by "the Catholic question," but I would have welcomed anything he had to say on the subject, however he defined it and however he might have chosen to explore it.[63]

McDonnell was Gutman's case study; Gutman's article about McDonnell is mine. Its failings are typical of much of American labor history, including the new. New labor historians, Gutman prominently among them, should have suspected that something more substantial—and doctrinal—was going on than just premodern people confronting modern economies. The new labor history was not new enough or adventurous enough. Its practitioners, even the best of them, were unwilling to jump over what Orsi said were the absolute limits imposed by Protestant = absence and look for points of entry into the world of Catholic = presence. They wouldn't have to stay in that uncomfortable Catholic space long; just long enough to have a feeling for what Orsi says "divided Catholic from Protestant in America." The equivalencies are not exact, but they're close enough: Catholic versus Protestant can be made to read working class versus employing class; antimodern traditionalists versus progressive modernists; erratic visitors versus owners of the nation's title deed.[64]

I mentioned in the Introduction that that there were many IrishCatholics in America who, like Joe McDonnell, routinely joined the Irish national cause to the cause of labor. The two were attached, sewn together on a tight seam line that James Connolly said could never be "dissevered." That was a definitional part of their erraticism. That was true among the more militant of nationalists in Ireland as well, but the topic at hand is the outside notions of the outside Irish in America. There was what Dorothy Thompson called a "radical cosmology" that pulled the two causes together. I suspect that Orsi would have called it a "subversive cosmology." To repeat something said earlier: For the IrishCatholics in America, the association of causes was neither transactional nor one of convenience. It was entirely predictable and natural, part of the social unconscious of a traditional, premodern, and good-hearted people whose gods were omnipresent. The Irish were a subject people; Ireland was a subject nation; workers were a subject class. The causes went together. I will follow the lead of the erratics and leave them that way.[65]

That was not the pattern in market economies. Modern capitalism required that the three causes occupied entirely separate planes. They belonged in different ideological jurisdictions and could not be joined. The seam had to be torn. The "great transformation" described by Polanyi included both the secularization of society, the banishment of the gods as well as the dead generations, and the compartmentalization of society, the separation of politics from morality, the separation of both from economics, and the assignment of each to what Jean Bethke Elshtain calls "separate spheres." Since the secularization of society accompanied and required its compartmentalization, I will take them up as the related issues they were.[66]

I begin with Robert Orsi and the "subversive" nature of Catholic = presence and the erratic nature of IrishCatholic = presence that followed from that. Orsi is here at his combative best. America's vaunted "freedom of religion" was inherently reformational. The Ahlstrom thesis applies. America was an anti-Catholic movement. The religious clause of the First Amendment didn't mean what it said; there was an ontological codicil. The Catholic belief in the real presence blasphemed; it was a superstition, not a religious doctrine. As Orsi writes, freedom of religion in America meant "liberation from . . . superstitions." The "free exercise" of religion meant none would be established, but it did not mean that false faiths would be accorded equal privileges. It did not apply to the inauthentic, of which Catholicism was foremost.[67]

Elshtain makes a similar argument. America was one of what she calls "Protestant nation-states," those brought to robust life by the Protestant Reformation. In the case of America, it was more Cromwell's and Locke's Reformation than Luther's. She quotes Locke's words: Religious faith was an "inward" matter; it was voluntaristic and had to be kept "'absolutely' separate and 'absolutely' distinct" from governance. It followed necessarily that in a properly constituted society, in Elshtain's words, "the Care of Souls is not committed to the Civil Magistrate." A true democracy could not tolerate any blending of disparate and often contradictory responsibilities.[68]

Obviously, by Locke's definition, there could be "absolutely no such thing . . . as a Christian Commonwealth." The idea of it contradicted a true democratic commonwealth. The Christian versions—and this was especially true if Catholic Christian—were "far too 'outward'; their faith and its clerical guardians were too much on display. They were, in Elshtain's word, a "strong *ecclesia*, [one with] communally endorsed habits." Those habits were not just communally endorsed, they were communally enforced. The divergence could not have been more complete. For IrishCatholics there could be "absolutely no such thing" as a commonwealth in the absence of those Locke and the Enlightenment had evicted: the gods, the ancestors, the neighbors, and the familiar places—all under their birth names—in sum, the ecclesia. It was their *presence* that made society a *commonwealth*; in their absence, there were only crowds of people, unconnected to the past, the place, and one another.[69]

Alexis de Tocqueville also had something to say on the issues raised by Locke; and, since he mentioned the Irish in his comments, I think them relevant here. The word *commonwealth* had a sense of democracy, of equality of rank, about it. American nativists insisted that Catholic inwardness subverted American democracy. Locke would doubtless have agreed. De

Tocqueville felt those fears were quite misplaced. His remarks were in the context of the Irish Catholic immigration. It was "pouring" into the United States when de Tocqueville wrote *Democracy in America* in 1835. He had visited Ireland that same year. The pour, as he likely could have predicted, would soon be a flood.[70]

Americans, even the most virulently anti-Catholic—*The Awful Disclosures of Maria Monk* had come out just a year before de Tocqueville's book—had nothing to fear from papists. "Catholics," he said, "form the most republican and democratic class there is in the United States." In fact, "Catholicism" was "most favorable" to democracy's foundational principle, "equality of conditions." The Church's hierarchy was limited entirely to the clergy; the laity, rich and poor and all in between, were equals—as in equally inferior and subordinate to priest, bishop, cardinal, and pope. That equality of station was why Mr. Dooley told Hinnissy that "I don't want ye iver to speak to me whin ye get rich." It clearly was why the Irish shunned the Irishman "fatted with riches." Locke and the Americans' democratic commonwealth was political; de Tocqueville's and the Irish Catholics' version of the same was social.[71]

To social democrats, inequalities of rank—like wealthy and powerful lay Protestants buying front-row pews and putting their names on them—were a greater risk to democracy than high-hatted and mitered bishops. If Americans at the time and later had not essentially ignored the section on Irish Catholics in de Tocqueville's great work, *Democracy in America*, they might have understood that there were different ways to define *commonwealth*. The debate over which was the true way availed little or nothing. The better discussion would have been how the social and political could be joined and the commonwealth made whole.

Modernity, Polanyi's great transformation, codified Lockean "inwardness," and delegitimized Catholic "outwardness." The economy was no longer embedded in society; that was a medieval relic. In modern societies, the economy was autonomous and entirely self-regulating. Society was embedded in it. The laws of supply and demand were made as universally applicable and as morally neutral as the law of gravity. Compartmentalizing was a modernist "imperative." Modernity "privatized" religion and "separated [it] from society," in the process secularizing both. People "seal[ed] themselves off into compartments." Americans did not attempt "to merge and blend" politics and matters of "conscience and moral purpose," to return to Gutman's language. They didn't even introduce the one to the other. In Elshtain's words, in modern America "never the twain shall meet." That was the new ideology.[72]

The twain still met and comingled in IrishCatholic America. Merging and blending the two was an erratic's imperative. Granted, the two were what Seamus Deane admitted were "opposing discourses"; the one had to do with culture, the other with economics or finance. But the Irish had had a lot of practice at stitching seams. They managed "a felicitous convergence of the two." In modern market-dominated societies, matters of finance and culture were "schismatically and disastrously ... divided from one another." I can't help thinking Deane chose "schismatically" to signal heretically, with its usual religious meaning intact. Certainly he chose it to indicate a very high level of ontological—or, to use his word, "cultural"—dissent. He quotes another Irish writer, Daniel Corkery who expanded the playing field by identifying the two "spheres" as the "emotional" and the "intellectual." Separating them, Corkery went on, was "the opposite of Irishness."[73]

Polanyi's explanation was less theological, though he gave ample space to the importance of religion and ritual to "tribal" societies and to the various— and felicitous—ways they converged the opposing discourses. The problem was that in Anglo-America "the institutional separation of the political from the economic sphere was constitutive to market society." *Constitutive* is a strong word. It was essential that there be an "'economic zone' and a 'political zone'; they had to be maintained." They were "the irrefragable condition of the existing system of society"—secular commandments of a sort.[74]

Brad Gregory brought Orsi and Polanyi together. Protestant (= absence) and capitalist market economies "segregate[d] economic behavior from interior dispositions. Then when asked about one's decisions or priorities, from a complementary and politically protected 'private sphere' [moderns] could utter a quintessential modern Western imperative ... 'Mind your own business.'" Or this one: "It's Your Misfortune and None of My Own." People coming from traditional societies would not have known what that meant. Societies were organic; "your" misfortune was very much "my own." IrishCatholics in America would learn soon enough that inorganic modern societies were zero-sum games, but knowing that and other of the modern imperatives did not make erratic Irish like them or want to act in accordance with them.[75]

In 1846, an Irish member of the British Parliament told his colleagues that, during the worst years of the Great Famine, starving cottier families often left their last edible potatoes outside their cabins for any "passing beggar," a habit which was unfathomable to the English, one of whom, also a member of Parliament, took the practice of sharing as evidence that the Irish had a surfeit of potatoes. In 1913, the top one-half percent of the American population held 40 percent of the nation's wealth. That half of one percent shared little of their wealth with passing beggars. There were certain erratics, some Irish, some not, who thought it was nearer the truth that, in fact, the half of one percent had taken their wealth from and created the passing beggars. The taking, however, was legal and the transformed economy of Anglo-America was unbothered by it.[76]

There were "laws" that governed modern, autonomous, and disembedded economies. They were irrefutable and universal: the law of supply and demand; the law of competition; the law of self-interest; the law sanctifying private property; the one entitling capital over labor. Anglo-America held that all those laws and all that arose from them were logical and empirically derived, intrinsically fair, even sanctioned by their God. And so, laissez-faire, let them be. Any interference in their self-regulating operations, in the name of fairness or even mercy, would not only itself be unfair, but utterly ineffective and hence unmerciful.[77]

Many Irish believe that obedience to the inviolate rules of laissez-faire was one of the reasons more than a million of their ancestors had died between 1846 and 1850. They had a point. Some believed that when applied to the modern American capitalist economy, those same economic laws created a system in which scarcity and hunger had become weapons of the rich. They had a point on that one too. The idea that the "free labor" economy was self-regulating and self-reforming, that there were "invisible laws" that "emancipated" labor, in Polanyi's harsh judgment, "made the threat of destruction through hunger"—one's own and one's family's—"effective." In other words, workers were left free to starve. Food went to those who could pay the price for it. It once went to those who were hungry. Semianarchists as they were said to be, the Irish had no more respect for these "natural" laws than they did for the statute laws in the civil and criminal codes.[78]

Everything that went into the making of an Irish Catholic worldview—culture, history, memory, tradition—made erratics of many of them. There was a moral dimension to everything. To separate traditional elements of fairness from politics was to render that moral dimension powerless and leave politics without a basis in justice. Democracy had no meaning in a society of such gross economic inequality. "Violent contrasts of wealth and power," in R. H. Tawney's words, "and an undiscriminating devotion to institutions by which such contrasts are maintained and heightened, do not promote the attainment of [equality], but thwart it." Those violent contrasts had no happier effect on democracy.[79]

The institutions Tawney had in mind were those that placed matters of conscience and matters of political governance in separate spheres. The two had to be joined and advanced simultaneously. The twain must always meet; indeed there was no twain; there was only the one. The public and the private had to be embedded—literally, in bed together. They had to be grafted, blended, melded, mixed, merged, converged, fused, woven warp and weft. Modern Anglo-Americans thought that a distinctly erratic way of thinking. Modernity had a different word list: the two had to be disembedded, divorced, zoned off, separated, divided, compartmentalized, kept distant and distinct. All of which recalls previously cited comments of Jackson

Lears: "The most powerful critics of capitalism have often looked backward rather than forward. . . . [T]he most profound radicalism is often the most profound conservatism."[80]

This divergence between the traditional Irish Catholic and the modern American Protestant versions of democratic governance also calls into question the notion that when the Irish got around to defining, declaring, and defending their democratic republic, the United States was always their model. Ireland, according to some at the time and since, would be America writ small, a neoliberal capitalist state, a scaled-down replica of modern America. The Irish would go from being West Brits to being East Americans. According to a recent historian, Irish Americans "longed to see their native land as a miniature America." They hoped "that at some point [Ireland] might offer the same" as America did. There were some Irish who thought that. They are, after all, a fissiparous people.[81]

The issue of what Free Ireland would be, other than a nation with its own flag, is one to which I will return. All that needs to be said at the moment is that the "Ireland as miniature America" idea ignores the deep divisions between IrishCatholic culture and the disembedded economy of modern capitalist Anglo-America. This was particularly the case with working-class Irish Americans who looked on the American system with considerable disaffection and for whom the idea that Ireland Free would be a classical liberal Anglo-American style nation was offensive—un-Irish, really. Kerby Miller cited thousands of Irish immigrant letters back to Ireland. This one, written in 1883 by Eugene O'Callaghan back to relatives considering emigrating, has always stuck with me. "This America," he wrote, "is not what it used to be; any person who can make a fair living at home are better Stay theire." I don't know what O'Callaghan thought America used to be, but it clearly was not what he wanted, or the Irish needed, it to be. By "fair living," O'Callaghan did not mean merely finding a job at a living wage. America was unfair, as in unjust. It was not a friendly place.[82]

For Irish like O'Callaghan, modern America was nearer the indispensable opposite, the negative referent to the model of what the new Ireland should be. It was one thing to admire what Americans had done in '76; the 4th of July was an Irish holiday as well as an American. Breaking out of the British Empire was heroic. The Irish should go and do likewise. It was quite another thing to admire what America had become after the break from empire—particularly what it had become after 1870 and Polanyi's "great transformation." A true republic, as dissident Irish defined it, had to be a society informed by moral and ethical values. America's was not. Why would the Irish want to copy it? They could never quite get their erratic sensibilities around the modern idea that human relationships should be consigned to separate and unconnected categories that never spoke to one another.

Americans had detached fairness from governance; they had separated the inseparable. In Orsi's language, they expelled the old gods and made new ones of the selfish and grasping; they tolerated glaring economic inequalities that mocked their pretensions of democracy and showed a strange preference for the company of stumps. A "fair living" came hard in such a place. Ireland had to try to do better. Its republic had to be its own; not French, not Russian, not American. The only model the erratics needed was the humane one that their sorrowing ancestors, their "dead generations," had bequeathed them. Some of the erratics drew a logical conclusion: Perhaps the United States could make itself into an Ireland writ very large. Modern Americans had much to learn from their IrishCatholic visitors with their accumulated sorrows. It would serve the Yankees well to listen to and heed the advice of the Irish dead. That may have been the single most erratic, subversive, and outside notion IrishCatholics ever brought to America.

CHAPTER TWO

"And a Fourth There Is Who Wants Me to Dig"
Patsy Caliban and the Limits of American Liberalism

> "The Irish . . . could patrol the streets, work on the railroads, put out the fires, carry the hod. . . . Their hands and feet were adaptable . . . but there was this mind lag. . . . They were . . . backward."
> —Francis Hackett, *American Rainbow* (1922, 1971) in Miller, *Emigrants and Exiles*, 519

The character of Caliban in Shakespeare's play *The Tempest* has been variously interpreted. Leo Marx said the play was Shakespeare's "American fable" and Caliban—who, it should be noted, was a slave—was one of the New World's most barbarous specimens. Ronald Takaki agrees with most of Marx's argument; *The Tempest* was Shakespeare's "wilderness epic." Caliban was fierce in nature and physiognomy, one of the first of the racialized Others who would wander through America's history. I do not discount either Marx's or Takaki's argument, but neither am I fully persuaded by them. Shakespeare described Caliban as an anthropoid, scarcely human. But he also provided some specifics: he was a whelp, but a *"freckled"* whelp, the son of Sycorax, a "hag," but a *"blue-ey'd"* hag.[1]

Shakespeare wrote *The Tempest* just as England was launching its empire by assaulting Ireland; the play may not have been an Irish fable, but it assuredly was an imperial and heavily racialized one. *The Tempest* is nearer Shakespeare's Hibernization of savagery, which means the Catholicization of savagery. The English definitely made that connection. An 1870 *Punch* cartoon by John Tenniel depicts a ferocious "Patsy O'Caliban" wearing a belt labeled "ultramontane." This Catholic primitive, wrote Tenniel, was the true "Rory of the Hills," the gallant Irish hero of one of Charles Kickham's sunbursting efforts at Irish nationalist poetry.[2]

From Shakespeare to James Joyce is not so great a leap, but this may be the first time these passages from *Ulysses* have been called on in the context of erratic Irish in America. In *Ulysses*, Stephen Dedalus refers to "Patsy Caliban our American cousin." Shakespeare's "freckled whelp" had an Irish nickname—a disdainful one, at that—an American place of residence, and some cousins in the home country. I am taken as well by the fact that Caliban was condemned to live on the rocky ground of the island—land beyond the pale perhaps?—the good land was reserved for those who had stolen it from Sycorax, Caliban's mother. And what is to be made of the curse Caliban wishes on his tormentors: May "the red plague rid you/ For learning me your language"? In the context of the "translation" or Ireland, that's anachronistic, but it does not affect the fact that *The Tempest* had an imperial aspect—as did Dedalus's reference to Caliban. Later in the book, Joyce included a reference to the "rage of Caliban at not seeing his face in a mirror," which suggests nothing so much as the inverse mirror of the imperial Other. Joyce's adaptation doesn't necessarily contradict either Marx's or Takaki's. The island is a New World—Patsy, after all, lives in America—and Caliban is a brute. More specifically, he's a hooligan.[3]

The other scene from *Ulysses* that deserves notice occurs very early in the book. Dedalus tells his English roommate that "I am a servant of two masters. One is "English. . . . the imperial British state. . . . A crazy queen, old and jealous." The second is "Italian . . . the holy Roman catholic and apostolic church. . . . Kneel down before me." That passage is frequently quoted. Dedalus meant that he was the colonial servant of an English monarch, the ecclesiastical servant of an Italian pope. Then came Dedalus's almost throwaway line; he said—in proper Hiberno-English, it should be noted—"And a third there is who wants me for odd jobs." He did not identify this third master, but that "third there is" was Ireland, "the old sow that eats her farrow," Dedalus's pervasively repressive home country.[4]

Stephen Dedalus, however, was not the only Irishman subservient to masters. When Joyce speaks of Patsy Caliban, his American cousin, he acknowledges that. Dedalus knew of Patsy. All Ireland did. So I'll add Patsy to the conversation. He is of far greater interest to me than hypersensitive poets with hurt feelings. I'll use Joyce's words as Patsy might have spoken them: "And a fourth there is who wants me to dig"; or these from Bridget: "who wants me to scrub." That gets Joyce wrong, but history right. It's America's odd jobs, of which it had an abundance, that I'm interested in, the ones Bridget did with wooden buckets, Patsy with long-handled tools—including military-issue long guns. Cousins Patsy and Bridget had not left Ireland because it was boring and unappreciative of them; they left because it couldn't be relied on to feed them. Ireland and the Irish were arguably more dependent on those odd jobs and the Anglo-American masters who controlled them than they were on the church, the crown, or a restive, intolerant, and fissiparous Ireland.

There is one other important question: Did the masters, Joyce's three and my additional one, connive? Were they a gang? Specifically—and, pulling the fourth American master into the discussion—did the English, the Italian, and the Irish have reasons to put the middling and poor on the road to America? To start with the Italian master: The Catholic clergy of Ireland had encouraged the "translation" of Irish to English; partly because it might help the popes undo the English Reformation, and partly because it would help the Church spread its evangelizing wings in the English-speaking parts of the world. As for Ireland, it was a nation ruled in the interests of the English but ruled by an Irish bourgeoisie whose economic interests were well served by setting the superfluous Irish to wandering. That was particularly the case when those taking their leave of Ireland blamed England and not other Irish for their misfortunes.[5]

But what of Patsy, what of the Irish in America who believed, many of them quite strongly, that the English master was running a labor bureau for the fourth, the American master. I want here to quote some others who addressed the possibility that England's Irish policy was designed at least in part—and possibly a very large part—to meet the labor needs of an expanding American economy. I have already noted that the more erratic of the Irish American working class connected the Irish national cause with the cause of American labor. It's what passed for an Irish American working-class ideology. It had its source in the idea of a hugger-mugger deal, a covert and sinister agreement, between the two parts of Anglo-America.

I cite first an anonymous Irishman who called himself "Ballaghaslane Beara." Ballaghaslane roughly translates as "evicted" or "expelled" from home, a victim of what Dedalus had called "the British imperial state." Beara was the place in West Cork where Ireland's richest copper mines were located. They were owned by a British company. In 1876, Beara sent a letter from Virginia City, Nevada, that was published in Patrick Ford's New York newspaper, *The Irish World and American Industrial Liberator*. The Irish, he said, "are slaves in the United States, and . . . the reason is plain." It was "because we haven't an Irish nation. England defrauded us . . . and we are . . . chained down to live in the [American] mire." Their imperial first master had passed them down to their capitalist fourth master, the one who wanted them to dig. Beara did not say that the arrangement was intentional, but the tone of his letter would suggest that he would not have been surprised to learn that it was.[6]

My second source was as angry as Beara. Michael Hannan was an Irish-born Catholic priest who presided over St. Mary's parish in Butte, Montana. I do not cite him as a credible source of historical truth, only as an example of politics on the radical edge of the seam. Hannan kept a diary from 1923 to 1927, very late in the Irish Americans odd-jobs era. But what he told himself in that diary and likely repeated in conversation—or homilies—would have applied equally at any time from 1870 to 1930. In his entry for April 12, 1923, he wrote this: "I can see clearly" that "Ireland must not be free." She is a good stock farm on which to raise wage slaves." Liam Mellows, a leading and decidedly left-leaning Irish Republican, called Hannan "a tower of strength to the [Republican] movement." Were the others in the movement of the same mind as Hannan on Ireland as a place kept by England to raise American wage slaves?[7]

I turn next to a fine and careful historian, John V. Kelleher. His language is more restrained than that of Beara and Hannan. And certainly he has far greater credibility than either. But there is anger in Kelleher's comments, too. From "the 1840s on," he wrote, "floods of Irish immigrants gave [the United States] . . . a huge fund of poor, unskilled, cheap, almost infinitely exploitable labor." The fund was well used "with a callousness now hard to comprehend . . . in crude, backbreaking jobs." He did not draw the date 1840s out of a hat. Beginning with the Famine immigration, the Irish served, as one interested party put it, as a "mobile 'reserve army' of labor . . . to supply cheap muscle power." That's Kelleher's point. The Irish contribution to the American economy was "real . . . but it would be difficult to distinguish it from the drafthorse contribution . . . and it was rewarded with about as many thanks."[8]

Kelleher is not arguing that the *intent* of England's Irish policy was supplying the American labor market. Neither am I. The English—and the Irish middle class—were not notoriously kind to the Irish poor, but they did not set them to wandering in order to provide America with cheap labor. At that, I think both Kelleher and I are more understanding of why it appeared that way to some Irish Americans at the time. One reason for our greater forbearance—if such it be—is that the erratics' idea that there were "masters" who did not grieve when the Irish left and other equally powerful masters who had plenty for those Irish to do upon arriving was not entirely fanciful.

• • •

Orsi's, Gregory's, and Elshtain's accounts of the origins of cultural divergence date back centuries. That does not affect their relevance, only their immediate applicability to Patsy Caliban, Ireland's American cousin. Herbert Gutman's emphasis on the divergence of premodern and preindustrial people coming into a modernizing and modern, industrializing, and industrial American economy moves the issue to and beyond 1870. Gutman, however, never defined what *premodern* and *preindustrial* meant, and he said little at all about the erratic cultural values of those who were both. He

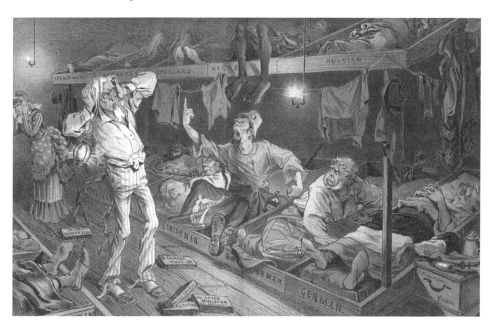

J. Kepler, "Uncle Sam's Lodging-House," 1882. The Irishman was the noisy and erratic outlier in an assembly of otherwise well-behaved workmen. Courtesy Library of Congress.

was interested in the fact that Irish Catholics, both immigrants and their descendants, came from a place that was neither modern nor industrial, but what made them such, other than chronology, was of less interest to him.

• • •

I chose to start this account at 1870 in part because it's close to when Jackson Lears began his study of American modernists taking up the cause of antimodernism, and because that's when the team of Polanyi and Arensberg would have started it. Here's a key passage from Polanyi's *Great Transformation*: The "origins of the cataclysm" that would transform societies "lay in the ... endeavor ... to set up a self-regulating market system" that would in time become the "one common matrix" of modern civilization. That market system was based on a "motive only rarely acknowledged as valid in the history of human societies ... namely, gain," production for individual financial gain not for use or consumption by the local society according to the traditions and rituals by which it governed itself. The new self-regulating market economy reported only to itself.

Polanyi then placed this cataclysmic change in time. "As everybody knows, it grew to maturity in England in the wake of the Industrial Revolution, during the first half of the nineteenth century." Which meant, among other things, that it determined the English response to an Gorta Mór. "It reached ... America about fifty years later. ... For the origins of the cataclysm we must turn to the rise ... of the market economy." Polanyi's theory incorporates elements of each of the others: Orsi's "ontological fault line" is there; so is Gregory's "unintended Reformation" and the expulsion of the gods. So is Elshtain's politics of "separate spheres," where "never the twain," namely, the moral and the economic, "shall meet." Fifty years after the English, America had an Industrial Revolution of its own. Its great transformation was complete. The transformation of those who would do the labor of it was not.[9]

The origins of the cultural divergence that is the topic here are to be found in the years immediately after the American Civil War. From then until 1920, another 7 million Irish, the vast majority Catholic, arrived and joined the more than 3 million who had come to America before them. The Irish economy and society had changed from 1845 to 1870, but only slightly. It was still nonmarket and, on the basis of Arensberg's description, it resembled that of the seventeenth century more than the economy of almost any other place in the western world. America may have been more unfathomable to an Irish immigrant of 1890 than it had been to an immigrant of 1850. It was also not conspicuously more tolerant of papists.

As in 1845, the Catholic Irish who came after the Civil War entered a Northern working class that consisted of what Americans zealously proclaimed were *free* laborers. They would have disputed vehemently my addition of that fourth American master who wanted Irish to dig and do other odd jobs. Free labor was a special and favored status. Freedom was what every American had; it was also all any of them had a right to. It bestowed equality of rank. The comparative base, of course, was slavery, a labor system recently and providentially abolished. Free labor was defined as the total opposite of slave labor. Capitalists were not buyers of workers at slave auctions, they were buyers of work in free labor markets. The American economy, as Polanyi described it, had "isolated the economic sphere entirely from the ... Constitution ... and created the only legally grounded market society in the world." Came next his judgment: "In spite of universal suffrage"—that is, political freedom and equality—"American [wage laborers] were powerless against owners." Measures to expand democracy through political rights would amount to little without an equal foundation in social and economic rights.[10]

The master-slave relationship was American capitalism's negative referent—and a very handy one it was. It allowed freedom to be defined by what it was not. It allowed even the emancipation of Black slaves to be seen as admission to an American peerage. The former slaves were free and thus, by definition, equal American citizens. There were some Northern free laborers who viewed this "antislavery theory of liberty" as a denial of reality, an illusion. If it was to have meaning, the Civil War had to be extended, in David Montgomery's words, "beyond equality." But it couldn't be. By the logic of the free labor ideology, there wasn't anything "beyond equality." There were no greater gifts. It was the ultimate endowment.[11]

The Union's victory would lead to a reconstruction of the feudal slave-owning South, but not of the modern and free labor North. There would be no reconstruction, no reordering, of the relationship between the working and the employing classes, North or South. The Civil War, in the words of the one-time Catholic, full-time Irish American socialist Michael Harrington, was a "triumph of Northern capitalism." It was more than that, of course. But it was assuredly that. The "free labor system" was the mid-nineteenth-century term for what later generations would call capitalism. To be on the side of free labor was not to be prolabor. It was very nearly its opposite.[12]

Robert Penn Warren, though hardly a disinterested observer, spoke to a central truth. The "legacy of the Civil War" was a mixed one. Union and emancipation were worthy goals; Warren granted that. But the detritus of modernity and unchecked capitalism had also to be granted: "ragged children"—North and South, Black and white—along with "shoddy aristocrats"—also without sectional distinction—were also the war's legacy. The Northern "reformers" who had led the assault on slavery before the war "shrink away from the besmirchments of the new society" that emerged after it. For them "to grapple with the concrete, immediate problem of poverty and exploitation would have been . . . too befouling, too full of the danger of involvement." Defending the Union and attacking slavery were easy because both were abstractions; "one could demand the total solution, the solution of absolute morality . . . the apocalyptic *frisson*." The "quest for social justice" was not abstract; it did not lend itself to a total solution. It would be put on hold.[13]

Warren, of course, wrote that in 1961, but if something like it had been written sixty to eighty years earlier, and if any Catholic Irish in the Northern working class could have been found reading it, Warren's discourse on the legacies of war would have resonated with them. Warren would have appeared as one like themselves: unwilling, or unable, to remove the idea of social justice from the idea of democracy. That Americans could compartmentalize and separate the two was incoherent at best, morally deficient at worse. A social order of shoddy aristocrats and ragged children could not be a democracy. Shouting "free labor" slogans, including the freedom to move out of the working class and move up socially—James Henretta's "new ideology"—did not change that. The postwar response to industrialization and its discontents—the "social question," in the polite language of the day, the unjust treatment of labor by capitalists in more direct language—was hamstrung by the commitment to the ideology of "free labor" among those who would reform the system.

There was a corollary to that ideology. The *Boston Daily Advertiser* put it this way in 1867: America was unique; "there is no such thing among us as a *hereditary* working class." Which meant essentially that there was no such thing as a working class at all. That comment returns the argument to a working class that consisted solely of strivers and failures. The statement enshrined the idea of social mobility. The American model was one of workers who freely sold their labor for the market price in the form of wages and worked for only the time it took them to become the buyers of the labor of others who, in their turn, would do likewise. All this would be free of any interference in the operation of labor markets whether by governments or unions—or by antimodern Irish Catholics who blended opposing discourses.[14]

Here is William Lloyd Garrison on the free labor market question in 1867, two years after slavery's end. He insisted that in America wage labor was only "a temporary condition from which the worker could 'rise to a higher social position.'" As he put it, "'may he not choose his employer? May he not contract for wages? May he not change his occupation, whenever he can improve his condition? . . . Does he not own himself?'" Did he not have the suffrage? Garrison was particularly outraged when free laborers used the language of race and bondage to make the case that they were not free in any meaningful sense of the word, as when they described themselves as "wage slaves," "white slaves," even "white niggers." All of this, Garrison said, was a "disgusting" form of 'cant,' an insult to the intelligence of every sane man."[15]

Wendell Phillips was another of the abolitionists who angrily condemned the talk of wage slavery as a cynical effort by a privileged class of free white laborers to co-opt the language of radical reform and to benefit from the immiseration of enslaved black labor. The free labor system could not lead to wage slavery. That was more paradox than the postwar generation could handle. Northern workers, Phillips contended, were "neither wronged nor oppressed." And if even minimally ill-used, they were American citizens with the right to vote and the option to flee and go in search of the American Big Rock Candy Mountain.

Worker complaints, Phillips insisted, were based on "'false doctrines' . . . derived from the habit of 'looking at American questions through European spectacles.'" I think he meant "Southern spectacles" as well, but no matter. Phillips acknowledged that in "'old world[s]' there were 'absurd and unjust institutions'" that were cruel and oppressive. But in the providentially favored parts of the New World, workers had the chance to become capitalists; they had only to practice "economy, self-denial, temperance, education, and moral character," everything, in other words, of which Patsy Caliban was thought incapable.[16]

For someone as "acutely sensitive to injustice" as Phillips, these statements were astonishingly myopic and lazy. His emphasis on social mobility as the reward for righteous behavior was not just culturally biased, it was a social-class conceit. As Christopher Lasch put it, there was clearly "a slackening of moral realism and resolve in [the] increasingly unconvincing celebration of free labor, a willingness to confuse the ideal with the reality." These free workers were "increasingly subject to the degrading effects of wage labor." The "'very foundation of [the American] 'industrial system' [was] a fixed"—that is, hereditary—"hopeless proletariat.'" The abolitionists' and later reformers' embrace of free labor did not translate into support for that free working class who did the laboring. Often it did the reverse.[17]

Free labor was a term and an ideology based on contrasts. The free labor system was filled with light and righteousness; other labor systems were dark and filled with iniquities. The biblical images are entirely appropriate. Postwar Northern reformers, like the abolitionists whose lead they followed, were holy warriors. Also like the abolitionists, they did not have to look hard to find dark places. To put it in historical or semigeopolitical terms, the Northern free labor ideology had coherence and political traction only in the context of its perceived opposites, the labor systems of Europe and the American South with their hereditary and fixed working class. In this context, there is enormous irony in the fact that no one, North or South, ever acknowledged that slavery was ended not just by invading Union, free state armies, but when two million Black slaves walked off the job, the largest general "strike" in history. The free labor ideology left no room for such an analysis. In fairness, given the absence of comment at the time, neither did any other ideology, Marxism included.

To put the matter simply—and to understate it—the "antislave theory of liberty" was an inadequate response to American industrialization and the social problems that came with it. Black Americans were the most profoundly and tragically affected, but the free labor ideology did no one in the working class any favors. It was not solely an Irish issue. The Catholic Irish in the working class, however, were a singular case; that was often the situation when the issue had to do with labor. Once again, blame history—and the Irish sensibilities that arose from it.

For a very specific and important example of the distinctiveness of Irish labor, listen to what E. L. Godkin had to say on the matter of the hundreds of thousands of Patsy Calibans in the American labor pool. Godkin was the founder of *The Nation*, the journal of record for the "best and brightest" of the reforming class. He spoke for that class. But Godkin was also born in Ireland to an Anglo-Irish Congregationalist minister of not-quite-Ascendancy status. He wanted it understood, as he put it, that though "I am an Irishman, . . . I am . . . English in blood." He may have said more than he intended by that racialized comment. But let it also be noted that he named *The Nation* after the Irish Home Rule journal of that title. All of which makes him my perfect spokesman for the post–Civil War Anglo-American liberal reformer.[18]

On the most basic of worker demands, the eight-hour day, Godkin took the side of capital, arguing that ten hours constituted a "natural" day's work. But it wasn't just a matter of shortening the length of a working day that Godkin rejected. The demand for eight hours came not from careful students of society, but from the working class, which, Godkin and other reformers insisted, should have been in the process of repealing itself. In fact, it came from organized—or semiorganized—labor, from unions of working people, the mere presence of which suggested a permanent laboring class. Those unions, moreover, were demanding, in the interests of justice, that state legislatures pass laws implementing the eight-hour day. Such laws wouldn't just violate free contract; they would take items from spheres kept separate and join them. Godkin then told his readers that everything about the agitation for an eight-hour law presaged the formation of a Workingmen's Party, the dangers arising from which were staggering. Such a party would impose moral social-class issues on a classless free labor economy and reduce society to "barbarism."[19]

But Godkin hadn't finished. He turned next to that peculiarly Irish convergence of causes, to the Irish tendency to demand not just labor's emancipation from "wage slavery," but Ireland's emancipation from imperial slavery. It was not just a workingmen's party that Godkin feared. There was also the prospect of what he called an "Irish Party," Fenian rebels who would agitate for an American involvement in the Irish national question. On this issue, Godkin identified the threat as being not just to the free labor ideology, but to "this Christian civilization of ours," by which he meant that of Protestant Albion and its American seed.

It may be that the workingmen's party that he feared and the Irish party he feared even more would have been separate and discrete. But Godkin included reference to both in the same sentence and it is far more likely that what he truly feared was the prospect of a blended and doubly threatening political presence: a single Irish Worker's Party dedicated to the simultaneous advance of both causes. Here was how he described the Irish Catholics in America's working class: They were "poor, ignorant, helpless, degraded, ... reckless, ... priest-ridden, whiskey-loving, thriftless Paddies." If only they had been "Protestants ... the American church organization" would have helped them, but the churches take "but little interest in the half-barbarous stranger." No civilization, certainly not "our Christian" one could survive the convergence, the partnership, of Paddy, the Fenian with a bomb, and Patsy Caliban, the hooligan with a muck stick.[20]

And that raises the issue of the second of the two problems internal to American reform that limited the reformers' ability to deal effectively with the American labor problem. The first was using slavery as "free labor's" antithesis. This second one was like the first in that both involved systems and institutions defined on the basis of their perceived opposites; both required looking at one's own world through the spectacles of another. This next limit to liberalism, however, arose from more than just the self-satisfaction that came with the victory of a free labor system over one based on slave labor. And it involved more than just the problems that were inherent in that free labor ideology. Defining free labor as "not slave labor" loses all coherence and relevance in the absence of a system of slavery near enough to serve the role of the defining negative. The end of slavery meant that the free labor ideology would have to be entirely self-justifying.

Perhaps that is what Godkin meant when he offered this remarkable comment in 1871. With slavery gone, he said, "Catholic [interests]" were the "most portentous of all the 'interests' which [then threatened] American society and government." By "portentous," he clearly meant ominous, a threat not just to America's social order, but to America's core values and institutions. This second inherent limit to a meaningful response to labor issues involved more than just the free labor ideology and an undifferentiated working class. This one was about Cousin Patsy Caliban and the legions of Irish like him. Godkin knew them well; they carried "in their blood traditions which give universal suffrage an air of menace." So much for suffrage as labor's salvation.[21]

E. L. Godkin was a liberal, a reformer, one of a recognizable type of Anglo-American race/religious patriots. The questions can be simply posed: How could reform movements based on Godkin's ideas and those similar to his be applied or even made comprehensible to IrishCatholic working people? Is it even conceivable that what the reformers witnessed and what they knew, or thought they knew, about Catholics did not affect how they would treat labor issues when the laborers were Catholics? I would ask those questions specifically of Godkin and of *The Nation*, the classiest of the journals of reform. Catholics not only had voted for the party of slavery before the war, they voted for the party of apartheid after it. Official Catholic doctrine did, in fact, run counter to America's constructed national image; that's the other half of the Ahlstrom thesis. That did not mean that postwar reformers had to malign and abuse individual Catholics; asking reformers to divide the faithful from the faith is not asking too much.[22]

American Protestant reformers didn't see the world the way immigrant and ethnic working-class Catholics did. Indeed, they didn't see the same world at all. There was no moral common ground; no shared ideological commitment; no agreement, or even the chance of agreement, on either methods or goals. If the only issues had been ones of social class, if the American labor force had been composed of undifferentiated native-born and Protestant workers, American reformers, including those of genuinely radical persuasion, would have had a freer hand. As statistics on immigrants in the unskilled work force indicate, however, it was not just a labor question; it was an immigrant, ethnic, and, most of all, a Catholic question.[23]

In a recent article, Gary Gerstle writes that America was a "version" of the "Enlightenment call for human emancipation.... At the level of mythology, emancipation is the very essence of 'America'"—which sounds a lot like a rider to the Ahlstrom thesis. Gerstle says the American essence arose from the Enlightenment. I have chosen to attribute that essence to the Reformation, the Enlightenment's religious foundation. American liberty, including prominently liberty of conscience, was an "inalienable right," an endowment of their creator, whom they took for granted was either Protestant or agnostic. Jefferson, after all, swore "eternal hostility" against "every form of tyranny over the mind of man" on the "altar of god." The Irish ideological matrix had no "inalienable rights"; the Irish claimed their right to liberty in "the name of God"—whom *most* took to be Catholic—and their "dead generations." As for individual liberty of conscience, the Irish Catholic Church, to understate, was not keen on that idea.[24]

It is unlikely that many Protestants read *The Irish World and American Industrial Liberator*, the newspaper published by Irish-born Patrick Ford, though some of the reformer types might have been intrigued by the second half of the paper's title. But whether they knew of Ford or not, none would have been surprised to read his only half-rhetorical question: "Can a man be a good Catholic who believes in the Declaration of Independence?" For that matter, could a Catholic, even a not very good one, believe in any part of America's core mission? As Robert Orsi writes, the "most fundamental" parts of being Catholic were "loyalty to the pope, obedience to authority, love of the Virgin Mary, and devotional practices addressed to the saints." But it was precisely such as those that "struck Americans as pagan, pre-modern, and perverse." They certainly struck Godkin and the rest of the Protestant campaigners for social improvement that way.[25]

• • •

That was particularly the case with the Protestant Social Gospel reformers. The United States had been invaded by millions of priest-ridden papists drawn from a benighted European peasantry. The issue was not, obviously, an exclusively Irish one. Indeed, the arrival of other Catholic peoples, particularly the "swarthier" of them like Italians, helped lift the Irish socially. But more than three million Irish immigrated to the United States between

1880 and 1920 and no one keeping track of cultural deviancy could have ignored that Celtic presence among the papist hordes. Besides, the Irish ran the American Catholic Church; they brought it over and they owned it. The bonded slavery of the American South had been partially undone by the Civil War, but Catholicism *qua* slavery had survived. In fact, the Church's numbers and influence had grown as a consequence of that "free labor revolution." It remained as easy to conjoin reform and anti-Catholicism after the "revolution" as it had been before.[26]

This was certainly the case with those Protestants whose liberalism arose from their belief that Gilded Age America, with its "ragged children" and its "shoddy aristocrats," faced multiple crises. The Gospels offered them more than spiritual solace. They were a primer of sorts; they instructed as well as inspired. Their message provided all that was needed to deal with the crises America faced. It awakened people to their Christian obligations and then directed their reform efforts. That this Protestant social gospel also aligned perfectly with America's "mystic chords" of memory gave added strength to its appeal. America, as one abolitionist had put it, was born "Protestant and free," the one a consequence of the other. Reforming it was only a matter of restoring it.[27]

There was nothing strikingly new in this use of the gospel as a blueprint for crafting a new and improved social order. Abolitionists had embraced a similar theology, one that was both emancipatory and redemptive, as America in its allegorical role as the empire of righteousness had once been and could be again. But the Social Gospelers of the 1880–1920 years inherited more than just a robust and activist theology from their prewar ideological ancestors. They also selected their targets from the same lineup: slavery was on it; so was exploitation and poverty. And so was Catholicism.

Recall E. L. Godkin's comment that with slavery gone, Catholic "interests" were the "most portentous" ones facing America. I have no idea of what he meant by either word. Did "interests" mean the Church's welfare or its ambitions? Did "portentous" mean ominous or merely pompous? Was he talking about the institutional Church or about the Catholic people? Was he concerned with doctrinal matters or social, cultural, and political ones? The safest course is to say that he likely meant all the above and that individually and collectively Catholics constituted a grave threat to post–Civil War America.

Certainly that was how the issue was framed by those whose gospel exegesis moved them toward liberal reform. As before the war, an informed or even semi-informed hostility to Catholics and Catholicism was a core part of the reform agenda. To put the matter as Thomas Leonard does in his important new book, *Illiberal Reformers: Race, Eugenics, and American Economics in the Progressive Era*, there were crusaders for justice whose policies and beliefs seem now contradictory. Leonard's account of these "illiberal reformers," as his subtitle indicates, gives more attention to racial and ethnic biases than to religious ones, but given the close association of race and religion, it is entirely fair for me to continue to conflate the two. I want to discuss a select and representative few of those illiberal reformers, but only in the context of their attitudes toward Catholicism and the Irish who embraced it.[28]

I begin with Josiah Strong and the menaces faced by the United States as outlined chapter by chapter in his 1885 book with the revealing title of *Our Country: Its Possible Future and Its Present Crisis*. Whom he meant by "our" did not have to be explained. Strong, in the words of Sydney Ahlstrom, was "the dynamo, the revivalist, the organizer, and altogether the most irrepressible spirit of the Protestant Social Gospel movement." Strong's book about his and his best friends' country was "almost certainly the most influential Social Gospel book of the nineteenth century." In it Strong counted eight major threats to the country's possible future, each identified rather ominously—or portentously—as a "peril." He devoted a full chapter to each of the eight. The first was immigration, followed by religion and the public schools, Mormonism, intemperance, socialism, wealth, the city," and this last one, out of its proper order in the book but central to all the others except Mormonism and wealth: "Romanism" and those who professed it.[29]

Strong did not say "Irish Romanism"; he didn't need to. In 1885, Irish-born and their descendants probably constituted two-thirds and certainly a majority of all the Catholics in the United States. Add to that the fact that the Irish were the ones most closely connected to the Roman Catholic Church in America (not, I would add, the American Catholic Church), and the ethnic component of Strong's chapter headings becomes obvious. The instinct for individual freedom present in all native-born Americans and inherent in the Americans-in-waiting among the immigrants had died aborning in the Irish. Or, rather, had been killed by the Catholic Church. Lay Catholics, Strong wrote, were "simply the instrument[s] of the absolute and intolerant papal will" (which would have been a surprise to the papacy); they were kept by the Church in a state of "besotted ignorance." "Everyone born a Roman Catholic is suckled on authority." Their "sympathies can assert themselves and control" their lives—in other words, they can become Americans—only if they stop being "Roman Catholic."[30]

He did not mean only the Irish when he said that, though "besotted" attached to "ignorance" was suggestive. He obviously did mean Irish when he commented on their breeding habits, which resembled those of the most high-volume of the world's animals. In a book written after *Our Country*, Strong said they were turning New England into a "New Ireland." For a race patriot as convinced of Anglo-Saxon superiority as Strong, this was a classic example of the "survival of the unfittest," or, in more fateful language, race suicide. Doctrinally, these ignorant, submissive, procreant, and boozy people were equally suspect. Catholicism was a "superstitious form of Christianity," a point Strong made in the same sentence in which he condemned the "superstitions of heathenism."[31]

I grant that Strong's anti-Catholicism was the most virulent of the Protestant Social Gospel reformers. The differences, however, between Strong's attitudes and those of the others in the movement were of degree not of kind. I can find none among the other Social Gospelers, even the gentlest and most tolerant, who ever reproached Strong or suggested that he should moderate some of his views. The entire Protestant Social Gospel reform movement was, to various degrees, anti-Catholic, anti-immigrant, and anti-Irish. It is impossible not to conclude that culturally at least the Social Gospelers were ill-disposed toward a very significant portion of the working class that they promised to save, if only from its Catholic self.

Walter Rauschenbusch, an avowed Christian Socialist, was a far abler and more temperate advocate of the Social Gospel than Strong. At that, his *Christianity and the Social Crisis* (1907) contained some unconcealed nativism: Catholicism was "decadent," "despotic," entirely "ceremonial," even "mystagogic." Its priests were a "hereditary pundit class" used principally as "plain-clothed policemen to club the people"—especially, it seemed, those in the hereditary working classes—"into spiritual submission to the ruling powers." Fortunately, in God's time, the sins and errors of this "pagan" church had been revealed to the world; its once potent influence had been enfeebled by the Protestant Reformation; soon it would be gone forever.[32]

Rauschenbusch was not referring to the Reformation as usually defined and placed historically as the agent of this happy development. The reformed Christianity he had in mind had come by way of Albion, but it was among Albion's American seed that it shone brightest. The American Church—for such it was that Rauschenbusch was describing—was the direct linear descendant of "the Puritan Revolution" and of "the marvelous army of Cromwell." That was "the spirit of its origin," and it has retained" that spirit, just as Catholicism had retained the "decadent spirit" of its Roman origin. It was the Puritan revolutionary spirit that made the American Church so democratic; it was that same spirit that guided them toward social reform. In Rauschenbusch's words, the "type of Christianity prevailing in America has one foot in the people's camp."[33]

I find no reason to doubt that Rauschenbusch believed all of what he wrote. He was not speaking in roundabout language. That said, his remarks had an important subtext that needs to be noted. My reference is to the "eleven years" (1886–97) he spent as a "pastor among the working people" of what he called "the West Side of New York City." He hoped that his book would "ease the pressures that wear ... down" those who lived there. The most revealing aspect of that remark was what he chose not to reveal. He was not just a pastor; he was the presiding minister of a German Baptist congregation. That congregation was not just on the west side of the city. It was on the edge of the overwhelmingly Irish and Catholic neighborhood known appropriately as Hell's Kitchen.[34]

The working-class Irish sections of New York were wayward and unruly on their best behavior. They were brutal and vicious on their worst. And Hell's Kitchen may have been the nastiest of them all, the "toughest" and "probably . . . the most violent Irish section of New York." The entire neighborhood was "afflicted with alcoholism, . . . crime, [and] despair. . . . Youngsters ran wild in the streets . . . gangs proliferated"; they were "impossible to control." The pressures brought to bear on the "plain people," as Rauschenbusch called them, of the West Side were intense. Rauschenbusch knew all that; but he said nothing about any of it other than "I shared their life." The "their" was left undefined but if he meant the lives of the Irish Catholic majority of the neighborhood, he cannot have shared much of it.[35]

But I'm curious. Why did he use the nondescriptive and meaningless phrase "working people on the West Side"? He had to have consciously chosen not to mention, or even to write the words, "Hell's Kitchen" or "Irish "or "Catholic." His comment that he had "used up the early strength of my life in [the] service" of these West Side working people requires some clarification. In whose service exactly did he use up his strength and what did he mean by service? His father had been an "immigrant missionary." Was the junior Rauschenbusch an urban "home missionary" sent to evangelize and convert the heathen of Hell's Kitchen? I think that peculiar and erratic neighborhood had to have taught him something; why didn't he say so directly? He notes frequently in his book that American Catholics were being "protestantized"; was that happening on the West Side?[36]

Christianity and the Social Crisis sold more than half a million copies. It is not likely that many of the Irish of Hell's Kitchen or anywhere else ever read it, but quite likely their priests at least read into it and reviewed it for them in conversations and at Mass. Those reviews cannot have endeared Rauschenbusch to the Irish or eased any of the pressures that "bore them down," assuming that Rauschenbusch included them among the "plain people" he hoped would be helped by his book. For an obvious example, it may have been possible to have conjured up someone more despised by Irish Catholics than Cromwell and his "marvelous army" of Puritans but I cannot imagine who that might have been. The idea that Rauschenbusch understood the Catholic Irish or was sympathetic to their needs is delusional.[37]

The Social Gospel reformism of Josiah Strong and Walter Rauschenbusch proved uncommonly durable. So did the illiberal nativist reformism that was fundamental to it, even indistinguishable from it. This was as true of those reformers who sat in Protestant pews as of those who preached from Protestant pulpits. The Social Gospel became a central part of the emerging academic discipline of social science, or at least a central part of the interpretive framework of many social scientists. We may now say that the theorists of Protestant Anglo-Saxon superiority were little more than xenophobic bigots. That is not, however, how they were perceived at the time. They were seen and saw themselves as objective and dispassionate scientists. They intended no offense to anyone. Science and the gospels—a strange pairing in some ways—had led them to the truth. They were obliged to report it.

And so the sociologist and reformer E. A. Ross, by all accounts a blunt-talking man, utterly convinced of his own rectitude and competency, could write in 1919 that "a centralized ecclesiastical machine," by which he meant the Catholic Church, was more than just a hindrance to reform; it "betrays the people to the Powers that Be.... The religion [the] hierarchy ladles out to the dupes is chloroform.... How cheering, then, is the fact that many Western peoples have already escaped the grip of centralized churches, and that there is no prospect of their ever again falling under priestly dictation. ... In all the forenoon lands the end of clericalism is in sight"—a Protestant version of sunburstery. There was, however, one threat of an early and soul-killing sunset. "Since half the nation's children come from a quarter of the families, race deterioration soon sets in if the successful withhold their quota while the stupid multiply like rabbits." He didn't say how many of these rabbits were Irish—"feckless Celts engrossed with an old-fashioned problem—that of freeing their country." He also didn't say anything about why he thought wanting to free Ireland was old-fashioned.[38]

Ross's blending of Protestant Christian reform with scientific racism was a prominent feature in the writings of social reformers. Their movement contained a large share of race "scientists" and other experts who conferred on themselves the responsibility of dividing the human populations of the world into hierarchically ranked racial blood groups. This has to be counted the ugliest aspect of an otherwise commendable effort by Social Gospel reformers to join what Polanyi called the "double movement" and bring a measure of fairness to America's patently unfair market capitalism. America's working class, however, contained millions of immigrant and ethnic Catholic peoples who ranked near or at the bottom of the eugenicists' *scala naturae*, that great natural stairway with God and God's celestial companions at the top and Protestant Anglo-Saxons only slightly below them—and moving up. Had the exploited not been so congenitally and incurably papist, a measure of noblesse oblige might have been possible—as it was in England where Protestant and secular reformers worked to improve the lives of Protestant labor.[39]

Being an illiberal liberal in America was not without its challenges. Some were internal to the movement; the reformers had to work their way through the contradictions created by their illiberalism. Did the more abhorrent features of industrial and urban societies victimize racially inferior people or were the racially inferior people to be counted among those abhorrent features, or both? Deciding one way or the other would have allowed liberal reformers to direct their energies, but the answer was frequently "both and both at the same time." Victims of evil were simultaneously agents of evil. The reformers were at cross-purposes with themselves.

Take, for example, two of E. A. Ross's closest colleagues, the economists Edward Bemis and John R. Commons. Leonard gives considerable attention to them in his *Illiberal Reformers*, noting that both thought that meaningful social reform had to begin with the imposition of severe restrictions on immigration. Those restrictions would be frankly and unapologetically based on nation of origin, which is to say based on race, ethnicity, culture, and religion. Once again, Irish Catholics were not the sole targets of the new exclusionary rules. They weren't even the most important targets. Commons and Bemis came to prominence after the immigration of Irish Catholics had been overwhelmed by the "new immigration" from southern and eastern Europe and Asia. It was that immigration—overwhelmingly not Protestant, it must be noted—that the reformers insisted had to be checked. Irish Catholics were collateral damage in the liberal's wholly illiberal campaign for immigration restriction.[40]

Americans never attempted to disguise their preference for immigrants from northern and western Europe. They were the chosen ones. The Irish, ironically the most northwesterly of them all, were the exceptions to this geographical rule. The racial biases of immigration restriction were covert, but the efforts to hide them could have fooled no one. Immigrants from the nations that had provided the greater and best part of the "old immigration" were to be privileged. Those from Asia were to be denied entry; those from southern and eastern Europe—Jews, Orthodox, and Catholics mostly—were to be granted limited entry. It was all based on "racial science," which was coming increasingly to mean eugenics and the great chain of racial being.

Bemis was obsessed with sorting out those races, ranking them according to their intelligence, manliness, robustness, and, for good measure, their physiognomies and hygienic habits: Were they comely or ugly; how often did they bathe? And the rankings all made the same point: America had been lucky, or especially blessed, in the immigrants it attracted. For its first two centuries, only those of "vigorous stock, descendants of the hardy yeomanry and best elements of *English* life ... [had taken] deep root in the land." That changed. "Now one half of our white population [is] of foreign birth or parentage." That was in 1889.[41]

By "foreign" he was not referring to nation of birth but rather to those "who come to us with different conceptions of government, ignorant of our institutions." It was they "who indulge in most of the mob violence in time of strikes and industrial depressions." That was not an ethnic-specific category, but Bemis was slightly more helpful later in his article. These miscreants were, "alas . . . controlled by the boodle and saloon element, these people stand in the way of needed improvements in legislation and administration, and by their votes keep our worst men in power." "Boodle and saloon" was unsubtly coded language; there was no mistaking that Bemis was saying that the people in the "new immigration" were being schooled and led about by IrishCatholics. The Irish were part of the "old immigration," but only as outliers to it. They had become the pied pipers to the unassimilated new.[42]

Irish Catholics are never counted, either at the time or later by historians, as part of the post-1889 "new immigration." They should be, and not just for what might be called their organizational ability with the newest immigrants. Between 1891 and 1920, 1.7 million Irish, most Catholic, came to the United States. Omitting them from the category leaves the history of the new immigration incomplete. Americans may have gotten more used to them, but they hadn't gotten to like them. *The Damnation of Theron Ware* was written in 1896 and Madison Grant's *Passing of the Great Race* in 1916; the head-counters who put together the *Dictionary of Races or Peoples* did their race/religion calculations in 1909. The Irish were still cultural outsiders.[43]

And they were still capable of doing great mischief. As Bemis hinted, one of the reasons the "new" newcomers were such a menace was that they were so easily corrupted by the fifth column of Irish Catholics already present. The America to which immigrants would adjust and conform was not that of Albion's seed. It was nearer that of Hibernia's. That the Irish would teach new immigrants how to be Americans pushes irony toward farce. The Strangers had become the Natives. Unfortunately, they were false ones, as unassimilated as any new immigrant. Call it the ultimate IrishCatholic revenge—or the ultimate IrishCatholic subversion.[44]

Either way, immigration restriction had somehow to be drafted to include both the new immigration and the IrishCatholic. That would not be easy. Immigration restriction based on a percentage of the number of any given ethnic or national group's present in, say, 1890 before the new immigration had begun, would clearly limit the number of Italians, Jews, Poles, and others judged to be part of America's "immigration problem." Unfortunately, however, a quota system based on numbers in 1890 would do nothing to limit the number of Irish papists who were in the United States in the millions as early as 1850. That was a major problem with basing immigration quotas on percentages of those already in squalid residence.

Bemis devised a solution. His first point was based on a fiction: He quoted "European statistics [that] show that the emigration from Ireland, which formerly came from the thrifty and intelligent of the North, comes now in far the largest measure from the poverty-stricken, illiterate counties of the west of the island." He wrote that in 1889, half a century after those European statistics had begun to show that Catholics dominated the Irish immigration, exactly the opposite of what Bemis said they had. Did he misread, or just mislead? He was a "social scientist"; independent variables and statistics were the essence of his academic profession. More important was the coy and encrypted language that came next. No one can have been fooled by it: "Thrifty and intelligent" from the "north" meant Protestants; "illiterates" from the "west" meant papists, the most "Irish of the Irish," as Henry Merwin had called them.[45]

Bemis was no more statistically accurate on the point of literacy than on his historically illiterate argument that Catholics had only recently become the larger share of the Irish immigration. In 1897, an American immigration official noted that more than 95 percent of the Irish who got off the boats in New York could read and write, and in English. Bemis clearly didn't know that and didn't care enough to inquire into it. His assumption was that when the Irish were the topic, popery and illiteracy were definitional parts of each other. Race and religion were the issues, not literacy or erudition. How, using national quotas, were the two very distinct categories of immigrants from Ireland to be kept separate? Misstating the issue, as Bemis did, also solved it. He proposed that the nation's immigration policy include a literacy test. As he explained, "nearly all the most undesirable classes of all nations would be excluded. The Swedes, Germans, English, Scots, and *most* of the Irish would not be left out ... we do not want to exclude them."[46]

As for the old argument that America needed the unskilled Catholic Irish "to take the pick and spade" and other long-handled tools "and do the work of excavation," Bemis noted simply that "our need for railroads has been ... fully met." In other words, the United States had no further use for Irish Catholic diggers and scrubbers. Bemis had found a way to disaggregate the Irish without having to raise the intertwined issues of race and religion. It was not that different from the various nonracial means white Southerners had found to disenfranchise Blacks. His literacy test became what Leonard calls the "centerpiece" of the immigration restriction movement generally and of the 1911 Dillingham Report on America's "Immigration Problem." In 1917, it became the law.[47]

But Bemis was also a Social Gospeler; immigration restriction had to be more than nondiscriminatory. It had to be—as Bemis professed himself to be—"Christ-like." And so he asked, "to restrict is said to be unchristian. ... Is it?" His answer was remarkable for what it said about Americans' overarching sense of self-importance: "Not if it can be shown ... that our national life, and consequently our power as a civilizing agency in the world, is lowered." If America continued to accept all who wished to immigrate, it would "seriously lower the civilization of our own people, and hence our influence for good among other peoples." Being as a holy city on a hill and serving as light to the world was a heavy responsibility. It was also wearying. America needed a rest. Bemis chose an interesting example; did not Christ "rest from his work and go apart to the mountains in order better to perform the work He did attempt?"[48]

That influence for good extended beyond just being a moral example. America also served as Europe's "safety valve"—those were Bemis's words—a role Europeans seldom acknowledged. The presence of America allowed Europe to delay the "abolition of standing armies, the reform ... of poor systems of land tenure, the necessity of society to educate and elevate the poorer classes." In his usual slanting way, Bemis was talking mostly about Ireland. Occasionally, he even admitted it. "Immigrants have come to us by the hundred thousand from Ireland, but the poverty there seems as great as ever. . . . [W]e are trying to drain an exhaustless sea." Which led him to this: Restricting immigration from Catholic Ireland "might force an Irish revolution, peaceable it is to be hoped, ... which would attack the causes of poverty and degradation. Looked at thus, restriction is not unchristian." He did not think the revolution he hoped for would be against the British and the Empire. He thought and doubtless prayed that it would be against the Catholic Church.[49]

John Roger Commons was a far better known and influential social economist than Edward Bemis. Their ideas on how best to meet the labor issue, however, were compatible, up to and including the strongly Protestant caste of those ideas. In his autobiography, Commons said he had been "brought up on Hoosierism, Republicanism, [and] Presbyterianism"; included in this last was a well-used copy of "Fox's *Book of Martyrs.*" He described his mother as the strictest of "Presbyterian Puritans." She may have been. She badly wanted him to be a Presbyterian minister, and it was she who named him after John Rogers "who was burned at Smithfield by Bloody Mary." John Roger was an appropriate name. Commons's approach to political economy was Calvinist. His approach to politics was Cromwellian. As the secretary of the American Institute of Christian Sociology, it was his "aim ... to present Christ as the living Master and King and Christian law" as the ultimate rule for human society, to bring God's salvific lessons to a world that badly needed them. Like Rauschenbusch, Commons was a "Christian Socialist [; his] socialism [was] based on Love of man."[50]

In 1906, Commons was part of a multidisciplinary team of social scientists working on what came to be known as the Pittsburgh Survey. Six large volumes, edited by Paul Kellogg, were produced detailing the ills of America's steel capital. The survey was funded by the Russell Sage Foundation and the researchers included the American settlement house organizer Robert A. Woods. He and Commons had very similar reform ideas. Both were enthusiastic members of the Immigration Restriction League and both were convinced that though Pittsburgh had a multitude of problems, its two largest were corruption in local government and, as Kellogg put it, the fact that "two-thirds of the steel workers are unskilled immigrants . . . as uncomprehending as horses."[51]

The issue was unique to America. Other industrial countries also had labor problems, but theirs were less difficult of solution than America's. The English working class—the one most often compared with the American—contained some recalcitrant sorts but, with the exception of the Catholic Irish and a few assorted others, they were not entirely uncomprehending ones. It was made up of Englishmen and English women. There was a share of "horses" among them, but they were comprehending ones, of a superior breed than those in America.

Woods addressed this issue directly, Commons more by implication. Let Woods speak for both of them; his race patriotism was excessive even for that time and place. So were his prejudices. "'English life,' he said, "was the best civilization offered." He greatly envied "the homogeneity of English society" and the better classes of its workers. The "price" the United States was paying for its open immigration policy "was the sacrifice of the superior Anglo-Saxon people in America." Woods's "own America was one of 'the other nations of Great Britain'; it should learn 'from the mother country' how to solve the even 'more difficult problems' of the New World"—America as Albion's apprentice.[52]

Commons was as explicit an Anglo-Saxonist as Woods, and, if anything, an even more fervent Calvinist. In his mind it was the "doctrines of the Reformation . . . [that had] prepared the hearts of men for the doctrines of . . . liberty and constitutional government." Some of the more protestant of those doctrines had done even more: It was "abstemious Puritans [who] were the founders of British capitalism," which, in its turn, was a large part of America's Anglo-Saxon inheritance. Commons commented on "the great strength of capitalism" and of how it had grown out "of our civil war for liberty and equality." He said very little about the irony of that war's legacy and nothing at all about the postwar reformers unwillingness to acknowledge it.[53]

Commons referred to his politics as centered on a "Love of Man." That love was entirely abstract, and it was applied selectively. Commons was mostly in love with Anglo-Saxons. "Unhampered by inroads of alien stock," they fashioned all the "democratic theories and forms of government." As for the racial inferiors, including the Catholic Irish, Commons found them "wholly incompetent as pioneers and independent proprietors," the two models of Americans moving out and moving up. The best the new races in America could hope for was to find a job with a "captain of industry to guide and supervise their semi-intelligent work," a tidy summary of the "new ideology."[54]

The politics of this new ideology were in separate but related categories. Commons said that America was founded by people "Teutonic in blood and Protestant in religion." "The doctrines of the Reformation, adapted as they were to the strong individualism of the Germanic races, prepared [their] hearts . . . for the doctrines of political liberty and constitutional government." In both religion and politics, these were people who "were literally 'protestant'"—which nicely brackets the essential Protestantism of the nation-state. Their dislike of absolute monarchs was matched only by their dislike of popes, even fallible ones. These "protesting" and dissenting Christians formed the nation and imprinted it with their own democratic moral code.[55]

The success of democracies, America's prominently included, depended entirely on the righteousness of those who made up the demos. Commons understood that democracy was a demanding system. It required "intelligence," "manliness," a "capacity for cooperation," and a "public spirit." Americans had those traits in abundance; they were not "peasants" but "yeomen"; they were "merchants," the "middle class." The "races who through mental or moral defect are unable to assert themselves" had to be taught those American virtues. The standard was not entirely racial. He allowed that a "great [democratic] nation" did not require that its people "be of one blood." But they did have to be "of one mind." In this instance, Americanized and of the American mind. Self-rule worked only if the people involved were virtuous and disciplined enough to rule themselves. Many of the new immigrants were neither.[56]

He could have stopped there and his standing as an Anglo-Saxonist would have been secure. But he went on. He drew a "line . . . separating Protestant Europe from Catholic Europe." On the Catholic side of the line, "illiteracy predominate[d]"; the people were "primitive," "backward," "unskilled," "scarcely a single generation removed from serfdom." They came in ragged heaps, "congeries," as he called them; they were from "races . . . accustomed to despotism and even savagery, and wholly unused to self-government." These "race differences" were ineradicable; they were "established in the very blood and physical constitution" of the "inferior lot" who carried them. In the 1914 Report of the Industrial Commission on which he served, Commons wrote that among America's greatest problems was the one "forced upon us by the large immigration of backward races or classes." He liked the word *backward*.[57]

It is the case that the most racist of Commons's comments were directed at African-Americans, Asians, and southeastern Europeans. But they suggest something about his feelings toward Irish Catholics. So does this comment on racially inferior people and their "inherited traits of physical and moral degeneracy," traits that "suited them to the ... tenement house, the saloon and the jail"—three unlovely environments closely associated with the Catholic Irish. Consider too his contention that the Irish were America's "most effective" union organizers, and among the most numerous and militant labor "agitators." More damning than that, they were preeminent "racial amalgamators," by which Commons meant America's urban political bosses. For Commons, as for Social Gospelers and Progressives generally, there was nothing in America more corrupt than machine rule. To Irish Catholics in the working class, with the exception of the Church, there was nothing more socially useful, evidence enough of "how different they were from the qualities of the typical American citizen."[58]

Then came Commons's remarkable conclusion. Race and religion were seldom so closely linked: "Religious differences in America are not ... theological ... [but] racial. ... The Judaism of the Jew, the Protestantism of the British ... the Roman Catholicism of the Irish." The "peasants of Catholic Europe ... have become almost a distinct race." But not just distinct, an inferior race, one "drained of those superior qualities which are the foundation of democratic institutions." In other words, the Catholic Church had single-handedly created a new race of lesser beings, undemocratic and uncivilized.[59]

The Irish were a subset of that "Catholic race." Commons mentioned the Great Irish Famine, not in terms of the suffering it had brought, only as the time when "began that exportation of paupers on a large scale against which our country has protested and finally legislated." He had to have chosen the word "pauper" purposefully. In context it meant not just a "poor person" but a dependent poor person, one living "on charitable assistance," "unemployable" and "unproductive" and hence "excluded." That was how Commons explained the Irish Catholics' matchless talent at organizing corrupt political machines and manipulating races only slightly more defective than themselves. John Commons appears to have genuinely loved the working class. It was the men and women in it whom he couldn't stand.[60]

• • •

For Social Gospel reformers, turning the multiethnic, multiracial, multicultural, multilingual United States into a Protestant Anglo-Saxon redoubt was obviously not going to be easy. But even Progressives who could not accept the eugenics and race theories or who were doubtful that the parable of the ten talents was "endorsed" and validated by "modern philosophy," as Edward

Bemis put it, seem to have caught the contagion of cultural intolerance. The positivist and exclusionist message of the Protestant Christian reformers found a receptive audience among otherwise quite secular reformers. I offer as examples two American activists of vastly different backgrounds and politics but who had similar preconceived notions, Eugene V. Debs and Walter Lippmann. The first was America's leading heartland socialist; the second, one of its most urban and urbane public intellectuals. Neither would have said that Irish Catholics were outside the broad reach of their reforms, but the ideas and prejudices of both, whether they were conscious of them or not, make it unlikely that either felt any genuine sympathy for or connection with the exiled and dissolute papists of Éire.

In his biography of Debs, Nick Salvatore emphasizes that Debs was an all-American boy. His socialism was straight out of Terre Haute, Indiana, a Midwest version of Tyre, New York, the fictional village where Theron Ware presided over the Methodist Church. Debs's socialism was from native ground. It owed very little, if anything, to radical ideas emanating from London or Paris or Moscow. It owed a lot, however, to the Protestant Social Gospel. Debs was unchurched and unbelieving, but the Christian socialism of Rauschenbusch and the others was still socialism, and the gospel message, properly interpreted, could be put to radical purposes. The Social Gospelers inspired him, and he inspired them. Rauschenbusch admired him greatly; at Debs's funeral service, a New York City Protestant minister offered a poetic tribute, declaring that God had first claims on Debs's great soul: "Gene! Dear Comrade!/ Come up here,/ beside me,/ you are worthy, Gene for you did good deeds of love." That was true. He had. And an absent God called him to a distant heaven.[61]

But, like the other doers of good deeds, Debs dispensed them selectively. He was anti-Semitic, anti-Asian, anti-Black, and keenly anti-Catholic. He did not escape the contagion of illiberal liberalism. There was something of the all-American boy in that too. Debs, writes Jacob Dorn, "accepted the view, widespread in [American] Protestant culture, that Roman Catholicism was "fundamentally corrupt." The fact that the Catholic Church was hostile to socialism had something to do with Debs's animus toward it; a great many European socialists were of like mind. But it wasn't so much the Church's war against international Marxism that upset Debs; it was its adversarial relationship to fundamental American principles, what he perceived as the Catholics' war against Jeffersonianism.[62]

In Debs's mind the Catholic Church wasn't really a church at all; it was a "political machine in ... partnership with the robber kings, barons, plutocrats and other ruling and exploiting classes." It was a "political hierarchy masquerading as a holy church ... [as] unclean and repulsive as a white sepulcher filled with dead men's bones." In a 1912 letter to Fred Warren,

Debs wrote that "It is this Roman machine we stand face to face with and we have got to . . . strip it of its religious mask and expose it as the rottenest political machine that ever stole the livery of heaven." Warren needed no convincing. He was the editor of the immensely popular reform and nativist journal *The Appeal to Reason*, founded in 1910 by J. A. Wayland. Wayland left the *Appeal* in 1912 and started another newspaper, the equally popular and equally bigoted *Menace*, which must be counted among the most venomous anti-Catholic sheets in American history.[63]

Debs's vigorous defense of industrial unionism involved necessarily a defense of the rights of overwhelmingly Catholic industrial workers. It would be useful to know how in his own mind he squared his love of the proletariat with his disdain for so many proletarians. Debs wrote of those in the working class who mistook "superstition for religion." Would he have included Catholic Irish among those? He also wrote of "parasite priests" and "plutocratic prelates"—he mentioned Cardinals John Ireland, James Gibbons, John Murphy Farley, and William Henry O'Connell by name—who "traffic in the ignorant reverence of the masses."[64]

Debs championed the rights of hard-rock miners and railroad workers, among whom were tens of thousands of Irish. Did he exempt them from the ignorant mass? Debs thought Catholics, Irish included, were obedient and dutiful, then added that "obedience" was "not religious duty but debasing slavery." Would he have said that of Ed Boyce, the Irish-born Catholic head of the radical Western Federation of Miners who escorted Debs on a harrowing, weeks-long tour of the Western mining districts? The mutual admiration of Debs and Rauschenbusch was important; so was Debs's close association with F. J. Wayland and Fred Warren. More revealing still was the fact that his association with Irish Catholic working people seems to have taught him nothing. Debs inherited his nativist sensibilities and he never shed them.[65]

Walter Lippmann's prejudices were of an altogether different sort. There were no Patsy Calibans in his narrative, though plenty of ignorant masses, the "dispossessed," as he called them, who on their own were incapable of functioning in a modern republic. These sorts needed to be managed. A great number of working-class Catholic immigrants were among those dispossessed. Lippman was certainly anti-Catholic, but mostly because he thought the Church a nonrational and backward-looking system. He would have had no quarrel with Chesterton's description of Catholic cultures, the Irish included, as based on traditional values passed down by dead generations; Chesterton's "democracy of the dead" was an apt phrase.

Chesterton admired that kind of democratic governance. It rooted people. Lippmann scorned it for exactly the same reason. What Chesterton and those like him wanted, Lippmann said, was "jolly beer and jolly dirt and jolly superstition." Traditionalism was the autocracy of the dead. It was acceptable for "men [to] reverence the dead if they are buried. But they [must] no longer sit at table with corpses, ghosts, and skeletons." Being rooted in the past was to be shackled to that past; the democracy of the dead was the politics of the dead hand. Consulting the dead, giving them a vote in counsels, was self-indulgent nonsense. Allowing them a veto, as the Irish did, was akin to madness. As Lippmann put it, "there can be no real cohesion . . . in following . . . inherited ideals." Jollity was for children.[66]

Drifting occurred because what people inherited were worn-out notions that stripped them of control and left them directionless. As he detailed in his 1914 book, *Drift and Mastery,* the efficient management of modern national systems required scientific managers, trained and literally masterful experts, who alone could combat the forces of societal drift. Nowhere was this truer or the issue more pressing than during the period of what the historical geographer James Scott called American "high modernism." The "mastery of human nature [and] the rational design of social order . . . required scientific understanding." So said all the scientists of society. Dogmas, both religious and secular, were not just useless, they were pernicious. Simpler worlds could live with them, modern worlds could not. As Lippmann put it, one could "talk about eternal principles of conduct in an old-world village where the son replaced the father generation after generation, where the only . . . emigrants [were] the dead." But America was no old-world village and the "fixed traditions of peasant life" were not relevant. Needing an example, he cited the west of Ireland.[67]

For Lippmann, most of the trappings of democratic theory, including securing the consent of the governed who were living, failed the "mastery test." In this sense, he was not a progressive at all, but more one of the "new radicals," as Christopher Lasch called them, "an . . . embodiment of the national purpose," a trailblazing member of an elite corps of "intellectuals as a social type." I cited earlier Gary Gerstle's comment that "emancipation is the very essence of America." For Lippmann, that included emancipation from the past. Another of those intellectuals as a social type, Randolph Bourne, once told Lippmann that *Drift and Mastery* went to the heart of "the great problem of the age": "what to do with your emancipation after you have got it.'" Lippmann knew what to do with his: "We inherit freedom, and have to use it." It was the only worthwhile inheritance we had because it and it alone could "blast" the others. Lippmann listed some of the worthless ones: "The sanctity of property"—he was a reformer, after all—"the patriarchal family, hereditary caste, the dogma of sin, obedience to authority—the rock of ages, in brief."[68]

In the narrower view here at issue, what mattered most was that there can have been no set of philosophical principles more utterly alien to Irish

Catholicism than those of Lippmann and the others of the new radicals. They had found "the root of error in contemporary thought in the acceptance of the tyranny of tradition and routine.... those venerable but antiquated institutions." And nothing was more venerable and more antiquated than the Catholic Church, what Lippmann called "the greatest piece of constructive psychology that the world has ever seen." He listed the particulars of Catholicism's appeal: "the cavernous mysteries of its cathedrals converging upon the enduring altar, the knowledge of an Eternal Family that survives the human one, the confessional where sin could be expressed therefore purged, the vicarious atonement by which the consequences of human weakness were lifted off men's shoulders, the obliteration of death, the sense that wisdom was there inexhaustible and infallible." All of that was designed to "make [human] weakness permanent"; Catholicism was "hostile... to every force that tended to make people self-sufficient."[69]

That criticism was tame in comparison with that of the Social Gospelers. But Lippmann wasn't done. He then quoted from what he called "the lovely little book" he was then holding in his hands. The book was the *Spiritual Exercises* of St. Ignatius of Loyola, the founder of the Jesuit Order. Lippmann said that it read that "to die... is to go... where you will become the prey of corruption and the food of the most hideous reptiles"; while lying on the slab with family and priests around you, a "public officer... writes in the register of the dead all the particulars of your decease." Lippmann said next that "this is recommended for daily contemplation, a capital way, it seems to me, of poisoning the human will." The *Exercises* were one of the ways the Catholic Church "tried to make weakness permanent," to strip people of "self-sufficiency." That sounded a lot like Josiah Strong's assertion that the Church "suppresses individuality."[70]

It is hard to know where to begin a review of Lippmann's comments. First, though something like the language he quoted could have been found in places in Catholic literature, there is nothing even remotely like it in the *Exercises*. Loyola asked that retreatants imagine themselves experiencing what Christ experienced; he did not prescribe or impose any images. Second, the *Exercises* were not recommended for daily contemplation, even by Jesuit priests. Third, the vast majority of Catholics, particularly working-class Irish Catholics in America, would never have heard of them. Fourth, and most important, the point of the exercises is to liberate the will, not suppress it. If "mastery" included playing fast and loose with the truth, then Lippmann had indeed achieved mastery.[71]

Lippmann had Ignatius's *Exercises* exactly backward. He didn't understand them; he didn't get what they were saying or trying to do. For the intellectually curious, not getting it, as Robert Darnton put it, is a signal to "know we are on to something" and that by "picking at the document where it is most opaque, we may be able to unravel an alien system of meaning. The thread might even lead into a strange and wonderful world view." Lippmann had no interest in strange and alien systems of meaning. And his world view was already wonderful. He had about the same intellectual curiosity quotient as Wendell Phillips or Josiah Strong.[72]

From what he knew of them, or thought he knew of them—or made up about them—Lippmann concluded that Catholics were among those "unfit for self-government, they are the most easily led, the most easily fooled and the most easily corrupted." He recalled a conversation he'd had with an eighteen-year-old boy from the "West of Ireland." The boy was about to emigrate from Queenstown (Cobh) harbor, bound for New Haven, Connecticut, a place, wrote Lippmann, "where his creeds do not work"—another useful synonym for erratic. The young Irishman was unmoored; his only support was "his parish priest." But of what use was he? The boy wasn't just going from one place to another; he was "going from one epoch into another. . . . If he becomes brutal, greedy, vulgar"—Patsy Caliban-like, in other words—will it be so surprising?" At least Lippmann didn't assign his hooliganism to race.

Whatever its cause, it was the ones like this Irish lad and his out-of-time traditions who "make a governing class essential." Lippmann was emphatic on this point, writing in one place that "whenever evil is defended or tyranny devised, it is done in the name of tradition," in another that the "loss of a sense of the past . . . [is] a definite emancipation." "We should live," he wrote, "not for our fatherland but for our children's land." It's hard for me not to conclude that he had Irish lads in mind when he wrote that.[73]

Two years after Lippmann wrote that, Patrick Pearse stood in front of the General Post Office Building in Dublin and declared that Ireland was "striking for its freedom." "She" (and Lippmann would have angrily denounced the gendering of nations) did so "in the name of God and of the dead generations from which she receives her old tradition of nationhood." Pearse then acknowledged the support Ireland had gotten from "her exiled children in America"—by which he meant Irish banished to a modern, faraway, and culturally vacuous place. There is no evidence that Lippmann read or even knew of Pearse's proclamation, but his response to it may be assumed.

Lippmann was not a callous or uncaring man. He was not suggesting that science be turned loose only to build better dynamos and more efficient steel mills. His was a science of society and he would use it in the interest of "abolishing poverty which . . . modern democrats recognize . . . is the most immediate question before the world to-day." The problem, of course, was that no solution to poverty or anything else was possible as long as the world, and the poverty-stricken within it, drifted. The poor must become "modern," at least to the degree that they would allow the managerial elite who had mastered the sciences to govern them. Catholics, however, in the words of

Robert Orsi, "make bad moderns" of whatever degree "because they have trouble forgetting." Modernity depended on forgetting. Mastery required a self-inflicted amnesia. Which meant that Irish American Catholics were "just destined to be impure citizens."[74]

• • •

There are times when the reformers' attacks on Catholicism and the Irish who professed it seem almost involuntary, rather like the Irish American radical Elizabeth Gurley Flynn's father who could not say the words "England" or "Britain" without adding "God damn her." Sensibilities are like that. People with strong "inner nonrational receptors" cannot help themselves; the attacks are pure reflex. Others of them arose from what Lippmann would have been obliged to call "traditions," ignoring the fact—assuming he was aware of it—that he too came out of a tradition and that he retained much of it.

Traditions, Flynn's or Lippmann's, can give rise to intolerance, an appalling lack of inquisitiveness, or both. In the case of Lippmann and others of the liberals, that lack may explain their assaults on Catholicism. But whatever explains them, they severely limited the liberals' ability to work with or for the Irish in the working class. There was no ideological common ground on which anti-Catholic reformers and Catholics, including particularly those who were themselves reform-minded, could stand. Common ground is possible only if those occupying it are on the same plane of existence, with no ontological fault lines dividing them.[75]

It would also help if those on the two sides of the line treated those opposite them with a measure of respect. Ontological fault lines don't have to mean the suspension of polite discourse. That is particularly the case when those on one side of the line are enduringly powerful Natives and those on the other considerably less powerful and enduringly erratic transnational Strangers. I make that point in the context of Pope Leo XIII's *Rerum Novarum*. That papal letter was a direct assault on socialism—as those on the left, then and now, are disposed to remind us. It was also, however, a direct assault on modern capitalism and an implied attack on imperialism—which those on the same left, then and now, are wont to ignore. It can and should be read as the Labor Manifesto of a majority of the American industrial working class.[76]

In fact, of course, it was scarcely read at all by those who said they wanted to help America's industrial workers drawn from the world. The encyclical was dismissed by the secular and Protestant American Left as nothing more than an expression of a tired Catholic antisocialism. The official Church *was* opposed to socialism—perhaps more than it should have been—but it was also opposed to the new modern ideology, to laissez-faire capitalism and the materialism, acquisitiveness, and lack of moral consciousness that arose from it. The encyclical said less about imperialism, capitalism's partner in what Leo essentially said were social crimes. There was also this, I think written with America's Irish and their nonseverable causes partly in mind: If capitalism was tamed and colonialism brought to an end, "men would cling to the country in which they were born. No one would exchange his country for a foreign land if his own afforded him the means of living a tolerable and happy life."—the Pope's take on social and economic democracy and "making a fair living." The dismissal of *Rerum Novarum* and the Church that issued it by radical and liberal reformers showed them to be lacking in tolerance and generosity of spirit—not to mention good judgment.[77]

On this point, I again enlist the services of Gary Gerstle. Gerstle makes the eminently sensible point that discrimination "against members of racially and religiously 'suspect' immigrant groups [made] the process of political incorporation [into new host societies] more fraught, and more complicated, than it otherwise would have been." Put simply, if a host society wants its immigrants to respect and embrace it and "incorporate" themselves into it, it should be a good host and not insult them. That sounded like Edmund Burke's good advice: To be loved a nation should be lovable. Gerstle goes on to note that "modes of incorporation arise out of situations in which immigrants possess formal citizenship rights but, for reasons of religion, nativity, or race, have not been fully accepted as Americans." There was "a disjuncture between their formal rights . . . and their experience of those rights." Gerstle extends that definition "even [to] Irish-Americans."[78]

In another article, Gerstle cites the American philosopher Horace Kallen, whose views on race, ethnicity, and American identity must be counted among "the strongest and most eloquent calling for cultural pluralism." Kallen celebrated "ethnic difference." Each ethnic group was a part of the "symphony of American civilization." There was, however, one part of the orchestra that played an occasional discordant note. That was the Irish part. In Gerstle's words, Kallen wondered, "was there something about Irish culture . . . that encouraged intolerance?" By that he meant, were they clannish? Was it possible, he wondered, whether "the hostile reception given [them] by their Protestant hosts had damaged Irish culture in ways not easily repaired." Is that what made Patsy a Caliban? Such as that passed for wisdom in these, the salad days of American exceptionalism.[79]

I am not arguing that reformers edged up to some cultural borderland between Catholic and Protestant poor and consciously and with malice declared that the Catholics were defective and not deserving of sympathetic attention, that they were ineligible for the reformers' brave new world. I am arguing that mixing the social question with the Catholic question, indeed making the Catholic question one of the social questions, was not just internally contradictory, it all but closed out a significant part of the American working class from those Protestant reformers who thought that labor was being treated unjustly. In the plainest possible language: Too many of those reformers were far more interested in saving the Irish working class from Catholicism and corruption than from capitalism and penury.

That was true of America's secular liberals as well. They had "sworn upon the altar of [that lower case] god eternal hostility against every form of tyranny over the mind of man." Among those forms of tyranny were tradition, philosophy, and religion, all the ancient myths masquerading as eternal truths. Thus they swore that the past had to nullify itself. American reformers answered essentially to the minimalist rules of pragmatism. Their sole objective truth was that there were no fixed objective truths. Irish Catholicism was a lot of things, but pragmatic and present-minded were not among them. In sum, any convergence—to return to that concept—between Irish Catholic workers and liberals of sundry sorts foundered because a common purpose is not enough in the absence of a common ideological denominator. Some things simply do not mix. Separate worlds can be bridged; separate world views cannot.

CHAPTER THREE

A Transnational "Freemasonry of the Disinherited"
The Premaking of an Oppositional Irish American Working Class

> "[A]lthough the Irish have little regard for Socialist theories they have a strong bias in favour of action on lines that are in essence lines of Socialist activity."
> —James Connolly, "Socialism in Ireland," 1908

In a 1989 review essay on a collection of the writings of Herbert Gutman, edited and introduced by Ira Berlin, Peter Rachleff made the point that of all the subject fields in American history, none had undergone more transformative changes than labor history. Begun in the 1960s and still ongoing, the study of work, workers, and working classes went through what Rachleff called an "internal revolution." Everything in the field from methodology to interpretive emphasis had been made over. Labor history had gone from "an economistic, institutional history of trade unions to a social history of working people." The old labor history, according to David Brody, had "left us ... nearly ignorant of the history of the American worker"—labor history, in other words, had no laborers in it. The revolution changed all that. Again quoting Brody, the "establishment monopoly over what constituted 'good history' ... had collapsed," or been collapsed. A people outside history had been let in. Telling the stories of people once ignored was suddenly respectable.[1]

Which was a very good thing, indeed. My account of the lives of Irish miners in Butte, Montana, would have been a hard sell otherwise. But the revolution brought other equally happy changes: The "revolutionists," the women and men writing the new labor history, also claimed the right to "intrude" on their work; in fact, they insisted on it. Their histories of working people were semiautobiographical. Much of that history was done by historians who came from working-class backgrounds and were often the first in their families to attend college. Many were the children or grandchildren of immigrants. The historical observers looked and thought like those they were observing. They were studying people who were their social, cultural, and intellectual antecedents. As Rachleff put it, "how *they* lost is how *we* lost." To put it less politically, how they thought is how we think. Orsi called it intersubjectivity; it was built into the methodology of the new labor historians.[2]

Which returns the discussion to working-class Irish Catholics and their erratic ways. My emphasis is on the cultural divergence between a Catholic subset of America's working class and its fractious relationship with the values of a Protestant-made nation. There's room for that in the new labor history "revolution." Rachleff writes this: Worker culture had its "own rules, ones which often clashed with the evolving mainstream of late nineteenth century America." As for immigrant workers specifically, they were "culturally independent"; they "resisted the encroachments of capital by relying on a traditional set of values and expectations which made sense . . . to them."[3]

Which immediately brings up the most significant point about American worker culture and its "rules" and "traditions." American workers were drawn from everywhere and every culture. Rachleff writes of working-class rules and traditions. Given the diversity of the American working class, one must ask: Whose rules? Whose traditions? America's "evolving cultural mainstream" was characterized and given a fixed label: it was modern and, using the term loosely, middle-class. America's workers, however, were visitors from everywhere. I wonder sometimes, when the Industrial Workers of the World were formed in 1905, whether the founders took that name to indicate their internationalism, or did they mean to signify America's reliance on industrial workers *from* the world? I decided the issue by concluding that they meant both.

The old, prerevolution, labor historians acknowledged the racial and ethnic diversity of the American working class, but they did not single out any of those diverse ethnicities for special attention, nor did they ask what unique perspectives those ethnic cultures might have brought to working-class consciousness. Immigration was discussed, as were its effects. But the cultural sensibilities of specific immigrant and ethnic groups were not. Which allows me to place myself in the company of the new labor historians. My emphasis is on the Catholic Irish, of which many millions worked for American wages. Did they bring any special Irish or Catholic perspective to labor issues? Did the fact that they had emigrated from a British colony have any effect on American labor generally? Did their anglophobia?

And a related point: What difference did their Catholicism, or that of the rest of the papist hordes among America's workers, have on those perspectives? Catholicism was discussed by labor historians, but too briefly and usually only in the context of the Church as a prominent institutional enemy of socialism, in league with reactionary capitalists and other malefactors of great wealth. I'm not sure why that was the case, why historians of American labor all but ignored the religion of millions of those who labored. But I suspect it had something to do with what Robert Orsi meant when he wrote that if "the presence of the gods in the old Catholic sense is an absolute limit that contemporary [historians] refuse to cross, then they will ... fail to understand much of human life." They will lose the chance to "break into time." They will certainly fail to understand the dissident Catholic Irish in Protestant and modern America.[4]

These are Robert Orsi's concluding sentences: "[The] future ... envisioned for the human race [by modernists] has not happened. The gods were not turned back at the borders. . . . The unseeing of the gods was an achievement," an event. It was not one greeted with unanimous approval, nor was it made a perpetual and unchanging part of the human condition. In Orsi's words, "the challenge" for historians is to acknowledge that truth—painful as it might be for some—and "to see [the gods] again." If historians refuse even to look, "then they will miss the empirical reality of religion ... and they will fail to understand much of human life."[5]

That's a harsher stricture than I would make, but not by much. My topic, however, is more limited than Orsi's. And so, my conclusion can be less universal: At the very least, Orsi's laggard historians will fail to understand much of the Catholic Irish in America. Simply calling them premodern—and thus precapitalist—won't do. I'm tempted to ask, "so what?" Pre- anything implies a process toward becoming whatever it is that follows the *pre*. Were Irish Catholics only premodern and precapitalist? I find them to have been more than a little skeptical of both—erratics, in other words. IrishCatholics in America must be seen as culture-bearing, that culture must be traced to its historical origins, and the effects of it on the time and place of its landing must be observed and analyzed.

Given the top-heavy Catholic presence in the working class, the problem is a particular one for historians of American labor. If the history of workers in America is to be understood, the Catholic belief in the real presence must also be understood—or at least accounted for—including by those for whom the real presence is a medieval leftover, an alien, even a sinister concept. That is a self-imposed "constraint on ... scholarship," which is unfortunate enough. Worse, it puts limits on the culture, the social unconscious, of many of those they're studying. Which is another way of saying that history is an interpretation of interpretation; historians interpreting as the subjects of their scholarly inquiries interpreted. Historians and other students of American labor should at least know enough about the gods present to know that that belief influenced Catholic workers' ideas about capitalism, wage labor, equity, and social justice—and everything else under the Catholic sun. It was part of the structure of feeling, the ecology that made up their lives.[6]

• • •

I begin with Selig Perlman, in many ways the founder of the "old" labor history. In 1928, Perlman offered an interesting and important observation about labor and ethnicity and the connections between the two in his *Theory of the Labor Movement*. He made the commonplace observation that America had "the most heterogeneous labor class in existence." That was its "condition" and, as he had put it six years earlier in his history of American trade unionism, it was "fatal to the develop[ment] of a cooperative spirit." It separated the American working class "into mutually isolated groups even as the social classes of England and Scotland are separated by class spirit."[7]

The absence of a "cooperative spirit," however, was not all that was at issue. Like everyone else who took up the subject of American labor, Perlman was obliged to offer an answer to the question in Werner Sombart's 1906 publication, *Why Is There No Socialism in the United States?*—a question based on the assumption that there should have been. Sombart was as aware as any of the racial and ethnic diversity of workers in the United States; he called the American labor force a "variegated mixture." But Sombart did not offer ethnic diversity as part of the answer to the question he had posed. In fact, a variegated mix, as he put it rather primly, was not one of the "circumstances of interest to us."[8]

It was not of surpassing interest to Perlman either. Perlman answered the issue this way: With "a working class of such a composition, socialism or communism" could never be "the official 'ism' of the [labor] movement." But what really made the American working class resistant to socialist solutions were the attitudes, the sensibilities—though Perlman never called them that—of a major component of America's multihued, multicultured industrial workers from the world. "The radicalization of the American labor movement," he said, was impossible because it would "deliberately drive the Catholics . . . out of the . . . movement, since with them an irreconcilable opposition to socialism is a matter of religious principle." He might also have said something about the fact that with the radicals, including some in the labor movement, an irreconcilable opposition to Catholicism was a matter of ideological principle. That seems not to have occurred to him, despite the fact of his close association with John Commons whose anti-Catholicism was a core value, as it was for many other American socialists.[9]

Curiously—at least to me—Perlman seems never to have read *Rerum Novarum*, the 1891 papal encyclical on the condition of labor. Nor, it seems, had he read any of the many responses to that letter by American Catholic prelates or any of the reports and recommendations that came out of the National Catholic War, later Welfare, Council formed during World War I. I cannot help returning to this point: Catholicism was the religious home of more workers than all the other denominations combined. Would anyone writing a history of American labor have ignored a long letter on "the condition of labor" written by the highest-ranking cleric of any other religious denomination?

Rerum Novarum needs to be—or at least can survive being—interpreted in the context of Catholic Workers, even of Irish Catholic workers specifically. In many respects, it was as much the Catholic laity's "Labor Manifesto" as the Vatican's. Irish erratics could also have written it; they were certainly the most prominent of the American Catholics to apply its lessons to the management of the American economy. I grant that this is an unorthodox argument; it suggests that the Catholic hierarchy ran in both directions—the ones at the bottom schooling those above them. But I have long thought that it would be an odd hierarchy indeed in which ideas didn't occasionally run uphill. The anticlericalism of that comment would not sit well with many of the Church's hierarchs. But how could Leo, or any others of them, know about the condition of the working class, except by reading what the working class had said on the matter?

Its phantom coauthors aside, *Rerum Novarum* strongly supported unions and as strongly denounced the excesses of capitalism—of which it cited many. How to account for Perlman's omission of it? On that subject, how to account for Perlman's failure even to mention the number of Irish Catholics—who were also Irish nationalists—in the British Chartist movement? Why did Perlman dismiss the Molly Maguires, Irish Catholic labor militants in the Pennsylvania coal fields, as "terrorists and assassins?" Perlman admired Terence Powderly, head of the Knights of Labor. He said that Powderly was a machinist and had been the mayor of Scranton and that he wanted to "circumscribe the wage system." He said nothing about Powderly's Catholicism or his Fenian-inspired devotion to Irish nationalism. I don't think that Perlman was one of the "scholars" who Orsi said would not "cross" the "absolute limit," the line drawn in the scholarly sand by those who live in the anti-Catholic world of "Absence." I also don't think he was as curious as he should have been.[10]

Take his brief and casual reference to antisocialism as a "matter of [Catholic] religious principle." That equates religious principles with political beliefs, something he would never do—or at least never did—with any other religious group. He also missed the important fact that what the official Catholic Church believed was not necessarily what the Catholic people, including Irish Catholic people, believed. Radical Fenian nationalists paid no attention to clerical interdictions; Irish Catholics in the working class were at least as free-spirited—and free-thinking—as even the most advanced of the Fenian nationalists. Perlman seems to have thought antisocialism a creedal or doctrinal commandment: a "thou shalt not embrace socialism" rule that admitted of no exceptions and required no analysis. His casual and lazy assumption was that Catholics—all of them, not just the Irish—did exactly as their church bid them to do.

On this issue, recall only the "old truism" cited by Declan Kiberd: In Ireland, "socialism never stood for much more than a fundamental goodness of heart." The Church had no objection to socialism so defined; it was the essence of community and of sharing. That the saying was not a revealed truth does not make Irish communalism less important—or less attestable. As a nonrevealed truth it, may be more of both. Perlman asked for a "cooperative spirit," some goodness of heart. The Irish in the American labor movement could have provided it, or at least the idea of it. Whether they could have been persuaded to extend their goodness of heart beyond their own neighborhood was a different matter entirely. That, however, was not Perlman's point. Perlman was unfamiliar with Irish truisms and would have been uninterested in the one Kiberd cited. Socialism as goodness of heart did not count much with him, or with any of the old labor historians and too few of the new ones.[11]

I again quote James Connolly—Irish, Catholic, and socialist—who wrote that the "'firm distinction in the minds of Irish Catholics between the *duties* of the Holy See and the *rights* of the individual Catholic has been a necessary and saving element in keeping Ireland Catholic." There was no conscious contradiction in that comment. The Church held its position in Ireland because, according to Connolly, the Irish laity were free to challenge it. The more erratic of them frequently did. Connolly then added this: "As long as the priest speaks to us . . . upon religious matters, we will listen to him . . . with reverence, . . . but the moment he . . . uses the altar . . . to tell us what to do with our political freedom, . . . he will cease to be a priest and be simply a politician."[12]

That the official Catholic Church was antisocialist is indisputable. That lay Catholics were antisocialist as a consequence is not. I would not call anticlericalism an Irish Catholic sensibility. That gives it too much credit. Clannishness and anglophobia were sensibilities. Anticlericalism was a habit. Sometimes the hierarchical ordering of doctrinal decision-making worked well; other times it did not. It depended on the doctrine. Many Irish working people rejected socialism because it offended *their* Catholicism, not because it offended their bishop's. Their rejection did not make them devoid of class consciousness or a cooperative spirit. It only reverses the assumed hierarchical order: It meant they thought themselves fortunate to have been born into so wise a church, one that had the great good sense to agree with them. Much of this Perlman could have learned. He had only to ask someone in the Irish Catholic working class.[13]

It would also have helped if Perlman had found some place in his account for Jim Larkin, and—for there were many with similar views—the likes of Jim Larkin. He had to have known of Larkin, the "Catholic Communist," as Bertram Wolfe called him, who spent considerable time in America confounding his socialist comrades with statements like these: "'There is no antagonism between the cross and Socialism. . . . There is no conflict between the religion of the Catholic Church and Marxism." "I stand by the cross and Marx. I belong to the Catholic Church. In Ireland that is not held against a Socialist." Larkin then went on to say that the same was not the case in America. In fact, he had "never found more bigotry and intolerance than [he had] . . . among a certain wing"—the non-Irish wing—"of the Socialist party."[14]

If the Irish majority within the AFL's Catholic majority was opposed to socialism, it was because individual Catholic Irish didn't think socialism a particularly effective system. Socialists would turn the economy over to the state; the Irish knew two states, England and the United States. They had no affection for either. Nor should they have had. There was also this: Many didn't like socialism because they didn't like socialists. American socialists were too literally modern; they lived under the sign of Absence. Following from that, they were too chic, too theoretical, too disrespectful of the Irish and their faith, too materialistic, and too solemn, which is to say, too joyless. IrishCatholics workers were not antireform, antiliberal, or even antisocialist; it was reformers, liberals, and socialists they could not abide. I grant the ad hominem aspect of that. I also contend that there was a lot of ad hominemism—to coin a word—to the liberals' and socialists' disdain for all things Catholic, including Catholics. Dueling prejudices aside, the history of American labor must take into account that ontological divide.

To return to Perlman's response to Sombart: the best that can be said of it is that Perlman had at least identified a "Catholic dimension" to the American labor movement; he had even made a start toward a "culture turn" in the study of American workers. It was just not a very probing or promising start. It is one thing to argue that Irish Catholic workers affected the American labor movement. They did. It is quite another to say that their only effect was to push the movement away from the socialism that it might have embraced if not for popery and all those papists—Perlman's bad answer to Sombart's bad question. It is yet another thing to skip over the Irish presence in all this, and then to ignore the fact that Catholic social teaching and Irish social practice were both intensely communal, certainly communal enough to accommodate a range of collectivist ideas.

Perlman's *History of the Labor Movement* was published in 1922; his *Theory of the Labor Movement* six years later. In 1930, a book far more significant than either, Max Weber's *Protestant Ethic and the Spirit of Capitalism* came out in its first English language edition. Weber's book appeared in German in 1904, and there are reasons to think that the multilingual Perlman had read it prior to its English-language release. Whatever his familiarity with it, Perlman did not cite Weber's book. Granted, there weren't too many places in either of his books when he would have had occasion to.

I am not arguing that Weber's sociology belongs with the old labor history; it's not history at all, and it's not about labor except indirectly. What it is about, and directly, is Protestantism and capitalism and their cultural antagonists, Catholicism by name, and Irish—occasionally by name, but always by clear inference. Since the American Irish were most often found in the employ of Protestant capitalists, Weber's book, though not exactly an antecedent of the new labor history, is very much an antecedent of the cultural divergence between Irish Catholics and Protestant Americans. It's a primer of sorts on erraticism. At the risk of hopelessly blurring disciplinary lines, and aware that I am being a bit loose with chronology and theme, I'm going to treat *The Protestant Ethic and the Spirit of Capitalism* in the context of the new labor history.

I also acknowledge that much of what Weber wrote about the connection between the ethic and the spirit is now thought to be either incomplete or simply wrong. But that there was a Protestant ethic and that capitalism had a spirit has not been challenged. Neither has the fact that Protestant=Absence was fundamental to both. That's the important matter here and I will proceed as if Weber had something useful to say about it.[15]

Weber was fond of quoting Benjamin Franklin, including Franklin's admonitory counsel: "'remember, that *time* is money." That was not just one of poor Richard's "Protestant" aphorisms; it was more nearly a creedal truth. Weber liked it. It confirmed what he thought was "the essence of the spirit of modern capitalism," which he summarized as "the making of money,... acquisition as *the ultimate purpose of... life*." It was not, however, the ultimate purpose of Irish Catholic lives, as Weber knew well. Catholicism was a world of what he called "enchantments"—the real presences (always plural) taking a lively interest in human affairs. Weber contrasted that with the Protestant and modern—and God-absent—world, which he called one of "disenchantment." There would have been nothing in the "Irish philosophy" of "paples" as "more coompany than sthumps" that would have surprised him. But good company was not enough to sustain a modern capitalist economy. As for stumps, they meant hewn trees, milled lumber, paid wages, finished buildings, and someone's profits. They weren't intended to be company.[16]

Weber knew Catholics and keeping company. He also knew about Catholic feast days—and about their fondness for statues, relics, holy oils, holy waters, and holy all the rest. There were major "differences between" what Weber called "the capitalistic and pre-capitalistic spirits...." More important than Weber's too casual use of "pre-capitalist" was his argument for what gave rise to that capitalist spirit. It was the "Calvinist *diaspora* [that was] the seed-bed of capitalist economy." That's a fascinating use of "diaspora." Why not just "Calvinism" or the "Calvinist Reformation"? Diaspora doesn't have to mean to America, but it certainly suggests that it was in America that Calvinism had its greatest influence. And maybe it was. Rauschenbusch thought so. Weber quoted Franklin far more often than he did Wesley—or Calvin. In America, the Protestant spirit had led to an "emancipation from economic traditionalism..." by endowing money—hence time—with a specific moral purpose. Time was never to be dissipated. Wasting it wasn't just "offensive" in a modern society; for people "merely to pass the time" was an offense against a Calvinist God.

For Protestant Anglo-Americans, time-keeping brought order out of the chaos of infinity. Weber gave Franklin's adage its necessary Reformation gloss: "Waste of time is thus the first and in principle the deadliest of sins. ... Loss of time through sociability, idle talk, ... even more sleep than is necessary ... is worthy of absolute moral condemnation." Irish Catholics, particularly those drawn from the peasantry, were willing to risk Protestant moral condemnation. They had a great fondness for "sociability," idle talk," and "sitting idly" passing the time in storytelling. The Irish American writer James Farrell called it the Irish "dichotomy: civilization or the clock." It goes without saying that the Irish had no firmer grasp on money, time's equivalent, or on the meaning of work without pause, or of thriftiness, and frugality, money's guardians.[17]

To return to David Hackett Fischer's folkways and the important ways that erraticism showed itself: Irish "time-ways" were "outside notions," the regressive ideas of an "outside people"—folkways with a social-class edge. Many in the west of Ireland had never paid or been paid a wage, some had never seen a coin or a bill. As for time and the work routines it tracked, "'they had no experience at keeping watch on a clock.... There was a certain timelessness about their lives. The Irish, said Leo Ward, "seem to exist like God in an eternal now." And Ward was talking about IrishCatholic farmers in Iowa, the same ones who played Sunday baseball.[18]

Tim Buckley was an Irish tailor; his and his wife Ansty's—for Anastasia—most prized possession was a grand and ornate clock, which they kept immaculately clean and wound, but which they never set. The tailor greeted each morning in the same way, with a recital of what could pass as an Irish ode to timelessness: "Come day. Go day. Let's have another day." There cannot be a better definition of what Walter Lippmann called "drift" than that one. There's a certain driftiness even to the saying of it—as I do at the beginning of each day. The tailor and Lippmann occupied separate planes of existence, as did the Irish and progressive Americans generally. Irish time happened. It passed and one passed it, often idly. American time did not just happen and Americans did not just pass it. Had the Irish ever heard it, they might have cheered Lippmann's derisive comment about drifty lives as being like "a bubble on the stream of time." Bubbles drifted. Drifting was friendlier and more neighborly than mastery.[19]

• • •

Obviously, the Catholic Irish were not the only divergent element in the American industrial labor force. I think they were the most *culturally* erratic, but what Polanyi called the "double movement," the effort to keep the economy embedded in society, took many forms. That forces the question: Was the American industrial labor force too racially, ethnically, and culturally diverse to enable a unified working-class component of the double movement to emerge? That component did not have to be "radical"—however radical might be defined; it did not even have to be self-consciously proletarian. It did, however, have to be coherent. There had at least to have been a recognizable American working class. I frame the question that way to evoke E. P. Thompson's 1963 study *The Making of the English Working Class*, his brilliant and theory-shifting account of the lives of English working people from the late 1780s to the early 1830s.

The new American labor history started with Thompson. It could have started with Weber, but it didn't. Thompson tells us that when he was putting a title to his book, he thought that "this [was a] clumsy" one. He chose "making" because he was describing "a study in an active process" and that required an active verb. Here is more of what he had to say: "The [English] working class [not the working class in England, note] did not rise like the sun at an appointed time." It was not summoned into being. Rather, it "was present at its own making." It was not an abstract thing generated from forces outside itself. It was "not ... a 'structure,' nor even ... a 'category.'" It was "a relationship, and not a thing; a *"historical* phenomenon," defined by people as "they live their own history." The English working class made itself out of the lives workers were leading—and *the lives they had led*. The past contained in their present counted.[20]

Thompson's book recast labor history. He moved it from the study of institutions—unions in particular—to the study of workers as a special and separate category of people fully deserving of historical attention. Their work lives alone did not make them. Neither did the "labor movement," variously defined. Neither did the "new ideologies" of industrial capitalism. The working class had to be studied before it was a working class. I think Thompson's book was read with particular reverence—or, at least, particular attention—by those historians who had themselves come out of the working class and had experienced or at least witnessed something of what went into the making and character of one. Those of us in that category have an advantage. Our approach to the topic is "affectionate," used theoretically. It signifies an understanding from experience. It should not be confused with approval. The opposite may be the case. What it does mean is that historians have pasts too; they and their topics often know one another.[21]

In one of his many analogies, Thompson emphasized that the "working class, does not exist . . . to lie as a patient on the Adjustor's table." I don't know what an "adjustor's" table was or is but I think I get the point: Adjustors wrote accounts of labor without any laborers in them. For them, the working class was a thing. They would measure it. Thompson saw it for what it was, a "relationship," a series of them, in fact. It defined itself by working people living "their own lives," not those assigned by "adjustors." We are back to cultural sensibilities, those nonrational receptors that real people use to filter experiences. They do not compute. Those relationships occurred within and between "communities" with "working-class community patterns," the places discussed earlier, the ones with a "working-class structure of feeling" to them. Those patterns arose from neighborhood institutions. Trade unions were among them, but so were "friendly societies, educational and religious movements, political organizations, periodicals."[22]

Labor historians before Thompson seldom entered those neighborhoods. And they would never have said there was "a working-class structure of feeling" to anything they were recounting. Thompson's use of that descriptive language produced one of the most notable images in his entire long book. The imprecision, even vagueness, of it gets it exactly right. "Feeling" is the only word that will do. Those neighborhoods did not just *come into being* as a result of people being thrown together; they were fashioned and formed and *brought into being*. Thompson, of course, never made that point—it didn't apply to England—but I must: In America, those communities with that working-class feel to them had also an ethnic feel to them. They weren't just working-class neighborhoods. They were tribal enclaves, sanctuaries really, filled with safe houses.

Class was not all that defined working people. They had had an identity before they ever took, in the wonderful phrase of past years, "a job of work." Consciousness of class is a part of their story, but it is futile—a form of imperialism, really—to deal with it on the basis of how well or how poorly it matched some invented working-class matrix. Class, Thompson told us, cannot be judged on the basis of hypotheses like "revolutionary class consciousness." That was the easy way, the old and tired way, the vulgar and "enormously condescending" way to define it. It allowed theorists to "deduce the class-consciousness [the working class] ought to have" had and would have had "if it was properly aware of its own position and real interests." But the working class "seldom does have" the consciousness of class deduced from some adjustor's mathematical model. And it was always aware of its own interests and of which ones were real.[23]

There was what Thompson called a "cultural superstructure" through which a recognition of class interests "dawns." "Cultural superstructure" is like a people having "their own history," a synonym for "cultural sensibilities." I take all of that to mean that working-class consciousness did not have to be anything and that it was a mistake for labor historians and theorists to assign to the proletariat a specific role and then work to explain why it didn't recite its lines as the theorists had written them. It may, in fact, have been a mistake to give people who work for wages an abstract label like proletariat. By whatever name, those in the working class who were not revolutionaries were not "class collaborationists;" they did not have a warped or "false" consciousness. Class consciousness could not be "false." It could only be. The social world of industrial workers did not compel them to be class warriors. It did not compel them to be anything.[24]

One final analogy presents itself here. It is irresistible—or at least I will not resist it: Like the British Empire which it resembled and with which it should be paired, the capitalist factory system was designed and expected to "translate" people, to teach them new words and new tricks and make them over. That is what the British military's "translation" of Brian Friel's fictional Ballybeg—and all Ireland—was intended to do. The procreant power of both systems, according to the directors of those systems, was enormous, magical, really. Hugh, Friel's Ballybeg hedge teacher, knew better. There was no magic. Being "translated" into English did not determine who the Irish were or who they would become. E.P. Thompson knew better, too. The idea that the factory system took "some nondescript undifferentiated raw material of humanity, and [turned] it out at the other end as a 'fresh *race* of beings'" gave that system far too much credit. I can't know if Thompson used the word "race" intending to make the point that the category of "industrial working class," imposed by forces external to it and without regard to preindustrial cultures, was as counterfeit as racial categories externally imposed. I like to think he did.[25]

For historians of American working people, the key word in Thompson's title is "English." Thompson described the formation of *the* English working class—note even the use of the definite article; the working class had only to be made once. That gave him an enormous advantage over historians of

American labor. He was studying English and Protestant employers buying the labor of mostly English and Protestant—usually Dissenters—working people. That did not mean that the making of an English working class was uncomplicated and stress-free. Native-born English workers were deeply divided internally by occupation, skill level, and union membership. They were even more deeply divided from the employing classes by language, dress, manners, and Protestant religious denomination—by culture generally. They could never "pass"—Eliza Doolittle-like—as anything other than what they were. But the conflicts were fought on native grounds. The culture of the English working class was decidedly oppositional but it was also identifiably English, contained within an enclosed English cultural system. In comparison with the American, it was a model of cultural similitude.

Huge sections of America's working class weren't American, they were only *in* America. They consisted of foster children, "alien citizens" and cultural misfits, "democracy's outcasts." Josiah Strong made the point in 1893: "In England, however widely classes may be separated socially . . . the lord and the peasant"—or the employer and the employee—"are . . . generally bound together by . . . the same national history," they "speak . . . the same tongue, and presumably they are both Protestants." Selig Perlman, he of the old, pre-Thompson, labor history, put it directly: "American labor [was] the most heterogeneous laboring class in existence—ethnically, linguistically, religiously, and culturally." That may have been part of why, in Eugene Debs's words, "American workers do not . . . think as English workers."[26]

Even Antonio Gramsci, the Italian Marxist, jumped in on the issue, explaining the "backward state" of the American [working] "masses" on "the absence of national homogeneity, the mixture of race-cultures." Herbert Gutman, the best-known of Thompson's American disciples, called this American working class a "mélange," a concoction of ethnic elements so wild and unstable that trying to "Americanize" Thompson and produce a synthetic history of the "making of the American working class" was a hopeless enterprise. The only outsiders in Thompson's historical world were Irish Catholics; they were the only ones who were not made, or did not make themselves, into *English* workers. America counted its outsider groups by the hundreds.[27]

The poststructuralist argument that experiences have "no objective reality except as perceived" carries the point too far, but to say that different people with a different set of cultural sensibilities respond to the same experiences differently is only to state the obvious. The point is not that there was no working class in America, or that America was a classless society. The point of the new labor historians was that there was an American working class, but it never sat still long enough and was never culturally homogeneous enough for a Thompson-like analysis of how and by whom it was made. In

Ira Berlin's words—and, it may be presumed, in Gutman's mind—the "diverse origins" of the American working class "overwhelmed the seemingly minor distinctions between the English, Welsh, Scots, and Irish" who made up the single and homogeneous English working class. As the American historian David Brody put it, "Thompson's orientation may serve admirably in the English setting" and up to the 1830s, but "can we share [the] confidence of discovering for American workers a basic consistency of outlook and a distinctive way of life?" The answer was "no, we cannot."[28]

That was particularly the case when the topic was American workers after about 1870, long after 1832, Thompson's terminal date, when he said he'd taken *The Making of the English Working Class* as far chronologically as he needed to. English and American industrialization did not proceed in lockstep; the English process began before the American. It exaggerates the case only slightly to say that in 1830 there was hardly an American working class to be made. In other words, the timing was off. Thompson's periodization didn't fit the American reality any better than his homogeneous working class fit America's heterogeneous one. It was thought that there were too many culturally diverse ethnic and racial parts to the American working class. Historians of American labor had to take the separate parts on one at a time, understanding that an account of any one of them could not be used as a stand-in for the mélange as a whole. American labor historians could ask Thompson-like questions, but they could not expect Thompson-like—which is to say English-labor-like—answers.

・・・

Or could they? I begin by returning to Thompson, the essential Englishness of his account notwithstanding. There is a small section of his book that, as far as I can tell, has been ignored by his legions of American admirers. In his examination of England's working-class communities, Thompson notes that there was one racial-ethnic "ingredient . . . [that] necessarily evaded [his] analysis." That ingredient was the Irish immigration. The Irish were the only immigrants, the only racial and cultural outliers in his otherwise all-English working class. Fortunately for him, they played so small a role in the making of the whole that they deserved no more than the fifteen-page addendum-like section he gave them.

But listen again to what he said: The Irish "*necessarily evaded* [his] analysis." He had brought a "fine meshed net" to the task of catching English workers and making sense of their lives. He didn't ignore the Irish. But he missed them when he cast his net, or rather, they evaded it. Why evaded? That's as active a verb as "making." Thompson, I am certain, thought about it as long and as hard as he thought about his book's title. And why "necessarily"? Why did they *have to* evade it? That suggests that there was something fundamental that explains Irish "evasiveness." There was. They dodged the net because they weren't English. They were only in England. And they were Catholic.[29]

On this point, Berlin and Gutman erred not only in their reading of the Irish in the American working class. They erred in their reading of Thompson and the Irish. They either did not notice or did not know what to do with that "necessary evasion." I just quoted Berlin's comment that there were only "minor distinctions" between "the English, Welsh, Scots, *and Irish*." Ira Berlin was one of America's finest historians; Gutman one of the most perceptive of America's historians of labor. What is there to say about that comment? And I'm assuming it represented Gutman's views as well as Berlin's own. What Berlin said would have surprised everyone on the list of Irish and labor historians, including Thompson—particularly Thompson. It's in the same class as Werner Sombart's remark in his 1896 book, *Why Is There No Socialism in the United States?* Sombart wrote that the "Irish ... make up more than half of the *Anglo-Saxon* total" among the American working class.

To the Berlin-Gutman point, I would say only that there were a great many distinctions between the Irish and the British, and the Irish insisted on a full accounting of every one of them. Berlin-Gutman turned the Irish into West Brits, than which there was no graver insult. Irish Catholic workers in America, Joe McDonnell among them, would have agreed with Gutman's self-assessment that he had not paid enough attention to the Catholic—or the Irish—issue. To Sombart's even more egregious error, I would note that the Irish were not Anglo-Saxons—a racial point of no great importance—and that they deeply resented any suggestion that they were—a cultural and political point of surpassing importance.[30]

Thompson knew and made quite specific allowances for all the distinctions Berlin-Gutman found minor. For a crucial example, his was an English, not a British, working class; he did not deal with the Scots and Welsh as in any way separate parts of it. That was something he felt compelled to explain, so he offered a "note of apology to [the] Scottish and Welsh." He was being glib. He "neglected [them] not out of chauvinism, but out of respect," respect, that is, for their likeness to the English. They were English in thought and manner and could thus be "neglected." They were a part of the English whole. That was not true of the Irish. He couldn't neglect them; not out of respect—he owed them none and paid them none. His net captured only English or English-like workers. The Irish's essential non-Englishness allowed them to slip through its mesh and compelled him to deal with them as a separate group. Imagine a people culturally remote from the English. The Chinese will do. Had there been Chinese workers in England in the years from the 1780s to the 1830s, Thompson would have had to deal with them too and in the same way he dealt with the Irish, as an addendum.

The Irish had nothing to do with the making of the English working class. The key issue—no surprise here—was religion. For another equally crucial example, Thompson's "Irish supplement" did not include the Protestant Irish from northeastern Ulster, some of whom immigrated to and were working in England. He made a specific point of telling his readers that. He mentioned "Irish Protestants" by that name. Unlike the Irish from other parts of Ireland, they did not evade his net. They were caught in it. They didn't need a special short section for the simple reason that they were a part of the whole very large book, part of the making of the English working class. They deserved and were paid the same respect he paid the Scots. They were, after all, indistinguishable from the Scots.[31]

Religion mattered greatly to Thompson. Scots and Welsh were Protestants; they could be benignly neglected. Not so the Catholic Irish. Papists had to be treated and they had to be treated separately. The working class, after all, made itself out of the cultural materials it had at hand. And those were considerable. They were "free-born Englishmen"—and free-born Englishmen "as Paine had left [them] or as the Methodists had moulded [them]." The English hired "hand" was also "the inheritor of Bunyan, of remembered village rights, of notions of equality before the law." This free-born Englishman had gone through a "massive religious indoctrination" and had created myriad "new political traditions" long before he ever entered through the factory gate.[32]

But what of the Catholic Irish who entered with him—or lingered outside the gate hoping to be taken on? Thompson said nothing about a structure of feeling—working-class or otherwise—in the neighborhoods in Britain where the Irish not from northeastern Ulster lived—largely, one suspects, because he found no working-class structure of feeling to their lives. He did say that "disasters" had "afflicted" them." He was dealing with the years prior to 1832, and so he obviously did not mean what he called only "the potato-blight." He could simply have pointed that out and left the matter there, but he did not. Thompson was something of a revisionist when it came to Irish history; he wrote that the afflicting disasters that led to the "immiseration of the Irish people" came from "the after-effects of the counter-revolution" after the Irish rebellion of 1798. I'll leave it to Irish historians—revisionists and postrevisionists alike—to interpret that. What matters to me is Thompson's three-word sketch of the Irish "peasantry" who migrated to England. With a brevity uncharacteristic of him, he said that they brought with them their "semi-feudal nationalist Church." That was it. That was all they had.[33]

What came next is one of the parts of Thompson's Irish addendum that his American adherents have missed, in large measure, I think, because, like Gutman, they could not bring themselves to cross Orsi's line and attend adequately to the Catholic question. The issue here is not just the mélange that was the American working class; American labor historians have a point when it comes to that. The issue is that Thompson shut down his analysis of the *English* working class in the 1830s, before an American working class had begun to form. He did not, however and with my emphasis, shut down his analysis of *Irish Catholic workers in England*. Listen to Thompson here: he contended that the "semi-feudal nationalist Church"—and both descriptive adjectives are critical—was the "most enduring" of the "cultural traditions" of the Irish. Indeed, they persisted for "four generations."[34]

However one counts a generation, that could mean up to a century past Thompson's end date of 1832. Implied by his comment about the persistence of Irish Catholic "cultural traditions," Thompson was of the opinion that until at least the 1930s, Irish Catholics in England would "necessarily" have "required an entirely separate" analytical net. To put it differently, the Irish would have evaded the net had he cast it out again and again and taken his story far beyond 1832. I wish Thompson had felt the need to say something more on that point—or had written a book-length sequel to *The Making*, carrying the story beyond 1832; perhaps even beyond England.

That sequel would have been crucial for American historians. True, the American working class formed itself after the English and after 1832. But, by 1870, it was in place, and the Irish were a major component in it. So I offer this brief—and presumptuous—summary of what lessons that casual reference to "cultural traditions" lasting "four generations" might have taught: "Semifeudal" as applied to Irish Catholicism meant preindustrial and premodern; Thompson meant it that way. To drag Weber back into the discussion, there was no "spirit of capitalism" among Irish Catholics. Americans thought that about them too. In addition to being semifeudal, the Irish Catholic Church was [Irish] "nationalist." Thompson did not mean by that that the Catholic Irish had any understanding of nationalism or any idea of what an Irish nation might look like. It was more nearly a "semifeudal anti-English" Church. I wonder why he didn't just say that. Maybe it was a given. Thompson's inference is unmistakable: their archaic Irish church explained their backwardness as a people. It was what led to their "segregation of (and by) religion."[35]

Thompson's Irish story—implicit only and short as it was—went on for a century after 1832. American labor historians have always said that Thompson was one of the first to ask the right questions of and about working people. They would ask similar questions, basing them on similar theoretical assumptions. They admired his fine-meshed analytical net and determined to devise ones that would fit the American circumstances. Thompson, however, gave them more than they knew or knew what to do with. The Irish in the English working class were semifeudal, but they were that because they were Catholic. The connection is not as tight, but many were also Irish nationalists because they were Catholic. And they were all of that for the next one hundred years. Which means that for all of the years of their diasporic wanderings among Albion's seed, working their odd American jobs, they were enduringly semifeudal and Irish.[36]

I think Thompson intended to be taken literally and seriously when he pushed his "Irish story" into the twentieth century. "Four generations" was not an approximation. Indeed, it was the minimum shelf-life of Irish Catholic anglophobiac nationalism, as Thompson knew well: It carried well into the late 1950s when he was writing his book. And, since it was the essence of being Irish, that "semi-feudal nationalist church" accompanied the Irish wherever their roving took them. Thompson's discussion of the persistence of Irish cultural traditions was only one short part of an 800-plus-page book, but that single reference makes Thompson more of a historian of American labor—or, at least, far more relevant to American labor historians—than has been previously thought. It doesn't do anything to solve the problem of making sense of America's working-class mélange, but it inserts Thompson directly into the study of the Irish Catholic components of that mélange.

I offer the following from Thompson's story of England and English working people in the implied context of America and American working people, with Irish Catholics as the indispensable others in both. The making of the English working class involved as well the premaking of a significant part of the American working class. Thompson's implied account of Irish Americans begins, as many do, with their Catholicism. It also ends there. In the case of the Irish variant, Catholicism was filled with what he called "the hocus-pocus of Romanism." Weber had called it "enchantments," but they meant the same thing, "the candlesticks, the crucifix and the 'prints of saints and martyrs.'" That was the semifeudal part; it was also predevotional revolution but that would not have mattered to Thompson. Much of the hocus-pocus survived the Irish ecclesiastical revolutionaries.[37]

But, according to Thompson, "alongside" those prints of saints and martyrs on the walls of Irish (and Irish American) cabins, huts, and hovels was one "of O'Connell." That was the nationalist part. That reference to Daniel O'Connell is itself revealing: There would have been very few pictures of the "Liberator," the "King of the [Irish] beggars," prior to 1828, and none at all prior to 1800 and the Act of Union. As for pictures of him in Irish America, they wouldn't have begun to appear in numbers until after 1850.[38]

"Hocus-pocus of Romanism" is a bit condescending for one who would rescue working people from the "enormous condescension of posterity," but the comment was not evidence of anti-Catholicism as such. Thompson's prejudices were remarkably multidenominational. The son of Methodist missionaries, he was no kinder in his treatment of Methodism, which in one memorable passage he called "a ritualized form of psychic masturbation." Religion generally, and of every sort, obstructed the full development not just of an English working class but of all classes, indeed of all of humankind. In context, and at their most innocent, his comments about Irish Catholicism were only a lapse in manners.[39]

And, for all his distaste for Methodism, he spent a great number of pages writing about its influence on the making of the English working class. No one could ever accuse him of not paying enough attention to the "Methodist issue," as Gutman and the rest did to the Catholic. In addition, some of what Thompson had to say about the Catholic Irish were compliments—backhanded ones, to be sure, but sincere. He noted their "physical gifts," their strength of body, if not of mind, as well as their "pre-industrial labour rhythms," essentially "an alternation of intensive labour and boisterous relaxation." For "boisterous" read "drunken." These "gifts" suited the needs of an industrial society far better than did the "weakened physique and Puritan temperament" of the English—something that never occurred to Weber. To put it slightly differently, the Irish worked hard, spent their meager wages for drink, and so had to work again.

They were an English employer's godsend, the perfect unskilled industrial laborers, ideally suited to do the "menial, unpleasant tasks" that the English either refused to do or were not strong enough to do—in short, the "odd" jobs. Granted, these Patsy Caliban types had what Thompson said was a fine "disregard for veracity," a polite way of saying they lied a lot. They also lacked the "Puritan virtues of thrift and sobriety . . . application and forethought." Puritan virtues, however—the "imprint of Baxter and Wesley," in Thompson's words—were overrated. What industrial societies required was a "spendthrift expense of sheer physical energy," uninhibited by Wesley, or anything else, including thrift and sobriety.[40]

If only the Irish social deficits had ended there. Unfortunately for making working classes, the Catholic Irish who were working in England were not just thriftless and besotted, they were also primitive rebels, not in the cause of labor but in the cause of Ireland. Here too Thompson's analysis extends to at least four generations—far beyond the 1830s—and so is directly relevant to American labor history. Thompson's description is notable: He writes of Irish outlawry, of secret societies like the "Threshers, Caravats, Shanavests, Tommy Downshires, Carders, Ribbon-men, and the later Molly Maguires" and of "the rapid movement of men with blackened faces at night, the robbery of arms, the houghing (hamstringing) of horses and cattle—these were methods in which many Irishmen had served an apprenticeship." The methods would change over time—though not by much—but training in semiorganized violence and "outrages" against the public order was also ongoing through the next four generations.[41]

The names of later outlaws were not as inspired. Fenians, Land Leaguers, even Invincibles and Moonlighters can't match Threshers and Shanavests for style, but, as nativist Americans learned the hard way—or came to convince themselves—scheming, plotting, and belligerence seemed fixed characteristics of a great number of Irish for at least the next century. The Irish remained what Thompson said of them, a people of "rebellious dispositions," more likely to bring a "revolutionary inheritance" to trade unions, among many other associations. Their clustered neighborhoods were like the headquarters of revolutionary corps, early versions of flying columns.

Taken all in all, Irish Catholics formed in late-nineteenth and early-twentieth-century America what Thompson said they had been a century earlier in England: a "natural freemasonry of the disinherited." The freemasonry comparison is perfect. The Irish, said Thompson, were "quick to come to each other's aid," at least as quick as the more socially ascendant—and anti-Catholic—gathered in their Masonic Lodges. As for disinheritance, I take that to mean they were divested and cut off from their British national inheritance. But let it also be noted that the Irish disinheritance was of their own doing and on their own terms. Theirs was a self-disinheritance. They didn't want to be British inheritors. However it happened, if there is a better turn of phrase than "natural freemasonry of the disinherited" to describe Irish Catholics in England and in Anglo-America, I don't know what it could be.[42]

Thompson's reference to four generations of uninterrupted Irishness must be kept in mind. His point was clear: The Irish would perhaps one day outgrow the semifeudalism of their church. They might even, one day, take down the images of O'Connell and other of their "nationalist" heroes and martyrs. To outgrow was to grow up. But they hadn't by the early 1830s. They hadn't even shown any signs of changing or maturing. Or was it evolving? In all events, it is unimaginable that Thompson would have disagreed with Marx's analysis from 1870. Marx was persuaded that the Irish were congenital rebels, that they were, for mysterious reasons of "race," "more passionate and revolutionary in character than the English"—the perfect spearpoints of revolutions, even ones they didn't understand. Engels was even more excited than Marx. The Irish were "real proletarians and sans culottes . . . wild, headstrong, fanatical Gaels," the sorts who hough horses and cattle.[43]

Eric Hobsbawm, another Marxian historian of English labor, explicitly pushed this analysis further into the late nineteenth and early twentieth centuries, and far beyond Britain's borders. The unskilled Irish were the ones who formed the "revolutionary" element in the British working class, but not for reasons having anything to do with class. They "sympathized with revolution not because they were labourers, but because they were Irish." In other words, they were very good at being angry; the source of their anger or at whom it was directed was less important than the mere fact of it. Then, in a comment that echoes Kevin Kenny's argument for the persistence of diasporic sensibilities, Hobsbawm writes that "as every Irishman knows, emigration does not snap the links between the exiles and the home country, not least in the history of its labour movement." Among those links was "a tradition of armed rebellion." It "formed part of the political experience of their country." It certainly did. Hobsbawm also stopped short of dealing with those who emigrated for America, but it is safe to add "American working class" to the labor movements in which Irish were conspicuous among the "revolutionary" elements.[44]

Like all historians of American labor, I am indebted to Thompson; not because his descriptions of Irish Catholics were accurate or without prejudice. A lot of what he had to say about them was not just ill-mannered but bigoted. That does not diminish their usefulness to new labor historians writing about the American working class from 1870 to 1930. And I have another reason for my high regard for his Irish addendum: Thompson put the maximum amount of cultural distance between Irish Catholics and British Protestants and, by inference, between Irish Catholics and American Protestants. There were times when he did so by putting the maximum amount of distance between the Irish and the rest of civilized humanity, but I'll gladly settle for his singularly persuasive argument for Irish Catholic erraticism.

His summary portrait of the "free-born Englishman" as Paine had left him and Methodism had molded him, creator of "new political traditions," has been cited. He never offered a comparable portrait of Irish Catholics, so I will draft one for him: "beggar-born Irishman, out of time and out of place, inheritor of ancestral sorrows, indoctrinated and molded by a devotional Catholicism that was backward looking, and creator of anarchic traditions." America's new labor historians need not agree entirely with that description, but if they are to make sense of the Irish contingent in the American working class, they have at least to make it part of their analytical net.

The English working class, as Thompson defined it, was "a social and cultural formation, arising from processes which can only be studied . . . over a considerable historical period." That formation was distinctly oppositional to the dominant creed of capitalism and market economics. At times, the conflicts resembled what one American historian called "cultural warfare at the highest level." The Catholic Irish working class in America was also a social and cultural formation and it also arose over time. The conflicting interests, however, not only originated outside of economics, they extended far beyond the economic. Labor versus capital, yes; but also Catholic versus Protestant; Irish versus American; Irish versus non-Irish; lawbreakers versus law keepers; those beyond versus those within the cultural pale, anglophobes versus Albion's seed.[45]

Thompson once wrote that the bearers of a culture can be likened to flying insects; society he likened to a windshield against which the insects were squashed—a metaphor to rival anything Peter Yorke ever come up with, including his menagerie. In Kevin Kenny's theoretical framework, the Irish with their diasporic sensibilities were the flying insects, the "enduring power of the American nation state" was the windshield. That windshield was a formidable barrier, "finished, complete, and single-minded." That it was also nativist and anti-Catholic need hardly be added. But the sensibilities of those aggravating swarms of Irish also endured, and they traveled well. Thompson asserted that those of the Irish assuredly did; squashing them had only made them uglier; it had not pacified them. Nor would the move to America. Their unlovely features were indestructible. Patsy Caliban, papist doer of America's odd jobs, was a premade and troublesome sort before he ever got off his America-bound ship. His children were only marginally less erratic.[46]

• • •

Walter Lippmann, in his discussion and contrast of "drift and mastery," said very little about the particulars of what the age of mastery would involve—other than that the real presences had all to be exorcised before the age could commence. Other modernizers were more specific. Mastery had a persona; there were parts to its makeup, cultural sensibilities that filtered experiences and judged their mastery quotient. There was a mastery tool kit and a set of hegemonic rules governing how the tools were to be used and for what purposes. One of the most important of the tools was the clock, and one of modernity's most important responsibilities was teaching the antimodern that they had to be mindful of it. *How* to tell time could be taught easily enough; in the meantime, whistles could be blown and bells rung that would tell even the most "chrono-illiterate" when to work, when to eat, when to go back to work, and when to go home.

Why to tell time, understanding that time needed to be told, was a far tougher lesson. Of all the things in modern capitalism's tool kit, or in its syllabus for "how to make and train a working class," the timepiece was the most important item. Working people had to understand that the modern world ran on clock-measured time. Gramsci, for example, spoke of the "ultramodern form . . . of working methods," established by the dominant employing class: those methods included keeping and scientifically managing time. Gramsci said it was part of turning workers into "trained gorillas." Jackson Lears writes that the "corporate drive for efficiency underwrote quantified time as a uniform standard of measurement." The "triumph of clock time" was a "key component" in the emergent culture of modern industrial capitalism." Modern capitalism had commodified work, work had become an item, something to be bought and sold. Modernism had also commodified time, and in the same way, using the same words.[47]

Reenter E. P. Thompson. I give "time" this amount of time because he did, not only in *The Making of the English Working Class*, but also in his 1967 article "Time, Work-Discipline, and Industrial Capitalism," an article that covered the modern industrial era, far beyond the early 1830s. In fact, the article, unlike the book, had no real end date. I have used Thompson's reference to four generations to extend his reach beyond England and beyond 1832. I turn now to his article on time and work discipline, not only because he pushed his analysis to the modern era of industrial capitalism but because he made the Irish central to that analysis. The Irish, in fact and by name, are the case study for his article, as Joe McDonnell was for Gutman's. Thompson said nothing directly about the Irish being a case study for American labor, but I'll presume to make the connection for him.

"Time, Work-Discipline, and Industrial Capitalism" was about America's Irish laborers as well as England's. They were the prototype contrarians: being undisciplined, heedless of clock time, and severely out of time and place in the world of industrial capitalism were parts of their personality as ecology. Of all the outward manifestations of Irish Catholic dissidence, their "time ways," to use David Hackett Fischer's term, were the most conspicuously—and infuriatingly—erratic. Mindfulness versus mindlessness of timekeeping was one of the widest of the gaps separating traditional Irish Catholic Strangers from modern American Protestant Natives.[48]

Thompson said this: "Without time-discipline we could not have the insistent energies of industrial man." "In mature capitalist society all time must be consumed, marketed, put to *use*; it was offensive for the labor force merely to 'pass the time.'" Modern industrial societies, America's in particular, ran on time. Time had been commodified. It was a thing. People could save it, have it, lose it, borrow it, waste it, make it, keep it, spend it, count it, track it, manage it, steal it; they could even buy it and kill it. Most of all, working people had to be "on time," an expression coined in the 1870s, not the 1830s. Thompson did not write a sequel to *Making*, but in this 1967 article, he hinted at where it would have gone had he done so. He also made explicit what he meant by Irish Catholic cultural traditions persisting for a hundred years.[49]

Sometime between 1897 and 1902, the Protestant Irish playwright John Millington Synge described with a mixture of affection and bemusement the people of the Aran Islands off the coast of County Galway in farthest western Ireland. Synge said that the islanders had a "disregard for clock time;" that "few" of them were "sufficiently used to modern time to understand in more than a vague way the convention of the hours." They wanted only to know "how long is left them before the twilight." Their "general knowledge of time ... depends ... on the direction of the wind" and which of their two cabin doors are left open to "give light to the interior." It was a complicated bit of home management, but the nub of it was this: if the wind changed direction, "the people, who never think of putting up a primitive dial, are at a loss."

They depended on their priests to advise them of "changes in time." They lived by the tailor's dictum, "Come day. Go day. Let's have another day."[50]

Thompson didn't know of the tailor and Ansty. But he knew of Synge, and he quoted Synge's passage in his article. The emphasis in both his book and his article was on the emergence of a modern working class from a cast of premodern workers and on how painful and difficult that emergence was. Which makes it important to emphasize again the relevance of Thompson to historians of American labor. Synge was not describing the Irish of the eighteenth century. He was writing about the late nineteenth century, and at a time when Irish were still emigrating to America in great numbers. By citing Synge—though he never put a date on the material cited—Thompson was saying that as late as the end of the nineteenth century, there was still an "inexhaustible flow of reinforcements to man the "Satanic battlements," the workshops of capitalism. The Irish reinforcements of the late nineteenth century, like the original recruits, were social primitives with "a different value-system." They were still a part of a "freemasonry of the disinherited," still in service to their semifeudal Church and to the Irish nationalism it embodied.[51]

Thompson's comments about Irish Catholics in the satanic battlements of Britain and, by inference, America, in the late nineteenth century call to mind the remark of Viscount James Bryce, who served both as Britain's chief secretary in Ireland and as ambassador to the United States. Perhaps Thompson had read Bryce. Sounding a proper Thompsonian note, Bryce wrote of the Irish working in America that they were "hardly to be reckoned with the working class [at all]." They were rather a kind of subset of workers, evaders of Thompson's net, "what is called in England 'the residuum,'" the residue, the dregs. Bryce wrote that in 1897, the same time as Synge's wandering in the Arans, less than a decade before Joyce wrote of "Patsy Caliban," the Irish's "American cousin."[52]

For Thompson, the Irish were outliers among the English working class. According to Bryce and countless others, they were the same in the United States. They were America's residuum and for the same reason of religion and driftiness. I particularly like Thompson's reference in the article on industrial conditions in the 1890s to the "reports of working men"—not necessarily Irish—who simply sat for hours, "annihilating those portions of time in utter vacancy and torpor." He then added that it "was worse than Bingo." Worse even than the tailor's command to the sun. I have absolutely no evidence for this, but I can't help thinking that Thompson chose bingo for a reason. (My thesis can survive my being wrong on this.)

Thompson said that the Irish Catholicism of the early nineteenth century was semifeudal; what might he have said of it in the late nineteenth century? What would he have made of emigrant wakes? Or of the persistence of a whole panoply of Irish folk beliefs? How would he have treated hunger striking, "biting at the grave," as Yeats described it, and obviously still a weapon of Irish protest as late as the 1980s? What would he do with the fairy faiths? At the same time Synge was visiting the Aran Islands and recording his images of the people, an Irish woman, said to be possessed by fairies, was burned to death by her husband and members of her family. The "hocus-pocus" quotient had not diminished. Thompson didn't cast his analytical net over those features of Irish culture because they were not even incidental sidenotes to the making of the English working class. They were, however, far more than incidental in the making of the American.[53]

• • •

In his book, Thompson referred to Catholicism as the Irish "nationalist church." The nation, needless to add—so he didn't—was Ireland. They worked in England, but they were not in the English working-class because they were not English. He said nothing directly about their being anti-English, but the inference was unmistakable. Thompson thought that a relevant point. So do I. And I apply it here. The Irish brought with them to America an implacable hatred of their "crazy queen, old and jealous," whose latest offense against them was to deport them. They had been expatriated. America became a launching pad for Irish patriotism. The American Irish were the quintessence of what Benedict Anderson called "long-distance nationalists." But they were also a dominant element in the American labor movement, which means, almost with the force of logic, that what happened regarding Ireland in British imperial offices directly affected American labor history. The "master-servant" relationship between the Irish and the Americans did not arise solely because the two were on opposite sides of a labor-management bargaining table; it arose because they were on opposite sides of the windshield—and of history.[54]

Herbert Gutman always insisted that American working-class culture was oppositional. It was not simply a "middle class without money." American workers had "unique values, institutions, and language" befitting—and explaining—the "working-class feel" of their neighborhoods. But Irish Catholics were also oppositional; they were not simply "deferred Protestants." Thompson's "natural freemasonry of the disinherited" was from a book about working people, but it was from a section of that book on Irish working people outside Ireland and so it applied to those in America as well. The Irish were doubly disinherited; I would say triply except that their Catholicism was inextricable from their Irishness. So also, however, was the fact that their being Irish and Catholic was scarcely ever in conflict with their being working-class. Labor historians tend sometimes to miss how very Irish those relationships were. That is particularly true when it comes to paying a proper attention to the Catholicism with which Irishness was paired.[55]

I am reminded of the "middle class without money" comment every time I consider the half-famous remark of G. K. Chesterton that in America "even the Catholics are Protestants." Chesterton clearly included the Irish among those apostate papists. They were no longer smashing themselves against the American windshield. They had become little more than Protestants with rosaries. Chesterton didn't say when it was that American Catholics had been undone, only that he was saddened by the fact that they had been. The world needed oppositional cultures, America more than most. Obviously, I think Chesterton was wrong.[56]

There was another English convert to Catholicism, one more backward-looking and eccentric even than Chesterton, who was of the opposite opinion, at least about the Irish of America's Catholics. Evelyn Waugh was writing in 1949, decades after Chesterton. He agreed that some of the Catholics in America had lost their Catholic way, but not the Irish. Indeed, in Waugh's mind, the Irish alone had remained defiant of America's Protestant culture. Add Waugh to the growing list of those who picked out the Irish as the poster children for an American countercultural. Irish defiance did not take violent and primitive form, as Thompson and Hobsbawm had emphasized. Hamstringing horses and cattle was not a part of it. It was not quite cerebral, or even conscious, but it didn't have to be to matter. And to Waugh, it mattered greatly.

Waugh first made an argument for the Reformation origins of the modern American state, in other words, for the Ahlstrom thesis: America's "history and psychology," he wrote, was "resolutely anti-Catholic." He then listed some of "the individual qualities that are ... characteristic of Americans," a list that reads like a composite of what made up their cultural windshield. It's a list that any one of Jackson Lear's antimodernists could have written. Waugh's was a catalog of modernity's sins, and he intended it to be read as such. But it is equally applicable to the narrower context of what Irish Catholics brought with them to modern American capitalism and to the evolution of an oppositional Irish Catholic worker culture. I offer it as part of the pre- and self-making of the "freemasonry of the disinherited" component of the American working class.

Waugh said that Americans had disenfranchised their dead; he called it their "psychopathic antagonism to paternity and all its symbols." He commented on the sheer busyness of Americans and their selfishness and celebration of money; their unexamined faith that nothing was a finished product, that everything could be improved on, and that change was always good, always progressive; their insistence that theirs was a classless society, that nothing divided Americans, not religion or culture or ethnicity or social class, and that any dogma that suggested otherwise was subversive and had to be put down; their lack of discipline and their resentment of any effort to discipline them; most of all, their studied unwillingness to make social justice an operative part of governance. All of that was "unsympathetic to the habits of the [Irish] Church." Waugh's language was severe. These American habits and ideas were counted among the very worst of what he called "the multifarious frauds of modernity"—what Jackson Lears called its "evasive banality." By whatever name, modernism was a giant and immoral con.[57]

Waugh reported that too many of the Catholics in America had fallen for it and made themselves over. But not the Irish. "The Irish . . . have never suffered a prick of shame in avowing their origins." They were what they had always been. Waugh did not mean angry and hate-filled primitive rebels, the bandit class; that was Thompson's and Hobsbawm's portrait of them. Waugh saw them differently: The Irish brought with them to America "all their ancient grudges and the melancholy of the bogs, but also their hard, ancient wisdom." America changed them, but only superficially. They went from being "peasants and soldiers" to being "townsmen." "At heart," however, the Irish, with their "truculence and good sense," remained what they were in the beginning, an "adroit and joyless race that broke the hearts of all who ever tried to help them." Freemasons of the disinherited, indeed.[58]

That sounded a gloomy note, but Waugh closed with this remarkable comment: They "alone of the newcomers [were] never for a moment taken in" by modernity's "multifarious frauds." It changes Waugh's meaning only slightly to substitute "capitalism" for "modernity." Indeed, in Robert Orsi's mind, it doesn't change much at all. Both existed under the sign of absence. Evelyn Waugh wasn't talking about class conflict; cultural struggles were his topic. What the new labor history has made clear is the relevance of the one to the other.

In Gramscian language, the dominant culture had no hegemonic control over them because they were outside that culture. That may assign more consciousness to the IrishCatholic erratics than they deserve. Their resistance to fraud was mostly inadvertent. Which only strengthens the argument for their role as counterhegemons. Traditionalism, loyalty to the dead, could not be something calculated. It could have its origins in hard, ancient wisdom, but unbroken faithfulness to tradition was not a call on wisdom; it was a call on instinct. It had to be spontaneous—literally thoughtless. Allen Tate, the southern antimodernist poet and, like Waugh, a convert to Catholicism, once wrote that "tradition must be automatically operative before it can be called tradition."[59]

The Irish did not carefully scrutinize the culture codes of modernity and then reject them because they found them misguided and foolish. That was Waugh's unfounded claim for them. They were not so much wise as they were bewildered. They were not "taken in" by the frauds because they had never encountered anything like them before and were culturally immunized against them. Cultural hegemony requires that the values of a society—fraudulent and otherwise—be expressed in a common language, that there be shared definitions and interpretations of words. There may have been far less of that than was once assumed. The Irish spoke the English language, but the words did not always mean to them what they meant to Americans. The erratic IrishCatholics in the American working class were counterhegemons by accident not intent. Blame history. Or, more specifically, blame "semifeudal hocus-pocus," two of the more conspicuous artifacts of that history.

The progressive and modernizing elements of American society—the Protestant=Absence equation—saw the world as linear and progressive. The purposeful "unseeing of the gods" eliminated, or at least severely attenuated, a past tense. "A corrupt Catholic *then*," writes Orsi, gave way "to a free and rational modern *now*." The present tense "now" was to be prized, not because of what had come before it and created it, but because of what would come after it, what it could create—and inevitably be undone by. *Now* was the staging ground for a brave new *will be*. Traditional cultures, by definition, had not come to grips with that reality; they were "nostalgic," and constantly mixing up their verb tenses.[60]

And that, to modernists, was manifestly unjust. The "present" wasn't just "a bubble on the stream of time," as Walter Lippmann called it. It was the essence of time. It was the "now," a precious and cherished commodity; one that had to be carefully and lovingly cared for. The "past" was "then;" it required no care, which was fortunate because, to modernity, none could be given it. Besides, it was an imposter. I again cite Lippmann: The traditionalist "is not devoted to a real past. He is devoted to his own comfortable image of it." To which the Catholic Irish response would have been "so what?" I wish I could show that Irish nonconformity with American values was the result of Irish=Presence, America=Absence, but even Orsi stopped short of providing particulars. Regardless of their origins, the following Irish offenses were more against modernism than against the capitalist system as such. But I repeat the noncontroversial point that to violate the rules of either was to violate the rules of both.[61]

Consider the following as parts of an index to Irish Catholic erraticism. America was a measuring society, and the Irish were not a measuring people—or at least not a people who measured in the same way and for the same reasons. Commodities, by definition, must be appraised and quantified. They are things that are to be exchanged for other appraised and quantified things in marketplaces that are themselves measured. Time was such a commodity. So was labor, and modern industrial America measured both. Time was tracked to the second and recorded. Labor was paid by hours of work rather than items made; and, like all commodities, it was disposable in theory and disposed of without hesitancy or remorse in fact. So was land

and the resources on it. Americans owned it individually, and they quantified and appraised it by the acre and by how many of those quite arbitrary things were listed on their title deed. The hard, ancient Irish way, as Conrad Arensberg described it, was to measure it by how many cattle, or sheep, or goats—or children—a parcel of land could pasture or feed.[62]

There were fundamental differences between societies that answered to clock-time and those who didn't know what time it was, between those who counted by size, preparatory to sale, and those who counted by function, preparatory to use. The contrasts extended beyond measuring. For an example, Americans saw the area to the west of their settlements as a grand stage for future American greatness. American images of the West were not just expectant, they were hallucinogenic. Westering—the idea of it as surely as the act—was emancipatory. The Irish looked to the west with dread. The devil came on them from the west—so had the potato blight; the west portals of their churches were guarded by St. Michael. In American space-time, the West was the glorious future. In Irish space-time, it was the sorrowful past.[63]

These were not just folksy superstitions of interest only to ethnologists. Attention must be paid them. Ira Berlin said that Herbert Gutman took every aspect of worker culture seriously. "Outside the context of class struggle, . . . cultural baggage," like Irish feelings about the devil sneaking up on them from the west, appears "merely as a collection of antiquarian curiosities." But "within [a working-class] context," these different perceptions of reality divided cultures and became "powerful instrument[s] of class warfare." Warfare may be too strong a word; working people were not going to make class war over "perceptions of reality." At that, marching to the ding-dong of all of those factory bells was more than an annoyance. It was disrespectful. So was being told to go West and "grow up with the country."[64]

A people's belief systems, their customs, rituals and traditions, their fables and fairytales, folk stories, legends, symbols, myths, and fantasies were the nonrational receptors with which they filtered experience and that colored their perceptions of reality and truth. Their collective memory cannot be erased from the historical record. Separating the Irish from their past was impossible; so was separating them from their home place. Indeed, their past was their home place. And they refused to walk or race or dance away from it. Saying that that refusal was "escapism" is not just deterministic; it is, to use Thompson's phrase again, "enormously condescending." Dismissing any "attachment to the past" as "nostalgia" is no less so. Nostalgia is not a pejorative. It needs to be rehabilitated, made respectable again, and restored to the political discourse.

Waugh insisted that the Irish's nostalgic attachment to the past was why they were resistant to modernity's frauds. He did not employ any theoretical framework in his analysis. Cultural hegemony would not have been a term of art for Waugh; it had too modern a ring to it. At that, "multifarious frauds" sounds a distinctly hegemonic note. As does "taken in." Gramscians use "spontaneous consent" and "acquiescence," rather than "taken in," but those are linguistic distinctions without a difference. Something immunized the Irish. Waugh says it was wisdom. That's too generous. More likely, it was a combination of confusion, incomprehension, and sheer otherworldliness.

I offer the following while not presuming that all or any were frauds in the conventional sense of lies, deceits, and trickeries. I do, however, offer them as products of modern American bourgeois and Protestant society, the cultural hegemony of which I take as a given. Consider the American emphasis on individualism, with "rugged" frequently attached, which to muddled and uncomprehending Irish Catholics was a celebration of selfishness. Personal identities were relational; they did not arise from the individual but from the communities, the neighborhoods in which individuals found their friends. It was also, of course, where they found themselves. Being neighborly carried with it certain obligations. One was expected to show some "goodness of heart." The "immutable" laws of the new ideology all too often profaned the moral laws—as when ships laden with food left the ports of a starving Ireland or when the laws of supply and demand drove the wages of free laborers below what was sufficient to buy enough food.[65]

I quoted Engels earlier when he wrote that when "suddenly cast into the modern great cities of England and America," Irishmen found themselves "among a population with entirely different moral and legal standards." Sixty years later, E. P. Thompson said the same thing and more about "Irish peasants" and the impossibility of incorporating them into a British working class. His short treatment of them in his book was a postscript, an afterthought that added nothing to his central theme. Irish Catholics didn't belong—in the book or anywhere else in English or American worlds. I'm surprised sometimes, though always grateful, that he had those afterthoughts and decided to share them.[66]

I'm equally grateful that he did not put the Protestant Irish, so identified, into that postscript. Nor, I would add, did he call them peasants, as he did the Catholics. They did not evade his net, necessarily or otherwise. As he explained, in a comment that should be read carefully, counting the Protestant Irish among the English was an "act of respect." Thompson seems never to have changed his mind about Irish Catholics and the "hocus-pocus" of their "semifeudal nationalist Church." He even extended his chronological reach and dealt with them in the context of the late 1890s and early twentieth century. They hadn't changed much; they were still a "natural freemasonry of the disinherited," they still couldn't—or didn't—tell time, and they still played bingo. Let an account of the making of an Irish American working class start with that.

CHAPTER FOUR

An Irish Catholic Working Class
The Butte "Rising" of 1917

"Don't stop in America, come straight to Butte."
—Advice from an Irish woman to her sister in
  Ireland preparing to emigrate

In 1916, just before the Easter Rising, in which he and his Marxist Irish Citizen Army (ICA) were participants and for which he was executed, James Connolly issued the first commandment of the Ireland that he wished to be: "The cause of labour is the cause of Ireland, the cause of Ireland is the cause of labour. They cannot be dissevered." He meant that literally. The relationship between the causes was not just transactional. They were inseverable to the point of indistinguishable. Should the Irish abandon the cause of labor, they would cease to be Irish; should any labor movement deny the right of all nations to govern themselves, it would lose its legitimacy in the cause of labor.[1]

Some, Connolly among them, were radical in both causes. He had never disguised that fact about his politics. Sean Cronin calls it "Marxist Fenianism." Others were more alliterative, labeling it "Celtic Communism." Connolly's brief commandment, however, left the meaning and purpose of the causes unstated. It may safely be assumed that the cause of labor was anticapital, the cause of Ireland, anticolonial. Those were definitional parts of both. But nothing more specific need be said about them. Celtic communists were always more Celtic than communist, more Fenian than Marxist. But what matters more is that severing the causes destroyed both. That's what made his commandment so erratic.[2]

Attention must be paid to the sentence that follows Connolly's comment about inseverable causes: "Ireland seeks freedom." That much went without saying. But freedom had no meaning unless it meant the freedom to be Irish, what the historian R. F. Foster calls "psychological autonomy." So what was it to be psychologically autonomous; in other words, to "be Irish"? Connolly's explanation was cultural, not political, and it was based on the deep antiquity of the Irish, not on the immediate needs of Easter 1916. Labor—and in this context that meant socialism—would "make the free Irish nation the guardian of the interests of the people of Ireland." By interests, Connolly did not mean only what he called the "material"; there were times when he didn't mean the material at all. He said that Ireland's critical interests, the ones that defined the Irish people, were "moral." Those were the twain that must forever meet.[3]

I think there were some Catholic aspects to what Connolly defined as "the cause of labor," but he kept them well hidden. For him, Catholicism and Ireland—faith and fatherland—were quite severable. Indeed, there were many on the Irish left who insisted that the two had to be severed if the second of them was to flourish. It was socialism and fatherland that could not be divided. Recall Polanyi's comment that nonmarket economies, "far from having a capitalistic psychology, had, in effect, a communistic one"; or that old "truism" quoted by Declan Kiberd that, for the Irish, socialism was a loose synonym for "fundamental goodness of heart," more a sensibility than an ideology. Connolly was counting on it. His definition of socialism was more doctrinally correct than that old saying, but not by much.[4]

If he is to be believed, and if he believed it himself, for Connolly communalism—to give it a less ideologically loaded term—was something the Irish were born to. It arose out of the melancholy bogs, or the Celtic mists, or what Connolly called "the genius of the Irish race." He didn't have to connect the causes of Ireland and labor. He had only to describe a connection that was already in place and had been for hundreds of years. Irish history had inscribed it into the Irish culture code. It is here worth asking whether Connolly's study of the Irish past led him to embrace Marxism or the other way around. Which came first, his radicalism or his "applied" ethnographic history? Connolly stretched the ancient precolonial history of Ireland to make it contain the basic features of communism. Was the stretch casuistic, even cynical? And a related point: Did Connolly push Ireland leftward or did Ireland push him? He would have to have said the latter. He followed where the "genius of the Irish race" and the trajectory of Irish history led him.

The connection between causes that Connolly described applied transnationally. Connolly provided the perfect epigrammatic expression of the point: The night before he was executed, in answering the charge that he had sacrificed the cause of labor to the cause of nationalism, Connolly gave his accusers a simple lesson in history: They had forgotten that he "was an Irishman." The fact that he didn't say *also* an Irishman was telling. He didn't need to say "also"; it was implied. The English and the Americans never quite understood this about Irish Catholics. Albion and her seed separated political questions from economic. Democracy was one thing; capitalism was another. The Irish did not frame statecraft in that way. Political freedom had to be paired with social and economic justice if it was to have any real meaning or coherence.⁵

This linkage and equation of causes distinguished the Irish from the other immigrant and ethnic groups in the American working class. No other ethnic component of that class was as passionately and as obsessively engaged with the motherland as were the Irish. Other immigrants had a catalog of ancestral sorrows, but they had not arisen because their nation of origin was a powerless and oppressed colony. It was usually quite the opposite; their homelands were autonomous; the oppressive polices that led them to leave were homegrown. Let that homeland, or at least its government, be damned for the evil it had done, not apotheosized for what evil was done to it. The sorrows of the Irish, however, were the sorrows of Ireland. Both were England's fault. Let England be damned. But so also let be damned the unjust practices of the employing classes in America. The cause of Ireland wasn't just a political question. It was a profoundly moral one—an ontological one. So was the cause of labor.⁶

• • •

Nowhere was that more true than in Butte, Montana—but for reasons that need to be briefly introduced. The cooperative spirit of the Irish, that fundamental goodness of their hearts, did not always apply outside IrishCatholic tribal limits. The favors done and the favors returned took place within narrowly bounded "neighborhood" worlds. Whether the Irish were more ethnocentric than the other elements of the variegated American working class is impossible to know. They may have been; they may also have had reason to be. Either way, by 1870, the Irish were central figures in every facet and phase of the shift of American labor toward "prudential," that is, pure and simple job-conscious unionism. American industry had become corporate; artisans had become workers. The asymmetries of economic and political power were never more obvious. A hereditary working class had become a fixture of American society. Unions had to turn away from abstract theories and toward union solidarity in the interests of job protection and worker security, the core issues of trade union organization, policies, and tactics—and the stuff of the old labor historians.⁷

One of the old labor historians in particular needs to be returned to the discussion. Selig Perlman wrote that Catholics "figured prominently" in that shift to prudential unionism. Other than in their related role as dogmatic antisocialists, that was the only place where Perlman identified Catholics by name. He should also have identified the Irish and by name, but that aside, there were aspects of labor's great shift that were clearly influenced by the Irish dimension in American labor, with a few tribal Catholic and preindustrial elements thrown in. To the undiscerning eye—and even a few of the discerning—there were no meaningful differences between Catholic preindustrial and medieval.[8]

According to Perlman, a new American "economic group psychology," one based on scarcity rather than abundance, had emerged after the Civil War. The only effective working-class response to scarcity was the adoption of a new labor group psychology, one also based on limits and on class consciousness stripped of theory and theorists, ideals, and idealists. Modern American industrial capitalism was no place for labor fabulists. What job- and wage-conscious workers "really wanted," as Perlman's close associate John Commons had put it, "was bread and butter" and they wanted them "right away." That was not just to the point of labor union policy. It was to the point of working-class self-awareness and culture.[9]

In a sentence, the first clause of which he italicized, Perlman described what the move from a theoretical to a more practical unionism involved. The relevance of his comment to an understanding of the Irish dimension in American labor seems now immediately apparent. It would not have seemed that when he wrote it: *"The group asserts its collective ownership over the whole amount of opportunity* and, having determined who are entitled to claim a share in that opportunity, undertakes to parcel it out fairly among its recognized members . . . on the basis of a 'common rule.'" Perlman called this a "collective disposal of opportunity." This collective ownership and distribution of limited opportunities was as "natural" to "manual" laborers as "*laissez-faire*' [was] to the business man." It was also nearly every bit as cold-hearted, including, as it did, "the power to keep out undesirables," to exclude them from the labor markets and from the limited supply of jobs in this new scarcity-based economy. A more forceful statement of a job- and wage-conscious unionism would be hard to find.[10]

But Perlman failed to define some key words. He never said who the undesirables were, only that they had to be "kept out." So also he did not define what he meant by parceling out opportunities *fairly* among *recognized* members and according to an agreed-upon rule. Using a common American idiom, he held that the opportunities had to be made available to the generic threesome of "Tom, Dick, and Harry." Those three constituted a hereditary working class, a proletariat in fact. "Unionism, perceiving the scarcity of opportunity," had to make jobs "the common patrimony of the group, to be administered in behalf of . . . that same Tom, Dick, and Harry." The tribal identities of those three were not noted because Perlman did not think that was relevant. In the world of the old labor historians—and some of the new—they weren't.[11]

"Prudential unionism" may have been where the Irish in America finally found their cultural niche—or rather a cultural niche found them. Who better to teach lessons in scarcity than they? Worlds of limited opportunities were an Irish specialty. The Irish, said Connolly, had served an "apprenticeship to misery"; the history of the race "reads like the record of a shambles." The "group psychology" of the Catholic Irish in the American working class—their natural freemasonry—had never been based on the presumption of a bountiful anything, America included. It was based on practicality, a presumption of scarcity, and an opposition to theorizing. In that regard, as in others, Perlman was wrong: Being Catholic didn't make the Irish practical and job conscious; being Irish did.[12]

• • •

So, what would an Irish American version of job-conscious and prudential unionism have looked like? Was there an archetype? Specifically, how was prudence defined? What were the "common rules" governing the "fair" parceling out of limited job opportunities among the "recognized members" of the "group?" And was every Tom, Dick, and Harry in the group treated fairly by it? These are critical questions in the history of American labor. What is needed here is a union, a place, and an industry all properly fitted out to answer them; in other words, a union run by Irish under Irish rules governing "group collective ownership" over the whole amount of job opportunities—a place where the whole of the Irish population had sufficient power to get away with that, and an industry in the managerial hands of other Irish. In other words, Butte, Montana.

Since some of what follows is taken from my 1989 book, *The Butte Irish: Class and Ethnicity in an American Mining Town*, a brief explanation is in order. Butte is obviously the place in Irish America that I have studied longest and about which I know the most. But the book is now more than thirty years old and it shows its age. It left some important questions unanswered or only partially answered, for the very good reason that they were hard questions and I wasn't ready to answer them. Most of those unanswered questions were contextual—placing the tangled world of Butte's Irish into a national narrative. Things that seemed jumbled, and which I dodged, now seem less opaque and ready to be taken on. Things that seemed settled then look different to me now. In addition to these interpretive revisions, what follows also carries the story beyond where I left it in the book.

Thirty years ago, I was far too uncritical of what might politely be called the Hiberno-centricism of the Butte Miners' Union; I privileged ethnicity over class and assumed that Butte's Irish miners did as well. I missed some of the factionalism that divided them; and I failed to recognize the full significance and meaning of Easter 1916 and of the events, including the Soviet Revolution, that followed it. In other words, this new edition is also a revised edition.

I begin with Butte itself, in percentage terms, the most Irish and the most Catholic city in America. Its city and county governments were firmly in Irish hands. Next, the Butte Miners' Union (BMU), formed in 1878, self-destructed in 1914, and during those thirty-six years was the largest and richest local union in the world, with a membership upwards of fifteen thousand. More than anything else, it was why Butte was known as the "Gibraltar of American Unionism." BMU officers were almost exclusively Irish, what one would expect given the Irish dominance of the mine workforce. As for the mining industry, it was dominated by the Anaconda Copper Mining Company (ACM), the fifth-largest corporation in the world, at one time the producer of more than 40 percent of the world's copper, and, for the first eighty years of its history, under the management of Irish Catholics.[13]

The charge was brought against the BMU that in all that mattered, the union was a partner of the corporation in an inter-class Irish freemasonry of the ethnically privileged. That the charge was occasionally made by Irish should be on the record. The BMU had a closed-shop agreement as well as a long-term contract with ACM; it even bought $50,000 worth of ACM's blue-chip stock. What was most revealing, however, was that in the first thirty-six years of its history, the BMU took no job action of any kind against ACM. There were no union-sanctioned slowdowns, no walkouts, no work to the rules, no boycotts, no sympathy strikes—though the BMU was frequently asked to mount one—and, obviously, no union-sponsored miners' strike or even a threat of one. Never did a large and important American union behave so prudentially.

In researching Butte's Irish, I encountered at various times and from various Irish sources Irishmen using the word *practical* in a way that required some decrypting. I found references to "practical Catholics," to "practical patriots"—of Ireland, needless to add—to "practical soldiers of Ireland," and, by the BMU, to "practical miners of good moral character"—which led me to ponder what an impractical miner might have been. I learned soon enough. "Practical miner" meant practical union man, the kind favored by all prudential unionists—no radical theorists, dreamers, and idealists need apply.[14]

Practicality and a distrust of theorists, however, was not the whole of prudential unionism. There was also the question of the "control and disposal of opportunities," meaning jobs. Here the issue becomes more tangled and contentious and the Butte Irish story more instructive. Eric Hobsbawm, writing from the perspective of Marx, not Perlman, contended that keeping the undesirables out by enforcing an "institutionalized scarcity on the labor market" created an "aristocracy of labor." Any difference between "institutionalized scarcity on the labor market" and Perlman's "collective ownership of [job] opportunities" is too slight to warrant attention.[15]

Hobsbawm's next comment, however, does require some attention. He said that workers had to have the "ability to exclude"—a point Perlman would not have contested—and that they need *"never mind how"* that exclusion was effected. If it was based on anything other than the ability to do the job, the result would be a "contrived aristocracy of labor," one destructive of working-class solidarity. Perlman hoped that the new unions would claim collective ownership of job opportunities—through "patrimony," no less—and that they would "dispose" of that limited number of jobs "fairly" by handing them around to members of the "group."

That may not have been how the system worked anywhere; it was certainly not how the BMU's critics said it worked in the Butte mines. In that job market, Pat, Mike, and Tim got and held jobs on ethnic privilege. The company was complicit in that. It was said that the Anaconda Company posted job notices in Irish. It may have. But that it gave hiring preference to Irish is certain. That that brought the company thirty-six years of industrial peace may not have been the policy's purpose, but it assuredly was its effect. From such evidence, charges of hugger-mugger deals arise naturally. It would not be far wrong to say that the BMU and ACM formed an ecclesia, a neighborhood, and that it endorsed and enforced communal habits. That was not what was intended by prudential unionism. It was a throwback, an antimodernist leftover.

It was also evidence of a seam that Connolly had anticipated but did not want. Butte's Irish miners were among America's stoutest and most militant Irish nationalists. Seeking steady work at good wages in strike-free mines was not evidence that the Irish had become submissive. Quite the opposite. The work they did would alone have ruled out the timid. Class collaborationism was not the issue. This was: Guaranteed and steady jobs meant more money for Irish nationalist militancy. It also increased substantially the amount and regularity of remittance checks back to Ireland. Irish labor was still enlisted in the cause of Ireland. Where it was not enlisted was in the cause of American labor in all its racial and ethnic variety. But, whatever the explanation, it must be granted—certainly I grant it—that turning the BMU into an Irish job fair in the interests of Irish nationalism was no way to run a modern industrial union.

The BMU made its Faustian pact with ACM in the interest of the Irish national cause as well as the interests of its thousands of Irish miners. The ACM gladly cooperated. At a time when the rest of America's hard-rock mining companies faced almost constant and often radical union resistance, Butte was an island of tranquility. ACM officers attended meetings of the Butte Clan na Gael with officers of the BMU. I often imagined them sitting next to one another and listening to the same sunbursting assaults on Brits behaving badly. There was a song about Miners' Union Day in Butte, June 13 of every year. The mines were closed, courtesy of a compliant ACM. There was a huge parade and day- and night-long festivities. Its only rival for size and enthusiasm was St. Patrick's Day. The Fourth of July was a distant third. In the song, a happy miner is getting ready to join the parade with his union mates. The occasion called for him to look his best, and so, "Me new green shirt I'll wear. / Six thousand miners will be marchin' / While I ride in stately ease, / Just like a Celtic warrior / As handsome as you please."[16]

In the minds of the more advanced—or creative—Irish nationalists, equating a labor union with a nationalist club did not affirm one's Irishness. It profaned it. The true cause of Ireland was not narrowly Hiberno-centric. Tom, Dick, and Harry and other non-Irish in the working class were as deserving of fair and impartial treatment as Pat, Mike, and Tim and others of Butte's Catholic Irish chosen ones. Even when done by a labor union—maybe particularly when done by a labor union—playing the Green Card, dividing the working class on the basis of race and ethnicity, was a *shoneen* trick, sham nationalism at its worst. Ireland's rightful and righteous cause was the cause of *all* labor.

That was what Connolly was saying in Ireland; "the socialist of another country is a fellow patriot, ... the capitalist of my own country is a natural enemy." Connolly was here connecting dots that he himself had penciled in. But the connected dots yielded this: The "capitalist class ... in its soulless lust for power and gold would bray the nations as in a mortar." To be Irish was to be a communalist, a socialist by whatever name. Ireland as a nation had to be centered on this fundamental Irish value. To be false to it was to be recreant. Connolly used the word *recreant* for a reason, meaning by it faithless, disloyal, apostate—in sum, an Ireland ruled by *shoneens* in Cromwellian dress. He might as well have said that "the capitalist of my own country is the enemy of my own country."[17]

It was one thing to hold those views in Ireland, where the only laborers in the vicinity were Irish. The best that Ireland could do was incite the workers of the world to rebellion. Connolly hoped it would. In particular, he hoped that the working classes of colonial nations would be inspired by the Irish example and strike for their freedom. Lenin hoped so too, as had Marx. Should their nation achieve its freedom at the same time, so much the better, as long as the new nation behaved humanely and protected its laboring poor, its men and women "of no property." But what of America and its working-class mélange, its workers from the world? Translating Connolly's notions of Ireland to Ireland's exiled children in America was going to require them to become less tribal, less clannish.

Nowhere was Connolly's "Irish nationalist internationalism" more ill suited to circumstances than in Butte. Some of its Irish miners—the less erratic—and all its mine owners—the *shoneens*—connected dots of their own and came to the conclusion that dividing the Irish American world on the basis of social class was no way to advance the national cause. Ireland free required Irish united. The cause of Butte Irish labor was connected to the cause of Ireland, but not as Connolly had connected it. In the BMU, the connection was entirely practical, the cause of Irish labor was the means of securing Irish ends, an independent Ireland among them. As for the cause of labor generally, it was on its own; it not only had no connection with Ireland free, it could be sacrificed to it. There would be time later for Irish fissiparousness—the fighting Irish fighting other Irish—as the Irish Civil War, with its obvious social-class aspects would show.

• • •

The earliest shots in the Butte Irish's "civil war" were fired by Ed Boyce, the first and ablest of Butte's Irish Catholic labor internationalists. No one applied Connolly's lessons, or Connolly's radical message, more determinedly than Ed Boyce. Indeed, there are places in this history where the chronology suggests that it was Connolly who applied the lessons of Boyce, not the other way around.

I didn't give Boyce enough attention in *The Butte Irish*. He was born in 1862 in Deeneystown, in an area of County Donegal that had been "ethnically cleansed" just a year earlier by a British landlord. He immigrated to the United States in 1883, tramped around the American West for a decade, ending up in the Idaho mining camp of Wardner, where, in 1892, he led a violent miners' strike that was brutally repressed and ended with Boyce in prison. In 1897, he became the president of the radical Western Federation of Miners (WFM), born in Butte in 1893, and headquartered until 1901 in the Union Hall of the BMU, Local Number 1 of the WFM's 120-plus local unions.

The relationship between the BMU and the WFM, theoretically the BMU's superior in rank, was always strained. The BMU was rich; the WFM was chronically broke. Number 1 had more members than the rest of the locals combined. But the differences between the Boyce-led WFM and the Irish-led BMU arose mostly because Butte was a town—the largest one between the Twin Cities and San Francisco. It was settled. The other WFM locals were in mining camps filled with transient workers from everywhere, some with advanced radical ideas, who encamped and decamped frequently. There were a number of Irish in that roaming proletariat. Boyce had been one of them.[18]

His union principles were at least as radical as the BMU's were prudential. He was an avowed socialist by 1897 and a vocal critic of the BMU and its sweetheart deal with ACM. The WFM he headed said nothing about "practical miners" or about "undesirables." Rather all "the wage slaves . . . working for wages in and around the mines, mills and smelters" were eligible to join WFM-affiliated locals. The WFM was an industrial union with a membership of 25,000 class-conscious proletariat warriors from all corners of the globe, a state-of-the-art mélange, the perfect representation of industrial workers of—and from—the world. Boyce had to represent all of them and lead them to socialism. His Catholicism, it should be added, was no hindrance to that.[19]

Nor did it interfere with his Irish nationalism, the Fenian side of his Marxist Fenianism. The year before he became head of the WFM, Boyce joined the Robert Emmet Literary Association (RELA), Butte's camp—the second-largest in the United States—of the radically nationalist Clan na Gael. He attended RELA meetings regularly; on one occasion, he spoke before the group and condemned British imperial policy in South Africa, concluding his remarks by identifying "our enemy, the British tyrannical government." By "our" he meant the Irish and Ireland. But Boyce's comment also made the connection between John Hays Hammond, American mining engineer, free-market capitalist, and Idaho strikebreaker, and the same John Hays Hammond who was second in command to Cecil Rhodes and a champion of British imperialism. Boyce made the connection between capitalism and imperialism central to the Irish national cause, as did the others of Ireland's new international nationalists.[20]

I'm sure Boyce read both Marx and Connolly. Marx, of course, was read by all on the American left. But Marx had had also written extensively on the Irish and the cause of Ireland—and on the usefulness of an Irish rising to a revolt of the British working class. Connolly, for his part, paid special attention to America; his writings came out in special American editions. He was more immediately relevant than Marx to the situation Boyce encountered in Butte. Like Ireland, Irish America had too many "sham nationalists," too many middle-class *shoneens* and gombeen men, renegades and collaborators, in Connolly's mind, the anti-Irish Irish. Their nationalism was counterfeit. It "emasculated the Irish national movement" and "distorted Irish history."[21]

These "recreants" liked to shake "their fists at England and whoop it up for liberty." But the Ireland they envisioned was nothing more than a miniature version of capitalist England—or, as Boyce would surely have added, capitalist Butte. "Our [English] oppressors," Connolly wrote in 1897, "had inoculated" some Irish "with their perverted conceptions of justice and morality" and with their "brutally materialistic" system of civilization. The Irish Workers' Republic proposed by Connolly would not only take Ireland out of the Empire, it would drive these *shoneen* Irish out of Ireland, that or make paupers of them.[22]

Boyce knew the type as well as Connolly did, maybe better. Some were in the Clan na Gael, the Ancient Order of Hibernians (AOH), or both; some were officers and rank and file of the BMU; but the *ard ríthe*, the high kings of the recreants, were the corporate heads of the Anaconda Copper Mining Company. They disarmed the real "cause of labor" by playing the green card of the "cause of Ireland." In the process they corrupted both. Boyce condemned them all. But he condemned with particular venom his countryman, Marcus Daly, founder of ACM and patron and protector of Butte's Irish.

Daly was born in 1841 in County Cavan, less than ninety miles from where Boyce was from in Donegal. Boyce's accusations against Daly were both personal and uniquely Irish. Daly was known variously as the "boss Irishman" or "Pope Marcus." Neither was intended as a compliment, but Boyce gave both a new descriptive edge. Daly, according to Boyce, was "using the green sunburst of Erin," as Connolly would put it later, as part of the management policy of his corporation. He resorted to the most "miserable [and] contemptible" of tactics pitting "one nationality against another": Pat, Mike, and Tim versus Tom, Dick, and Harry. It was the kind of "religious bigotry that has proved the ruination of the laboring people for centuries."[23]

Daly was "lauded" among Butte's Irish "for his friendliness towards organized labor." Boyce found that risible. In fact, Daly "never did anything for ... workingmen ... except as it advance[d] his personal aggrandizement." That thousands of Butte's Irish miners were contributing money to build a statue to him was infuriating to Boyce. The "promoters of the Marcus Daly memorial fund," including a number of BMU officers, needed only to "visit the cemetery" where thousands of Irish headstones marked the graves of those who had "sacrificed their lives in Marcus Daly's mines, working like slaves to make him a millionaire." Let them be Daly's monument and epitaph. It was the only fitting one.[24]

Then came Boyce's ultimate rebuke: "Like millions of his countrymen, ... Daly was forced to leave the land of his birth on account of an unjust tyrannical system of landlordism and oppression." In other words, he was exiled. But the minute he had "accumulated wealth ... he became the equal of the worst Irish landlord that ever lived." He was tolerant only of those unions "he could ... control." Witness the Butte Miners' Union, run by "Mr. Daly's deluded slaves." Marcus Daly was a *shoneen*, a bad Irishman; a gombeen man, an Irish exploiter of Irish, a traitor to his heritage and his people. Not many Americans would have understood the severity of Boyce's charge, but every Irishman would have. Boyce's attack on Daly was uniquely Irish. His charge that Daly was a bad Irishman would not have been replicated by any other ethnic radical. Jewish radicals accused capitalists, including Jewish capitalists, of multiple sins. But I know of no Jewish radical who accused capitalist Jews of being "bad Jews." Being unfaithful to some theoretical Jewishness was not among their sins.[25]

Boyce was utterly convinced that there could be "no harmony between organized capitalists and organized labor" and that "nothing short of the complete abolishment of the present wage system will ever adjust it.... Our present wage system is slavery in its worst form." Great corporate trusts had emerged; they "oppress labor ... and rob the people, [all] that a few unnatural tyrants may roll in luxury and revel in wealth." Boyce insisted that only industrial unions could solve the "class war"; trade unions were wholly inadequate to the task. He bemoaned the fact that of the "many gold, silver and copper mines" of the West, "not one" was owned by the WFM or any of its locals. It would have been useful had he elaborated on that point. Miners' unions owning mines was a form of syndicalism; their mines would have been soviets.[26]

Boyce was playing high-stakes labor politics and his language reflected it: "There is a class struggle in Society and this struggle will continue until the producer is recognized as the sole master of his product"; the working class and *it alone* can achieve its "emancipation,"—a comment that had a kind of Irish ring to it, a *Sinn Féin* for labor. In 1901, Boyce told the locals of the WFM to "let the rallying cry be Labor, the overthrow of the whole profit-making system, equality for all and the land for the people"—which also had an Irish ring to it. Boyce understood that whatever action was taken "in the interests of labor, the trained beagles in the employ of capital from behind their loathsome fortress of disguised patriotism will howl their tirade of condemnation." He said that in a labor newspaper, but by disguised patriots he meant only Irish.[27]

In 1900, Boyce wrote the introduction to Job Harriman's short and radical pamphlet on the 1892 strike in the Coeur d'Alenes. Boyce praised Harriman's "fair and logical presentation" as the only "true history of this great struggle." He hoped that every laboring man and woman in the United States could read" it. (His inclusion of "laboring women" should be noted. Connolly and others on the left were routinely doing the same.) Harriman's pamphlet deserved a wide readership. Perhaps then there would be "fewer volunteers to shoot down workingmen by such combines as the Standard Oil Company." The Standard Oil allusion was straight from Butte. Shooting down workmen was a reference to strikes in Idaho and Colorado earlier in the 1890s.[28]

Boyce was not the only one in the American labor movement to say that workingmen were being shot down. He was, however, one of the few who suggested that they shoot back. Earlier, in an 1897 letter to Samuel Gompers—whom he despised—Boyce told the head of the American Federation of Labor that American workers had to possess "the manhood to get out and fight with the sword." He meant that literally. Later that year, at the WFM convention in Salt Lake City, Boyce ratcheted up the arms race: He directed attention to "Article 2 of the Constitutional Amendments" of the United States—the "right of the people to keep and bear arms." He then told the heads of the unions in the federation that "every [local] should have a rifle club. I strongly advise you to provide every member with the latest improved rifle, which can be obtained from the factory at a nominal price. I entreat you to take action on this important question, so that in two years we can hear the inspiring music of the martial tread of 25,000 armed men in the ranks of labor."²⁹

Given the ethnic makeup of the Western hard rock mining workforce, there would have been a great number of Irish, perhaps as many as ten thousand in that twenty-five-thousand-man army. The BMU "division" alone would have had at least five thousand. E. L Godkin of the *Nation* had worried that a Workingman's Party could become an Irish Party. He had more to worry about than an Irish Party. This was an Irish Workers Army, Patsy Calibans with guns. Boyce, moreover, was not being theatrical. Take him literally. He wanted miners' unions to become armies or at least syndicalist militias. That was a truly remarkable suggestion, then or later. The entire US Army had only twenty-eight thousand men under arms in 1897. When Gompers heard of the rifle-club speech, he publicly declared that Boyce was "either a traitor or clearly insane." Whether Gompers intended that to mean a traitor to prudential unionism or to the American nation is uncertain. He may well have meant both.³⁰

There is no way of knowing whether Boyce was "being Irish" when he proposed his miners' defense force. Did the idea arise from a "rebellious disposition" brought with him from Donegal? He may also have been caught up in the mythical wild West. But I'm struck by how similar Boyce's armed soviets would have been to Connolly's and Jim Larkin's 1913 ICA. Even Boyce's idea of forming rifle clubs as a means of disguising intent was used by rebels in Ireland—both Protestant loyalists in the northeast and republicans in the rest. As noted, maybe it was Connolly who was reading Boyce.

By 1900, Boyce had compiled an interesting mix of enemies, ranging from Marcus Daly to Samuel Gompers. With his rifle-club speech, he earned another. M. J. Burke was the Irish-born president of both the BMU and of the Butte chapter of the Ancient Order of Hibernians. He also resided on a seam line joining ethnicity and class. It just wasn't the same seam line that Boyce was on. In response to Boyce's rifle-club idea and to his occasionally overheated rhetoric, including his assertion that the "conservatism" of the BMU was a form of "moral cowardice," Burke moved to "withdraw the [BMU] from the Federation." That motion failed, but Burke then moved to evict the WFM from BMU Hall. That motion passed. The BMU had kicked the WFM out of town. Boyce packed his bags and moved the Federation to Denver.³¹

Butte, as Boyce could have predicted, did not change after the expulsion of the WFM. As for the BMU, if anything, it grew even closer to ACM after the WFM left town and quit nagging it. One labor radical claimed that by 1905 the BMU was not "merely reactionary." Its leadership and "four-fifths" of its rank and file were "on the payroll of the ACM." That was the year the Butte Miners' Union bought ACM stock; two years later, it negotiated five-year contracts; in 1912, it acquiesced in—if it hadn't actually requested—the adoption of a company rustling card used to blacklist radicals and other "impractical" unionists. The BMU continued to provide Irish answers to labor issues, provide Irish working-class answers to Irish nationalist issues, and to behave like the eminently prudential union it had always been.[32]

I quoted earlier the lyrics to that Miners' Union Day song with the Irish miner wearing his Irish clothes and identity to a working-class party. The song is undated, but it could have been sung any year from the mid-1880s to 1913. Miners' Union Day, 1914, would not have been a good day to be singing it. A sizable number of "insurgent" elements in the BMU boycotted the parade. Most were not Irish, but there were enough Irish among them that *boycott* is the entirely appropriate word. At the end of the festive day, those who sat out the parade sent another and more forceful message: They dynamited Miners' Union Hall. It was a large building, able to hold meetings of up to eight hundred union men, and stoutly built. It teetered but only part of it collapsed, and so ten days later the same union rebels dynamited what was left of it. They took the safe with all the union's money as well as the membership lists. After thirty-six years, the Gibraltar of Unionism had been laid waste.[33]

Later in that summer of discontent, the IWW sent the Italian anarchist Arturo Giovannetti to Butte to preside over and celebrate the burial of the BMU. Giovannetti spoke before what was left of the Union Hall and proposed an epitaph. He told those gathered to hear him, including many hundreds of Irish miners, that the BMU was "an obsolete union." Then, pointing to the rubble behind him, he told them that "Here lie the remains of 36 years of peace and prosperity; the working men of Butte should be ashamed of those thirty-six years." The remark doubtless left many who heard it speechless. It leaves me speechless.[34]

• • •

Two months after Giovannetti's eulogy, Butte's "respectable" Irish began a determined effort to restore the old order. The counterattack against the forces of labor radicalism, whether socialist or IWW, was led by Irish-born James B. Mulcahy. Mulcahy had come to Butte in 1910 and bought a small, struggling newspaper, the *Butte Independent*. As with Boyce and a few others, I've always wondered whether he was sent and, if so, by whom. I would note only that by 1910 ACM hiring practices had grown more modern and "scientific," which meant the Irish were being given fewer favors, and some Irish in the BMU were tilting leftward and questioning the union's chumminess with the corporation. Mulcahy kept the paper's name but added to the masthead "devoted to the interests of Ireland and the advancement of true American ideals." In May 1917, after the United States had entered the war,

The dynamited Butte Miners' Union Hall, July 23, 1914, "the remains of thirty-six years of peace and prosperity." The safe holding the union's money was stolen and the dues and membership lists were destroyed to shouts of "you're all paid up now!" Courtesy Butte/Silver Bow Archives.

that was later changed to "the organ of uncompromising Irish nationalism and virile American democracy."

Mulcahy's commitment to Irish nationalism was entirely severed from labor's cause. The Ireland Mulcahy envisioned would be respectably middle-class, more nearly a Catholic theocracy than a democratic, not to mention workers', republic. The cause of Ireland for Mulcahy was the cause of labor only if the laborers were Irish—and Catholic—as well as enterprising and eager to rise in the world. Everything, in other words, that Connolly's true Irish were not. Mulcahy kept his paper alive until 1937, when he returned to Ireland. During all those years, the *Butte Independent* was the journalistic mouthpiece for the interests of the Anaconda Copper Mining Company and the Irish gentlemen of property who ran it.

In 1910, the year Mulcahy began publishing Butte's Irish "paper of record," Connolly came to Butte on an organizing trip for the WFM; this, of course, after Boyce. He told an enthusiastic Butte crowd what Boyce had preached more than a decade earlier: Irish bosses could be as bad as any other kind. The *Butte Independent* did not even cover the event, and from that time forward, Connolly was a frequent target of Mulcahy's attacks. Not as frequent a target, however, as Jim Larkin, who, for Mulcahy, was the embodiment of the Irish Left at its most reckless; Larkin's cause of labor would be the annihilator of the cause of Ireland.

With Connolly, Larkin had led the Irish Transit and General Workers Union (ITGWU) in its bitter and unsuccessful resistance to the Dublin lockout of 1913. After the ITGWU called off the resistance, and at the invitation of the IWW, Larkin came to America, where he stayed until 1923, spending the last three of those years in a federal penitentiary. Between 1914 and 1916, Larkin made four trips to Butte. His message was always the same: Connolly had said that "the Socialist message to Ireland and to America is identical." Larkin put it more dramatically, telling a Butte crowd that "the struggle you have here is the same you knew in Ireland—the struggle against economic and political tyranny." Larkin told a large audience that "you lose your class ... and race solidarity" when you allow "mercenary phrase mongers, to talk about Irish freedom."[35]

Larkin all but danced along seam lines, linking Ireland's woes with those of Irish Americans; equating the economic and the political; and, most important, appealing for the solidarity of both race and class. When Mulcahy rose to condemn such remarks as "demagoguery," Larkin shouted back that "true Irish patriots" would "spit in the faces of a renegade shoneen Irish" like Mulcahy. Mulcahy answered in kind. Larkin, he wrote in his paper, was a "blasphem[er] ..., a man "dwarfed in intellect, barren of spiritual vision, devoid of patriotic instinct," a "most vulgar ... ignorant ... conceited and pitiable little atom." Put simply—and Mulcahy never put the cause of Ireland any other way—Connolly and Larkin, as Boyce had before them, were dividing the Irish on the basis of social class, and that was no way to fight a war of national liberation. Irish making enemies of other Irish was no way to fight the only enemy that mattered.[36]

There was something of the stage-Irish about the Larkin versus Mulcahy duel. But their exchange took place in Butte and it included, as it had to, the motives of the insurgent dynamitards who blew up Miners' Union Hall. Not all of Mulcahy's remarks on this topic came in response to Larkin; a few came even before the hall was blown up. Those that came after that event were a bit anticlimactic, but no less revealing, primarily because Mulcahy supplemented his one-dimensional nationalism with a boundless admiration for and fidelity to the mostly Irish officer corps of the Anaconda Copper Mining Company. Mulcahy's praise of ACM presidents John Ryan and Con Kelley bordered on sycophancy. He was convinced—or ACM had convinced him—that socialism was "nothing more than a sniveling manifestation of defunct and discredited APAism." His reference was to the intensely anti-Catholic American Protective Association. Had too many socialists not also been nativists, that remark could have been dismissed as cheap politics.[37]

But it wasn't just the latent nativism of the socialists—or of the IWW, of which both Connolly and Larkin were members—that was at issue. Mulcahy claimed that left-wing unionists ignored the fact that there was a "most amicable relationship . . . between employer and employee" in Butte, that the company paid the highest industrial wages in the world, and that it had "met every reasonable and just demand of the [miners] . . . in a spirit of magnanimity." Implied was that a free Ireland could be like that too. In Mulcahy's mind, to be anti-BMU and anti-Anaconda Company was, by definition, to be anti-Irish. There were no meaningful differences between them. Those comments came before the destruction of Union Hall. Indeed, the beliefs behind Mulcahy's comments were among the reasons the hall was blown up.[38]

It was that act that explained Mulcahy's extraordinary charge that the leftist insurgents' "aim [was] to undermine Irish influence and exterminate our people from Butte . . . by "tax[ing] to the breaking point the great company that has offered every Irishman the chance of procuring a competent livelihood." If by "chance of" Mulcahy meant "guarantee of"—and he did—he may have been right. Then came a more specific claim. Mulcahy noted with undisguised pride that the Anaconda Copper Mining Company, the corporate giant brought to life by Marcus Daly, sustained in power and influence by John Ryan and Cornelius Kelley, middle-managed by scores of others as Irish as they, "has placed the Irishman at the forefront of every great enterprise and lavishly rewarded Irish genius and ability with the most responsible and lucrative positions at its disposal." So it had—and with the full and enthusiastic support of its genial partners in the Irish-run Butte Miners' Union. It was unusual, even in Butte, to see so frank an admission of ethnic job preference, of an interclass Irish deal that struck at the heart of working-class solidarity.[39]

That brought Larkin back to center stage. Whether he knew it or not, Larkin, the "peripatetic anarchist," as Mulcahy called him, had allied himself with Butte's "foul-mouthed anti-Irish coterie." Larkin said he stood for labor, that his intent in coming to Butte was to speak on labor's cause. Mulcahy refused even to grant him that. He claimed that Larkin's intent was the same as the other foul-mouthed ones. He wanted to "undermine the source of livelihood for" Irishmen and their families. Mulcahy contrasted this with the role of Con Kelley, Anaconda's chief counsel and second-in-command to John Ryan. Kelley was a "kindly Irish of the Irish, neither Saxon nor Italian." He was a "citizen and man of great achievement." The reference to not-Saxon was to be expected; that to not-Italian may have been in the context of the BMU insurgency—or Mulcahy's prejudices. As for great achievement, that was an American specialty. Which raises another interesting and related point: Larkin's comments were not carried in Mulcahy's paper; I read them in the *Butte Socialist*. Mulcahy's responses were in his *Butte Independent*. I think there is a good chance that Ed Boyce, comfortably retired by then and living in Portland, Oregon, subscribed to both. I hope he did.[40]

• • •

Two months after the destruction of the Butte Miners' Union Hall, and the union along with it, World War I began. The Irish in America described the conflict more narrowly: The Irish Left saw the conflict as an imperialists' war and condemned it. The more common Irish response was that Germany had gone to war against Great Britain and that the United States wasn't in it. Those two facts together allowed them to fantasize once again that England's distress was Ireland's opportunity—and England was most sorely distressed. In Butte, the Irish, to a person, it seems, totally ignored President Woodrow Wilson's insistence that Americans remain "neutral in thought, word, and deed." (In truth, Wilson ignored his own stated position.) Butte's Irish were exceptional in their defiance.

The city's annual St. Patrick's Day parade in 1915, for example, proceeded under the flags of the United States, Germany, Austria, and Ireland—three nations and one nation-hoping-to-be. Speeches included a fervent prayer from Fr. James English, an Irish-born priest, that "the sons of imperial Germany under the eagle of the Fatherland, will soon be in a position to help restore to Ireland that precious boon of freedom and independence." A year later, and after the Wilson administration had secured passage of the National Defense Act essentially putting the United States on a war footing, Father English was more specific: "Today we recognize Germany as an ally. ... [W]e claim her." He did not have to explain whom he meant when he said "we," which, in the geographic and political context where he said it, makes his comment even more notable, if not notorious.[41]

A little over a month later, on April 24, 1916, the day after Easter, around eight hundred Irish rebels, many armed with rifles supplied by Germany, entered Dublin and occupied the city. Connolly and his ICA were among them. On that first day, the young Irish poet Patrick Pearse read a proclamation that he and Connolly had prepared, announcing to the world the birth of *an Poblacht na h-Éireann*, an Irish Republic. As Father English had, the proclamation also thanked Ireland's "gallant allies in Europe," that is, Germany, as well as its "exiled children in America." The children, for their part, chose to interpret Pearse literally and make Germany the ally of an Irish Republic, which, by a bit of only semitortured logic, made the enemies of Germany the enemies of Ireland, which, by impeccable logic, left those exiled children to face a severe test.[42]

Robert Schmuhl claims that, after America's entry into World War I in April 1917, the American Irish "subordinated ancestral considerations to the cause of [an American] victory." I disagree. The United States had gone to war in defense of the British Empire, from which Irish nationalists were striving mightily to escape. A great number of the American Irish tied those considerations to an American victory, but they did not subordinate them to it. The proclaimed Irish nation was the gift of dead ancestors to their grateful neighbors and friends still living. An American victory would be welcome only if it honored and redeemed that gift. The Irish loved America most—it's tempting to say only—when it was on the right side of causes dear to Ireland. To quote from James Barrett's recent study, *The Irish Way*, "The Irish were most loyal to U.S. policy when their own cause could be squared with it." That was especially true among the erratics.[43]

The Easter Rising in all its aspects has received a vast amount of attention from historians. No attempt will be made to cover it here. Rather, the concentration will be on two aspects: first, the Rising as Connolly and the Irish Left defined it. And second, the effect of that Leftist aspect of the Rising on Butte's Irish working class. Regarding this second issue: I am allowing Butte's Irish to speak for more than themselves; indeed, I am insisting they do. What they said and what they did informs—*in extremis*, I grant—our understanding of a very large percentage of nationalist Irish America, particularly working-class and left-leaning Irish America.

That returns the story to James Connolly, ably assisted by Patrick Pearse. Connolly had woven together radical social reforms with physical-force nationalism, found Irish racial and historical roots for both, and made the case to the world that a war of national liberation, if it was to have any real and enduring meaning, had also to be a social revolution. I have already alluded to his 1897 comment that "'nationalism without Socialism ... is ... recreancy." By his reckoning, "Irish capitalism" was an existential contradiction. An Irish nation formed by the likes of these, or an Ireland led by them, would not be a good-hearted nation; capitalism was, by definition, hard-hearted when not heartless. The *Poblacht na h-Éireann*, as Connolly envisioned it, could never be such a nation, for the simple reason that if it ever became such, it would no longer be Irish. It would be a different and lesser place, one without enchantments, morally and culturally unmoored. Marx counted, but so did Fionn mac Cumhaill, the Counsels of Cormac, and others in the repository of the Irish past.[44]

There was genuine radicalism in that. I do not mean to be excessively formulaic, but consider, as Connolly clearly did: By its very nature, the cause of the Irish nation would be a subheading under the cause of anti-imperialism, which, by *its* very nature, was a partner of the cause of anticapitalism. Those too could also not be dissevered. That's why there was no contradiction between Connolly's nationalism and his socialism. His nationalism was entirely consistent with his internationalism; in fact, the one was inseparable from the other.

Many on the left, including Marxist internationalists, agreed. Lenin, for example, writing in 1914, claimed that for "centuries England has enslaved Ireland." Note the verb in a present tense. Lenin went on—now in past tense— that England "condemned the Irish peasants to unparalleled misery and gradual extinction from starvation, drove them off the land and compelled hundreds of thousands and even millions of them to leave their native country and emigrate to America. . . . Ireland has become depopulated. . . . Britain owes her 'brilliant' economic development and the 'prosperity' of her industry and commerce largely to their treatment of the Irish peasantry." I know that Lenin read Connolly; I would like to know how many Irish in America—or in Butte—read Lenin.[45]

Trotsky may have expressed the conjoined causes more clearly even than Lenin. In a passage so like a Connolly historical exegesis on Cromwell that it could have been lifted from *The Re-conquest of Ireland*, Trotsky wrote that the "young Irish working class, . . . saturated with the heroic traditions of national revolt . . . was always ready to link syndicalism and nationalism . . . together in its revolutionary consciousness. . . . Thus the 'national revolution' in Ireland . . . has amounted, in practice, to a revolt of the workers." There was, said Trotsky, an unbreakable "relation between the social rights of the Irish toilers and the political rights of the Irish nation." The *poblacht* for Trotsky was what Connolly called it, *an Poblacht Oibrithe na h-Éireann*, a *Workers*' Republic, Jacobinism in Irish dress.[46]

In the final analysis, this assessment by Sean Cronin seems not only the simplest but the fairest: James Connolly was an "anarcho-syndicalist" who "hated imperialism . . . hated capitalism . . . hated Britain, and . . . wanted an independent Ireland even if it was non-socialist." There is nothing internally inconsistent in that list, though that "even if non-socialist" point needs an explanation. Here's the most uncomplicated one: Connolly wanted Ireland to be Irish. He was always an Irish nationalist. Connolly believed in "direct action" because "*out of it* [would] arise... the spirit of Irish revolution." The events of 1916 were the direct action textbook anarchist propaganda of the deed. It was not the revolution but rather the catalyst for the revolution, what Connolly called in 1899 "a means to an end."[47]

But what of Connolly's coconspirator and corevolutionary? Patrick Pearse was routinely described—or is it dismissed?—as a mystic Catholic poet with a death wish, a non- or even antiradical fantasist who dreamt of an Ireland that never was and never would be. The proclamation that he cowrote and read contained only one sentence that could be said to express an economic principle. The "Irish people" had the sole right to the "ownership of Ireland." What he meant by "ownership" or even "of Ireland" is uncertain, but a less adventurous principle would be difficult to find. It was closer to Woody Guthrie than to Marx and Mao—or Lalor and Davitt. It didn't even reach the low bar for radicalism.

But read Pearse's language as a great many of the British did. They had reason to be worried about what the Rising and Pearse's proclamation of a republic might mean. A republic, by definition, would mean Ireland was completely removed from the Empire and as completely removed from the mentality of empire as the postcolonial blues would allow them to be. It was also, however, and more immediately, an act of treason. And treason without ideological purpose. The Irish were what they had always been: English-hating papists of evil and violent dispositions. That was all. That summed them up. The year 1916 simply marked another periodic instance of their coming out. The English would have had no quarrel with the dismissive judgment of Karl Radek, the Marxist revolutionary. The Rising, Radek wrote, was a "bourgeois putsch," a mindless act of adult delinquency, Irish howling at the moon. That did not, however, eliminate the Irish threat to the Empire. That was especially true after Lenin set Radek straight. Lenin saw the Easter Rising as an event of great significance. Connolly and Pearse's Ireland had a special role to play in the coming revolution. Pearse's Ireland was also an *Poblacht Oibrithe na h-Éireann*, the uniquely Irish Workers' Republic.[48]

Pearse's proclamation didn't say that, but three weeks before the Rising, Pearse had published a short and "startlingly radical" pamphlet, "The Sovereign People." He was considerably more forthcoming in the pamphlet than in the proclamation that followed it. "The Sovereign People" included this: In the new Ireland, "no private right to property is good as against the public right of the nation," which certainly extended and clarified what the proclamation intended by "the right of the people of Ireland to the ownership of Ireland." Pearse meant that those he called "the actual people" of Ireland owned the material resources of Ireland. He then made specific reference to who those "actual people" were—and who they were not. Among the latter, he mentioned specifically "the [Irish] gentry," many of them "corrupted... by England." He went next to "the merchants and middle class capitalists" who "when not corrupted, [had] been uniformly intimidated."[49]

Lest there be any mistake about what *shoneen* types were about to lose, he listed what "other nations" had identified to be among the material resources rightfully belonging to the actual—the real—people. He mentioned specifically "railways and waterways." Then, perhaps because a full list would be unwieldy, summed it up with "all sources of wealth whatsoever." "Control" of all sources of wealth whatsoever by the sovereign people of a sovereign state sounded a distinctly collectivist, even syndicalist, note. I wish Pearse had said which "other nations" he had consulted, but I do so while pointing out the obvious: The United States was not one of them. There was nothing in America's sacred texts that said what Pearse had said.[50]

J. J. Lee wrote that Pearse's "Proclamation... appeared, however vaguely, to commit the rebels to building a new society, promising equality of social and economic opportunity." This would have had little appeal to the "established interests," including the "capitalists" whom Pearse had all but purged from the ranks of the *pobal*, the true Irish of the *poblacht*. Connolly's radicalism is established. The only doubt is over whether he sold it out in 1916. Pearse was not as radical; he was certainly not a communist. But consider that Pearse had "stood shoulder to shoulder" with Connolly "in defense of the Irish Republic they had [both] proclaimed in arms." Pearse liked to say he was just an "old-fashioned Irish Catholic nationalist." That was either a very circumspect self-characterization or it's time for a reevaluation of what was involved in old-fashioned Irish Catholic nationalism.[51]

If the effect of Easter 1916 on the Irish in America is to be understood, the advanced radicalism of Connolly and the somewhat more subdued radicalism of Pearse must be taken into account. The year 1916 was not simply a matter of Irish Americans one day having an Irish flag to salute; it meant having an Ireland committed to establishing a social order uniquely Irish and, as a result, ideologically leftist. The Irish had not just outgrown what might be called the dominionism of the Parnellite Home Rulers; they had moved beyond an American-style capitalist Irish Republic and toward an Irish Workers' Republic that was outside both the British Empire and the capitalist world that accompanied empire. And all this in the midst of a great war between rival imperial nations. The events of 1916 had a global reach, one beyond anything Connolly could have envisioned. That reach was particularly apparent in places where the cause of Ireland and the cause of labor were already mixed—not to mention mixed up—where the Connolly formula, the radical conjoining of social revolution and national liberation, had had a head start.

∴

Butte, Montana, was a place like that. I begin with the fact that there was a perceptible increase in RELA membership and a decline in AOH membership after the Easter Rising. The RELA was Clan na Gael; it had always been the party of Irish Republicanism. A republic—any republic—took Ireland out of the British Empire. The one proclaimed in 1916, however, did more than that, and the RELA was faced with being outflanked on the left. As for the AOH, it had always consisted of the United Irish League–Home Rule sorts of Irish nationalists, the dominionists of above. Nationally, the Hibernians were telling Americans that they were the Irish club of choice for "judges, lawyers, bankers, railroad magnates, . . . businessmen, and Bishops." The labor situation in Butte essentially took the AOH out of play. This new Irish world belonged to those Connolly and Pearse had identified as the "actual people" of Ireland, those who were "actually" Irish in their sensibilities and not just *shoneen* nationalist posers.[52]

In late 1916, just months after the executions of Connolly and Pearse and not long after Jim Larkin's tumultuous third visit to Butte, another Irish communist, one of Larkin's and Connolly's closest allies, Con Lehane (or O'Lyhane), came to Butte. Lehane had been there before the Rising, probably as part of Larkin's "campaign of agitation" among "western miners," a campaign that was more antiwar—or anti-England-winning-the-war—than it was prolabor. This time, it was the Rising and the executions following it that moved Larkin to urge Lehane to make a return visit. Lehane brought one simple message, the same that Larkin had been preaching: Working-class Irish could honor Connolly best by forming Connolly Workers' Clubs, organizations that would carry the banner of Celtic communism.[53]

Lehane apparently said nothing about Patrick Pearse. Mystic Catholic poets seeking a "glorious sacrifice" and a "blood[y] redemption" were not important to him. That Pearse was more than that did not matter. Lehane did not want Pearse and poetry. He wanted Connolly and class war. Butte's erratic Irish were receptive, but only to part of what Lehane was promoting. Typical of Butte, they split the differences between Pearse and Connolly without splitting the causes by naming their new organization after both of them, then adding "Irish Independence," not "Workers'," Club to the whole of it. The cause of independence came first; it was a condition of the cause of the worker. The Pearse-Connolly Irish Independence Club of Butte (P-Cs, or Pearse-Connollys) bought some green sashes to wear on parade, then set themselves up in Finlander Hall, sharing space with Finnish radicals, the IWW, and the remnant and tattered parts of what remained of Butte unionism. There is no evidence that the Pearse-Connollys even asked the RELA and AOH whether they could share Hibernia Hall; no evidence, in fact, that they had any contact with those established Irish fraternities about anything.[54]

On April 6, 1917, the United States declared war against Germany, gallant ally of Revolutionary Ireland. The declaration broke the hearts of Irish and Irish American republicans everywhere and called the Pearse-Connolly Club to new duties. Ireland's "old traditions of nationhood" still needed to be tended to. The RELA did a dizzying about face: Germany could no longer be Ireland's liberator. Only the United States could. The Pearse-Connollys understood that as well, but they emphatically did not subordinate the cause of Ireland to the cause of an American victory. Four days after the US declaration, the P-Cs called for a "monster parade and exercise" in opposition to the war. Almost a thousand people watched as the new Irish club in town marched under the flag of the Irish Republic.[55]

On June 2, the Wilson administration issued an executive order that all immigrants not nationalized had until June 6 to be registered. Registered for what was not made entirely clear and it was easy to interpret the order as registration for a draft. That was not a dishonest or misleading representation of the order. Conscripting noncitizens was and remained a possibility. Butte, with a population of just under one hundred thousand, had the fourth-largest alien registry list in the United States. On it were thousands of immigrants from what was still the Austro-Hungarian Empire, against which the United States would also be fighting; at least an equal number of Finns, many of them socialists, none of them friendly to the idea of America allying itself with what was still a Czarist Russia; and thousands of young, footloose, and angry Irish, who had multiple objections to being registered for anything having to do with this war. Many hundreds of those were in the P-C Club. This was the ethnically mixed crowd that had blown up Miners' Union Hall in 1914.[56]

On June 3, the Pearse-Connolly Club, in a single-page hand-typed flyer circulated throughout Butte, called for "a silent strike against the war" generally and against the alien draft registration order specifically. "Silent strike" sounds a bit like a boycott; that may have been the point: Irish miners being called on to leave the mines "severely alone" by walking off the hill would turn a labor action into an antiwar protest. Whether that was intended or not, the writer of the flyer made clear that he wanted a job action that would shut down the Butte mines, this just after the Wilson administration had listed copper and steel as the two most vital materials of war. There were more than twelve thousand men working underground in those mines; that number would grow to eighteen thousand; thousands more were working topside. This strike, said the call, would be "the greatest step ever taken by the American working class."[57]

Step toward what was not made explicit, but consider that the alien registry was condemned as an examination "as to our fitness to kill and murder workingmen of other countries." But the flyer also said that it was an examination to see who would be fit to kill on the side of the nation that had "riveted the chains of slavery around Ireland." On June 5, thousands in Butte responded to the call and demonstrated in protest of the war. It was later claimed, likely with cause, that some of the resisters were beaten. Twenty-five men, most with Irish surnames, were arrested and jailed for leading a protest against an American war.[58]

One of the demonstrators that night was William Francis Dunne, son of an Irish immigrant, an officer of the International Brotherhood of Electrical Workers and, since 1910, a member of the Socialist Party. In 1916, Dunne had moved to Butte. Why is uncertain, but the mines employed hundreds of electricians, and he may simply have been looking for work. It may also be that he—like others for myriad reasons—was sent. By whom also is unknown, but Dunne, as Butte was about to learn, was a skilled writer and a fearless agitator of advanced radical views. Regardless of what explains his presence in Butte, Bill Dunne clearly knew Con Lehane and Jim Larkin. In 1916, all three were antiwar socialists. By 1919, all three were avowed communists. The questions ask themselves: was Dunne part of Larkin's plan "to slow up the American effort to aid the Allies" and to "obstruct the manufacture of war material, etc., and to use as confederates persons of German extraction and Irishmen belonging to the Sinn Fein faction"?

It's not on that topic, however, that I first advert to Dunne. Much later in his venturesome—and underreported—life, he recalled some of the events of June 3 to June 6, 1917. What struck me was this story he told about the night of the antiwar protest: "The parade started to gather on Upper Main Street. It [looked very] bad for a while because the police and county [sheriff's officers?] were acting very tough." Labor radicals never expected anything else from the police, but Dunne quickly changed the subject to one far more important to Irish American and American labor history generally than any account of tough acting police.[59]

This, he said, was "probably . . . the first time [that] Irish women and . . . Finnish women [had] ever met one another. Old Irish women were standing on the sidewalks and saying: 'what is the world coming to! The Finns are carrying guns and the Irish are packing knives!'" He remembered that "one of [the women] had a banner wound around her. The other women got hold of one end of it and unwound it and she spun around it like a top. She was a husky Finnish woman. When they got the banner hoisted it said 'Down with War.' Then these Irish, Finnish and Montenegrin and native-born American women, with their crudely lettered banner went down the street to meet the police and county deputies."[60]

In context, there's something affectionate, almost tender, about Dunne's story. The insurgents within the BMU were convinced that a kind of ethnic blacklist, enforced by the union, had long been part of the Butte labor market. In 1912, blacklisting became a company policy. Its first victims were Finnish socialists, hundreds of whom were fired in 1912, not because they were socialists, but because they were Finns and socially "undesirable," and that word was used—though not as Perlman had intended it. When a delegation of Finnish miners approached the BMU leadership and demanded that the union avenge them—as Finns, not as socialists—shouts were heard in Miners' Union Hall: "They're all Socialists, Finlanders. To Hell with them." In other words, they were "impractical." That was what "peace and prosperity" looked like in Butte.[61]

And that is what makes Dunne's story so important. Irish and Finnish women were strangers to one another. So were Irish and Finnish men. And so I add this story to Dunne's. Among those arrested after the antiwar protest were Denis Harrington, an Irish former city policeman, and John Korki, a Finn, recently arrived in Butte. Harrington, who had a Pearse-Connolly Club application in his pocket, said he "was looking for Irishmen of the proper kind," which can only have meant of the same kind as Larkin and Lehane were looking for. As for Korki, he told authorities that he had marched because he "wanted to help free Ireland." He may even have been serious.[62]

The Pearse-Connolly Club flyer calling for the walkout had a title on its banner; it was "The Butte Strike Bulletin." It is the first frame of the microfilmed copy of what became the *Butte Bulletin*, the radical newspaper edited off-and-on for the next ten years by Bill Dunne. That and similarities of style and content are enough to convince me that Dunne wrote the flyer as a member of the Pearse-Connollys. The P-C Club's friends and office mates from the Finnish socialists, the IWW, and what was left of Butte miner unionism also were involved, but the demonstration and the strike call were P-C Club initiatives.

There is a wonderful irony to this demand for a work stoppage coming from an Irish club. The BMU, after all, was charged by many with having been infiltrated by the RELA and the AOH—with, it was assumed, a helping hand by ACM—and turned into little more than a poorly disguised Irish nationalist club with no inclination to strike. Why not an Irish club taking a job action? There were many strictly labor issues still festering in Butte: blacklisting, inflation, wages, occupational safety issues, and more. And the Pearse-Connolly strike call included references to all of them. In the final analysis, however, this strike was to be an Irish protest based on the seamless connection between the cause of labor and the cause of Ireland.

• • •

On June 8, three days after the Pearse-Connolly Club's strike call and the violent protest against the alien registration order, a fire broke out 2,400 feet underground in the Granite Mountain shaft of the Speculator Mine. The fire started accidentally, sparked by the carbide lamp of a mine foreman, a German immigrant named Ernest Sallau. One hundred sixty-eight men were incinerated in that fire. It remains the worst tragedy in the history of American hard-rock mining. On June 14—the day after Miners' Union Day, as it happened—the recently formed Metal Mine Workers' Union (MMWU) called for a strike against all of Butte's mines. The new union claimed a membership of a thousand men. It may have had that many, but that was considerably less than 10 percent of those working on and under the Butte hill. The union had no formal affiliation with the AFL or the WFM (now known as the International Union of Mine, Mill, and Smelter Workers—"Mine-Mill"); it had no affiliation with any labor federation, including the IWW with which it and the Pearse-Connolly Club shared office space in Finlander Hall.

Technically, this was a wildcat strike against the largest copper mines in the world at a time when the United States and its allies needed, and by law insisted on having, all the copper they could get their hands on. Which returns the discussion to the IWW and more specifically to Con Lehane and Jim Larkin and their determined efforts to interfere with war production. US military intelligence agents, on the basis of information provided by the Thiel Detective Agency, were operating on the assumption that the IWW was going to strike the "copper mines in Montana, Arizona, and Utah." A further assumption was that Butte's striking miners "would get money from the German Government." The MMWU denied any association with the IWW, but the office space it shared with the Wobblies occasioned considerable speculation. It was the third office mate, however, that deserves the most notice. A Butte newspaperman reported that the "leaders of the P-C Club were also the leaders of the IWW in Butte." He may have been right. Certainly that was what Lehane and Larkin had wanted to happen.[63]

The great Butte copper strike of 1917 idled twelve thousand workers, "tying up," as Bill Dunne said later, "the biggest copper mining camp in the world." It was led by a new and unrecognized union without a strike fund. It took place while thousands of federal and state troops were patrolling Butte's streets, while strict curfews and limits on crowd size were in effect, and during a time when an IWW militant by the name of Frank Little was hauled out of his boardinghouse by parties unknown and hanged. Despite all that, the strike lasted until December 18, seven months, which is itself very nearly a record for an American strike. All of which suggests a number of other things, some of them suppositional: Strikes of that length always require working-class neighborhoods to remain neighborly and "ecclesial," with grocers extending credit; women taking care of children other than their own; wives and children bringing food to strikers on picket lines. They require, in other words, the symbiotic relationship between being a worker and, in this instance, being Irish, a part of the single platoon of class and ethnicity, this in a place the "social structure" of which indicated it belonged to both.[64]

Most of all, it demonstrates that in 1917 the same established, predominantly Irish, mine work force that had never taken a single job action against the company walked out. A strike requires strikers. That's not the tautology it seems. A strike needs a picket line, a line in the sand beyond which only scabs ventured. Western mining "camps"—they were called that for a reason—were filled with transient young men. They didn't wander in because they wanted to make those camps their home. They came because they wanted and needed to work. They would throw their bindle on a bunk in a boardinghouse and rustle a job. If, for whatever reason, there were no jobs, they left. A strike did not put transient workers on the picket line. It put them on the road.

Which means that for the 1917 strike to have gone on for as long as it did, there had to have been working miners who stayed in town but did not report to work. There had to have been established Irish miners—the same who had never gone on strike—who walked off the hill and formed a union picket line. The events 1917 were not a general strike, but they came very close to having the effect of one. Closing down Butte copper closed down Butte. A decent case could be made that it closed down the state of Montana. The closest parallel to it, however, particularly in context, is the 1916 Irish Rising with the Pearse-Connolly Club playing the role of the Butte division of Connolly's ICA. The United States was at war and had made it clear that that war could be won only if America's mines and smelters produced the maximum amount of copper. The Butte strike affected the American war effort in the same way the Rising affected the British and was met with the same charges of German conspiracy and treason.[65]

Unanswered by all of that is why, for the first time in their history, Butte's miners went out on strike. What were the causes of the strike? The MMWU issued strike demands: The miners wanted a closed shop, a union hiring hall, and a near doubling of wages. The union leaders even considered demanding a six-hour workday, collar to collar. They held off on that last one until the strike of 1918. They also demanded—168 dead miners later—the enforcement of occupational safety rules already on the books. In a fair and just world, those labor demands would have been entirely defensible. But this world was neither fair nor just, and what the MMWU was demanding had a certain otherworldly character about it.

The MMWU had to have known that it was asking for more than the going rates for unskilled industrial workers. Consider only the six-hour day—and at a daily wage that was triple that of other unskilled workers in the United States. Which leaves open for discussion the possibility that the war, the production of materials for the conduct of it, the selection of the men who would fight it, and the short- and long-term consequences of it—including consequences for Ireland—were also in play. To pose only half-rhetorical questions: Why did established Irish miners, old men as Butte counted old, "peaceful and prosperous," join this strike? And would they have joined any other?

My reference, of course, is to the fact that *a* strike was called *before* the Speculator disaster. Twenty years after the fact, Bill Dunne said this first strike was called because peaceful antiwar demonstrators were "clubbed and bayonetted" by Butte police and federal national guardsmen. A year after the events, he testified at the trial of an IWW officer that an "Irish group" had wanted to protest the war and the alien registration order but was denied a parade permit and so determined to force a strike. The only group that fits that description was the Pearse-Connolly Club. An IWW representative sent to Butte testified at that same trial that "the Irish had got together in the churches and had meeting in opposition to the draft" four days before the Speculator fire. Future Montana governor Burton K. Wheeler, in his autobiography, mentioned the "Pearse-Connelly [*sic*] club" and its antidraft pamphlet and said that the local papers were reporting that Butte was "on the verge of a serious riot"—of an antiwar, pro-Irish sort.[66]

The "cause of Ireland," as James Connolly had called it, was the reason for the first strike call. It was not, however, the reason for the strike that eventually came. To pose a counterfactual history: Suppose that Ernest Sallau's carbide lamp had not ignited a fire in the Granite Mountain shaft on June 8 and that the miners on that shift were hoisted out of the mine safely and went home. Would there even have been a MMWU? Would it have called a strike? That's one hypothetical. Here's another: would Butte's old-time Irish miners have answered the strike call if only the "cause of labor" had been the reasons for it? The Speculator was not an Anaconda Company Mine; it was not known as an "Irish" mine, that is, one in which the work crews were predominantly Irish—though more than fifty men with unmistakable Irish surnames were among the 168 dead. Would the disaster that occurred in the Granite Mountain shaft have been sufficient to turn workers once thought ethnically privileged and compliant into militants?

I can't know the answer to that last one. No one can. My point, however, is not that the established Irish miners of Butte walked off the job solely or even partly to deny the United States the copper it needed to win Britain's war. But they also knew this: They knew about the still entirely provisional Irish Republic. They knew that it had claimed Germany as a gallant ally. They knew that Irishmen—their countrymen—had been martyred in defense of it.

They knew that the government of their fosterland had declared war against Germany, which, according to their reading of the rules of war, meant against both the *Poblacht*, the Irish Republic, and the *pobal na h-Éireann*, the Irish people, a category in which they included themselves. And they knew that that same government was demanding that they—or their sons—fight that war.

Bill Dunne claimed that the antiwar strike would be the "greatest step ever taken by the American working class." There's more than a little sunburstery in that, but what matters more is whether that step was taken in the cause of Ireland, the cause of labor, or the cause of both. That was left uncertain, perhaps purposefully; it didn't really matter. Consider also the Butte miners' strikes that followed 1917, one per year for the next three years. An issue in all the strikes was the unfair imprisonment of California labor radical Tom Mooney, the once-Catholic son of Irish immigrants. Mooney, let it be noted with emphasis, was in jail for protesting the war. Add his name to the list of Irish Catholic working-class erratics. Butte's miners surely did.

A few things, however, must be reemphasized: the strike was called by the Pearse-Connolly Irish Independence Club. It was not called by the nationalists of the RELA. One of them had once advocated that the RELA buy a small blimp, fly it over the British Houses of Parliament, and drop dynamite down the chimneys and stacks, but even the most zealous of them would never have thought of such an action as the Pearse-Connollys did. But that first strike was also not called by a union. The Wobblies were indirectly involved, but there was little chance that Butte's established miners would have responded to an IWW strike. How much Jim Larkin and Con Lehane personally had to do with it is hard to know—maybe a lot. The ghosts of Pearse and Connolly, however, had everything to do with it.

As for the second strike—the one that did happen, with the active support of the Pearse-Connolly Club—it should be counted among the most important work stoppages in American history. The deep cultural rift between Irish and American sensibilities was put on full display. So was the related and equally deep social-class divide. So was the "enduring power of the [American] national-state," particularly its inability to decide how it felt about immigration generally and about all the racial and cultural Others that had made their way to its factories and mines. The Butte copper strike held up a mirror to America. It revealed that racial identities and working-class consciousness were interchangeable and, at times, impossible to differentiate.

The historian James Barrett recently wrote that the "key to labor reform in the late nineteenth century, was its relationship with Irish nationalist organizations.... [T]he two movements shared personnel and resources and often acted out of similar impulses." "Similar impulses" certainly strikes a proper tone. Barrett's reference is to labor reform in real time. Which means, of course, that if labor reform in the nineteenth century is to be understood, the relationship of labor reformers and Irish nationalists must be a part of the historical inquiry. A new element has been added to the study of American labor and working-class history and to transnational history more generally: England's Irish problem—and Ireland's English problem—had a decisive effect on American history generally, American *labor* history in particular.[67]

To make a more specific point, sense can be made of the Butte Rising of 1917 only if the Easter Rising of 1916 is factored into the analysis. The established Irish miners responded to the MMWU strike call as they did because, like the rest of the men, they were overworked and underpaid and because that was the only right response to the death of 168 of their working-class comrades. Those were their reasons. The cause of Ireland may have made their decision easier, but it did not determine it.

I would add a more general point and a more general explanation: Being Irish in America involved more than just Irish nationalism and the anglophobia that was central to it. The cultural divide between Catholic Irish and Protestant America was still there. So were the assumptions that the only thing that made the Irish useful was their ability to dig. The Irish were what they had always been: foster children, alien citizens, commuters and guest workers with long-term visas, erratics, in other words. In 1917 in Butte, as workers and as Irish, they went out on strike. Put simply, America had not yet given them sufficient reason not to.[68]

CHAPTER FIVE

Celtic Communists
"The Irish Contingent" among America's Radicals

"Lenin's prophetic word was fulfilled. The Easter rising marked the beginning of a new epoch."
—Bill Dunne, *The Red Easter*, 1952

In her book *The Radical Persuasion*, Aileen Kraditor wrote that there were immigrants who arrived in America as fully formed social-class radicals. America didn't radicalize them; Europe did. There were three ethnic/national groups that Kraditor put on her list of the preradicalized: "east European Jews, Finns, and Franco-Belgians." Many of the immigrants from each group arrived in America holding "theories about capitalist society [that] applied to whatever country they might live in." In other words, the three groups were transnational before they ever arrived in America. Radicalism was a global road show, geographically unbound, the same actors reading the same lines regardless of where they were.[1]

The Irish were not on her list. All that she said about them was that there was a "small handful" of "Irish socialists" with revolutionary ideas in their heads. Kraditor needed more than a small handful to justify inclusion among her radicals-on-arrival. But that wasn't the only reason the Irish were not among her immigrant groups with a "large radical element." Kraditor noted as well that the Irish, including those on the political left, diluted whatever influence they might have had by "insistently link[ing] Irish nationalism, culture, and history with their radical beliefs."[2]

That misses the point. Irish radicalism was neither diminished nor compromised by being linked with Irish history and culture. On the contrary, it arose from both. Similarly, Irish nationalism did not dilute Irish radicalism. It validated it. That was the way with causes on a seam. Each validated the other. That's not the only seam line she missed. Kraditor's is an account of three American radical organizations, the IWW, the Socialist Party, and the

Socialist Labor Party. She pillories them for insulting the working people whose interests they were supposed to be serving. But she chose to "omit ... their views ... concerning religion." Why she omitted their religious prejudices, particularly their anti-Catholicism, is a mystery to me. I assume that religion was included in her "culture" category, but, since the majority of American industrial workers were Catholic, it is easier to deal with American radicalism if the religious issue is confronted directly.[3]

It is in this context that I enter into the discussion the New York City-based Irish Progressive League (IPL), founded in 1917—the end-year of Kraditor's book—and active until 1921. The League was never very large, perhaps 150 members at its peak. It was created in part to give Irish support to the New York mayoral candidacy of Morris Hillquit, a Jewish Socialist who has a starring role in Kraditor's book and was running against two Irish Catholics, who have—and deserved—no role at all. The IPL's support of Hillquit bespeaks a certain cosmopolitanism not usually associated with the Irish. But it wasn't just its openness that distinguished the IPL; its politics were a perfect blend of collectivist ideas and Irish nationalism.

I am not claiming for the IPL the radicalism of, say, the IWW; nor am I suggesting that, had Kraditor extended her account, she would have made that claim. Let the IPL be judged on the basis of what it fought for—and what it fought against, including the bigotry and condescension that Kraditor exposed and condemned in the radical organizations she studied. The league opposed the war; hated imperialism; opposed the conscription of Irish to serve in the British military; vocally supported women's and Black rights; championed both the Irish and the Soviet republics; had no affection for American capitalism; and took strong positions on issues of labor and social justice, for the United States, for Ireland and for the world. That's basically the same list that Sean Cronin compiled to describe Connolly. If "radical" seems to fit, apply it. There are two other issues: First, some of the IPL's nonconforming ideas sounded vaguely Catholic or came from Irish who were or had been Catholic. Often, it was their Catholicism that made them nonconforming. Occasionally, it was what made them radical. And, second, no other ethnic group in America ever formed anything like it. No other ethnic group in America can be imagined forming anything like it.[4]

Whether the league's radicalism was the real article depends on definition, and a precise one doesn't exist. In this case, however, none is needed. I use the word *radical* because that is the conventional thing to do. If referring to "Irish radicals" is unfair to the genuine version, or to the word itself, substitute something like ideological nonconformists, troublemakers, alien and alienated citizens. Under whatever heading, let the IPL stand as a final bit of evidence that Irish nationalism and Irish communalism—to give it a less loaded label—were ideologically harmonious and mixed easily.

"Radicals *in* America," Kraditor also wrote, were "part of the American class structure. A commitment to fight against something" implies a "form of acceptance . . . of the personal significance of what one is fighting." She concludes that it was America's radicals, not America's workers, who "labored under the ideological—or psychological—hegemony of the bourgeoisie." That ideology and that psychology were professedly and undeviatingly modern. Working-class Irish did not so much fight against that "ideological version of modernity" as reject it and then ignore it. They did not accept the American "class structure" against which they fought; most didn't even understand it. Their assaults on imperialism and capitalism arose from Irish ground. They constituted a Left, to be sure, but it was an *Irish* Left.[5]

It was also, however, and to a degree that was and is too seldom acknowledged, a Catholic Left. Larkin wasn't the only "Catholic communist," as Bertram Wolfe called him. Catholicism, Wolfe went on to add, was the "unifying creed of Irishmen." It, not class consciousness, was "the foundation of [their] simple socialism." Irish socialism was a lot of things; "simple," as in arising from a goodness of heart, may have been one of them. Wolfe may also have been patronizing. That aside, Wolfe deserves praise merely for mentioning that the Irish Left had a "unifying creed" and that being or having been Catholic and for being aware that the Church's teaching on social justice, broadly interpreted, was part of it.[6]

And consider the lasting and patently radical effects of that unifying reformist creed, whatever its origins. In 1916, Irish rebels set in motion a series of events that eventually took down the entire British imperial system. The Easter Rising was more than just another instance of Irish ill temper and lack of restraint. In a recent presentation before the Irish Centre for the Histories of Class and Labor, Luke Gibbons made precisely that argument. He quoted US secretary of state Robert Lansing, who, in 1920, connected the Easter Rising to Asia and Africa as well as Eastern Europe and then warned that if the Irish got away with 1916 by sustaining their republic, other British colonies in India, Egypt, and South Africa would be inspired to go and do likewise. If anything, Lansing underestimated the Rising's full, long-term effects. I acknowledge that that is an Irish, not an Irish American, story, but it's also one marks the place from which Irish Americans had come and to which they still looked.[7]

Gibbons also emphasized the fact that, in 1916, the Irish revealed to the world that radical ideas could come from backward-looking traditionalists. Insurgent movements did not have to start—indeed, frequently did not start—among the ideologues in the metropolitan centers of industrial capitalism. Ireland was on the colonial periphery, a subject state, noncapitalist rather than overtly and loudly anticapitalist. The same was said of Russia. Consider, too, as the Irish Left frequently reminded people: the Bolsheviks,

St. Petersburg, and the Red October, 1917, were a year and a half later than the Irish Citizen Army (ICA), Dublin, and Easter 1916. What came next also mattered greatly. Gibbons stated the obvious corollary to Irish anti-imperialism and asked that it too be acknowledged: 1916 was the "entering wedge directed straight at the heart of British *capitalism*." It would not take capitalism down with the Empire. It would only stagger and redirect it. But that does not diminish the enormity and the sheer—and complex—radicalism of the Irish Left.[8]

That returns the discussion to Kraditor and the omission of the Irish from her ranks of American immigrant radicals. Kraditor was writing two decades before Kevin Kenny began to think about how the transnational and the cross national had both to be considered if sense was to be made of American immigrant history. Kenny does not cite Kraditor's book; it was not central to his task. But Kenny writes specifically of the way issues like "women's rights, an income tax, [and] an eight-hour workday for American workers" were linked—to use Kraditor's word—to the cause of "Irish land reform and national liberation." He then goes on to describe this blending as a "genuinely transnational working-class movement, . . . [one] that combined ethnic nationalism, trade unionism, and social activism"—which sounds a lot like Kraditor's point about the nexus of "nationalism, culture, and history"—and "radical beliefs."[9]

I return to Kenny's brief but telling discussion of "the syndicalist James Larkin and the republican socialist James Connolly," both, I must again add, Catholics. Larkin's Catholicism is acknowledged; Connolly's is not. Another Irish socialist, Jack Carney, who knew Connolly well, says that Connolly "believed in Catholicism with all the faith of a simple Irish servant girl"—than whom none had a greater abundance of faith. The Irish American writer and leftist James Farrell agrees with Carney, and quotes Connolly in doing so. Obviously, I am on the side of Carney and Farrell. There are too many places in his writing where Connolly simply sounds Catholic. Mixing up Catholicism with politics did not disqualify one from being radical. Anglo-America was about to learn that.[10]

• • •

In February 1917, revolutionary forces in Russia overthrew the tsar. Eight months later, in what the American radical and Larkin ally John Reed called the "ten days that shook the world," hardline communist Bolsheviks under Vladimir Lenin seized and consolidated power. Socialists everywhere were jubilant. Antiwar activists were no less so. There were cadres of both in Ireland, and they were among the celebrants. But the Irish had more to cheer than "bread and peace." By the time of the Red October, Lenin had come to see the Irish Easter Rising of 1916 as nationalism in the service of an Irish workers' revolution. The Irish revolt, Lenin had written, like all such "mass struggles," had its share of "petty bourgeoisie and backward workers," but "*objectively* [it would] attack *capital*." It would "seize the banks . . . appropriate the trusts" and ultimately "'purge' itself of petty-bourgeois slag," for which read purge itself of *shoneens*, a word Lenin probably knew.[11]

Lenin may have cared nothing for Ireland or the Irish. That can be said of Marx as well. But both cared mightily about a worldwide proletarian revolution, and Lenin had begun to believe that Irish nationalism and "secession" from the British Empire would advance that revolution. As he put it on May 9, 1916, three days before Connolly was executed, "a blow delivered against the English imperialist bourgeoisie by a rebellion in Ireland is a hundred times more significant politically than a blow of equal weight delivered in Asia or in Africa." The inclusion of "bourgeoisie" with "imperialist" was significant. That the British Empire was the partner of British capitalism was an idea embraced by all sides, imperialists as well as Marxists and everyone in between. Theoretically, and whether they knew it or not, the acknowledgment of that partnership turned a lot of Irish nationalists into anticapitalists or, at least, agents of anticapitalism. That was Gibbons's point. It was Lenin's too. As he had put it in 1916, "Socialism will be achieved by the united action of the proletarians . . . of the countries that have reached the stage of development of *advanced* capitalism." Russia was not one of those. Neither was Ireland. But England was.[12]

Connolly had written similarly in January 1916: The "battle line of England is weakest at the point nearest its heart . . . [namely] Ireland." An English "'defeat in India, Egypt, the Balkans or Flanders would not be so dangerous to the . . . Empire as any conflict of armed forces in Ireland. . . . [A] strong man . . . will succumb if a child sticks a pin in his heart.'" The child had stuck the pin. A year and a half later came the Lenin-led communist takeover of Russia. Ireland's Republicans suddenly had another gallant ally, one far more ideologically compatible than the Germans—or, for that matter, the Americans—could ever have been.[13]

"Nowhere," one Irishman reported, "was the Bolshevik revolution more sympathetically saluted" than in Ireland. It was a strange pairing, Ireland and Russia. Both sides to it should have been more careful. Neither knew much about the other. As the Irish historian Emmet O'Connor has written, "What did the Irish understand of Bolshevism? What did [international communism] know of Ireland? . . . was it possible to run an Irish movement from Moscow?" The answers would turn out to be "very little," "almost nothing," and "no." But that was not the way the Irish Left and the Russian "friends of Irish freedom" saw the matter in 1917.[14]

The "alliance" of Irish leftist nationalists with Russia became significantly less strange in December 1917 when the Soviet government declared that its policy on the postwar settlement and its ongoing governing philosophy would be "no annexations, no indemnities, and the right of every nation to determine its own destiny." In other words, Germany was to get out of Belgium and England was to get out of Ireland. Lenin next surrendered all of Russia's imperialist claims in Central Asia and then granted all of Russia's former colonies the right of self-determination. Annexation, he explained, "involves the concept of an 'alien' people, a people that has preserved its peculiarities"—its erraticism—"and its wish for independent existence." The timing and the content make it unimaginable to me that he did not have Ireland partly in mind when he said that.[15]

Engels had written that the "only point where one can hit official England really hard is *Ireland*." "Ireland lost, the British 'Empire' is gone, and the class war in England, till now somnolent and chronic, will assume acute forms." Thirty years later, the Bolsheviks reopened the conversation and initiated the relationship with the Irish. In 1918, the Executive Committee of the Third Communist International told the world that the Bolsheviks were ready to "assist by all means in [their] power the National Revolutionary movement in Ireland." That anti-imperialist manifesto was followed the next year by the Soviets' recognition of the Irish Republic; Russia was the first nation to extend that favor. On February 4, 1918, ten thousand enthusiastic Irish gathered at a rally at the Mansion House in Dublin. They had come to hear an impressive roster of rebel Irish and to join them in "hailing with delight the advent of the Russian Bolshevik Revolution," particularly, one suspects, its professed "principles of self-determination of subject races and territories . . . that fearlessly challenged the British . . . grip on Ireland."[16]

The Irish were to be courted; that it was a courtship of convenience, not affection, made it only slightly less fervent. That was as true of Lenin as of Marx. Like Marx, he had never set foot in Ireland. Like Marx, he wanted the "separation of Ireland" from Great Britain, "not in order to secure 'justice for Ireland,' but in the interests of the revolutionary struggle of the British proletariat." Indeed, he warned that though the "resistance of a nationally oppressed population . . . *tends* towards national revolt," those revolts frequently fell into the hands of "the bourgeoisie . . . of the oppressed nations . . . [who] enter into reactionary agreements with the bourgeoisie of the oppressing nations behind the backs of, *and against*, [their] own people." To translate into Irish, the *seoininí*, both in Ireland and in Irish America, wrap themselves in the nationalist flag and "degrade, vulgarize," and subvert the entire enterprise.[17]

Lenin was clear on this: It was *not* a Marxist's "duty to support every struggle against imperialism. We will *not* support an uprising of the reactionary classes against imperialism and capitalism." That Lenin supported Ireland's uprising makes it clear that he did not perceive it as an uprising of the reactionary classes, the *shoneens* and bourgeoisie. Of course, it says nothing about whether he perceived it correctly. For the moment, that was less important than the fact that Ireland, in Nicholas Mansergh's words, was "'of *immense practical* importance" in determining "the attitude the proletariat of the *oppressing* nations should adopt towards national movements." Freeing Ireland freed the British proletariat. It is not too much to say that when Marx and Lenin made room for some wars of national liberation, they—particularly Lenin—did so largely because of Ireland. As Lenin had put it in 1916, the "emancipation of ... oppressed classes was inextricably tied to the 'right' of "oppressed nations ... to secede" from the empires that held them. Let the "emancipation" of Ireland start the worldwide proletarian Revolution.[18]

• • •

Larkin said that the Irish had already given what Marx and Lenin wanted from them, that 1916 was the Revolution's effective date, not 1917. Red Easter was the cradle-ground of Red October. The Mansion House rally was a proper ceremonial tribute to both. Larkin was fantasizing. Marx and Lenin's problem with Ireland was of an entirely different sort. In Mansergh's words, their "inflexibility of mind, ... their ideological approach to political problems" had led them to error. Neither understood "the fanatical character, the emotional side of Irish nationalism." For *emotional*, substitute *moral*, even *enchanted*. True psychological autonomy required both ideology and emotion, both politics and poetics. The result was that the communist tactics "were suited to a situation which in fact did not exist." As an example, it is highly unlikely that more than a Kraditor-like handful among the ten thousand celebrants at the Mansion House that evening were hardline communists there to hail the Bolshevik Revolution. That the Irish had found their revolution in Irish History rather than *Das Kapital* should have been of more interest to Marx and Lenin than it was.[19]

The Bolsheviks misread Ireland. The Mansion House meeting recalls nothing so much as a remark Shane Leslie had made just the year previous. The Irish, he said, "'would have declared themselves pro-Hell had they sufficient proof that the devil was anti-British." Nonetheless, ten thousand Irish men and women cheering communist revolutionaries was a noteworthy event, not least to the British government, and not without causing growing concern to the American one. The Republic would take Ireland out of the Empire; if all that followed went as the Irish Left hoped it would, the working classes who would come to rule that republic would remove the capitalists from Ireland.[20]

That was as close as the nationalist cause of Ireland would ever come to the cause of international Marxism. A year after the rally at the Mansion

House, the Irish Labour Party told a socialist conference in Germany that the Irish revolt was based "on the historic nationality, separate and distinct, of the Irish people." Irish nationality came "first." It was still true that the Irish people had a special "genius" and thus a special calling. Ireland could be "the basis for a solution to national questions elsewhere." I read "national questions" as the Irish Progressive League meant it, as including labor and social questions. Irish labor was actively engaged in "calling upon all Irishmen and Irishwomen outside Ireland," including prominently the United States, "to support" two equally worthy and mutually reinforcing causes. The first was "the heroic Russian Revolutionists." The second and more immediate one was the "claim of Ireland to self-determination." That was also the more important one.[21]

In 1917, an anonymous Irishman calling himself "Spailpín" (Spalpeen) wrote a pamphlet with the nondescript but revealing title of "Sinn Féin and the Labour Movement." Sinn Féin had become the label and the political party of Irish republican nationalists; that is what Spalpeen meant by its use. By the "Labour Movement," he meant the Marxist and hence internationalist Irish Labour Party and Trade Union Congress (ILPTUC). Not all of Ireland's working people were in the party. The pamphlet writer wasn't, though was almost surely a member of Sinn Féin. He was a spalpeen, an itinerant laborer, one of Ireland's rambling proletarians. Spalpeen, however, can also mean rascal, mischief-maker. Often, spalpeens were all the above.

This one said he had "marched out with a loaded rifle in hand on a certain Easter Monday morning." He did not say with which of the "revolutionary organizations" he marched, but he did say that he grew up poor and his perspective was very much that of a working-class nationalist. There is no evidence in his pamphlet that he was a labor unionist. If he was a socialist, he was a most uncommon one, and I doubt that he was with Connolly's Reds, the ICA. Which leaves either the Irish Volunteers or Sinn Féin. Even though I have no idea who or what he was, there are good reasons to think that Spalpeen's opinions were shared by a great many Irish, including a good share of the ten thousand at the Mansion House who cheered the Russian Revolution.[22]

Regardless of whose "army" he was with on Easter Monday, Spalpeen certainly knew the Pearse-Connolly catechism and that Irish nationalism was a fight for the restoration of moral as well as political and material resources. It was the separateness, the genius, of the race, that mattered. The demand for independence did not arise because the Irish found the British administration of Irish affairs to be "bad and injurious." It was that, but even if it were to reform itself and rule efficiently and fairly, it would still be what it had always been, not Irish, and "ruin[ous] to the [Irish] race." For Spalpeen, 1916 was about "poetics." Political autonomy was meaningless in the absence of "psychological autonomy."[23]

Two aspects of the Irish race were of concern to him. The first was the non-Englishness of it. The second was its interclass nature, and it was here that the Spalpeen parted ideological company with Irish socialists. The "workers of Ireland," he insisted, "cannot be regarded as a 'Class'—they are the Nation"; in other words, part of the "native people." They were fighting as Irish, not as proletarians. But equally Irish were those nationalist "Sinn Féiners" who were not of the working class. "The genius of . . . all [Ireland's] children must have full play." Ireland needed all its native people to be patriots, and Spalpeen wasn't entirely sure the Marxists among the Irish laboring class were. They seemed to him to be far too cosmopolitan, too internationalist, too in thrall to those "uplifters of humanity" who would "cover up the oppression of Small Nations" with the "cant" of "the Brotherhood of Man." They and Irish labor generally had put the social-class cart ahead of the nationalist horse.[24]

The labor movement, including its most radical wing, had nothing to fear from Sinn Féin nationalists, and for reasons of which Connolly would have approved. Spalpeen said there was not the remotest chance "that an Irish Republic would be established by . . . capitalists." Indeed, it "would be established in spite of, and in the teeth of, opposition from the aristocratic and capitalistic classes." It was unimaginable to him "to suppose that the evils from which we have suffered under a foreign flag should be perpetuated under our own." Then came, however, his predictable conclusion—what was increasingly becoming Ireland's only conclusion: "It must be obvious that economic freedom is contingent upon political independence." Contingency did not mean that "Labour must wait," nor did Sinn Féin ever say that it must. But neither was it fair for labor to argue that "independence must wait." No one had to wait. The "heroic combination . . . of Pearse and Connolly" would be restored, and the "sunshine of Freedom, . . . [and] truth will be revealed." "Sinn Féin and Labour can go hand-in-hand."[25]

There were and are a great number of ways to describe the joining of the political and the social aspects of the Irish resistance. Spalpeen has them "holding hands." The political and the social were one cause, as mysterious in its way as the Catholic trinity, and, if culture and language are worked into the amalgam—and they should be—as literally three-sided. Regardless of descriptive language, Ireland came first, first in order and first to mind. Sinn Féin and Labor were hand-in-hand, but Sinn Féin's was the guiding hand. That was what Marx and Lenin didn't get; they didn't understand that Ireland was a world unto itself, known only to itself. The Irish were radical enough but it was a Celtic-style radicalism. It was of their own devising, arising out of the Irish race. Spalpeen left the issue there.[26]

Not all of the Irish did. Many took the racial aspect a long step beyond where Spalpeen had left it. The Irish weren't just exploited colonials. They were exploited *white* colonials, the last such in all of Western Europe, if not the world. By definition, theirs was a "white" rebellion, and in a highly racialized and racist world, that was worth a great deal. They rebelled because they had genuine grievances, not because they were savages. There was no one among these Irish patriots who looked like or played the role of Toussaint L'Ouverture, or Crazy Horse, or Cetshwayo. (The Irish would have been better off had there been.) The year 1916 had the same legitimacy that Americans claimed for 1776. Both rebellions were in a just cause, both were led by honorable white men. The British ignored the Irish argument from whiteness, as they had every other defense the Irish had made for the righteousness of their cause. That was predictable. That some Irish made an argument from race was less so, but regardless of that, some did and it diminished the moral force of the entirety of their rebellion, particularly the anti-imperialism that was part of it.[27]

• • •

In April 1918, the government of British prime minister David Lloyd George attempted to restore the Irish to their proper standing as subordinate colonial West Brits by preparing legislation that would extend military conscription to Ireland. The Irish response was swift and fiercely hostile. The provisional government of the rebel Irish Republic said that "the passing of the Conscription Bill ... must be regarded as a declaration of war on the Irish nation." To accept it was "to acknowledge ourselves as slaves"—a loaded term with obvious racial overtones. The Catholic hierarchy jumped in, calling conscription a "crisis of unparalleled gravity," a "scourge" that had to be resisted in "every way possible." Sinn Féin said that the British wanted "to harness the people of Ireland to England's war-chariot.... don the uniform of our seven-century-old oppressor, and place ... [Irish] lives at the disposal of the military machine that holds our nation in bondage." I am struck by how like rebel Butte in 1917 all of that sounds.[28]

There were some "cause of labor" aspects to this nationalist controversy. Connolly had spoken of "hunger-scription," of capital laying men off in order to drive up enlistments. But the threat of conscription was almost entirely a national issue, not a labor one. And that makes it more important that it was met on the ground not by a Sinn Féin–sponsored protest march but by a general strike of Irish workers, the same who had led the Irish cheers for the Bolsheviks and had openly consorted with internationalists as well as with British labor. On April 23, "all work and all business ceased for 24 hours throughout the whole country except the Unionist districts in Ulster." (E. P. Thompson—"out of respect," one would presume—would have understood perfectly). "The stoppage was complete and entire, an unprecedented event outside the continental countries." Britain backed down and Ireland was "preserved ... as the only unconscripted country in Europe." Labor had shown itself to be "an invaluable industrial auxiliary to the other militant forces." It should be added that "industrial auxiliary" was the language of the ILPTUC, not of Sinn Féin.[29]

Labor seems also to have gotten Spalpeen's point about contingency and first things coming first. I can't know whether Spalpeen had anything to do with putting labor in the streets in protest of the draft. His arguments, however, have resonance regardless of who made them. They and others like them pushed Irish labor toward radical nationalism. The working-class "auxiliaries" would, in time, demand a full and coequal partnership with Sinn Féin. Emmet O'Connor writes that the conscription crisis drove Irish labor toward a "consensus nationalism." But it also pushed a larger segment of Irish nationalism than before toward a consensus labor radicalism: Sinn Féiners hand-in-hand with labor, both, to an extent, now hand-in-hand with Russia.[30]

Later that year, in the December 1918 general elections, the ILP and Sinn Féin had another opportunity to demonstrate that new understanding. The election was of Irish representatives to the British Parliament. The candidates of Sinn Féin ran on the promise that, if elected, they would take their seats not in London but in Dublin, in an Irish parliament, a *Dáil Éireann*. The election was a referendum on radical Irish nationalism, on 1916—both the Rising and the executions of its leaders—and on the conscription crisis. In order not to split the nationalist and anti-imperialist vote, the Labor Party withdrew from the contest, leaving the nationalist field entirely to Sinn Féin.

The ILP explained itself simply: On the national question, Ireland required "unity"; thus, and only for the moment, the unions "willingly sacrifice[d] ... their aspirations towards political power" in order that "fortunes of the nation ... be enhanced." Obviously, the Labour Party still had aspirations to political power, but it was as confident as Spalpeen that Sinn Féin was led by "men and women who view problems from the standpoint of the working-class" and that the Irish Republic that would emerge from the 1918 election would "be a Workers' Republic, not an imitation of those republics of Europe and America, where political democracy is but a cloak for "capitalist oligarchy." No "miniature" American republic was envisioned by either side.[31]

Sinn Féin won an important victory in 1918: Of the 105 contested seats, 73 were won by rebels, 37 of whom were still in jail. The popular vote behind those totals can be confusing—as they were in 1918. Sinn Féin won less than half of the votes cast, but it also won in twenty-five districts that it dominated but where no votes were cast because it was unopposed. To no one's surprise, the vote from Protestant-held districts in Ulster was overwhelmingly for Unionists. E. P. Thompson would have understood that too. As for the rest of Ireland, what would become the Free State, the Republican Sinn Féiners had the support of 70 percent of the voters. As for the "dominionists" in the

Irish Parliamentary Party, they had 73 seats in 1910, 6 in 1918. In short, the election was every bit the triumph the rebels claimed for it.[32]

Sinn Féin's victory was due in large part to the withdrawal of the Irish Labour Party. The members of Sinn Féin were in labor's debt. In January 1919, they discharged a part of that debt by drafting the Democratic Programme, a blueprint of the Irish Republic to come. The program did not go as far toward a socialist republic as many in the labor movement wanted, but, as Cronin put it, there was a "radical ring" to it—as there was to the 1916 Proclamation and Pearse's pamphlet "The Sovereign People" on which it was based. Later critics charged that the Democratic Programme was mere "poetry," Sinn Féin's way of appeasing labor by establishing a set of governing principles that the ILPTUC wanted but that Sinn Féin had no intention of implementing. It does not appear that way to me, but I will leave that issue to Irish historians to sort out.[33]

There are four parts of the Democratic Programme that are striking and deserving of notice. The first came in the Irish text of the program. Its official title in Irish was *Clar Oibre Poblacnaighe*, the Program of the Workers' Republic. A Workers' Republic, in general and in this Irish context, meant a socialist republic and was occasionally used as a synonym for one. Proclaiming it in Irish was a clear signal that this was to be an *Irish* workers'/socialist republic; tossing *oibre*, workers, into the title was not done casually. The second section worthy of notice was predictable and came straight from Pearse: The members of the *Dáil* "reaffirm[ed] that all right to private property must be subordinated to the public right and welfare." They *re*affirmed that Irish truth. Was that a bow toward Ireland 1916 or Ireland 1116? Either way, that was not the language of bomb-throwing Jacobins, but of a mystic Catholic poet with a radical edge and a strong sense of the Irish past.[34]

The next two notable sections are different, less leftist but no less revealing of the Irish war on the seam. The *Dáil* said that it was going to "abolish the present odious, degrading and *foreign* Poor Law System" and substitute for it a "sympathetic *native* scheme for the case of the Nation's aged and infirm." I will dodge the questions of whether "foreign" meant Protestant as well as English, and that "native" meant Catholic as well as Irish. Either way, the infirm needed the nation's help; the aged deserved the nation's gratitude. That was a native Irish sensibility, part of the Irish contribution to what Polanyi called the "double movement." There was a stark contrast between it and the modern system of the market-ruled British economy. This next provision was also native, but it arose less from leftovers from nonmarket economies than from the sturdiness of Irish memory and the depth of Irish rage. There is power and sadness in it: "It shall be the duty of the Republic to prevent the shipment from Ireland of food . . . until the wants of the Irish people are fully satisfied and the future provided for."[35]

Not long after the Democratic Programme was passed, the ILPTUC sent delegates to report on the labor movement in Ireland before the International Labour and Socialist Conference in Berne, Germany. The ILP delegates had a lot to say. Total membership in the TUC unions had reached 250,000 up from 50,000 in 1911, 150,000 in 1917. As nationalist fervor increased, so did union membership. They were in lockstep. The Irish then told the attendees that "in no country was the overthrow of . . . Tsardom hailed more gladly than in Ireland, and by no working class was the triumph of the Workers, Soldiers and Peasants of Russia . . . more enthusiastically welcomed than by Irish Labour." That was followed by effusive praise of Lenin and Trotsky and a promise that Ireland was ready to play its part in the "new era in proletarian history" that was then opening.[36]

The Irish labor delegates next put their nationalist credentials on display. The new Ireland would have a starring role in that opening. The Irish representatives recalled the time in 1897 when the Labor Party had led the nationalist protest of Queen Victoria's Jubilee celebration, and, in general, schooled the gathered socialist internationalists on the association of causes. They pointed out specifically that, "although no union, as such, had any part in the [1916] insurrection . . ., it is certain that the majority of the insurgents were Trade Unionists." Connolly's ICA was "solely . . . proletarian," and the Irish Volunteers were "largely proletarian." In other words, 1916 was the Irish version of a general strike as well as a blood sacrifice in the name of a *Poblacht na h-Éireann*.[37]

Then followed a reference to the "re-conquest of Ireland by the working class" and the stripping of all control by any "imperialist Power." "Re-conquest" is a peculiar and seldom-used word. The Irish delegates took it directly from Connolly's 1913 pamphlet of that title. Then came a statement directly attributed to Patrick Pearse: "Property must always be subordinate to Humanity, and Private Gain must ever give place to the Welfare of the People." Compare that line with this one from Pope Leo's *Rerum Novarum*: "Man should not consider his . . . possessions as is own, but as common to all, so as to share them." The delegation from the ILPTUC also put special emphasis on the generic anti-imperialism that was built into the Irish revolt and on its potential usefulness to the cause of socialism. It concluded by speaking again to the eagerness of the Irish to "carry [the socialist message] to the proletariats of other lands."[38]

• • •

The other land they had most in mind was the United States, for the obvious reason that there were millions of Irish there. Many, in Britain as well as in America, were convinced that Irish America was a kind of de facto "New Ireland" and, in some ways, more important to the cause of radical nationalism than the old one. Which leads to an important question: As noted, Lenin had said that Irish nationalist rebels could be "'of *immense practical* importance'" in mobilizing the British proletariat. The quote is from Mansergh; the italicized emphasis was Lenin's. Is it possible that Lenin thought Irish Americans could be of equal practical importance and in a similar cause? In 1882, the Anglo-Irishman Philip Bagenal had written that those he called America's Irish "exiles" had entered into "an alliance ... with what is known in America as the Labour party [and] ... in the interests of the most Radical of the democratic political section. The cause of the Irish tenants was identified with the cause of American labour, and Fenianism *joined hands* with the most violent advocates of revolution *all over the world*."[39]

Thirty-five years later, nothing had changed. Another Englishman, Hugh Pollard, wrote in 1922 that "in America" there was "an identity of interests between Irish-Catholic communities and extreme Labour organizations." Both Bagenal and Pollard also said the American Irish were more radical in their nationalist demands and more willing to use physical force to win them than were the Old Country Irish. The seam was tighter, and both sides of it more militant among the exiles. Bagenal and Pollard made E. L. Godkin seem prescient.[40]

It is extremely doubtful that Lenin had read either Bagenal or Pollard. But was he of similar mind? Connolly had spent seven years in America; Larkin was in America from 1915 to 1923. There were hundreds of other Irish as radical as those two and hundreds of thousands more who linked causes as they had. Were they Lenin's point of entry into the American industrial proletariat? The representatives of the ILPTUC thought they were, or could be made to be. They spoke frequently of the martyred Connolly, calling him "the most brilliant and ablest thinker Irish labour has ever produced." He was that. But he was also "the mentor of many of the best men and women in the movement in ... the United States." Among "the Irish workers in the United States[,] ... Connolly" had carried on "a successful Socialist propaganda."[41]

They noted as well the work of the Irish labor movement in "circulat[ing] ... in the United States, etc., regular supplies of news and views of its activities in Ireland." It is unimaginable that the Irish leftward tilt was not known among the Irish in America, including those in Butte. There was even in 1909 an American edition of Connolly's 1897 pamphlet "Erin's Hope," still the best short account of Connolly's ambitions for Ireland and the Irish. How many American Irish approved of what they were learning is unknowable, but Celtic communism—or Celtic habits of the heart—were clearly pushing a sizable number of them leftward.[42]

Whether the American Irish were pushed as far leftward as Kraditor's preradicalized immigrant Jews, Finns, and Franco-Belgians is unknowable. But specific to the Jews, I would note that Pollard was convinced that

"Socialist propagandism has been mainly carried on by [people] of Celtic or Semitic blood"—again, the focus on race. Brendan Behan may have been right—he frequently was: "The Hebrews and the Gaels have much in common. Both are exotic enough to be interesting and foreign enough to be alarming." In this connection, it's also worth quoting a couple of lines from a poem by Michael Gold, an American Jew and a founder of the American Communist Party. In his "Ode to Walt Whitman," Gold wrote of the "greenbaums and kelleys," and of their "Lenin dreams / Deep in the gangrened basements / Where Walt Whitman's America / Aches to be born." Gold's paean to Whitman doesn't indicate whether "Kelley" was *preradicalized* by what he had known in and of Ireland or radicalized by what he encountered in America. Either way, like Greenbaum, he belonged on the list of those with "Lenin dreams." (Adding a second "e" to Irish surnames was a *shoneen* trick to disguise their Irishness; Gold may be excused for not knowing that).[43]

There were a lot of Irish like Mike Gold's "Kelley." Kraditor's "handful" seriously underestimates the number of Irish American "Lenin dreamers." I repeat Emmet Larkin's definitive claim: Jim Larkin was not an "aberration." There were a lot like him. And in almost every instance, their introduction to leftist labor politics began with lessons taught by Fenians—that is, physical force Irish nationalists. As important, their labor radicalism never lost its Fenian accent. William Z. Foster, the American Communist son of Galway immigrants, explained it simply: It was "as natural to hate capitalistic tyranny in the United States as English tyranny in Ireland." One needn't have shared Foster's radicalism to understand his point.[44]

In his 1939 *Pages of a Worker's Life,* Foster wrote that by about 1910 there was an "Irish Federation" of the left wing of the American Socialist Party; this quite unofficial "federation" had a "high back[ed] ... soap-box" near Times Square and various of its "soap-boxers" spoke from it almost nightly. The platform was "surmounted by three flags—the Irish on one side, the American on the other and the red flag in the center." The presence of the American flag was not entirely a matter of custom and good manners, but neither was it well-fitted to the other two—or they to it. That the red flag was accorded prominence of place would have surprised no one. These were Marxist platforms. It was that green flag next to the red one that is the issue here. Someone in the American socialist movement must have thought that the green flag and the red flag went well together. That someone was probably a part of the "Irish federation," but Irish or not, putting the sign of Irish resistance next to the emblem of Marxist revolution said something important about both. Doing it in the United States added to that importance.[45]

Contemporary American radicals knew of these Irish, knew even a little about Ireland, about Brits behaving badly, and about America's working-class Irish and the gangrened tenement basements where they lived. One of those was the communist Benjamin Gitlow, son of one of Kraditor's radical-on-arrival Russian immigrant Jews. Gitlow would have agreed with Emmet Larkin; Irish radicals were "numerous and significant." In place of Foster's "Irish federation" reference, Gitlow wrote of the "Irish contingent" within American communism. "The American communist movement," he said, owed "a great deal to "Irish and the Irish-American radicals." From them "the communists got organizers, writers, editors, speakers, trade union leaders and valuable contacts with important elements in other . . . unions."[46]

The Irish, Gitlow went on, "constituted a virile, aggressive element which boasted of revolutionary traditions and was proud of the achievements of the Irish revolutionists." The first part of that comment—the list of useful services and the "virility and aggressiveness" with which they carried them out—was close to cartoon Irishry. It was the second part of Gitlow's remark—that oddly phrased history lesson—that makes what he said important. By the "revolutionary traditions" of the Irish and all those "Irish revolutionists," Gitlow can only have meant that 1916 was the Irish version of Jacobinism or the Red October. The Easter Rising was as much a socialist revolt as a "strike for national freedom."[47]

Gitlow was not the only American leftist who would have thought that. Irish rebels were becoming something resembling cult figures. They were seen not just as "virile" Marxist warriors and esteemed as such, they were also aesthetes. The combination proved irresistible to some of those who merged the political with the poetic and assumed that the Irish were both. Emma Goldman, than whom few in America were more radical, convinced herself that the Irish were "unspoiled by the dulling hand of civilization and free from artifice." They retained a "simplicity of faith—in what, she did not say—and "were full of fancy and dreams." They were "wild and fiery." Louise Bryant, feminist social critic, wife of John Reed, and committed Bolshevik, said that the Easter Rising was "led by poets and scholars . . . fighting with . . . a copy of Sophocles in one hand and a rifle in the other." The choice of Sophocles was to make a scholarly point. Bryant simply assumed that they had already read all of Marx and Lenin. Even H. L. Mencken abandoned his hard-hitting journalistic style to make the same argument. The Irish, he wrote, "face a firing-squad with sheaves of sonnets under their arms."[48]

There was a great deal of silliness in all that. But it counts far less than the fact that those so remote from the Irish made the case. Gitlow's reading of Easter 1916 recapitulated Connolly's nonseverable causes, Irish nationalism holding hands with socialism. Bryant's recalled the point about saints, scholars, and subversives and arose from wishful thinking. Both, however, suggest that the "communist movement" was aware not only of what the Irish Left wanted 1916 to be, but of the transnational sensibilities and "Lenin-dreams" that made them think that they could have what they wanted. But add the

"The Irish Contingent" among America's Radicals 163

James Connolly speaking on behalf of the IWW, Union Square, Greenwich Village, New York, May 1, 1908. Next to the podium is the banner of the Irish Socialist Club. It read *"Fag a'Beáloc,"* "Clear the Way." American capitalism honed the radicalism that Connolly read into Irish history. Connolly, to an extent, "Celticized" the radicalism of American labor. Photo courtesy of Library of Congress.

corollary: The power brokers of Britain and of America were equally aware of joined causes and of the transatlantic reach of those causes. The capitalists and imperialists, the *shoneen* Irish and the anti-Irish, the anglophiles and the Anglo-Saxon supremacists, all who were lined up against both communist revolutions and Irish revolutionists, also knew what "Celtic communism" was and that there was an American version of it.

Gitlow identified two of those Celtic revolutionists: James Connolly and Jim Larkin. He identified Connolly as "a scholar and revolutionary leader[,] ... the Lenin of the Irish radicals." Connolly had "studied the words of Marx and applied his *special brand of Irish Marxism* to the Irish revolutionary cause for independence." The Irish, in America as surely as in Ireland, "looked up to James Connolly." Certainly, some did. The same ones, joined by a great many non-Irish others, also looked up to Jim Larkin. Gitlow pointed out, with justice, that Larkin "must be considered one of the founders of the American communist movement," followed—without pause for explanation—by a reference to Larkin's "'devoutly adhering' Catholicism." Then came another of Gitlow's contributions to transnational sensibilities and preradicalization: "Larkin's tactics and policies sprang from Irish experiences rather than from what the conditions in the U.S. demanded." As with many, their erraticism antedated their immigration.[49]

• • •

Ten years before his comments on Larkin, Gitlow had written about another Irish American communist, William Francis Dunne. He said nothing about Dunne's Irishness or about his Catholic upbringing or about the time Dunne had spent working as a skilled electrician three thousand feet underground in the Anaconda Company's Neversweat Mine in Butte. But what he did say was significant. Dunne had been the editor of the "famous labor paper, the *Butte Daily Bulletin*," one of the founding journals of the left-wing Federated Press, and, as Gitlow pointed out, "the largest labor daily in the United States at that time." It was also, as Joseph Freeman, another Jewish-American communist, pointed out, the "only daily of any kind which supported the Bolshevik revolution in Russia from the beginning."[50]

That wasn't all that commended Dunne. Gitlow noted with approval Dunne's "appearance." It "was the opposite of what a Communist was expected to look like." Dunne looked like the amateur boxer he had been, a "proletarian rough-neck," the "'wild bull from Montana,' as he was known." Freeman spoke similarly. Dunne was "the hero of Bloody Butte, . . . a short and stocky" man "with a tremendous barrel-chest, solid as a rock, and a dark, heavy Irish face. [His] reading was wide, ranging from Lenin to Joyce." "He had in him the traditional Irish poetry. . . . Yet his contempt for the literary triflers of bohemia was boundless." In Dunne's mind "good literature . . . could arise only out of the class war." Dunne reviled the "phony arrogance of certain bohemians who fancied they had a monopoly of brains and knowledge, when they actually understood nothing of the essential struggles of our epoch."[51]

There was more to those comments than just casual description. Clearly, communists were "expected to look" a certain way, in large measure because they did look a certain way. There was a chic-chic quality to being an American Communist. It was role-play for many, and there were American leftists who acted and dressed the part. Elizabeth Gurley Flynn, of radical Irish descent, called some of them "intellectual dilettanti," and "infantile Leftists." William Foster said many on the American left came from what he contemptuously called the "better clawses," as unfamiliar with workers as they were with work. Connolly said the American radical movement was filled with "faddists and cranks," dabblers who saw communism as a forum, a "means of ventilating their theories on . . . sex, religion, vaccination, vegetarianism, etc." Larkin agreed, adding to the list of cranks those so-called leaders who "loved . . . long words and abstract reasoning which went over the head of the masses."[52]

Like the others of the "Irish contingent," Dunne was not that sort of communist. He thought of himself as a writer with a genuine and informed interest in literature and culture. "Intellectual," however, was "a term of contempt." And never would he act like one. Indeed, he acted like Patsy Caliban. Gitlow told of the time that Dunne "took the floor [to speak] in his stocking feet and with his shirt tails out of his pants—drunk of course." He mentioned that Stalin liked Dunne, in large part because Dunne was not a Jew. Stalin was also convinced that Dunne's radical credentials, including his distaste for the radical haute couture of Greenwich Village, were entirely genuine. Unfortunately, Stalin learned that the Irishman drank too much—which, coming from that source, spoke volumes. He once dispatched Dunne to Outer Mongolia, ostensibly in the interests of the Comintern, in fact to dry out in a Mongolian sanitarium.[53]

His personal habits aside, Dunne's *Butte Bulletin* was as furiously radical as Gitlow portrayed it. In 1920, Colonel A. S. Peake, a military intelligence officer stationed in occupied Butte, called the *Bulletin* "one of the most radical papers published in the United States. It is thoroughly seditious." The war had been over for a year and a half when Peake filed his report; the reference to sedition can only have been to comments such as the workers "must take over and operate the mines, mills, and factories for the good of society" or Dunne's call for the striking miners of Butte each to buy a "Springfield rifle and 1000 rounds of ammo." It might have been that editorial that prompted the Anaconda Company to put gun turrets on some of its mine head frames and station armed company riflemen in them. As Gitlow said, Dunne's was a "famous labor paper." He didn't add "radical" to that; he didn't need to.[54]

It was also, however, if far less famously, a radical *Irish* paper. Dunne's labor militancy was joined to an equally militant Irish republican nationalism. Workers taking over the mines "for the good of society" was standard Marxist fare. It was also, however, the specific language Pearse and Connolly—and Sinn Féin—had used. Similarly, his idea of arming strikers was obviously not original with Dunne, but it had an Irish connection with Connolly's ICA, not to mention Ed Boyce's plan to build a twenty-five-thousand-member WFM militia. Dunne had to have known something of Boyce's plan and he certainly knew of what Connolly had done, or tried to do, with the ICA.

Which returns the discussion to Colonel Peake and the meaning of "thoroughly seditious." In 1919, the socialist *New York Call* carried a short account of "'Fighting Dunne,' editor of the *Butte Bulletin*," the "only paper in the U.S. to support without reservation the Russian Revolution ... and the program of the Bolsheviks." Dunne, the paper continued, had "fought the cruel Anaconda Copper Company," which was not work for the faint of heart. The offices of the *Bulletin* had to be heavily guarded, and Dunne was "often compelled to edit his paper with a gun by his side." But then the

Call said this: "He is as enthusiastic a supporter of the movement for Irish freedom as he is of the cause of freedom for the people of America." Note, "the people of America," not the "Irish people," but note more closely the reference to Irish nationalism. The *Call* then asked the question I implied above: "Which is his offense in the eyes of Bourbon democracy? We do not know. Probably both." I don't know either. Probably both.[55]

What became the *Butte Bulletin* began life as the "Butte Strike Bulletin," the flyer announcing not that a union had called a strike against the mines but that the Pearse-Connolly Irish Independence Club had. As noted, I think that Dunne wrote the Pearse-Connolly strike notice. That's what makes the editorial policy of the paper so important. The *Butte Bulletin*, both during and after Dunne's editorship, was filled with news about Ireland and the Irish people, exiles and home guards alike. Dunne even carried stories about movies that were filled with "stage Irish." These were "insults to Ireland and the Irish." But Dunne did not blame nativists for this outrage. The attacks on the Irish were straight from the "capitalist" party platform. They were the products of "obnoxious . . . British . . . imperialistic propaganda . . . and the picture show trust." Predictably, given the source, it wasn't just the Irish who were being maligned. "Russia and labor generally," along with the Irish—"three movements for freedom," Dunne called them—were all being "shown in dark colors."[56]

Dunne did that sort of thing all the time. He moved from Irish topics to labor topics in the same sentence. His coverage of them was as seamless as the topics themselves. The issue from Mar. 11, 1919, carried a banner headline, "IRELAND WILL BE FREE." Free of what or from what, he didn't say. Six days later, on St. Patrick's Day, he explained that the only thing "that stops the 'Land of the Shamrock' from being a 'Haven of Joy'" was not the curse of English imperialism—the usual assigned villain—but "the curse of capitalism," America's prominently included. That curse was also about to be lifted. Dunne was sure of it. Irish nationalism was "swinging rapidly to the left," he said. It was "oriented towards labor." Then came his addition to the concordance of nonseverable causes: "The fusing process at which Connolly worked has held firm." "Fusing" was the way a skilled electrician would be expected to describe a nonseverable seam. On another occasion, Dunne used a more common metaphor: "We have today woven in with the national aspirations of the Irish people, a hatred of capitalism."[57]

Dunne took his next theme directly from the Celtic communist playbook: "The ancient Irish," wrote Dunne, "were a communistic people." Even Connolly had not pushed them that far. "You cannot have the spirt of old Irish life without restoring the communal spirit . . . the old communal traditions . . . and you cannot do this without utterly destroying capitalism." "Not Ireland for the . . . capitalists of Ireland," he wrote in a close paraphrase of Connolly, whose writings he clearly had read, and of Spalpeen, whose pamphlet he may have read.

Dunne, however, wasn't finished. He carried the Irish story far beyond where Connolly had left it and toward internationalism, what Spalpeen had rejected as the ideology of believers in the "brotherhood of man." Dunne's ideology was professedly that "Ireland free" would mean—and Dunne put this in large, bolded capital letters—"THE WORLD FOR THE WORKERS." Small colonial nations in revolt ordinarily do not have such outsized influence. But Ireland did. In Dunne's mind, anything short of the world for the workers would be a betrayal of the genius of the Irish race. This was Dunne's "Lenin dream." That he chose to express it using Irish images and Irish events matters greatly. The radicalism of the *Butte Bulletin* was obvious, but so was the fact that its radicalism was expressed on the seam lines between nationalism and socialism and between Irish nationalism and anticolonialism internationally.[58]

I offer one literally graphic example: In the issue of February 17, 1922, the *Bulletin* carried a political cartoon by the left-wing socialist artist Hugo Gellert. It's a simple illustration with three characters: A powerfully built young Irishman is in harness, straining to pull a primitive plow. A pudgy Englishman, prosperously dressed and looking a lot like David Lloyd George, is handing the reins and whip to an equally pudgy, bulbous-nosed Irishman wearing a shirt with a picture of a harp on it, and with a visage strikingly similar to one of Thomas Nast's simian Irish—a stage Irish *shoneen*. The caption reads "John Bull to the Irish Bourgeois: 'You Drive Him Now!'"[59]

The content and context of the cartoon were entirely Irish. It attested to Ireland's lasting relevance to leftist ideologues, in part because of the essential rightness of the Irish cause, in larger part because of its usefulness as a case study. Granted, radicals had to pound a lot of square Irish pegs into round Marxist holes, but those with Leninist dreams—including Lenin—were well practiced at constructing reality and making it do what they wanted it to do. Gellert's cartoon applied everywhere for the simple reason that the bourgeoisie wrapped themselves in their nation's flag and controlled the nationalist discourse according to their own class interests everywhere.

Hugo Gellert was the cartoonist of record for radicals wherever found; he chose Ireland intentionally and for reasons that radicals well understood. Dunne had to have loved Gellert's cartoon, both for its ideological message and for Gellert's choice of Ireland as his example. It's even possible that Dunne was among those who commissioned the piece. As he wrote in the same issue in which the cartoon appeared, it made no difference whether "the arm that cracks the whip wears a sleeve of green instead of a sleeve of red." He had direct knowledge of sleeves of green cracking whips over Irish

Hugo Gellert, "John Bull to the Irish Bourgeois: 'You Drive Him Now!'" 1922. Gellert was a well-known left-wing cartoonist. The subject matter here is entirely Irish, but it appeared in Bill Dunne's *Butte Bulletin*, which circulated widely. Obviously, it was thought to have relevance to an American audience. Courtesy Butte/Silver Bow Archives.

labor. Gellert's message would make more tangible sense in Butte than anywhere else in America. For more than forty years, hundreds of green-sleeved Irish mine bosses had driven thousands of Irish laborers. The lesson for the Irish working class was clear.[60]

Those of Butte's Irish not blinded by the sunburstery of recreant and false patriots had learned that lesson years earlier. In the 1890s, Ed Boyce condemned Marcus Daly for being a bad Irishman. Larkin and Dunne went after John Ryan and Con Kelley, Daly's successors as managers of the Anaconda, for the same offense. Shane Leslie had described Ryan as one of the "Irish millionaires, the type of silent, indefatigable business man that the Celtic race is supposed to be unable to produce." Dunne hoped the race would never produce another one. Dunne condemned to labor's hell, as had Boyce, "the sickening sycophancy" of those in the Butte Miners' Union who had fastened the "coils of treachery" around the miners, and "fawned" over Ryan as the previous generation had fawned over Daly.[61]

Dunne was no kinder to Con Kelley. He wrote that though he was the "chairman of one of the local bodies favoring Irish independence, his black and tans commit the same crimes on the bodies of Irishmen in Butte that the British government commits in Ireland." A week later, Kelley told the *Engineering and Mining Journal* that the new and radical unions of Butte were giving their "financial support to a . . . Soviet newspaper whose avowed object was destruction of the Anaconda Company and the AFofL." By "Soviet newspaper," he can only have meant the *Bulletin* and he wasn't far wrong.[62]

Dunne also attacked Silver Bow County (Butte) Sheriff John K. O'Rourke, who "did ACM's bidding in firing" on striking miners. O'Rourke "supports freedom for Ireland, but favors the shooting of Irish in Butte." He assailed James B. Mulcahy of the *Butte Independent* as a "slimy unmentionable" who took his "orders from the 6th floor of the Hennessey Building," ACM's headquarters in Butte. Dunne spelled Mulcahy as "Mulcahey."[63]

As Gitlow had said, the *Bulletin* was the largest labor daily in the United States. Dunne said another American left-wing newspaper, was "the most hated labor man of the West." The paper was not just Butte's bulletin; it was a message from Butte to workers everywhere. That was especially the case if the workers were Irish, not because Dunne loved them more or thought them singularly afflicted—though he may have. His internationalism was genuine. He meant it when he proclaimed that Ireland would be free and that the result of Irish freedom would be that the workers would own the world. That appeared to be a leap of faith—and logic—only to those not of the erratic Irish Left.[64]

Dunne's responsibility was to convince working-class Irish Americans that the "great mass of the Irish working class ... in the United States ... had to be made to understand [that] the [radical labor] movement in Ireland" was the same as the "movement here in America." American Irish workers had to learn that there were no bourgeois Irish nationalists because by all that was held holy, there could not be. It was a contradiction in terms. Unfortunately, too many Irish American working people had become "the unconscious tools of cheap politicians," too attendant on the "hypocritical whines of Irish-American ... 'shoneens.'" Once the Irish American working class "closed their ears" to those barroom and polling-booth patriots, "the reign of industrial autocracy [would be] over," over in Ireland, over in America, over everywhere. As Irish labor was tutor to American, so American labor—with some welcome help from the movement in Britain—would be tutor to the world. That, too, was part of Lenin's dream, as it had been part of Marx's.[65]

Which raises an obvious and intriguing question: Is it possible that the Communist International (Comintern) financed and, in a sense, ran the *Butte Bulletin*? Con Kelley had said that the *Bulletin*, the official organ of the very Soviet-sounding "Workers, Soldiers, and Sailors Councils," was a "Soviet newspaper" and that Bill Dunne was being paid in "Moscow gold." There were rumors in Butte that *Bulletin* bank deposits were "a consignment of Russian rubles." That's unlikely, but obviously the Comintern was involved in American affairs; it did look for America's alienated and preradicalized.

Did the Comintern regard the Irish as among them? Did it pay any attention to Irish nationalist clubs, the radical physical force nationalists of the Clan na Gael, for an obvious example? Or the various Connolly Clubs, including Butte's Pearse Connolly Irish Independence Club, for a more obvious example? Did the communists insinuate themselves into and provide copy to and pay the bills of left-wing Irish American as well as labor newspapers?[66]

Bill Dunne and the *Butte Bulletin* are the matters at hand here, and there is no direct evidence from the archives of the Communist International that any money was ever sent directly to the *Butte Bulletin* and its combative editor. Documents were found indicating that the Comintern budget included sums of money for "Negro" and "Irish" propaganda efforts and for unnamed English language newspapers in the United States. Some of that money was routed through John Reed, whose close ties to Larkin and Gitlow—and probably to Dunne—should be mentioned. That, however, is all that is known. Dunne was a communist, and the *Bulletin* was a communist newspaper. That he was sent to Butte on assignment, as it were, by American or even Russian communists is possible. The important issue, however, is not "the Soviet versus home-grown world of American communism," or even who paid Bill Dunne's bills, but the fact that a radical American labor paper would carry so many Irish stories. The Reds wore green.[67]

• • •

Had Bill Dunne's *Butte Bulletin* been the only example of an American newspaper operating on the radical edge of both the Irish national cause and the cause of labor, it could be explained on the basis of the sui generis history of Butte—the state-of-the-art working-class Irish town. There weren't many other papers that pushed "fused" causes as far leftward as Dunne had. But there were a couple and, like the *Bulletin*, they say something important about Celtic communists in America. One of those papers was *The Truth*, published in Duluth, Minnesota, by the Workers' Socialist Publishing Company and edited by a "feisty little Irishman," Dublin-born Jack Carney—"Comrade Carney," as he called himself. The paper began life in 1912 as the left-wing *Labor Leader*. In 1917, it was renamed *The Truth* and in 1918 Carney assumed its editorship.[68]

Carney had been in Dublin on Easter Monday, 1916, but not as an active participant in the rebellion. He had known James Connolly well and had campaigned with him in Belfast in 1913. More important, he was Jim Larkin's personal secretary. Larkin had converted Carney to socialism and the two remained close friends. Later in 1916, Carney immigrated to Chicago, where he joined Larkin in editing the American version of the *Irish Worker*. Like Larkin, Carney affiliated with the Communist Labor Party (CLP) rather than the more doctrinaire and "intellectual" Communist Party (CP). By 1920, after three years with *The Truth*, Carney was in Butte as coeditor with Bill Dunne of the *Butte Bulletin*. In 1923, he returned to Ireland, where he continued his active involvement in the international communist movement. His radical credentials, in other words, were intact and well known.[69]

Carney's years in Duluth are of greatest importance to this discussion. That he was sent there seems obvious; sent by whom is considerably less so, though it's safe to assume that Larkin and Dunne had something to do with it. The headline of *The Truth* after the armistice—and just after Carney's release from jail, where he was serving time on a sedition charge—was "The War Is Dead. Vive Revolution." But whose revolution and what of the gospel according to Connolly and Larkin and the others on the Irish left? He answered those questions on Easter Sunday, 1919, "the third year of the Irish Republic," when he issued what appears to have been the only edition of the *Irish Felon*. It was a commemoration of 1916, what Carney called the "first bright star that appeared through the dark clouds of militarism," imperialism, and capitalism.[70]

In a later issue of *The Truth*, Carney elaborated on that theme. The occasion was the death on a hunger strike of Cork's mayor, the Republican nationalist Terrence MacSwiney. Carney's account was another model of his sunburstery and rhetorical excess. "Within [MacSwiney]," he told his readers, "was Ireland; a Free Ireland. The Ireland of his love. Strong and mighty Ireland; suffering and bleeding Ireland. Hopeful Ireland. . . . Outside stood England—brutal, heartless England . . . stiff and stony. . . . Raw, uncultured, beastlike, murderous, she licked her vulgar lips like a canibal [*sic*; perhaps he meant 'a caliban'?]. . . . And now she feasts upon the flesh of starved MacSwiney." How this played in St. Louis County (Duluth), with eighteen thousand Finnish-born to its five thousand Irish-born, is uncertain.[71]

In 1918, not long after he got to Duluth, Carney wrote a long article, "In Memory of the Irish Rebellion." Coming as it did from one who knew Connolly and Larkin intimately, Carney's piece reveals a great deal about the Irish Left and about the underlying theme of its propaganda in America. The "Rebels," Carney claimed, "knew they were marching to their deaths." He was certainly right about some of them. His next comment spoke of different sensibilities. "Many in [the United States—note that he did not say 'many Irish'] condemned them as foolish nationalists." Those Irish like himself, "who have lived and worked with [the Irish rebels]" knew better. "They were not nationalists" in the usual sense. "They rightly believed that before you can have the freedom of the whole world, nations must gain their freedom"—nationalism in the service of internationalism—Lenin's "oppressed nations" in the service of the world's "oppressed classes."[72]

It's that "freedom of the whole world" reference that mattered most. The story of "the great struggle for the emancipation *of the workers* from economic thralldom ... cannot be written without Irish names." Carney wrote of the "Irish race" and of its special and unique "genius." Indeed, he shouted it out in capital letters—"THE SOUL OF A NATION" would "LIVE AS LONG AS ITS PEOPLE LIVE." The soul of the Irish people was communal. They were good-hearted, born communists—and, as such, born to be communists. It was Carney's task to teach Irish Americans this truth and then to send them out to teach it to the entire American working class.[73]

He would, of course, have to deal with the Irish American bourgeois capitalists—he called them "scab herders"—as well as the multitude of Irish American politicians who did their bidding. The nationalism of these "professional" Irish was counterfeit. They would create an Ireland in the style of America. In another issue of *The Truth*, Carney argued that America could be a useful model for Ireland only if it had a "new Lady Liberty," this one holding the true "'lantern of freedom'—the tablet of Soviet Russia." At the bottom of the page was a cartoon drawing of a statue in New York Harbor: Lady Liberty, with a broad smile, is raising her lantern with one hand and holding the Communist Manifesto tightly to her breast with the other. By Carney's Irish reckoning, the United States was run on the "*shoneen* principle," Americans exploiting other Americans with impunity, then buying off those they had methodically abused by giving them political "freedom," the right to vote for the capitalist of their choice.[74]

In 1919, Nora Connolly, the daughter of the martyred James, was part of a May Day celebration in Ireland. Her prepared remarks before an Irish audience were a summary of her father's dream of Ireland as a symbol of hope to the dispossessed and disconnected—to all the foster children of the world. What she said in Ireland demanded to be heard in America, by Irish and non-Irish alike. Carney reprinted her comments in their entirety. His headline read "The Red Flag in Ireland." Nora Connolly began on this International Workers "feast day" (an interesting use of "feast day") by congratulating the "Irish people." For the first time in Ireland's long history, "the people have demonstrated their comradeship with the workers of the world.... That was required and wishful rhetoric. This was not: "It spells the awakening ... to the fact that political freedom is not the be-all of freedom, that to be truly free, economic freedom must be linked with ... political freedom." Again, and always, those twain must meet.[75]

Nora Connolly went on: The Easter Rising primed the Irish, it was also preparation for what happened in Russia in 1917. The Bolsheviks made it "easy for [the Irish] to understand" what her father had been saying to them for more than two decades. The Irish placed those lessons "side by side with the system that prevails in America, and [they] have decided that the Russian system is ... the most just. And we in Ireland have long been hungry for justice." Implied by that comment is that the same was true of working-class Irish in America. Nora Connolly's remarks—and Carney's—deserve some attention, not because they were accurate descriptions of events, but because they reveal, as much as the accounts by Bill Dunne, the association of the Red and the Green and the importance attached to that association by the Red.[76]

There is one other radical newspaper meriting discussion. The *Producers' News* was a weekly journal of advanced left-wing politics published by the People's Publishing Company in Plentywood, Montana, the seat of Sheridan County in the far northeastern corner of the state, very near the North Dakota and Saskatchewan borders and overwhelmingly Scandinavian in ethnicity. There are more remote parts of the globe than Plentywood, Montana, but not many. The *Producers' News* began weekly publication in 1918 as the official organ of the Nonpartisan League. Its first editor was the aptly nicknamed Charles (Red Flag) Taylor. It was the league that sent Taylor to Plentywood to establish the *Producers' News* as a Nonpartisan League newspaper; it was also Taylor who, as he put it, "'took a step to the left,' joined the Communist Party USA, and made the *News* an openly communist newspaper. A half-century after the fact, Taylor told a researcher that the *Producers' News* was "financed directly by the Communist Party," and the Party "demanded and had direct supervision over it."[77]

Financed or not, controlled or not, the *News* followed the party line. Which lends a special interest to the fact that in 1925 Taylor was joined as editor by Irish-born "Colonel" Patrick J. Wallace—Pay Jay, or Paddy to his friends—and that in 1926, Wallace took over as full-time editor of the *News*. Taylor said Wallace was "'a smart Irishman,' but also an "opportunist" "freelancer and intriguer" who caused radicals "a lot of troubles." By the time Wallace got to Plentywood and the *Producers' News*, the dream of an Irish Workers' Republic was gone or at least forced underground—a new version of Hidden Ireland. The new recently christened Irish Free State, the one above ground and in the open was not a *Poblacht Oibrithe na h-Éireann*, an Irish Workers Republic; it was not even a *Poblacht* of whatever sort.

All that is known about Pat Wallace is taken from the biographical accounts he would occasionally put in the paper. To take the most charitable view of them, his accounts tended to exaggerate Wallace's career, particularly his role as a swashbuckling Marxist rapparee in various of the Irish rebellions. Wallace stayed in Plentywood until 1928. He wrote frequently on Irish issues, especially the more sorrowful of them. But his specific assignment seems to have been to write on the importance of building socialist coalitions of beleaguered farmers and exploited industrial workers. In Montana, that meant the Norwegian wheat farmers of Sheridan County and the Irish copper miners in Bill Dunne's Butte. Fortunately, this was a natural, almost heaven-sent, racial match. Taken together, according to Wallace, "the Irish and the Scandinavians . . . have done more to build up this republic than all the witch burning Anglo Saxons who ever landed at Plymouth Rock." That statement was likely as well received in Sheridan County as in Butte.[78]

In 1925, early in his tenure as editor, Wallace invited Tom O'Flaherty to speak in Plentywood. I've already introduced O'Flaherty: He and his older brother Liam were native Irish speakers, left-wing Irish nationalists, avowed communists who were convinced that the historians were bribed. By the mid-1920s, Tom O'Flaherty was an important part of the "Irish contingent" in the American communist movement. He had very complimentary things to say about the *Producers' News*. He called it "the best paper of its kind that I have seen anywhere." And he had seen the *Butte Bulletin*. As for Sheridan County, it was "Little Russia" (its climate made that true in more ways than politically), the "one bright spot . . . in the dreary . . . wastes of the Anaconda Company's State." That last part he probably learned from reading Bill Dunne, whom he knew well. I raise again a point that applies to many in this discussion: O'Flaherty had to have been sent to Plentywood as a roving reporter and radical columnist by the Communist Party. Whether the Russian or the American is unclear and unimportant.[79]

By 1927, O'Flaherty's column—which reads like it was written in Plentywood—appeared regularly in the *Producers' News*. His name was also on the masthead. In a 1927 column, he wrote of the "martyred" James Connolly and called Connolly a "practical revolutionist," one who "did not permit his knowledge of Marxist economics to excuse him from participating in the Nationalist struggle against the British Empire." That was a very revealing use of "to excuse." O'Flaherty explained what he meant by it: The "radical wing of Irish labor . . . was organizing" for "the final overthrow of British imperialism in Ireland and the abolition of Irish capitalism as well." He was quite wrong on both counts, but his conjoining of causes was revealing.[80]

In his 1934 book *Aranmen All*, O'Flaherty wrote—with no great affection—of his twenty years in America. "One moment I am in Aran, the next in Boston, New York, Chicago, . . . London, Paris, Berlin, Moscow." He seemed to be recording his stops in the order he made them. Tucked between Chicago and London, in that elided space, he listed Montana, a state among very large cities. I wish he'd said "Plentywood"; the incongruity would have been more striking. But "Montana" does that almost as well. For communists in league with Irish, it does so even better.[81]

• • •

What is important about Dunne, Carney, Wallace, and O'Flaherty is not just what they said but that it was they who said it, and that the Communist Party had chosen them to say it. It was remarkable that four Irishmen would be sent to distant American places to sound Marxist notes, and that they were sent because they were Irish and, it would appear, assumed to be naturally suited to the task. If certain reactionary elements in Britain and America conflated Irish nationalism and labor radicalism, it was partly because Irish nationalists and labor radicals conflated themselves. For Anglo-Americans, a free Ireland was bad enough; a Marxist free Ireland was horrible to contemplate. 1916 joined to 1917 had created something new and significantly more menacing.

The four Irish American radicals I have cut out from the pack—or the clan—spoke to the related truth that 1916/1917 had also created a new and more menacing Irish America. The alien and alienated in America were of interest to the Bolsheviks; they must have thought there were a few Irish among those alienated, some likely "Lenin dreamers." People treated as aliens tend to be alienated, whether in the Marxian sense or in the less ideologically loaded sense of social estrangement and cultural isolation. The radicals, of course, were a minority of these. That was true of radicals in Ireland as well. Being in the minority is a definitional part of being a radical. There didn't have to be many for those there were to be important. That was also true of every racial and ethnic group in America—including Kraditor's pre-radicalized Jews, Finns, and Franco-Belgians. But note too, as Kraditor did not, that these others never said, as the Irish did, that their radicalism was a consequence of who they were. They never said that they were radical *because* Jewish, Finnish, and Franco-Belgian.

There were Irish who were radical because they were Irish, as if it were a special racial calling. That in itself, in an American context, was outlandish and deserving of the attention I've given it. Irish radicals need only speak to their minority selves. I do not offer up the *Butte Bulletin, The Truth,* and *The Producers News* as typical of the Irish American press. For every Bill Dunne and the *Butte Bulletin* there were dozens of James Mulcahys and the *Butte Independent*. That is no reason to dismiss the Dunnes as aberrant and bring the Mulcahys forward as representative. It's a reason to study Dunne and go look for more like him, erratic Irish, America's useful misfits, guest workers with long-term visas, Patsy Calibans with an Irish collectivist sensibility and a rebellious disposition. It's not important—and the question of to what extent they were radicalized in Ireland and to what extent in America would have to be resolved—but I think there were enough of them to have earned for the Irish a place on Kraditor's list.

CHAPTER SIX

A "People Very Unlike Any Other People"
The Irish Catholic Challenge to American Capitalism

> "[T]his heart-destroying, soul-shriveling idea of production solely for . . . profits may give way to production for the good of all mankind."
> —Frank Walsh, *Lawson and Liberty* (1915) in McCartin, *Labor's Great War*, 22

Arthur Balfour, the English chief secretary for Ireland between 1887 and 1891, once said that Ireland "is the Ireland *we* made." He didn't indicate whether that was for better or worse, but the italicized *we* was his. In other words, Ireland was born in a British prison. Or, to switch metaphors, England was the ventriloquist, Ireland was one of its colonial dummies. As scholars of colonialism and postcolonialism have found, even after the imperial strings have been cut, the dummies continue to dance as before. Balfour's imperious comment was more to the point of Ireland and Irish nationalism than to the Irish people. But implied by what he said was that the people, the Irish as a race, were also English-made. Race and nation were separate, but they overlapped; each shaped the other. In that context, Balfour's comment may be applied to both. The Irish people thought and acted as their English masters bade them. They spoke the lines that the English had written for them.[1]

The national or political cause had dominated Ireland's English problem for centuries. It was occasionally accompanied by references to Irishness, but Ireland as an independent political entity was one thing, being culturally Irish was a separate thing. Theoretically, Ireland could be free and the Irish thoroughly anglicized; or Ireland could be a subject colony and thoroughly Irish. In the real world, however, the political and the cultural were mutually dependent. Each led inexorably to the other. Beginning in the 1880s, and continuing in fits and starts until well into the 1920s, the national cause was joined by a variety of Irish cultural nationalists—xenophobic Celticists in some instances—women and men with "vivid faces," said Yeats, who demanded that the Irish be restored to "psychological as well was political autonomy."[2]

The name usually given this cultural restoration is the Irish Literary Revival; on occasion, "Celtic" and "Renaissance" were added. It would be a stretch to call the Revival a movement, though it bore some of the features of a movement culture. Speaking generally, however, the Revival was too divided and factional, too amorphous, too unstructured; in other words, too Irish, to qualify. It was more nearly the Irish version of the antimodernist "movement" in America: the socially well-placed seeking the "real" Ireland and finding it either in the lives of the socially and culturally out of place or in the uncontaminated Irish past—modern antimodernists in an unauthentic search for the authentic.[3]

In the poetic language that fits, the Revival was more about Ireland's soul, its vital center, and the freedom of the Irish people to be their true and better Irish selves, free of the British, the Empire, and the mentality of both. Balfour said that "we English" made Ireland; now was the time for the Irish to remake themselves and build a "de-Anglicized" Ireland. That the Revivalists frequently idealized, romanticized, and sanitized Ireland as some mystical fairyland is important, but not as important as how politically and culturally deviant their ideas were. It was crucial that *sinn féin*, our (Irish) selves, be erratic; those out of time and out of place were self-defining. They also stood out from the modernist crowd and so were easier to spot.[4]

The English, said Augusta Gregory, had "thrust a mask upon us. . . . We had "worn [it] too long. . . . [I]t was time to appear in our own form." If only they knew what that was. As Agnes O'Farrelly wrote, "we do our best to be Irish people, but somehow, we do not properly understand how to be so." Constance Gore-Booth (Countess Markievicz) didn't understand either. The Irish knew "that the government of England [was] responsible for the famine." They also knew that the English system of government was "calculated to foster all . . . the petty, mean vices that follow on the idea that commercial prosperity and nothing else is the highest ideal of life. These ideas and many more, we have been allowing a subtle foe to graft on our national character at her will." In other words, England had made *shoneens* of too many Irish. More was involved and needed, however, than simply defining Irish as being not-English.[5]

The English, Gore-Booth went on, were like "slugs in our garden" to be "crushed . . . with . . . the tread of . . . fairy feet." The "fairy feet" reference with its clear allusion to Irish myth was a nice antimodern "psychological" touch. As for her politics, the countess stood with Connolly for a "Workers' Republic . . . a Soviet Republic! . . . a cooperative commonwealth."—a nice politically radical Republican touch—with some obvious psychological aspects to it as well. Irish Revivalists and Republicans alike blended the cause of Ireland and the cause of the Irish people, many, as with Countess Markievicz, in the same sentence, very nearly the same breath.[6]

Whether Revivalist or Republican, Irish and Ireland's erraticism was a recurring theme. Ireland would be different as the Irish people were different. Éamon de Valera said that the new Ireland would "show the world the might of moral beauty." It would be "the home of a people who valued material wealth only as a basis for right living, or a people who, satisfied with frugal comfort, devoted their leisure to the things of the spirit." Ireland, he told an American audience, had replaced the United States as the ruling city on a hill: "*We* are the spear-points of the hosts of political slavery, . . . we can be the shafts of dawn for the despairing and wretched everywhere."[7]

The "work of Ireland," wrote Yeats, "is to lift up its voice for spirituality, for ideality, for simplicity." It is not surprising that James Connolly had caught the contagion; he wanted "every man to live, if not under his own vine and fig tree, upon his own potato patch," surrounded by the "green fields of Erin," fields uncontaminated by "huge, ugly factories, with chimneys belching forth volumes of poisonous smoke and coating the [land] with a sooty desolation." Connolly may well be the only communist who ever protested factories and their smoke-belching chimneys. Belfast or Liverpool might have been on his mind. So might Butte.[8]

Irish-born Liam Mellows, who lived in the United States from 1917 until 1921 and accompanied de Valera on his extended American tour in 1919–1920, insisted that the Irish did "not seek to make [Ireland] a materially great country . . . following in the footsteps of all the rotten nations of today." He included America among the rotten. "It would be far better to have an Irish republic that was "poor and indigent," with "the people eking out a poor existence on the soil," than a dominion ruled by those Irish who had lost "their souls, their minds, their honour." For Peter Golden, also Irish-born but living in America, the Irish struggle was one of "polarities": "'simplicity' versus 'subtlety,' 'things of the mind and . . . spirit' versus 'a crass and narrow materialism.'" Michael Collins, who was on the other side of the Irish Civil War from all of the above, wrote that he stood "for an Irish civilization based on the people" and "embodying and maintaining the . . . habits, ways of thought, customs, that *make them different*." He celebrated those differences. The Irish, said Collins, had to "become Gaels again," they had to awaken "the vital indestructible Gaelicism within us struggling to life and expression."[9]

That meant throwing off everything that the British had inflicted on them from social-class haughtiness to bad manners and worse literature. There was an aesthetic to Irish cultural nationalism. Ireland free and collectivist, yes, but the "poetic" qualities of the Irish soul had also to be reawakened. This Irish imagined community was to be a cultural bellwether, Éire as creative muse: artistic and daring, tolerant, inclusive, open, intellectually curious and diverse, spiritually aware but fundamentally secular, in sum, a dreamscape. It would be a place that thoughtful people paid attention to, an *interesting* place, what it had been before the English (the *Sassenach*) conquest, a nation without bourgeois philistines and repressive clerics to censor its aesthetic instincts. All of this, the democratic, the communal, the poetic, and the sociable went together; each sustained the others. Lady Gregory offered an interesting literary analogy: The Gaels, in her mind, were like "Sancho and Quixote"—and Pope Leo XIII—the "champions of lost causes and shadowy ideals." That sounded a lot like drifters. Perhaps it was intended to: Ireland as an "imagined community" of the perpetually nonconforming. Either way, Irishness had clearly become an intoxicant.[10]

Benedict Anderson wrote that creating national communities among people who don't know one another was something of a conjurer's trick. It involved "awakening from . . . an epochal . . . sleep . . . behind [which] . . . was an immense antiquity." "New" and "historical" nations must "loom out of an immemorial . . . horizonless past." In the case of Ireland, the reawakening was nearer a disinterment, but the point is the same. Ireland never came up in Anderson's account, but it could have. His words apply. Which is why the last conjuring declarations should be those of Liam Mellows: Ireland, he told a gathering of wavering Irish rebels, "this miserable country, as some of you called it," had awakened from its long sleep and "rediscovered its ancient self." The key word was "rediscovered." Nostalgia was their driving impulse. They weren't looking for bright and shiny new objects.[11]

There were quite a number of Irish, both in Ireland and in America, who were like Mellows. They found that what counted as modern was both vacuous and morally bankrupt. They wanted nothing to do with it, which explained how it was, in Mellows's words again, that Ireland, "during the last few years," had become "the greatest country in God's earth." It had put itself "forth to the world . . . as a beacon to guide all those who were downtrodden," those who, like the Irish, were about to be run over by "progress"—the tranquilizer of the modern masses—efficiency, rationality, and other "crackpot obsessions" of modernity. The Irish revolt had taken in the world and all in it. It would be an inspiration to rebellious colonials everywhere, militant labor everywhere, feminist women everywhere, racial and religious outliers everywhere. Giving proper allowance to the fact that Mellows was one of the dreamiest and most literally quixotic of the Irish conjurers, he did speak for many more than just himself.[12]

To Mellows and others of the noncommunist Irish Left, the Irish resistance, both the "Celtic Renaissance" and the Republican revolt, had also changed the way national communities should relate to one another. In 1900, the standard and ruling definition of nationalism was close to what Voltaire had said a century and a half earlier. Nationalists strove to have their nation "enriched by commerce, and [made] powerful by arms." Patriots played a zero-sum game. National "greatness" required that "patriots wish evil to [their] neighbors." He had English patriots in mind, but Mellow might easily have applied the lesson to America.[13]

Mellows contrasted that Anglo-American style of "patriots" with those Voltaire had called "citizens of the universe," the ones who wished only that their "nation"—and themselves—should always "remain as it is, neither . . . richer nor poorer." Max Weber applied Voltaire's lesson on a proper foreign policy to personal relationships and concluded that "the doctrines of Voltaire are . . . the common property . . . in . . . Catholic countries." It was one of their enchantments. He didn't mean just Ireland, but he certainly included Ireland. Material success was a poor standard by which to judge either nations or people. Relationships based on reciprocity were better than those based on markets.[14]

I quoted earlier from the pamphlet "Sinn Féin and Labor," written by that anonymous Irishman who called himself the Spalpeen. He wanted the Irish Labor Party to understand that Sinn Féiners were not bourgeois nationalists; they were nationalists of a special Irish kind. He admitted that there were some of them who were "economically content," but he did not mean by that that they had "wealth." The economically content were "those who desire no wealth." To define what made one "wealthy" as having no desire to be wealthy was to say that having capital did not make one a capitalist. Chasing after more capital, being economically *discontented*, was what defined being a capitalist. Ireland had a few of those types—some of them Catholic nationalists—but they weren't part of Sinn Féin, not part of Our (true Irish) selves.[15]

Deciding winners and losers was the sport of capitalists and imperialists. The new Ireland would not play it. The Irish, they told themselves, wished no evil on anyone. Rather, Ireland would return to what it had been before the English translated it. That was its lesson and gift to the world. Irish patriots not only *could* be internationalists and nationalist at the same time, Irish republicanism and the social radicalism on which it was based *required* that they be. Irishness in the service of social justice, and Ireland as a corrective to the worst and most unlovely of the excesses of modernity were becoming Republican and Revivalist tropes. More to the present point, as Benedict Anderson puts it, those unifying themes were "wholly foreign to the Americans."[16]

• • •

The Irish Revivalists made few direct references to America, but English ideas and vices were not unique to the English, and applying what the Irish said about Albion to Albion's Seed came easily. Retranslating Ireland involved purging the nation of the values of a world Max Weber, no less, had said was run by "specialists without spirit, sensualists without heart," the ones Lippmann called masters. America had at least as high a percentage of those as did England. Lady Gregory had described the English-made mask: "They see in us one part boastful quarrelsome adventurer, one part vulgar rollicking buffoon." Many Americans saw them that way too. And that wasn't the only, or even the most disparaging, of the masks.[17]

America also had a full share of those who thought like Balfour. It is entirely right to ask whether Irish Americans were something that America had made. Were Irish Americans wearing masks fashioned by the Native host society? The assimilation of immigrants and ethnics involved making "transnationalists" of them. Was that not itself a "translation"? Assimilation—transnationalization—is a form of colonization; somewhat more benign than the imperial variety, but similarly motivated. Both were efforts at conversion. More specifically in the case of Anglo-America, both were efforts at Anglicization.

The Irish Revival had what one historian has called "a New World cousin, American Celticism." As was true of cultural awakenings in other parts of the postcolonial nation-imagining world, the Revival and its antimodernism came to America via some very modern contrivances: Irish American newspapers, including "missionaries of nationalism" like the *Gaelic American* and the *Irish World* as well as local and Catholic diocesan papers, carried Revivalists' articles to a literate Irish American audience. The transatlantic cable brought news from England and Ireland; so did print journalists and newspapers with overseas bureaus and correspondents in Ireland. Steamships full of arriving Irish immigrants carried news from home—and in the accents of home—as did Irish writers and nationalists on American speaking tours. There were Gaelic League and Gaelic Athletic Association chapters in American cities; compulsory Irish history and Irish language courses in parochial schools, most run by Irish-born Christian Brothers priests. Many of those schools, as in Ireland, were madrasa-like in their revolutionary nationalism. The American Irish were given a multidisciplinary education in Irishness.[18]

Some of it came from the prolific pen of Seumas MacManus, a Donegal folklorist and storyteller (*seanchaí*), and the husband of the Revivalist poet Ethna Carbery. MacManus was a regular and well-paid speaker on the Irish American lecture circuit and a contributor to American literary magazines. In a 1907 article in the *North American Review*, he wrote of the Irish Revival and of the Sinn Féin movement that he said arose from it. Sinn Féin was taking the Irish national cause away from a "fight in the Parliament of the stranger, . . . a foreign Parliament," and returning it to home ground, "wrought out by the people and upon the soil of [the Irish] nation." Special attention should be given to his use of "stranger" and "foreign" and to the fact that this was for an American audience. "The indomitable soul of the race" had to be "regenerated"—by which MacManus obviously meant something different from "reawakened." The folklorist had become the racialist.[19]

In 1921, he published his eight-hundred-page *Story of the Irish Race*. The book was still in print in 2009 and it must have been on parlor tables—for those Irish who had a parlor—and elsewhere in the homes of many thousands of Ireland's "far-wandering children." It is doubtful that many read it through, but it can be picked up at almost any page and skimmed. MacManus said that he was "impelled" to write for the American Irish. His heavily racialized nationalism required it. "Gaelic Ireland," he told his readers, "is the real Ireland." The rest of it was a place of "soulless nondescripts," a "pseudo-Ireland," the superficial, historically insignificant English-speaking Ireland," a western annex of what MacManus called "Saxonland."[20]

There is one brief sketch in *The Story of the Irish Race* that is typical of the whole, and directly to the point of the cultural contrariness of the Catholic Irish. It tells of a Munster Irishman, "a rude, wild mountaineer, who visited England four or five centuries ago." MacManus's chronology was vague, but this was probably pre-Reformation; the story is about the English race, not about some emerging "Cromwellian-Protestant ethic." On his return to Ireland, the wild Munster mountaineer had many "wonderful tales" to tell. One can imagine. But "none [was] more extraordinary, more unbelievable, than that the English people actually charged for the food, liquor, and bed, which they provided for a stranger!"[21]

The English, it seems, were born a commercial people; hospitality and neighborliness, as the Irish defined them, were not a part of their social calculus. The Irish did not belong among them. That was MacManus's lesson throughout the book. And he went out of his way to make clear that it applied to America as surely as to Britain. His book, as he admitted, was designed to safeguard the Irish "from the *intrusion of Americans* and other common peoples of [the] earth."[22]

• • •

No one made more obvious the incompatibility of the "common Irish people," and the Anglo-Americans, than Sir Horace Plunkett in his book, *Ireland in the New Century* (1904). Plunkett was an Anglo-Irish Ascendancy Protestant; he served as an Irish representative to the British Parliament and, after the formation of the Irish Free State, as an officer of the new Irish government. He was also, because of the work of his Irish Agricultural Organization Society (IAOS), a major player in the Irish Revival. In his book, Plunkett laid out a grand design for a new Ireland and a new type of Irish, ones capable at least of surviving in the twentieth century. His plan centered on the founding of agricultural cooperatives, both consumer and producer, and of credit unions that would replace an archaic system of lending and borrowing. His book, along with the many articles that appeared in his influential Revivalist newspaper the *Irish Homestead*, are frequently consulted. Those are the reasons he is remembered well in Irish history. He should be. I cite him, however, less as an architect of a new Ireland and more as a spokesman for some very old Anglo-Protestant ideas about Irish Catholics, including prominently those in America.[23]

Plunkett was born in England but he was raised in County Meath; he knew the Irish people—nationalists, unionists, Catholics, Protestants, Dissenters, peasants, Ascendancy bon vivants, squires, and squireens. I also presume, given his prominence in Ireland, England, and the United States, that his views were those of many in the Anglo-American world he inhabited and that he knew it. He was a race patriot, a representative figure in the culture wars between the Irish and the Anglo-Americans, and he spoke from authority.

Saving Ireland was the topic of his book. But that required saving the Irish people, mostly from themselves. And that, in its turn, makes everything Plunkett said relevant to the Irish in America. Indeed, he asked early in his book whether "we could not learn something from a study of what our (!) people were doing abroad?" He said he wanted to know more about "his people," more about the "manifest destiny of the [Irish] race." The reference to race was to be expected. But what of his use of the phrase "manifest destiny"? From 1879 to 1889 Plunkett owned a large ranch in Wyoming; he spent his summers in the American West playing cowboy and cattle baron. American shibboleths may have come easily to him, but to apply this one and in this context is especially revealing.[24]

The Irish problem was that their destiny was manifestly less promising than the American because Irish culture was so manifestly inferior to the American. Success in the "new century" would require modern attributes: individualism, striving, and grit. Irish culture was built around their opposites. It was a culture of "pleasant amenities." He mentioned specifically "the courtesies, the leisureliness, the associations of religion, and the familiar faces of the neighbours, whose ways and minds are like his"—and like no one else's. The Irish mind "tenaciously adhered" to these antimodern "relics of the tribal days," among which relics was the "feeling of communistic ownership." This Irish paean to the "really simple life" of the Irish past had "its commonest manifestation" among "rather simple people." That was the "Irish character as we find it to-day."[25]

But what specifically did *"we"* find that character to be? Plunkett found "a striking absence of individualism, self-reliance and moral courage; a lack of serious thought on public questions; a listlessness and apathy in regard to economic improvement which amount to a form of fatalism; and, in backward districts, a survival of superstition, which saps all strength of will and purpose." And then this—which requires little comment: By backward districts, he meant all those outside the northeast, where the "Presbyterian ... communities ... have developed the essentially strenuous qualities which, no doubt, they brought from England and Scotland."

In Plunkett's words, these "Presbyterian communities" of northeastern Ulster were "no part of what is ... understood by the Irish Question." They were not part of Plunkett's "Irish question" for the same reason they were not part of E. P. Thompson's: They weren't Irish. Plunkett, in fact, again like Thompson after him, was not describing an "Irish question." He was describing a "Catholic question." That was not quite a distinction without a difference, but it was close, and in Plunkett's case, it applied to both Ireland and Irish America.[26]

Plunkett's book came out just two years before Weber published the German-language edition of *The Protestant Ethic and the Spirit of Capitalism*. Plunkett almost certainly knew something of Weber's thesis, even going as far as to say that he wanted to investigate "the direct influence which the creed of each of the two sections of Irishmen produces on the industrial character of its adherents." The influences were obvious to all. The Catholic and Protestant Irish were "two races, two creeds, and, what is too little considered, two separate spheres of economic interest and pursuit."—the "two-nation" theory made all-embracing.[27]

The Catholics of these two races and two creeds had only one chance of making their way in the new century. Plunkett said that he knew from their history that they were a "leader-following people." Like his references to Irish sociability, that was not a compliment. Neither was it perceptive, or even accurate. His point was that once Ireland's "leaders," of which he counted himself one, had made the people understand the new realities, and once his economic innovations had been given a fair trial, he was sure that the "material conditions of the great body of our countrymen ... [would be] advanced." He was counting on those like himself to lead the Irish to rationalism and prepare them for the modern twentieth century and the "dawn of the practical," as he called it.[28]

The Irish people would develop "industrial instincts" and embrace a "commercial morality." They would "put away childish things and learn to behave like grown-up Englishmen"—a comment that should be given special notice and a special ranking, and to which "grown-up Americans" should be added. He was convinced that "in proportion to their natural intelligence," the Irish would "see that a political development on lines similar to those adopted in England was best for Ireland" and they "would cease to desire what is ordinarily understood as Home Rule." The key was that "proportion of natural intelligence." There had to be enough of it for the Irish to know how to protect their material interests.[29]

His reference to "what is ordinarily understood as Home Rule" requires some clarification. He clearly meant by it "rule from home," home rule in lowercase, everything that came under the generic heading of Irish nationalism from the Home Rule bill then being debated to an independent republic. The national issue, however, confused him. On the first page of his book Plunkett wrote that Irish nationalist "aspirations" would come "to nought" because the Irish race had no understanding of what nationalism meant. Since he thought those aspirations ignoble and senseless, one would think that that would have pleased him—racial defects as the deathblow of the Irish national cause.

He changed his mind midbook. By the time he got to the specifics of "what is ordinarily understood as Home Rule," he was of the mind that Irish nationalism would come to nothing because the Irish were a sensible race; one might even have called them shrewd and progressing toward masterful. They understood their physical needs and could be taught how to advance them. The British had once attempted to "kill Home Rule"—and home rule—"with [British] kindness"; that hadn't worked. Plunkett's better idea was to kill Irish nationalism with British efficiency. Once his economic reforms were in place, the Irish would have a chance to see "that development on lines similar to those adopted in England was best" for them. The Irish would prosper within the Empire; indeed, they would prosper only because they were in the Empire. And they would want to stay there. The brightest of them would even insist on staying there. They would abandon the nationalist fantasy. It would "come to naught."[30]

A more complete misreading of Irish nationalism—in Ireland surely, but in America as well—can hardly be imagined. Even had everything Plunkett promised come true, even if the Irish were to prosper economically by giving up their nationalist and cultural pipedreams, the status of colonial accessory was soul-killing. The Irish didn't hate British rule because it was inefficient and left them poor. It was and it did, but they hated British rule because it was *British* rule. It was that Irish emphasis on the "foreignness" of the Empire that Plunkett found irrational or, at best, nonrational, and he made no allowances for it. Except for those in the "Presbyterian communities" and thus possessed of "strenuous blood," Plunkett made no allowances for most of what the Irish thought—or for most of the Irish.[31]

Plunkett's blooded racialism, however, was more nuanced than that of many of his fellow Anglo-Saxonists. Obviously, he thought he had isolated an Irish race, but it wasn't just Celtic "blood" that decided it. Some of the race's origins were outside itself; Plunkett even said that the British governance of Ireland had often been oppressive. He agreed with Balfour that the English had been part of what made Ireland. That was a crime of which Plunkett held them accused. Having paid his respects to history as the source of Irish racial sensibilities, he then turned his attention to the far greater and proximate cause of Irish waywardness, the "Irish Catholic Church."

Plunkett's assessment was closer to racialized antipopery—or anti-Catholicism as a source of racism. It was Plunkett's judgment that Catholicism had infantilized the Irish, crippled them emotionally and intellectually. What R. F. Foster called the "psychology" over which they wanted "autonomy" was a collective mental disorder. The Irish Catholic Church had checked "the growth of . . . initiative and self-reliance, especially amongst a people whose lack of education"—a lack that he also laid at the feet of the Church—"unfits them for resisting the influence of fatalism with resignation as its paramount virtue."[32]

The Church had done all that on purpose. What that purpose might have been, Plunkett did not say, but it was sinister. Irish-style "Roman Catholicism," wherever found, "strikes an outsider as being in some of its tendencies non-economic, if not actually anti-economic." There's a remarkable indirectness to that comment. It separates Plunkett from what he was saying, but clearly, he was his own "outsider." And Plunkett didn't find "some" of Irish Catholicism's tendencies to be antieconomic. He found all of them to be that. And finally, what is to be made of the singularly empty terms, "noneconomic" and "antieconomic"? Everything else in his book makes it clear that he meant noncapitalist and anticapitalist. One is left to wonder why he didn't just say that.[33]

That was not the full extent of the Church's crimes—sins, really—against the Irish and Ireland. The "simpler Christianity . . . of we[!] Protestants" saw Catholic churches, filled as they were with "marbles and mosaics," as both "gaudy" and a colossal waste of money, money of which the Irish—particularly those in America where their churches were even larger and more gaudy even than those in Ireland—had too little. That was not all that was wrong with Irish Catholic church and parish buildings. Next came this: Too often they were built for "motives which have but a remote connection with religion." In other words, they weren't really churches at all. He left unsaid what they were, noting only that what went on within the walls of these impersonators of churches and pretenders of schools was wholly useless in teaching the Irish how to handle "the trials and temptations of life," wherever found.[34]

From this point forward, his book is given over almost entirely to those found in America. The behavior of those childlike creatures in the United States only confirmed what Plunkett had convinced himself he already knew. He did, however, offer this insightful comparative comment about the American Irish: They "are not in the same position as [other] ... immigrants who have no cause at home which they wish to forward." That, of course, was not quite true, as America's Jews and Poles, among others, would have been quick to tell him. At that, Plunkett had touched on something important. The Irish nationalism of Irish Americans was more directly anticolonial and was more strongly felt than the home-country patriot games. And on this next point, Plunkett was exactly right: "Every echo in the States of political or social disturbance in Ireland rouses the immigrant and he becomes an Irishman once more."[35]

There were a lot of those kinds of echoes; enough that Plunkett could only conclude that the American "Irishman is not a citizen of the country of his adoption." He was a visitor. "His views and votes ... are not [based on] any right understanding of the interests of the new country in which he and his children must live." (Why he used "must live" in that sentence was something he never explored.) The American Irish belonged to a "kind of *imperium in imperia*." That was what Henry Childs Merwin had also said about them. They "carr[ied] into American politics ideas which are not American, and which might easily become an embarrassment if not a danger to America." The "views and votes on international issues" of these clustered and unassimilated Irish were "dictated ... by a passionate sympathy for and remembrance of the land [they] no longer [live] in." All that was followed by this crucial fact: "Hence the powerful interest which America shares with England." America's "Irish question" was the result of too many homesick Irish with a passionate sympathy for the place where they no longer lived and a nonchalance about the interests of the place where they did live. The definition of erraticism can be carried no further than that.[36]

Unfortunately for all concerned, cultural nonconformity and a confusion over where their allegiance should lie was not the only Irish American defect. A fondness for hocus-pocus and semifeudalism was also apparent. The Irish had brought their church to America too. That, not some racial defect, was why they were as "helpless in the fierce current of [American] industrial life" as they were in the British currents running through Ireland. Plunkett mentioned their "lack of initiative, shrinking from responsibility, moral timidity[,] ... and a dread of public opinion." How could the likes of these "deal with the rawness and eagerness of" America, "the lust of the eye and the pride of life"?

He wrote specifically of the "early hours" of an American workday and of the "few holidays"—in other words, of clock time and of little time off. In addition, the "Irish people have never had the opportunity of developing [a] strong and salutary individualism." The Church had left Ireland in a "primitive social state, one in which the individual was nothing and the community everything." It had made defectives of them. They did not accept American capitalism; they challenged it, not so much from defiance as from incomprehension. America as a whole was "a rude shock upon the ill-balanced refinement of the Irish immigrant." Irish erraticism has never been given a more polished definition than "ill-balanced refinement."[37]

What came next was straight from the modernists' chorus: Catholicism was why the Irish "missed the greatest opportunity which ever fell to . . . a people agriculturally inclined." Plunkett's reference was to America's "veritable Promised Land . . . gradually opened up between the Alleghanies [sic] and the Rocky Mountains, [land] which [the Catholic Irish] had only to occupy in order to possess." That was precisely the argument that Merwin had made in 1896; Merwin attributed it to Irish clannishness, meaning that Merwin did not have Plunkett's understanding of the ultimate cause. They were clannish because the Irish Church wanted them to be. The Church had "functionally deranged" them; "the tenement house, with all its domestic abominations, provided the social order which they brought with them from Ireland, and the lack of which on the western prairie"—or the stump-filled cut-over district—"no immediate or prospective physical comfort could make good."[38]

Irish Catholics confounded Plunkett not because he didn't understand them but because, in important ways, he did. He said, "they belonged to a different world" and were hopelessly unprepared to enter the new one. They were, in fact, *"very unlike . . . any other people"* anywhere. Plunkett's despairing comment would have brought joy to the Irish and only added to precisely what the Irish celebrated.[39]

Plunkett was joined in it by an American writer whom he met in London sometime during "the rise and fall of Parnell." The American was Harold Frederic, the author of *The Damnation of Theron Ware*. Frederic, Plunkett wrote, "left some deep impressions on my mind." He followed that with a long passage from Frederick's *Damnation of Theron Ware*, "published in England," Plunkett wrote, "under the title of *Illuminations*—a nice discrimination!" Plunkett was happy to report that Frederic was "in entire accord with my view" that there were some serious "defect[s] in the Irish character"; the "psychology of the Celt," Plunkett recalled Frederic saying, was "chaotic." Why the Irish would want "autonomy" over it was evidence of how chaotic.[40]

The Irish race, according to Frederic, was "a strange mixture of elementary early peoples, walled off from the outer world by the four seas, and free to work out their own racial amalgam." "Irish, alone on their island"—a phrase that permits of more than one reading—"kept [the amalgam] alive. [They] brooded on it, and rooted their whole spiritual side in it. Their religion is full of it; their blood is full of it. The Ireland of two thousand years ago is incarnated in her." It flows "ceaselessly in their blood." It left them "unfitted" for the "political changes" that Plunkett and Frederic thought could alone save them.[41]

I have never seen Plunkett's association with Frederic referenced by historians. It should be. Here were two Anglo-Saxon race patriots declaiming on the moral and cultural inadequacies of Irish foster children in Anglo-America. It makes the connection between what Plunkett said about the Irish in Ireland and what he thought about them in America. His book could easily be retitled from *Ireland in the New Century* to *The Irish in the New Century*" But note one other aspect of the analysis of both Plunkett and Frederic: If the Irish gave up their erratic ways, they would cease to be themselves. But if they didn't become more like other people—particularly those others who ruled them—they would be racially destroyed. Either way, Plunkett and Frederic were describing a doomed race. As Luke Gibbons put it "Irish Catholicism ... [was] ... perceived as immersed in ... the general credulousness associated with ... 'doomed races.'" Ireland could succeed as a nation only if the Irish people stopped being Irish.[42]

In 1906, two years after Plunkett's *Ireland in the New Century*, Father Michael O'Riordan, an Irish Catholic priest, answered Plunkett's charges in a book titled *Catholicism and Irish Progress*. For all that "Sir Horace" (his favorite name for Plunkett) was born and lived in Ireland, the "real" Irish were unknown to him. Plunkett looked at Ireland "through the coloured glasses of a Unionist and a Protestant." There was no need for O'Riordan to add "colonialist" or "imperialist" to the list; they were implied. He "cannot understand us; but he evidently thinks he does." He "has 'standardised' us." Plunkett's values were "utilitarian"; they were "low and narrow" and "incommensurable ... with the "Catholic religious ideal." Plunkett had "link[ed] character with the industrial spirit, but in that he [was] plainly wrong." "Capital is not the ruler of the world." The "Almighty has no pecuniary interest in the stability of the funds or in the European balance of power." That last reference to balance of power added a proper anti-imperial aspect to O'Riordan's critique.[43]

Americans were not O'Riordan's topic. But had they been, he was certain that he "could produce pictures of American life quite of a piece with those I have shown regarding England." There too the "industrial spirit sacrifices every other human interest on the altar of Mammon." Specifically, and with the American economy in mind, O'Riordan asked—in the name of multitudes of Irish Catholics—if "an economic system ... which sanctions usury, or finds a place for trusts and monopolies which place the public at the mercy of a grinding industrialism is right and moral?" A system which "makes millionaires of a few and begets misery for" the masses must have within it "the germs of corruption." "The egoism of initiative and self-reliance will end in the survival of the fittest, will in the long run disregard the interests of the many who are down unless as levers to elevate still more the few who are up." A democracy in which there are "many who are down" but only a "few who are up" was an Irish contradiction in terms.[44]

O'Riordan concluded his lesson in erratic economics by insisting that "social economies imply distribution as well as accumulation." Americans were first-class accumulators, the best in the world. But they were seriously deficient distributors. They privileged those who produced tangible and socially useful things like railroads and corn—and stumps—but cared little for those whose contributions to society were less measurable. Good company comes to mind. O'Riordan based his arguments on doctrinal Catholic notions of social justice, with a substantial assist from what might be called doctrinal Irish notions of neighborliness and hospitality, alien concepts in Saxonlands. A proper social order was one based on equity and reciprocity, on favors done and favors returned.[45]

• • •

I alluded earlier to a second seam line, one connecting Irish nationalism to nationalist wars among colonial and submerged peoples everywhere. It's time to make this association of causes as explicit as the association of Irish nationalism with the cause of labor. America's racial and ethnic diversity required the American Irish to address colonial and working-class issues that went far beyond Ireland and the Irish. In shorthand language, the working-class "neighborhood" in which Irish Catholic workers lived had a number of non–Irish Catholics in it. The idea of neighborhood hadn't changed, but its cultural boundaries had. This is a central point in Bruce Nelson's brilliant *Irish Nationalists and the Making of the Irish Race*. I will use his language: There were some Irish in America whose "vision of the Irish nation ... turned outward as well as inward ... that spoke, 'gingerly,' of a common struggle for liberty. ... for freedom everywhere.'" Every part of that is important—including the use of "gingerly," set apart by commas.[46]

Here is Connolly on the topic: "in every enemy of tyranny we recognize a brother, wherever be his birthplace; in every enemy of freedom we ... recognize our enemy, though he were as Irish as our hills." James Farrell, the Irish American writer and political radical, said of Connolly that his "nationalism was ... consistent with his internationalism." So was Liam Mellows's, though without all of Connolly's socialist shadings. Mellows and the Ireland he envisioned would be rebels not just against England, but against every "form of injustice in any country the world over."[47]

This "merging of nationalism and internationalism" did not affect the long-standing convergence of nationalism and social-labor reform, except perhaps to strengthen both. Neither did it affect the Irish insistence that gross inequalities in the distribution of a nation's material wealth nullified any claims of democracy that that nation might make and parade before the world. Obviously, not all Irish were party to any of this, but Nelson's argument that many were is persuasive and "further complicates the narrative of Ireland as '*sacra insula*' and of Irish emigrants as narrowly conservative." Note particularly his subtle use of the word *further*; it implies that the American Irish had always included a significant number of "citizens of the universe," women and men who extended the definition of democracy to the economy, then joined the cause of Ireland and the cause of labor, and then internationalized all the above.[48]

Nelson is too modest. His analysis does more than just "complicate the narrative of Irish emigrants as narrowly conservative"; it upends it. My focus, however, is narrower than his. I acknowledge the seam line joining Ireland's cause with anticolonialism everywhere, but my emphases remain where they've been from the beginning, on "domestic" issues: first, on the Irish Catholic assumption that distributive justice was a definitional part of a properly structured political democracy; second, on the insistence of the Irish erratics that the cause of Ireland and the cause of American labor were nonseverable; and third, on the belief that blending causes was not a tactic; that it arose naturally—it's tempting to say organically—from Robert Orsi's "Catholic=Presence." I am contending for an Irish Catholic ontology as well as a doctrinally Catholic one. That may be squeezing ontology into too tight a space, so I will return to Irish sensibilities, the inner nonrational receptors they used to filter realities.

Horace Plunkett said that he could always distinguish between "political leaders" and "industrial leaders." He could tell them apart at a glance. I would use different labels; he could distinguish between nationalist fantasists and economic realists, which is to say between moralists and materialists, traditionalists and modernists, drifters and masters, the poetic and the practical. They were on opposite sides of the ontological divide; if Ireland was to prosper, they had to be kept apart, the dreamers put in a corner by themselves, there to talk only to each other. As soon as the better part of the Irish began to realize the practical and material benefits that came from being in the Empire, they would abandon the poetic and moral cause of getting out of it. They would take out the seam lines and, to borrow again from Jean Elshtain, never let the twain meet.[49]

The erratic Irish could not imagine a just system where they didn't meet. Certainly they did not want to see an Ireland in which moral issues had been "privatized" and removed from public discourse. In *Ireland in the New*

Century, Plunkett had written that "The more business in politics, and the less politics in business, the better for both." That was "a maxim which [he] brought home from the Far West." He liked and "advocated" for its adoption by the Irish. It's unfortunate that Polanyi had never heard it; it was the essence of disembeddedness. The Irish reversed the maxim, concluding that the more politics and economics converged, the better for all. As Lady Gregory put it in a passage quoted by Plunkett as evidence of Irish irrationality, "history, religion and politics grow on one stem in Ireland." It is interesting that those three, plus "law," were what Plunkett and his cowboy friends insisted had to be kept on separate stems. The Irish preferred the single-stem metaphor.[50]

There were two organizations, formed within a couple of weeks of each other in the fall of 1917, that gave public expression to this Irish Catholic unwillingness—or inability—to detach morality and matters of conscience from politics and assign their care and keeping exclusively to the "soul-keepers." The first, the Irish Progressive League (IPL), has already been introduced. Liam Mellows, Peter Golden, and a number of other Irish Republicans were early members. The leadership of the league, however, was mostly in the hands of Irish and Irish American women. Many of those were inspired by the example set by the women of the Literary Revival who were making the case for a revitalized—and radicalized—Ireland.

The Irish nationalism of the IPL was strongly international; what Ireland was demanding was what the rest of the British colonies deserved—Brits out of India and the end of the Raj as well as Brits out of Ireland and the end of the Ascendancy. It was at least as "cosmopolitan" in its domestic politics. It supported all workers—Tom, Dick, and Harry as well as Pat, Mike, and Tim. For the IPL, these policies were not denials of tribal Irishness. They were expressions of a new variant of it. Modern Anglo-Americans were individualists; they cared for themselves. IrishCatholics were traditionalists and communalists; they cared for their own, their friends and neighbors, those like themselves. The IPL's radical challenge to America's capitalist culture was to extend the neighborhood, to care for all who needed care and to do so in the name of Irish Catholicism.[51]

In August 1920, the British government court-martialed and imprisoned Terence MacSwiney, lord mayor of Cork City and a member of the Irish Republican Army. The charge was sedition. MacSwiney protested his sentence by "refusing to eat or drink." MacSwiney's hunger strike—and that is an interesting use of the word *strike*—would last for seventy-four days. He died "biting at the grave" on October 25. Hunger striking is impossible for rationalists and other modernists and self-appointed masters to comprehend; this "old and foolish custom" was irrational, literally out of their world. "Ontological fault line" does not cover it. Starving oneself is not just drifty; it's more than just a revolt against modernity. It is protest of an entirely different order, one more "wholly foreign to Americans" than anything on Benedict Anderson's list.[52]

For the women of the IPL, MacSwiney's strike became a totem of the mystical otherworldliness of Celts and the spiritual poverty of Anglo-Americans. During the summer of his self-starvation, they formed an affiliated group called the Women Pickets for the Enforcement of America's War Aims. The women engaged in various forms of political theater, protesting the imprisonment of MacSwiney as well as the denial of a travel permit to Irish Australian archbishop Daniel Mannix. They also called for a boycott of British goods, "occupied" the British embassy in New York, marched on the US capital, and conducted street protests in and around New York City. On August 27, 1920, the women moved beyond street shows, boycotts, and pickets. They went to the Chelsea Docks on the west side of Manhattan and there persuaded the largely Irish coal stokers aboard a British passenger liner to strike in support of MacSwiney and everything else connected to the cause of an anti-imperialist, antipatriarchal Irish Workers' Republic.

The strikers were quickly joined by the overwhelmingly Irish American longshoremen, many of them young Irishmen recently arrived in America, who refused to unload British ships. As one Irish American leftist put it, "the old Fenian dream of striking the blow from America that would free Ireland had been realized that day on the Chelsea docks." Irish American women, wrote the *New York Sun*, had set in motion events that would culminate in "the first purely political strike of workingmen in the history of the United States." I still think the Butte strike call of 1917 was first, but what matters is that both work stoppages were blended products, labor actions in the cause of Ireland in support of an Irish workers' republic.[53]

That same convergence of causes was also evident in the second organization, formed at the same time as the IPL. Four American Catholic bishops established the National Catholic War Council (CWC; after the war, the Catholic Welfare Council) to deal with "Catholic activities incidental to the war" and the immediate postwar period. Since everything the bishops did was based on *Rerum Novarum*, that included labor activities, broadly defined. In 1919, the bishops turned their attention from war to what they called "reconstruction," lifting "the yoke little better than that of slavery," as Pope Leo had written, from American industrial laborers. The bishops' "Program of Reconstruction" was *Rerum Novarum* brought to America. The Pope's message was a Catholic document, not an Irish one. But it had a certain Irish structure of feeling to it; it sounded Irish. That is not reason enough to treat the bishops' plan as an Irish American document. It is, however, reason enough to decode the Irish elements in it and to include the Plan in this discussion.[54]

Irish women protesters, New York, 1920. The tactics of these protesters were those of the suffragettes. So was the attire. Tearing apart the Union Jack was radical political theater. The way in which it was done, however, was decorous. Courtesy Library of Congress.

My decoding begins with James Connolly's 1913 pamphlet, "The Re-conquest of Ireland," a short account of the most unpardonable of the British sins against Ireland, and of what the new Ireland would have to do to be made whole and wholly Irish again. As stated earlier, it wasn't just the loss of Irish lives and the theft of Irish lands that mattered to Connolly. The conquest had inflicted less visible wounds. It was the "victory of the capitalist conception of law and the functions of law." James Farrell wrote that for Connolly the "Reformation was 'the capitalist ideas appearing in the religious field.'" By reformation, Connolly did not mean Luther or the Tudors. The capitalist conquest came with the "Cromwellian settlement in 1654 . . . [I]t was then [that] the conquest reached its highest and completest point." The lesson was unambiguous: Irish Catholics did not share the Cromwellian "Protestant ethic." The "spirit of capitalism" and imperialism was not on them.[55]

In 1920, Father John Ryan, born on a Minnesota farm to Irish immigrants, his father a member of the American Land League, edited a collection of documents called *The Church and Labor*. Ryan was a key figure in the CWC and Leo's entire encyclical was reprinted in his book, as was the whole of the bishop's plan and documents on the labor question by Church leaders of six countries. There are two things that are especially striking about the selections in *The Church and Labor*. The first is how many of the Catholic priests who contributed to it said what Connolly had said: the source of modern economies and thus of the social injustices endemic to them were to be found in what one of them called the "so-called Reformation." It was then that "capitalism began." England came under the dominion of a capitalistic regime that "enthroned an individualistic principle of life"; the "democratic and co-operative institutions" that might have challenged that principle were "upon their death bed" and had been "ever since the Reformation." And all of that without so much as a footnote to Weber.[56]

The second significant shared opinion was related to this first. All the documents in the book took as a given the cultural and ideological differences between an idealized "Catholic way" and that of the "fierce individualism" of Protestantism and its ugly offspring, modern American capitalism. Ryan said that the "laissez faire" theory to which England and America have been so long accustomed" was contrary to the "teachings" contained in the "ancient treasury of the Church." Laissez faire—what Ryan also called "non-intervention"—was a "perverted modern notion," a "purely commercial and pagan ethic." The idea that the Catholic Church had ever believed in it was a "calumny." Capitalist economies had to be changed—transformed and reembedded in society, to use Polanyi's language. The transformation would be drawn from the deep well of Catholic ideas of the commonweal and the distributive justice that sustained it.[57]

Connolly believed the same. He just gave it a different name. His transformation would be drawn from an equally deep well, the "deep antiquity" of Irishness. Like Ryan's, the changes he spoke of would do more than just modify the system. They would transform it. Connolly's "modifications" were the same as the Church's: building cooperative commonwealths and insisting that democracy be extended to include social as well as political equality. The ideal world was one of peasants, village communities, guilds, and small shops. It was all a dream but, in the context of American industrial capitalism, not an unworthy one. To those who doubted that pre-Reformation Europe, or Ireland before Cromwell, had anything useful to say about the modern world and its social question, Leo offered the assurance of the traditionalists: "It is not rash to conjecture the future from the past." Not rash perhaps, but in modern and rationalized capitalist states, certainly drifty.[58]

The point is not that the bishops were inspired or even influenced by Connolly—or Connolly by them. What matters is that they thought alike on the role of the Reformation in the coming of capitalism. Connolly's "Reconquest" could have been relabeled "The Irish Ethic and the Spirit of Cooperation"—or "Socialism." The bishops' plan and *Rerum Novarum* could well have been subtitled "The Catholic Ethic and the Spirit of Distributism"—or at least "Noncapitalism." Edward Keating, the Irish Catholic editor of the magazine *Labor*, called *Rerum Novarum* a Catholic manifesto on labor, and this in the same speech where he insisted that the Catholic Church "did not suddenly turn 'liberal' in 1891."[59]

James Barrett, in his book *The Irish Way*, says of the bishops' plan that it had its "roots in the church's ancient hostility to materialism," whether as the foundation of socialism or unregulated capitalism. *Ancient* was the governing word. That doesn't turn the bishops' plan into an Irish plan, but it certainly mixes up the two categories. Barrett goes on to write that the bishops' proposal "reads like a blueprint for the coming welfare state; it called for workers' legal rights to organize, bargain collectively, and strike; a living wage; old-age pensions; public housing; social insurance; and the regulation of public utilities."[60]

Taken all in all, I think a good case can be made that John Ryan and the other bishops in that near-totally Irish clerical platoon went further leftward than Barrett's reference to "the coming welfare state" suggests. Ryan carefully discussed every aspect of the bishops' Plan in his book *Social Reconstruction*. Early on in the book he wrote that the bishops wanted capital to grant to labor the right to "adequate participation . . . in all the industrial aspects of business management." This meant "to a great extent the abolition of the wage system." Ryan even quoted with approval a newspaper account that said that the bishops' plan "proposes not merely to make Capitalism good, but to make it less." The National Civic Federation thought the bishops' ideas were "near-Bolsheviki." The federation was the easily frightened voice of reactionary capitalism, and its reference to Bolshevism need not be taken seriously. But that the ideas of Ryan and the bishops were radical and "un-American" must be. The Catholic Irish were once again playing the role of cultural fifth columnists, nonconforming, and erratic.[61]

• • •

Summarizing the history of American labor from 1916 to 1921 and making clear the social crisis created by the labor wars of those years is impossible, so numbers will have to do. In 1919, there were over 3,600 strikes and walkouts, involving more than 4 million workers; more than one in every five Americans working for wages went out on strike that year. Taking the six years from 1916 to 1921, there were more than 22,000 strikes and walkouts involving more than 12 plus workers. The Commission on Industrial Relations Report of 1915 revealed that 2 percent of the nation owned 60 percent of the wealth; 65 percent owned 2 percent of the wealth. One-third of America's laborers took home less than $10 a week, and most workers were jobless for more than two months out of the year. Those were not numbers that squared with America's claims to be a democracy.[62]

That was the context for labor's struggle for industrial democracy, the right of wage workers to "participate ... in all the industrial aspects of business management." "Industrial democracy" had an abundance of meanings. Even Walter Lippmann used it. The phrase itself re-embedded economies in society and directly challenged the hegemons of both modern American capitalism and of the Protestant nation-state in which capitalism was housed and kept well-fed. Labor historians have begun to pay more attention to this issue, none to better effect than Joseph McCartin in his *Labor's Great War*.[63]

But there is one aspect of the struggle for industrial democracy that has not gotten the consideration it deserves. Early in 1919, the still highly provisional Sinn Féin government in Ireland adopted the "Democratic Programme of Dáil Éireann." As noted earlier, the Program "reaffirmed" that everyone living in Ireland would have an "adequate share of the produce of the Nation's labour." Ireland was not breaking new ground. It was only restoring old Irish truths and correlating them with a restored Ireland. Bruce Nelson tightens the correlation—and then transnationalizes it. The Irish "Democratic Programme," he writes, "invoked a far more radical vision of democracy than the one that prevailed in the United States, a vision that had much in common with the proposals emanating from American proponents of industrial democracy and a workers' republic." Earlier in his book, Nelson had written of the "widespread demands" by American labor for "industrial democracy even a workers' republic." Nelson's use of *even* suggests that there was a distinction between industrial democracy and a workers' republic, and that the first came up short of the second.[64]

I grant that there is a distinction, but only a slight one. Connolly had for years insisted that American democracy, by its toleration of huge economic inequality, mocked itself. His workers' republic would enshrine both political and economic democracy. Michael Collins, in the last speech he would give, said he wanted an Ireland with full "worker participation in management," by which he meant a workers' republic very much like Connolly's. I think the phrases may be taken as nearly synonymous. And so I join Nelson in connecting the Irish and the American movements: "Industrial democracy" was an American version of an Irish "workers' republic." This Irish connection adds to and advances McCartin's account of American "labor's great war for industrial democracy."[65]

John Ryan, this time without clerical collar, strongly advocated "complete cooperative ownership and management" of production, adding that the "indispensable first step [toward] industrial harmony . . . is to make the worker . . . not a mere executor of orders or . . . instrument of production," but a partner. And not a silent or junior one. In Ryan's plan, workers were to have "control of processes and machinery; nature of product; engagement and dismissal of employees; hours of work, rates of pay, bonuses, etc.; welfare work; shop discipline; relations with trade unions;. . . . safety and sanitation in work places." That was as close to what capital condemned as a "Wobbly shop" where the workers made all the management decisions that one could get. Ryan had stretched industrial democracy as far as it could go, nearly as far as any on the Irish Left ever took it.[66]

Industrial democracy had an American ring to it. Any reference to any kind of democracy did. Had the United States not just fought and won a war to make the world safe for it? Did Whitman's "chants democratic" not incorporate the industrial? Was not the "artisanal republicanism" of American society in the early part of the nineteenth century not based on something akin to it? Ryan's restatement of worker control as a critical component of democracy, however, said nothing about any of that. He never looked to any part of the American experience. Rather, he spoke of "the system that developed . . . in the later Middle Ages," a system "in which the masses of the workers . . . owned and managed the tools and the land"; when "workers . . . exercised individual ownership and management through cooperation." To be even more specific, the "system" that Ryan had in mind was "Ireland prior to the conquest," the Ireland that Plunkett, among many others, insisted had to be entirely undone. Ryan did not identify Cromwell as Ireland's Protestant "conqueror," but he could have. Ryan's contentions were the same as Connolly's had been, if more gently expressed. As surely as for Connolly, "ancient"—read medieval—Ireland was his model, what he called a "partial solvent to capitalism."[67]

Ryan wrote that at a time when the vast majority of Anglo-Americans, when they considered the Middle Ages at all, thought of them as a benighted Dark Ages from which only the Reformation and its sequel, the Enlightenment, saved the world. As for Irish tribal ownership, they didn't think of that at all. Ryan and the bishops, however, held the Reformation responsible for the worst features of modern capitalism. So, to a lesser extent, had the Pope. There was only one cure for America's industrial crisis: a "return" not to the artisan republicanism of early-nineteenth-century America. Ryan did not quote de Tocqueville on preindustrial Americans' generosity and charitable instincts. He quoted Thomas Aquinas. His references were "to Christian life and institutions" to "a revival of genuine religion," to a world in "harmony with the kind of . . . system that obtained when the Church was most powerful in Europe." In other words, the world before the "great transformation" to a market economy.[68]

Consider what Ryan and the bishops were saying: The Reformation prepared the ground for imperialism and its injustices and for modern industrial capitalism and the "galling slavery" it imposed on working people. The bishops held the Reformation responsible for all of that and more. That was a very hard sell even among those others in Polanyi's double movement who themselves spoke out against the uglier aspects of modern American society. In a country that was literally a child of the Reformation, the idea of returning to institutions in place "when Catholic principles and ... social influence ... were at their zenith" was evidence of a disordered and erratic mind. The bishops, of course, were not suggesting a return to medieval life, only to its Catholic beliefs and values. That can have eased no Protestant fears. By Americans' reckoning, and contrary to Pope Leo's self-assured comment, one century was not "wonderfully like those of another." Only a people "very unlike any other people" thought as Leo did.[69]

Bruce Nelson's association of Sinn Féin's Irish Democratic Programme with American industrial democracy makes a crucial point, particularly in that the American struggle for giving labor a voice in management frequently involved Irish Americans. It doesn't make industrial democracy an Irish invention but it does suggest that a lot of Irish Catholics challenged the capitalists' orthodoxy that labor and management also occupied separate worlds and should never be introduced to one another. The Irish view of democracy was more expansive than the American. It connected "poetics," variously defined, with democratic politics, private morality with public governance. The two knew one another intimately. Find one, find both.

• • •

No one, on either side of the Atlantic, expressed the Irish sense of democracy as a social as well as a political system more vigorously than did Francis Patrick Walsh. I would say the same when it came to the seam line connecting the cause of Ireland and the cause of labor. The seams were more tightly sewn, more literally nonseverable, in the career of Frank Walsh than in that of any of the other Irish who operated along those seam lines. That does not make him more radical than the others on either cause, though his standing among the Irish Left is secure. It only makes him a more consistent and thus a more coherent seam stitcher.[70]

Frank Walsh was born in 1864 in the St. Louis Kerry Patch to Irish immigrants, one of the eleven children "of an old Catholic family." According to someone who knew him well, Walsh had experienced "life ... at its hard angles. ... it taught him to" hate poverty." Walsh himself put it simply: "'poverty was an unnecessary evil.'" So too were the conditions, the social systems, that created it. Walsh, said another, "hates oppression... with the strength of his entire being." And he saw "no difference... between a wrongful act committed by a nation and one committed by a man." Empires were also unnecessary evils.[71]

Trying to separate Walsh into his component parts, ethnic, religious, and political, is not worth the effort. He was an Irish Catholic advocate for a poetic Ireland and for the rights and welfare of Ireland and of working and misused people everywhere. The reigning values of America did not fit him or he them. It's the source of his politics that is at issue. The historian Joseph McCartin, who has studied him carefully, said Walsh "never completely [broke] his ties to his Irish Catholic culture." Ex-president William Taft said he could "not help liking the Irishman in him." In other words, Frank Walsh was a recognizable type: an Irish citizen of the universe.[72]

In 1913, Woodrow Wilson appointed Walsh to chair the US Commission on Industrial Relations (CIR); later, during the war, Wilson made Walsh the labor representative on the War Labor Board (WLB). Walsh's service with the CIR is particularly important. In a little more than two years while it was in place, the commission's members traveled to hundreds of cities, interviewed thousands of representatives of both labor and industry, and issued an eleven-volume final report containing tens of thousands of pages of testimony, the recommendations of the commission's majority, and a dissenting set of recommendations by its minority.

There had been nothing like the CIR before, and there has been nothing like it since. Walsh called the final majority report "more radical than any report upon industrial subjects ever made by any government agency." McCartin says that "not since Reconstruction had the report of any federal body seemed more radical." Melvyn Dubofsky claimed that it was "perhaps the most radical document ever released by a federal commission." American leftists, Dubofsky goes on, were convinced that it was the "beginning of an indigenous American revolutionary movement."[73]

The majority report came to be known as the Walsh Plan; that was a fair designation. His spirit and ideas animated everything in it. For Walsh and the majority of the commission, the "causes of industrial unrest" in America came down to four issues: an "unjust distribution of wealth and income... unemployment and denial of opportunity to earn a living... denial of justice... [and] denial of the right... to enter into [labor] organization." Stated that matter-of-factly, the claim that the majority report was radical seems overstated. But account must also be taken of the majority's recommendations for remedying those four defects: a vastly expanded role for the state, including the nationalization of certain industries; a judicial or legislative reversal of the laws governing everything from labor contracts and due process to workers' contributory negligence and assumption of risk, to the legal ban on secondary boycotts. And finally, consider the most basic part of the Walsh Plan: a fully democratized industrial system, one with at least a part of "the manager's brain under the workman's cap."[74]

What is intriguing in all that ascribed radicalism is that it seemed to have affected both John Ryan and the US bishops. Ryan may or may not have read the Dáil's 1919 Democratic Programme for Ireland, but it's certain that he and the other bishops read the majority report of the Frank Walsh–led CIR. It is at least possible, even likely, that the Irish Sinn Féiners who drafted the Democratic Programme had also read the Walsh Plan. Which adds up to a lot of Irish Catholics in both Ireland and America who thought, as Walsh put it, that "political Democracy is an illusion . . . unless builded upon and guaranteed by a free and virile Industrial Democracy."[75]

Compare that with John Ryan's contention in *Social Reconstruction* that the "theory . . . that the industrial population is divided into two classes, a few supermen who . . . direct, and the great masses who . . . carry out the commands imposed from above" was undemocratic and unjust. He also said it had "been rejected"; he was getting ahead of himself on that one. He then spoiled the progressive sound of his criticism of the theory by pointing out that it "came in" not with the Industrial Revolution but with the Reformation and that the rejection of it was by counterreformation Catholics "many centuries ago." Looking backward was seldom so forward looking than which John Ryan was involved.[76]

Walsh called the economic system established in the United States "industrial despotism"; on another occasion he chose "industrial feudalism"; dressed-up versions of the heavily loaded "wage slavery." He wasn't being reserved. He also wrote, in language that recalls *Rerum Novarum*, that the "man who toils is little better than the slave unless he has a voice in the conditions of labor." "The house he lives in, the food he eats, the clothing he wears, the environment of his wife and children, and his own health and safety, are in the hands of the employer." His conviction that "industry must be democratized" arose from that. It was a "call for justice, for opportunities to lead full and free lives, to develop the best that is in [people]." Walsh would have called industrial democracy emancipatory.[77]

The connections are there: *Rerum Novarum* and Catholic social teaching, Fr. John Ryan, Frank Walsh, the Report of the Industrial Commission. Ryan wrote even that the idea of a living wage, not a market-driven one, "is almost identical with that of Pope Leo," adding that "I suppose that Mr. Frank Walsh was responsible for that." Which leaves American labor historians with a huge irony to deal with: what Dubofsky called the "most radical document ever released by a federal commission," what American leftists were sure was the "beginning of an indigenous American revolutionary movement," Polanyi's entire double movement, owed an uncommonly large debt to an encyclical letter of a Catholic pope as read and interpreted by an erratic Irishman from the Kerry Patch.[78]

The question of sequence and of cause and effect can be asked of every Irish Catholic on the seam. Did a commitment to the cause of labor lead to the cause of Ireland or the other way around? In the case of Walsh, the evidence is strong that labor was first, followed quickly by anti-imperialism and internationalism generally defined, which led to Ireland Free. He came late to this last one, at least in his public life. He was never indifferent to it, but a free Ireland was never enough for him. He wanted a humane Ireland, partly as a guide to a more humane world. He would fully embrace the national cause the moment it fully embraced labor's and then internationalized both. A narrowly nationalist Ireland, run by and for the bourgeois and propertied Irish, would have nothing to teach the world. There were lessons in what Lady Gregory had called Ireland's "lost causes and shadowy ideals." Victims had much to teach; victimizers very little. Walsh agreed.[79]

In a 1920 address in Montreal, Walsh spoke of the "wrongs" Ireland and the Irish had suffered "through almost a thousand years" and of the "glories of her sons and daughters." Those glories were evident "in the realm of... propaganda for liberty all over the world... as well as statesmanship, letters and art." That was "the very soul, the pure white soul... of the Irish nation." Ireland had "never lost her soul." Then came the connection: Ireland was "a working nation; the handful of financiers that control the destinies of Ireland"—the *shoneens*—"are on their way out."[80]

The next year, 1921, Walsh elaborated on that theme: "The Irish Labor party is officially committed to Irish independence, and on national issues is allied with the Republicans." On another occasion, Walsh turned alliance into something far more fundamental. First, he reported that "Ireland has the most intellectual, significant and coherent labor movement in the world today." Then he cinched up the ties: "Labor in its organized sense, and republicanism in its militant arm, are one and the same thing in Ireland." "The workers of Ireland revolt against the idea of being wage slaves." They rebel against "absentee capital" as against absentee landlords and absentee managers of an empire. The "ancient Irish spirit as expressed by its poets and philosophers [was] the soul of the Irish revolution.... [But the] labor movement [was] its backbone, lungs, and heart."[81]

Walsh followed that with this ambiguous comment: "The Irish workers ... have a wonderful feeling of kinship for their brothers across the sea." Which sea? And were the brothers national-ethnic or social-class? It would have been useful had he said. The evidence, however, is on the side of "all the seas" and with social-class brothers (and sisters), Irish or not. For Walsh, the labor movement that was the backbone, lungs, and heart of the Irish national movement was international. He was as much a citizen of the universe as

Francis Patrick Walsh, n.d., ca. 1905. A relaxed Frank Walsh: portrait of an erratic. Courtesy Library of Congress.

Liam Mellows and the rest of the most fervent of the IPL. In Walsh's case, that led to a condemnation of all notions of white supremacy, not just of Anglo-Saxon supremacy; of all ethnic prejudices, not just those against the Irish; of imperialism generally, England's to be sure, but everyone else's too; and of male dominance and privilege in all its forms.[82]

But recall too his references to the Irish "soul," to philosophy, statesmanship, letters, poetry, and art—Éire as creative muse and catalyst. He was a revivalist as surely as Lady Gregory or Countess Markiewicz. "The sacred fire was still burning . . . after all these thousand years of darkness. . . . 'A thousand years are as yesterday.'"—a very Irish and very Catholic thing to say. As Pope Leo had insisted, the future could be "conjectured" from the past. That was not something anyone figured to hear from many modern American Protestants—which is one very good reason why calling Walsh or anyone else on the Irish left a "liberal" or a "progressive" makes absolutely no sense. This vision of a brave new Old Ireland turned out to be hallucinatory, but, looking back on it, who could dispute its—or Walsh's—very unlikeness to any others?[83]

• • •

Over the course of its two-and-a-half-year history, the CIR, chaired by Walsh, called 740 witnesses. Picking out one of them for special attention is not easy. The emphasis here, however, is on IrishCatholic outsideness generally, industrial democracy and the Irish-labor seam line specifically. For that reason, John Hays Hammond is an appropriate choice. Hammond was a mining engineer and mine owner, a member of the conservative National Civic Federation, the chairman of the federation's industrial and economic department. He had also managed mining operations in Mexico, California, Idaho—where he directly confronted Ed Boyce—and South Africa, where he was the manager of the properties of Cecil Rhodes. He had a well-deserved reputation as an imperial intriguer and capitalist strike breaker. He was alleged to have precipitated the Boer War in defense of British imperial interests. It's a certainty that he used Pinkerton detectives and heavily armed corporate gangsters against striking miners and that he played on ethnic and religious differences to divide the workforce. Hammond may have been as close to the quintessence of the Anglo-American capitalist and imperialist as could be found.[84]

When asked his opinion of "what has been termed 'industrial democracy,' giving labor a voice in the management of the industry," Hammond answered simply, "I do not believe in that. . . . Even in the political realm, democracy is not the expression of . . . equality." That was even truer in the entirely separate industrial realm. The distribution of wealth might become fairer but the accumulator index would suffer. "The average laborers," the "common man and common woman," Hammond said, "could not produce profit. Aristocracy not democracy, is the cause of profit." The test is "efficiency of operation, not fairness."[85]

I wish Frank Walsh had asked more questions of Hammond. There was only this one short exchange. Walsh wanted to know whether Hammond thought those in the American working class were all "well fed and housed." Hammond answered "No." Walsh moved from there to distributive justice: "Until they are so, can there be any such thing as over production . . . of wealth? Is not the inequality of distribution of wealth responsible for . . . unemployed factories existing at the same time with unemployed men and women?" Hammond's only answer was that production was set by management. So was hiring; so were wages. All were prerogatives of those in boardrooms, not of those on shop floors.

Walsh then asked Hammond what he considered "to be the standard wage for ... American ... unskilled labor. If you can fix it (the standard), I wish you would." By fix it, Walsh meant make the standard wage a living wage, another of John Ryan's quixotic notions. Hammond's response was—to give it a name—managerial: "The corporations would have to fix that." It would depend on the local "standard of living," which made it "difficult to establish just what the standards were" in the case of unskilled industrial labor. Wages had to be enough that an industrial worker "not ... simply become an animal, ... and worked to death." That was the best Hammond could come up with regarding distributive justice.[86]

John Rogers Commons was not called as a witness. He was one of the commissioners and he testified in that capacity. It was he who was most responsible for the dissenting minority report that Walsh entered into the final report of the CIR. I discussed Commons earlier in the context of "illiberal liberals," as I renamed Thomas Leonard's "illiberal reformers." Commons was a professed socialist, strongly influenced by the Social Gospel; he was as far removed ideologically from John Hays Hammond as he was culturally removed from Frank Walsh. He did, however, share one thing with Hammond, a deep hostility to labor running the store—whatever the store might be. With Hammond, that was entirely the responsibility of capitalist managers who would run it in the interests of capital. Government had only a small role in Hammond's modern economic system, and labor had no role at all. Commons was of a different mind. For him, well-trained government administrators, in the interests of efficiency and guided by theories of political economy, would impose limits—sometimes severe ones—on capitalists' authority. Labor, however, the third player in this economic system, would do what it had always done: work and make things and trust that the "new ideology" would sustain them.[87]

Walsh disagreed with both, with Commons as severely as with Hammond. The labor historian Shelton Stromquist writes that, for Walsh, "America [was] a profoundly class-divided society in which the problems of democratic reform could only be addressed by a fundamental re-distribution of power," which could only be achieved by giving workers "'a voice in the conditions of labor." The disagreement between Commons and Walsh could not have been more basic and has been given a great deal of attention by historians. What has not are the origins of that disagreement. The majority report of the CIR, written by Basil Manly but with Walsh's imprimatur—and that's the word for it—was passionate and angry; it could hardly be called drifty, but neither was it scientific and "masterful."[88]

It was important to Walsh that people knew that he was not a "political economist," that he studied "life itself," and that "you cannot card-index ... hopes, aspirations, happiness, miseries, laughter and tears." Commons's minority report was the opposite of the majority one in tone and style as well as substance. It was filled with card indexes and adjustors' tables. There was almost nothing in it on the causes of social unrest, and nothing at all on laughter and tears. Commons was interested in remedying the social problem, not in reconstructing society and life itself. He approved of the fact that "employers control the jobs. They hire whom they please." Indeed, they did. Commons "knew," and expected everyone else to know as well, "that . . . unions had always been unsuccessful when they ventured into business," meaning "management." Why would "anyone think that labor had suddenly grown wise?"[89]

Commons wanted to "save Capitalism by making it good," which contrasts nicely with what John Ryan had said, that it would make capitalism good by making it less. For Walsh and others on the left, the cause of industrial discontent was simple and basic: A decades-old "domestic war of classes" had reached a point of crisis; "the workers of the nation, through compulsory and oppressive methods, legal and illegal, are denied the full product of their toil." This was not a problem that could be solved by structural tinkering. But that was all that Commons offered. His report reads like a primer in political science. Walsh thought it went far deeper into the social-scientific weeds than was useful. As for Commons, he thought Walsh's "political program . . . pointed toward communism and socialism"— that from Commons's 1934 autobiography, twenty years after the report and during the first New Deal.[90]

If this were all that separated Walsh and Commons, the whole dispute could be explained as a disagreement on policy arising from different economic philosophies. That's Shelton Stromquist's contention in his recent and excellent *Re-inventing the People*. But there was a lot more than that. Commons's nativism profoundly influenced his economic analysis. And Walsh's quite Irish Catholic sensibilities profoundly influenced his. I have already quoted Commons on race generally; what follows are some of what he had to say on race as it affected industrial relations and industrial democracy.

He granted that "the people from backward nationalities" had a very large capacity for hard and dangerous industrial labor, plus a willingness to do it for considerably less than a "living wage." But they had "an incapacity for self-government." To give them any role in the management of American industry was madness. Indeed, Commons's report urged the passage of "very substantial restrictions on immigration." "Ancestry," after all, was the *"most important cause of eminence"*; it was time for the "thrifty, hardworking and intelligent American or Teutonic" races to guard the nation against the "backward, thriftless, and unintelligent races." Those are remarkable comments from one always and legitimately associated with American reformism.[91]

Ineradicable race and religious prejudice explains some of Commons's hostility to the idea of industrial democracy. "Self-government [required] intelligence, self-control, and capacity for cooperation." Without those, you get "boss rule"—which itself had ethnic implications. Industrial democracy threw the labor movement into politics and politics were not to be trusted; there were too many undesirables in it, too many "amalgamators of races" serving as politicians, by which he meant the bosses of urban political machines, many of them Irish. "Mr. Walsh," wrote Commons, "seemed to me to typify the politician." As for Walsh's "political program," as noted, Commons thought it "pointed toward communism and socialism."[92]

It didn't. It pointed the way to a measure of equality and social justice. Consider Commons's next: "Infatuated by an 'economic interpretation of history,' Walsh and those like him *overlook the racial interpretation*"—a comment that should be carefully scrutinized. In John Commons's world, some races were born to ride; others to be ridden. Socialists "hope to see the dispossessed . . . take possession." But, as those familiar with the "racial interpretation" could have told them, "the 'masses' would not be equal to the task." I said earlier and repeat it now: John Commons was a self-described progressive who loved the working class. He did not, however, like the people in it.[93]

The majority report of the CIR was written by a young attorney, Basil Maxwell Manly, who shared Walsh's reformist vision. Manly's contribution to the Walsh Plan is acknowledged by historians. But it was his background that caught my attention. Manly was the great-grandson of Basil Manly Sr., the founder of the Southern Baptist Theological Seminary in Louisville. His uncle, Basil Manly Jr., was an Alabama Baptist preacher who in 1861 administered the oath of office to Confederate president Jefferson Davis, prayed ardently for the Confederacy's success and the future of slavery, and then took the post of the Confederacy's Chaplain. One of Basil Manly, Jr.'s sons, was the founder of the University of Alabama and later its president. All the Manlys, including Charles, Basil Maxwell Manly's father, owned slaves and strongly supported secession and slavery.[94]

We can account for the motives of Walsh, Hammond, and Commons. But what explains Basil Manly? Perhaps he saw the CIR as another chance to take down the Northern industrial capitalism that had tried to translate the agrarian and traditional Old South and turn it into a New South, modern, and industrial. It is interesting to note that it was Manly who pointed out what had happened to the Fourteenth Amendment, noting that what he called this "negro civil rights" amendment that had been "forced upon [the South] by the Northern States"—Manly as aggrieved Southron.

Black civil rights, however, had been abandoned; the amendment had been "practically appropriated by the corporations. It operates today to protect the rights of property to the detriment of the rights of man." The "charter of liberty for human rights against property rights"—an interesting reading of abolition—is now "the Magna Charta of accumulated and organized capital." That's not an inaccurate analysis of what it had become—not inaccurate, but confusing. Did Manly object to the Fourteenth Amendment because it was a protector of Black civil rights or because it was the Magna Carta of corporate privilege? Or both? Basil Manly deserves more attention from historians than he's gotten. The irony—or is it the inexplicability?—quotient in the teaming of Manly with Frank Walsh is substantial. It speaks of the protean nature not just of American liberalism but of American antimodernism and anticapitalism.[95]

Manly seemed to want to see the Fourteenth Amendment, in both of its roles, undone. His reasons are uncertain. He was less indecipherable when it came to the Second Amendment. He didn't cite Ed Boyce and the WFM, but he pointed out that the Second Amendment allowed "'every union local [to] be a voluntary military company and every union hall an armory." He followed that with his formal recommendation—in a federal report, no less— that local unions arm themselves. "There would be no Colorados or West Virginias with such a democratic army in existence." The references were to violence against strikers and their families at Ludlow, Colorado, and Cabin Creek, West Virginia.[96]

Walsh included Commons's minority report, complete and unedited, in the Final Report of the CIS. He then rejected it *"in toto."* Manly's report, on the other hand, he praised as "an unassailable statement of the existing industrial situation." The statement may have been unassailable, but two of Manly's recommendations on how to deal with the existing situation were not. Walsh appended his two objections to the end of Manly's three-hundred-plus-page report. The idea of turning union halls into ordnance depots and arming American labor was not among them. Walsh said nothing about Manly's call to arms. Nor did Walsh say anything about Manly's dance around the Fourteenth Amendment, which, given Walsh's support of Black rights, surprised me.[97]

What he did say should have surprised no one. First of all, Walsh "wish[ed] to record [his] opposition, as a matter of principle" to Manly's recommendation for a literacy test as "a method of restricting immigration." Indeed, Walsh wanted to be on the record as opposing any and "all restrictions upon immigration." He thought they were based on racial prejudice. He was right. They were. Like poverty, they were "unnecessary [and] evil." His second objection was equally revealing, both of his politics and of Manly's: Manly had made "suggestions regarding civil government in isolated communities like coal camps." Many of those local governments were prolabor, but they were routinely overruled by state and/or federal officials. Walsh thought Manly's suggested reforms inadequate. The problem, Walsh said could only be dealt with "by the [federal] Government taking over all coal lands and leasing them upon terms which will make possible their operation *upon a cooperative basis by the workers."* Walsh, in sum, wanted open borders for all immigrants, the nationalization of a key industry, cooperative management, and industrial democracy. Five years later, the Democratic Programme of Sinn Féin advocated the same for the Irish Republic.[98]

· · ·

Frank Walsh was not the only leftist Irish Catholic in America. Like Jim Larkin, he was not aberrant. I return also to Bruce Nelson's comment about the Catholic Irish generally. Many of their critics, particularly from the reformer class, argued that the Irish were descended from some sacred isle, walled off from the world. Their origins, especially the more doctrinally Catholic of them, had made them "narrowly conservative," the inveterate and witless opponents of modernity, including modern reform. I join Nelson in rejected that idea; it is an artifact of the illiberality of American liberals. It needs to be discarded, and not just in fairness to Frank Walsh.

As for Walsh specifically, citing to the near poverty of Walsh's family or his professed "hatred of all oppression" also won't do. Irish "ancestral sorrows" have also to be invoked. As must the Irish ancestral faith. That Walsh became the lead defense attorney for both Tom Mooney and Jim Larkin wasn't just predictable; it was inevitable. If it is right to argue, as many have, that Social Gospelers were bringing their Protestants' "absent" God's message to the world, then it is equally fair to argue that Walsh was summoning the spirit of the Catholics' living and "present" God to his. Walsh's Catholicism was worn lightly, but it appears to have been felt deeply. Like Commons, Walsh loved the working class; unlike Commons, he also loved those in it. As a young man, he was of that class. It is uncertain that Commons, or the other Social Gospelers, even knew anyone in it.

Walsh was equally fervent about a free Ireland, a cause he believed inseparable from all the other good causes requiring his attention. He was actively involved in compiling evidence of British atrocities during the Irish War of Independence and providing that evidence to the 1921 American Commission on Conditions in Ireland. For Walsh, Ireland's was no ordinary national movement. As one of the witnesses before the commission put it, the war was a "struggle between two civilizations, capitalist and cooperative." Walsh agreed entirely. The Republic and the Irish who would direct its course had more to do than form a government. The national movement, Walsh wrote, "had been touched by God himself." It was an "instrument in God's hand." Through it, "the world would be made free." Frank Walsh was the model Catholic Irish contrarian and occasional subversive. More theoretically, he was the ultimate ontological dissentient and "philosopher" of Irishness. He was as close to being the sum of all the parts of the Irish Catholic Left, including prominently its erraticism, as anyone in either Ireland or Irish America. Credit history, the merry prankster.[99]

CHAPTER SEVEN

"The Irish Movement Has Forgotten to Be American"
Woodrow Wilson and the Transatlantic Great Red Green Scare

> "There will be sufficient pressure at home to keep the Irish question well in the forefront. . . . President Wilson cannot turn a deaf ear."
> —Hannah Sheehy-Skeffington, "Impressions of Sinn Féin in America," 1918

The Risings of 1916 and 1917, the Celtic in Dublin, the Bolshevik in St. Petersburg, both during World War I, gave the link between Irish nationalism and labor radicalism a new significance. Irish leftists were waging a war of national liberation. They were also and simultaneously engaged in a movement for radical social change—to use parallel language, a war of working-class liberation. There was nothing new about either war. Subject nations and subject peoples had been demanding their freedom for millennia. What was singular about the Irish struggle was that both wars were being fought at the same time by the same people flying the same flag, singing the same battle hymns, and convinced that victory in either conflict meant victory in the other.

Ireland was a disaffected colony, a nation without nationhood. There were a lot of those in that age of empires. The Irish people, regardless of where found, belonged to disaffected working classes. There were a lot of those too in that age of capital. In Ireland, the proletariat was not a large one; it was outnumbered substantially by the Irish peasantry. But it was conscious of itself and, theoretically at least, its ranks held room for a peasantry. Whether rebel Irish were the first ones to fight for both and at the same time can be debated, but not productively and not here. Mine is an argument for the rarity, not the uniqueness, of the Irish Left's resistance on the seam.[1]

The other singular feature of this resistance was the fact that the number of Irish who saw themselves as doubly misused was not limited to Ireland.

It extended to its exiled children in America, the shamed descendants of a "slave nation." Whatever the shortfall in Ireland's industrial labor force, it was more than made up for by the abundance of Irish in the American one, many of whom saw themselves as the victims of British colonialism as surely as any landless tenant in Connemara or impoverished dockworker in Dublin. The cause of Ireland was their cause as well. That these gave far more generously to the cause of Ireland than did those Irish Americans with pianos in their parlors should have surprised no one. It assuredly did not surprise anyone of the erratic Irish. Irish nationalism was nationalism of a special kind; it was not only compatible with socialist reforms, it was a social reform. It figured to have a special appeal for those who thought society needed reforming.[2]

This is the right time to take another look at the socialist *New York Call*'s 1919 story about William Francis Dunne, the "hero of Bloody Butte," the simultaneous supporter of a republic for Ireland and socialism for the world. The writer for the *Call* insisted, quite rightly, that Dunne believe that the freedom of Ireland and the freedom of the *American* working class were connected. The next point was a bit uncertain: the *Call* wondered which of Dunne's advocacies, in the cause of anticolonialism or of anticapitalism, was "more offensive" to Woodrow Wilson and his administration's war against radicals, real and imagined. Dunne didn't distinguish between the two; perhaps Wilson didn't either.[3]

Wilson is the key player in all this. His presidency lasted from 1913 until 1921, busy years for Americans and Irish by any accounting. World War I between England and its allies—including Tsarist Russia—and Germany and its allies began in the summer of 1914. The Easter Rising and revolutionary Ireland's "alliance" with Germany was in 1916. In February 1917, Russia abandoned its war against Germany. Two months later, in April, partly in response to Russia's withdrawal, Woodrow Wilson took America into the war against Germany. In November 1917, the Bolsheviks took over Russia; two months later, they recognized the still quite provisional Irish Republic. Obviously, Wilson had more important things to think about during these years than Ireland. But at its core, and for a decade after the war ended, America's "Irish policy"—if it can be called that—was of Wilson's design. It was not always statesmanlike.[4]

Irish erraticism, including that personified by Bill Dunne's conjoining of causes, offended Wilson. It violated his sense of national purpose. He made the problem far more serious by racializing it. He couldn't help it. He racialized—or ethnocized, to coin an ugly word—everything. For Wilson, race was determinative. It explained why people looked the way they did, why their head was a certain size, their nose a certain shape. It determined why they acted as they did. Race identity was a secular version of Calvinist predestination. Indeed, because for Wilson race had a religious component and religion a racial one, it was only semisecular. A "man's rootage," he said once, "means more than his leafage." Wilson's rootage was proudly Cromwellian. He was a "spiritual heir of [John] Knox, a dissenting Protestant of Covenanter blood," a "confirmed and confounded Calvinist," as Edward Bellamy called him.[5]

He was also a confirmed and quite unconfounded believer in the superiority of the Anglo-Saxon race. Anglo-Saxonism was Wilson's race standard. And a very high standard it was. The hard question is how many of Wilson's racial theories were taken from Anglo-Saxon supremacists whose racism was far more advanced than his own. There had always been something farcical about theories of racial supremacy. In certain hands, however, the senseless became also the malicious. In the case of Thomas Dixon, a North Carolina Baptist minister and Wilson's classmate, colleague, and friend, race science became pseudoscientific racism. In his 1902 novel, *The Leopard's Spots*, Dixon made the case that the post–Civil War reconciliation of North and South was in its essence a coming together of white men as white men. Black Americans would pay a heavy price for that racial reunion.[6]

Wilson also wrote a book in 1902. His five-volume text, *A History of the American People*, defined America as a glorious example of what happens when Anglo-Saxons are turned loose. As the historian Cara Lea Burnidge put it recently, Wilson's "view of the nation . . . was a racialized" one "which privileged white Anglo-Saxon Protestants." In the last few years, that has become the consensus among Wilson scholars. Lloyd Ambrosius, in his account of Wilson, defines the cultural background that produced *The Birth of a Nation*: white people over Black people; men over women; Protestants over non-Protestants; Anglo-Saxons over all. Ambrosius's conclusion is unnerving: "Out of this culture emerged both Dixon and . . . Wilson."[7]

Wilson's articles of faith were uncomplicated and unexamined. Cecil Spring-Rice, Britain's ambassador to the United States, once remarked that Wilson "is by descent an Orangeman and by education a Presbyterian." That was a redundancy. It was also a revealing use of the words *Orangeman* and *education*. By the time Spring-Rice offered his comment, "Orange" meant not just Irish Protestant, but Irish Protestant of advanced anti-Catholic beliefs. By "education," there is reason to think Spring-Rice used it as Henry Adams did, a cultural inheritance, something ongoing, unsanctioned, experiential—and an impediment to adjusting to new realities. Wilson took his ethnic identity from that correlation. He was a descendant of Lowland Scottish Presbyterians. The fact that these forebears—a word he would have favored—were born in Ireland was of no moment. They were Scots, and Anglo-Saxon to their very bones.[8]

That was not just Wilson's "rootage." In his mind, it was America's rootage as well. Wilson's America at its origins was Anglo-Saxon and Protestant. It was still that. American history was an Anglo-Saxon hero saga. As Wilson framed it, the truest American was an Anglo-Saxon Protestant living in an American forest or on an American prairie—the right people in the right place at the right time. America was made for such as these. America was their providential gift. It allowed them to experience "sooner than the mass of Englishmen at home what real freedom and self government meant." The American Revolution, by Wilson's reading of it, was one of *England's* finest hours. It had "made Englishmen"—those in England, that is—"feel like free men." Albion's seed was tutoring the English in freedom and thus strengthening the root stock.[9]

Wilson was one of the first Anglo-American race patriots. The glorious reconciliation of white men after the American Civil War had witnessed what the movie based on Dixon's book called the "birth of a nation"—white America. The reconciliation of English and American Anglo-Saxons witnessed the equally glorious birth of Anglo-America—Cromwelliana, to give it an impolite name. Rapprochement and détente do not go far enough. England and America did not just reconcile and patch up a few old animosities. They came together in what I called earlier a racial love-fest. Irish Catholics would pay for this reunion as Blacks paid for the sectional and racial reconciliation of North and South.[10]

The best that Wilson could say about the Irish was that they took "the strain off [his] Scotch conscience" and taught him "to love a good scrap." They were clownish and had "afforded me periods of most enjoyable irresponsibility when I do not care whether school keeps or not, or whether anybody gets educated or not." In Irish frailties was to be found Irish charm. The Irish made him laugh. He was almost certainly speaking only of the Catholics; the Protestant Irish shared his "Scotch conscience." Perhaps the Catholics made them laugh too. Overtime, they were unable to do even that. According to Dr. Cary Grayson, Wilson's personal physician, Wilson came finally to think of the Irish not as childishly irresponsible but rather "as a race very hard to deal with owing to their inconsiderateness, their unreasonable demands and their jealousies." By then, of course, he was talking only about the Catholics.[11]

The important part of that comment is not the list of Irish deficiencies but that Wilson ascribed them to race. All he really needed to say was that, "as a race," they are not Anglo-Saxon. In fact, they were intensely anti-Anglo-Saxon. There were reasons for that, but none that Wilson was intellectually curious enough to inquire about. All he knew or cared to know was that, by definition, it was impossible to be anglophobiac and not be hostile to Anglo-America. Which placed Irish hatred of England perilously close to disloyalty to America's racial pillar and its founding principles.

Take, for example—as Wilson surely did—Irish anti-imperialism. The assumption in America had always been that the Irish objected to the British

Empire only as that empire affected Ireland. Anti-imperialism was no more than a rhetorical accessory to Irish nationalism. In truth, it had always been more than that. And, as Wilson was coming to understand, it was assuredly more than that by 1913. Irish anti-imperialism was an assault on imperialism in general, including the American version of it, and the "cant of conquest" used to defend it. Irish anti-imperialism struck at the heart of what was to be the Anglo-American century. That Wilson thought of himself and his nation as part of that imperial destiny is indisputable. Americans may have been new to an imperial frame of mind, but after a century of expansionism as a frame of mind approaching a national duty, they proved a quick study.

Wilson transferred expansionism effortlessly to an overseas empire. "Of a sudden," he said, and without premeditation, "the United States had given themselves a colonial empire, and taken their place of power in the field of international politics." "Given themselves" was an interesting way to put it. It recalls nothing so much as John Seeley's claim about the English that "we seem . . . to have conquered half the world in a 'fit of absence of mind.'" Wilson was not disposed to challenge England's empire, regardless of how conquered. If anything, he seemed to be preparing America to help itself to the half of the world England had not taken. This was more than just a policy issue. To give it a grander label than it deserves, for Wilson and the other race patriots, building and defending Anglo-Saxon empires—or a shared Anglo-American Empire—was a matter of racial destiny.[12]

Wilson viewed the world through that Anglocentric lens. As for America's racial and ethnic others, he judged them on how well they understood the racial order and how quickly they adjusted to it. Some did better at that than others. For Wilson, immigration and assimilation were self-selecting and self-winnowing. Kraditor wrote of the preradicalized; Wilson of the pre-Americanized. Eagerness to be an American was the first step to becoming one. In a 1914 address to a largely Irish audience, Wilson said that America "appropriated" the "best impulses" of its immigrants and "Americanized and translated them into the glory and the majesty of a great country."[13]

I would note particularly his use of the word *translated*. It recalls Brian Friel's play, *Translations* and what the English did to the Irish of Ballybegs. For Friel, translating was an act of cultural appropriation, of theft. Wilson saw it as a gift, an act of great kindness. Wilson acknowledged that there might have been some "push" factors in the Irish immigration. But he never inquired into what they might have been because they should have had no effect on the transfer of political allegiance. He noted that there were some immigrants—the reference was mostly to Germans—"whom revolution [of 1848] had thrust . . . out of the old world." But the circumstances of the Irish diaspora escaped his attention. In his 1902 five-volume history of the United States, he wrote of the "great flood" of immigrants in the late 1840s but made no reference to Irish; in fact, he made no reference to the Great Famine at all. His conclusion applied to all immigrants; the best of them were "carried to western farms and the open regions of the interior." The "most unwholesome deposits" were left at "eastern ports"—where most of the Irish were to be found.[14]

That was the occasion for another of his serious quarrels with America's wayward and literally outlandish Irish. He could not explain and could not accommodate their communal instincts, their remarkable clannishness. Of all their bad impulses, this was the most unfathomable and the most threatening, more so even than their Catholicism. That clannishness and Catholicism might be related phenomena—or related defects—was not investigated. The Irish made themselves up in "groups." So did other immigrants, but they broke out of them. The Irish never did. Wilson's America did not consist of groups. As Wilson told an audience of new immigrants in 1915, "You cannot become thorough Americans if you think of yourselves in groups. America does not consist of groups. A man who thinks of himself as belonging to a particular . . . group in America has not yet become an American." It may be presumed that "working class" was also a "group."[15]

The question all but asks itself: How was it conceivable, even for one as incurious and certain of himself as Wilson, that a people condemned both in Britain and in America as a racial and cultural group would not develop racial and cultural group attitudes? The topic never came up. Wilson paid only slightly more attention to America's nativism than to Ireland's sorrows. He wrote, without a trace of disapproval, of the Know-Nothing Party as a welcome diversion from the slavery debates, nothing more. The leaders of the Ku Klux Klan of the Reconstruction Era were near-heroic figures. As for the xenophobes of the American Protective Association and the reborn KKK, he made no references to them at all. American nativists were trying only to ensure what Wilson said was the "maintenance of a safe ascendency in affairs for those born and bred to the politics and manners of America." I assume that his use of *ascendency* was entirely innocent and not a subtle allusion to the Anglo-Irish Protestant Ascendency class in Ireland. That's the only innocent thing he said in that entire comment.[16]

• • •

Easter 1916 and the rebel Irish "alliance" with Fr. James English's "gallant" Germany and the Irish American support for and entanglement in that alliance was followed by the American declaration of war against Germany, the Russian Revolution, and the Bolsheviks' dalliance with Ireland and its rebels. There was an old bit of what passed for Irish wisdom to the effect that "England's distress is Ireland's opportunity." The English were aware of it. They thought it passed for an Irish strategy. Wilson had to have been aware of it too; aware, in other words, that, as of April 1917, there may have been Irish in the United States who now saw *America's* distress as Ireland's opportunity.

The person who spoke most clearly on these issues was not Wilson but one of his staunchest friends and political allies, Walter Hines Page. Wilson had appointed Page the US ambassador to Great Britain in 1913; it was a post Page would hold throughout the war. Like Wilson, Page was a southerner and an ardent friend of the Anglo-Saxon race and of Anglo-America as its hybridized homeland. According to his adulatory biographer, Page had "the profoundest respect for the British character and British institutions." Like the other Anglo-Saxon supremacists, Page was convinced that "British conceptions of liberty and government and British ideals of life represented the fine flower of human progress."[17]

Page followed that sentiment with the requisite Anglo-American hymn of praise and thanksgiving: The best of America, he said, "[our] speech and . . . literature . . . our political institutions, our liberty, our law, our conception of morality and of life are . . . derived from the British Isles," of which Ireland was not one—perhaps the only thing on which Page and the Irish were agreed. Page's comment took Anglocentric history further even than had Wilson. America was one of Britain's crowning achievements. So was the British Empire. America and the British Empire were indivisible. America had left that empire only in an administrative sense. Culturally, where it counted, it was still in and of it. In Page's mind, the Empire was living proof of what the application of British "ideals of life" could do.

In 1914, World War I put this God-favored Empire at risk. In 1916, the Irish rebellion increased that risk. For Page, England's distress demanded America's assistance. Americans shared fully in the British imperial birthright and, with Wilson's April 1917 declaration of war against Germany, they proved themselves worthy of it. Page knew they would. That's what kindred did. "Blood," as he had told an English audience in 1913, "carries with it that particular trick of thought which makes us all English in the last resort. . . . The United States is yet English-led and English-ruled." He said that he didn't mean that last comment literally, but it's easy to see how some might have misinterpreted it.[18]

According to Page, it was intentionally and egregiously misinterpreted by certain "anti-British elements on [the American] side of the water." Everyone knew which elements he had in mind. He said there were "Irish societies" who "clogged the pages of the *Congressional Record*" with their protests and their demands that England's Anglo-Saxon cry from the heart be spurned. On May 3, 1917, soon after the United States entered the war, Page wrote a revealing letter that indicated just how detached the Catholic Irish were from the Wilson administration, if not from the entire American nation.

He wasn't speaking for Wilson officially, but he could have been. His sentiments echoed Wilson's own, and his letter can be read as what Page may have intended it to be: a statement of the administration's position on Anglo-America, race patriotism, the war, the Irish question, the preservation of the British Empire, and the effect each of those topics had on the others.[19]

He began by stating that the war had called Anglo-Americans to their duty and their destiny. Victory—and with America's entry, it was all but assured—would bring an era of Anglo-American dominance: "We can now begin a distinctly New Era in the world's history." Americans "can play a part bigger than we have yet dreamed of if we prove big enough." No Anglo-Saxon chest-beating followed that, but what Page offered next implied some of it. Playing that "bigger part" required that Americans "simply . . . conduct our affairs by a large national policy and not by . . . listening to the complaints of . . . *really non-American* people," in which category he placed, by name, "the Irish." The war would flush out these miscreants. "See how the declaration of war has cleared the atmosphere!" There is no mistaking Page's meaning, or the joy he took from being able to express it: The war would finally force the "really non-American" Irish to make up their minds and decide where their hearts lay.[20]

It appears obvious now that, from the beginning of the war—indeed, for at least a couple of decades before the war—Wilson was on the side of Anglo-America and his fellow Anglo-Saxon race patriots. Richard Drake, a careful and perceptive historian of imperialism, puts it this way: "In effect, Wilson wanted the United States to sign on for gendarme duty in the campaign to preserve the British Empire in Ireland, Egypt, and India." The English needed America to serve as a cavalry unit, racing to protect the British imperium threatened by the brutishness of the Germans and the faithlessness of the Irish. Wilson obliged. The German threat to Britain's Empire was grave; the Irish Republican threat was only slightly less so—and no less real.[21]

Which raises an important point: A republic, by definition, cannot be a colony of another nation. Republics can fight to defend another's empire, but they cannot be in one. Ireland had declared itself a republic—of which sort didn't matter—and that placed it out of and free from British imperial authority. Might not other colonies do as Ireland had done? How might the British working class respond? Marx had said it; Lenin was about to say it again: freeing Ireland freed the world. The proclaimed Irish Republic, moreover, was of a distinctly collectivist sort. How might the Irish American working class respond? Some of this Wilson couldn't even have known; the US State Department didn't receive consular reports from Ireland until months after the 1916 Rising, an act of administrative delinquency difficult to explain. At the least, however, news of the Easter Rebellion can only have added to Wilson's decision to intervene and make Britain's war America's war.

The US declaration of war on Germany not only broke Irish American hearts, it forced a radical shift in their allegiance and affections. Ireland's freedom was still tied to the war; it just wasn't tied to the same side winning it. Freedom now had to come as a consequence of an American victory, not a German one. Ireland had a new ally; the Yanks were coming. Switching sides that rapidly was vertiginous for Irish America. Two weeks after the American declaration of war, the Clan na Gael issued secret instructions to its scattered camps: The policies and the actions of the Clan were from that point forward to be "devoted entirely to securing the National Independence of Ireland through the intervention of the Government of the United States." It is interesting that the Clan did not say "our" government.[22]

There was a strong element of fantasy in that Irish American belief. It ignored the alliance between the United States and Great Britain, the newly effected racial entente cordiale, the family reunion of Anglo-Saxons. It also ignored the fact that an American victory would be a British victory. The Irish should have asked themselves when the last time was that a victorious nation was stripped of colonies as a consequence of its victory. More specifically, they should have considered that Great Britain could and likely did agree with all of Wilson's principles, including the right of self-determination for small colonial nations, as long as they were small colonies belonging to nations that lost the war. The evidence is now incontrovertible that Wilson was on the English side of that one too.[23]

Irish credulity, however, is not all that was at issue. Wilson should have been less vague—and more honest—in what he told the Irish and the world to believe. As in 1910, when he said that "no little group of men like the English . . . have the right to government in [other] parts of the world." Or in May 1916, a month after the suppression of the Rising and short weeks after England executed those who led it, when he repeated his belief "that every people has a right to choose the sovereignty under which they shall live. . . . [T]he small States of the world have a right to enjoy . . . respect for their sovereignty and for their territorial integrity." The Irish had been told that "national aspirations must be respected." In the future, people would be "dominated and governed only by their own consent." *Dominated* was a confusing word in that context, but *consent* was not. Wilson elaborated on it. "Self-determination, he asserted, "is not a mere phrase. It is an imperative principle." In April 1917, when he called for a declaration of war on Germany, he said he wanted "to make the world safe for democracy." Was Ireland not a democracy-in-waiting?[24]

Wilson never retreated from that anticolonial stance. And most of the Irish never stopped doubting that he meant what he said. That was particularly true when the Irish read his Fourteen Points, presented to the Congress on January 8, 1918. I offer them up without comment. Their meaning to the

Irish would have been obvious: "The day of conquest and aggrandizement is gone by"; a world made safe "for every peace-loving nation which, like ours, wishes to live its own life, determine its own institutions"; a "free, open-minded, and absolutely impartial adjustment of all colonial claims based upon ... the principle that ... the interests of the populations must have equal weight" with those of the "imperial power." In regard to Russia, Wilson demanded the "evacuation of all Russian territory" that the Russian people might have "an unhampered ... opportunity for the independent determination of [their] own political development and national policy."[25]

There were repeated references to "race" as the determinant of new national borders, along with phrases like "autonomous development," "political independence and territorial integrity," "peoples associated together against the Imperialists." Wilson pledged "equality among the peoples of the world ... whether they be strong or weak." Walter Hines Page had said that the war was going to force the Irish to make up their minds: Were they Irish or American? The Irish could now say that Page was wrong, that that was a false dichotomy. They could be both. Indeed, with America as liberator, they could only be both.[26]

I repeat: Irish Americans should have known better. They should at least have figured out that the Bolshevik "Rising" of 1917 would be of far greater concern to Wilson than anything that happened in Ireland. The United States entered the war when it did partly in response to the possibility that Russia might be leaving it. That they might be leaving it in order to export Bolshevism made that an even more fearsome prospect. Wilson's Fourteen Points were in part Wilson's response to what he perceived as a Bolshevik "new world order" as a rival to his own. January 1918, however, was also right in the middle of the communist courtship of the Irish and the favorable response of the Irish to that courtship. The interesting possibility must at least be raised that Ireland must also have been on Wilson's mind when he issued his Fourteen Points. Certainly Wilson was on Ireland's mind.

That Wilson believed all that he said at the time he said it is likely. That he did not believe it when it came time to act on what he had said is certain. By then he knew that principles, even imperative ones, have sometimes to give way to realities. That possibility had already occurred to Robert Lansing, Wilson's secretary of state, who, in a diary entry, noted that the principle of self-determination was "loaded with dynamite" and that he wished Wilson would stop putting "such ideas into the mind of certain races." Most prominent among the "certain races" likely to make "impossible demands" were the Irish.[27]

Other of Wilson's friends were of the same mind as Lansing, and there was at least one semiofficial effort to temper—if not entirely walk back—Wilson's loose language on self-determination. Sometime later in 1918, Colonel

Edward House, joined by Frank Cobb and Walter Lippmann, presented an "American Interpretation of the Fourteen Points." It appeared in a Supplement to the *Foreign Relations of the United States* of 1918. The Irish were not on the State Department's mailing list, and it is unlikely that any of them knew how "America interpreted" what Wilson had so clearly stated. The document included this most revealing statement: There was "some fear . . . expressed . . . that Wilson's promises "involve[d] reopening . . . all colonial questions. Obviously it is not so intended. It applies clearly"—and only— "to those colonial claims . . . created by the war. That means the German colonies."[28]

. . .

I quoted earlier Dr. Cary Grayson's March 1919 comment on Wilson's feelings about the Irish race: They were inconsiderate, made unreasonable demands, and were jealous of others. There is no reason to doubt Grayson's account, particularly as I decipher it: By inconsiderate, Wilson did not mean discourteous. The Irish were that too but, in this context, the word meant selfish. By unreasonable demands, he did not mean Irish demands were arbitrary, even irrational. They were, but he used *unreasonable* as meaning unwarranted and unjust. As for jealousies, Wilson wasn't just saying the Irish were an envious race—though he thought they were and had ample reasons to think so. The word signified dishonesty. Irish jealousy was a base element, a racial blemish. They didn't play fair. Once only silly and irresponsible, Irish Americans had turned sinister.

Horace Plunkett was right; Ireland was first in Irish American hearts; Shane Leslie, as quoted earlier, was also right: the Irish would happily have made a pact with hell if proof could be found that the devil was anti-British. By the spring of 1918, Sinn Féin proved the accuracy of Leslie's prediction. Communist Russia—the nearest thing to an ideological underworld—having already recognized the legitimacy of the Republic of Ireland, lined up in strong support of the anticonscription movement led by the joint forces of Sinn Féin and the Irish labor movement. It wasn't just the satanic Bolshevik support for the Irish that raised the alarm. It was that the Irish so eagerly accepted that support. Russia had become Ireland's patron. The Irish national movement had again been indiscriminate in its selection of allies.[29]

But it wasn't just the pragmatism of the weak that determined the Irish response to the support given them by the Bolsheviks. The Irish were not without political ideals. A leftist workers' republic was among them. That some Irish nationalists, whether in Ireland or the New Ireland in America, were leaning leftward was one big reason for Wilson's growing distrust of the entire national movement. Ireland's leftward plunge was taking it perilously closer to revolutionary Bolshevism. Even Cardinal James Gibbons, the most restrained of Irish American nationalists, was reported by a British Embassy official to be afraid "lest Ireland may turn to Bolshevism unless her nationalistic aspirations can be satisfied." To Wilson, that was less a prediction than a threat, and a cynical and manipulative threat, at that.[30]

Some of this can be explained as two sides speaking the same language and not understanding a word the other was saying. I offer as an example Father Peter Yorke—chieftain of the "plain Irish people" of San Francisco—and the widely circulated article he wrote in 1918 on how the Irish in America should conduct themselves during the war. He first tried to make an argument that Wilson had promised that the war would free Ireland. Wilson hadn't, but he'd come close enough, and Yorke's argument was not specious. But then came Yorke's bow to the Bolsheviks, thanking them for recognizing the Irish Republic and adding that Russia was the only nation of the "original Entente that accomplished anything worth while in this war." Since the war wasn't over, that comment about Russia and 1917 had some ominous implications for both ruling imperialist nations and the ruling capitalist classes within them. Yorke was making a connection: Ireland 1916–Russia 1917.[31]

He then further raised the stakes, saying that he was worried about "the morale of our people," by which he clearly meant the Irish people, including and with emphasis, the exiled Irish in America. "You see [their morale] threatened because of Irish exasperation and fury"—the consequences of England's refusal to deal fairly with the Irish issue. That was the negative aspect. But there was a positive, perhaps even morale-boosting, alternative for the Irish. Yorke cited "the economic revolution," a reference that set up his version of causes seamlessly joined: "Do not imagine that the masses of America to-day are any more immune from ideas coming out of Russia than they were a century and a third ago from ideas coming out of France."[32]

There were a lot of Irish in those American masses, as Bolshevik-sponsored Irish propaganda campaigns attested. Yorke, however, then turned the Russian connection to a different purpose. His "Irish people" had a special role to play among the masses of an otherwise undifferentiated American working class. The "Irish element" in the labor movement could be "the saving salt of the American mass." By "saving salt" I presume he meant "salvation." By salvation he meant that the Irish had "always stood for conservatism." Perhaps he had the Butte Miners' Union in mind. Irish conservatism could now save America from the "economic revolution." That's what Wilson didn't get. It was urgent that the "unrest" among the American Irish "caused by the fury and exasperation at England's misrule of Ireland" be "removed." "Men with Irish names" were being "driv[en] . . . with accelerated velocity . . . to the side of the economic revolution."[33]

It was quite unlike Yorke to be so circumspect in his language: "Ideas coming out of Russia" and "economic revolution" do not adequately convey his point. I will presume to speak for him: All that was standing between the United States and a communist Armageddon was the Irish element in the American labor movement. The United States would be wise to tend to that element carefully by answering its righteous demand that Ireland be a free republic. If that was a socialist workers' republic, so be it. Yorke was less troubled by the prospect of the Irish turning toward the "economic revolution" than Cardinal Gibbons was, but the two clerics were saying the same thing.

It was Yorke's contention that the Irish dominance of America's working class had kept the unions "conservative." Their "conservativism," however, was solely a function of their Irish nationalism. It was in service to the needs of Ireland. As those needs changed, it would change in response. If Ireland needed Irish American workers to be radical, then radical they would be. They would march American labor toward Marxism and revolution. According to Yorke, the furious and exasperated Irish had the power to take the whole of the American labor movement with them into the economic revolution.

The Irish would move left, not because a grossly unjust capitalist society had beggared them, but because Anglo-Saxon deal-making had left Ireland in the Empire. Wilson would have found those arguments incoherent and based on totally unconnected grievances. In plainest terms, Yorke was engaged in political extortion. Threatening to turn to communism if Ireland was not set free was Yorke's quid pro quo; and it put Wilson in an absolutely untenable place: The Irish in America would do the right thing and turn American labor away from communism only if Wilson did the wrong thing—indeed, the impossible thing—by recognizing the Irish Republic and pressuring Britain to do the same. That was the deal as Yorke presented it. A little over a month after Yorke offered his quid pro quo, Secretary of State Lansing, in a letter to Wilson, explained that the Irish were willing "to sacrifice democracy to their own selfish ends." Lansing likely used the word *democracy* as Wilson had when he promised to make the world safe for it.[34]

As Wilson left for Versailles in January 1919, the Sinn Féin–dominated Irish Parliament issued a "Message to the Free Nations of the World." The free nation of greatest importance to them was the United States. And the American that Sinn Féin most wanted to read and hear what it had to say was Wilson. The message avowed that the Irish were a people "radically distinct" from the English in "race, . . . language, . . . customs and traditions." That may have been largely true. But they directed this to one who believed that the Americans were radically *indistinct* from the English race in those same categories. Ireland then "demanded to be confronted publicly with England at the Congress of Nations ... in order that the civilized world" could "judge between English wrong and Irish right."[35]

Less than a month later, Irish labor radicals told the socialist conference in Berne that being "right" had a distinctly social-class and revolutionary cast to it. The Irish Left wasn't just firing a shot across England's bow; America and Wilson were put on warning. The world was "at the dawn of the promised era of self-determination and liberty," and Ireland was "resolutely and irrevocably determined ... to suffer foreign dominion no longer." Every "free nation" was called on to uphold Ireland's "national claim to complete independence as a ... Republic against the arrogant pretentions of England." England wasn't about to uphold anything like that, which implied that England was neither a part of the "civilized world" nor a "free nation." It was the United States, the free nation of record, that was being called to its moral duty.[36]

Later in that same session, the Irish Parliament passed the Democratic Programme. Politically expedient though it may have been, and as far short of Marxist as it assuredly was, the program also cited the pledge of Patrick Pearse ("Pádraig Mac Phiarais" for these purposes) that the "Nation's sovereignty extend[ed] not only to all men and women ... but to all its material possessions," the "Nation's soil and all its resources ... and all the wealth-producing processes." Irish inscrutability was seldom on fuller display. Did sovereignty mean ownership? Were "wealth-producing processes" the same as the "means of production"? Elusiveness aside, this much is certain: No American congress and no British parliament at any time in the history of either would have passed such a resolution. The Irish *Dáil*, however, provisional though it was, was now on record: The *Poblacht na h-Éireann* would be no miniature Anglo-America.[37]

The Irish parliament and a significant percentage of the Irish people were taking a distinctly leftist and poetic path toward nationhood. Since Ireland's more poetic instincts had always had a ready market in Irish America, Wilson's Irish problem was going with him to Versailles. Ireland 1916 and Russia 1917 were still conjoined, or at least spoken of in the same sentences. The threats each posed to American interests as Wilson defined them were real, especially the threat of Bolshevik propaganda directed at the great many Irish in the American labor movement, or the large contingent of them among American communists. That's why Ireland counted for so much and why Wilson had to pay such an inordinate amount of attention to it. He had a lot of reasons not to like or trust the Irish for the unassimilable, clannish, regressive, and disloyal sorts he thought them to be. This last defect, however, this leftward lurch toward something Celtic and ideologically deviant, was something that Wilson simply could not let stand.

• • •

In the normal order of things, Ireland and its proclaimed republic would have been a sideshow at Versailles. Germany—and Russia—occupied center stage. The only thing that made rebel Ireland important was Russia's interest in it. In 1943, more than two decades after Versailles, an Irishman, John Sherry Mangan, under the name "Terence Phelan," wrote a short piece on Woodrow Wilson and the Bolsheviks. That same year, 1943, the Comintern included Phelan's article in its "Reports of the Fourth Communist International." In it, Phelan listed what the Communist Party believed had been Wilson's most important issues at the Versailles Peace talks. Ireland was not on the list. But note what was: "1. Crush the Soviet Union"; "2. head off a Socialist revolution in defeated Germany"; "3. strangle Soviet Hungary"; "4. smash revolutions [it didn't say "Communist revolutions"] and aid counterrevolutions elsewhere"; and "5. redivide the world according to the demands of the three most powerful imperialisms."[38]

Phelan and the Comintern are not unimpeachable sources. But the accuracy of the list is not the issue. Phelan wanted to make the point that the treaty's purpose was to destroy communism. That was the party's view in 1943, but it reflected the Bolsheviks' view in 1919. Versailles was essentially an early phase of what would be a domestic Great Red Scare and a foreign policy cold war. It's in that context that room may be found to append Ireland to objects 4 and 5 on Phelan's list. The Irish revolution was to be "smashed"; the English counterrevolution "aided"; and Ireland was to be sacrificed at the command of Britain, the most powerful of the three "imperialisms," ably assisted by the United States, only scarcely less powerful and gaining. Phelan put Wilson's name in the title of his report for a reason. The United States and Wilson were still on gendarme duty for the British Empire. The Comintern may be forgiven for thinking that. Many of the Irish living in the two most powerful of the imperia thought so too.

What makes Phelan's account more credible are the remarks of three of Wilson's closest friends and allies as well as of Wilson himself. Ray Stannard Baker was in Versailles as Wilson's personal secretary, and the two men apparently talked daily. Baker would later write an admiring biography of Wilson and edit a multivolume edition of Wilson's private papers. In 1922, he wrote that during the Versailles Treaty talks the effects of "the Russian problem," as he called it, were "profound.... Russia played a more vital part at Paris than Prussia.... Without ever being represented in Paris at all, the Bolshevik and Bolshevism were powerful elements at every turn." The negotiations in Paris could not be understood "without Moscow." "Bolshevism, he said, was "everywhere spreading like an infection from Russia," "like a black cloud over Europe."[39]

Wilson agreed. "Bolshevism" was a "poison" and he feared "the susceptibility of the people of Europe" to it. The Irish were not the most important, and certainly not the most numerous, of those Europeans. But, few as they might be, they were also the Russians' entry to American labor and the American Left. The Irish could simply, almost casually, usher them in and escort them through. Celtic communism could become a transnational Irish (hyphen) American phenomenon, and that had to have been deeply unsettling to Wilson.

On September 11, 1919, during his nationwide tour to sell the treaty and the League of Nations, Wilson told a crowd in Billings, Montana, that he wanted to "speak of Russia." He asked, "Have you seen no symptoms of the spread of that ... chaotic spirit into other countries? ... [T]he dread of every thoughtful man in Europe is that the distemper will spread to their countries. Have you heard nothing of the propaganda of that sort of belief in the United States?" There were "apostles of Lenin in our own midst." Billings was a distance from Butte geographically; ideologically, it was another planet. But the audience in Billings would have known of Bill Dunne and of the Butte Rising of 1917. It's more than just likely that Wilson had both in mind when he warned of Lenin's apostles in their midst.[40]

Two weeks after his talk in Billings, in what he called his "Final Address in Support of the League of Nations," Wilson returned to a well-used theme. "There is an organized propaganda against the League ... proceeding from ... disloyalty." But disloyalty of a particular sort and of particular origin. "Any man who carries a hyphen about ... carries a dagger that he is ready to plunge into the vitals of this Republic." Wilson intended that remark to apply to all immigrants, but the figurative use of "hyphen" recalled his 1914 scolding of the Irish and was associated—by Wilson assuredly and by most of those who heard him—with Irish-hyphen-Americans. Turning all of them into dagger-wielding assassins of the republic was new, but not the idea that they were unassimilated and unassimilable cultural subversives. There had always been a certain apocalyptic quality to American nativism, but this last comment by Wilson set a new standard.[41]

Wilson's animosity toward Irish America was intensely personal and racially charged—closer to a border war between Orange and Green than a policy dispute. Allusions to it can be found in the diary entries of two other of Wilson's closest associates, Dr. Cary Grayson and Ray Stannard Baker, both in attendance with Wilson at Versailles, and in letters written after the fact by others who knew Wilson well. The Grayson and Baker diary entries are from May 31 to June 27, 1919. I assume they were made in real time and not after the facts they describe, and that these "notes to self" were not self-deceptions.

I begin with the June 11 entry in the diary of Grayson. The *Dáil Éireann* had declared Irish independence; the guerilla war in defense of that declaration, the Irish War of Independence, was in its fourth month. On this particular day, Grayson's diary entry concerned the conversation about the cause of the Irish Republic that occurred between Wilson and Frank Walsh, the chair of the US Commission on Industrial Relations, then in Versailles along with Michael Ryan and Edward Dunne. The three had been sent to the Peace Conference by the Irish Race Convention to remind Wilson of what he had been saying for the last decade about imperialism, imperialists, and the right of self-determination.[42]

According to Grayson, Walsh on that day had told Wilson that the Irish were suffering severely as England tried to suppress its rebellious and warring colony. Walsh then said that the suffering was such that there "is nothing for the Irish farmers and producers to do but turn to Sovietism if this state of affairs is allowed to continue." The word *allowed* had to mean that Walsh thought Wilson could "disallow" and reverse what was happening. Indeed, it implies that Wilson could preclude anything like it from ever happening again by contesting Britain's imperial claims on Ireland and become the sworn ally of the Irish Republic. Walsh then told Wilson that he had also spoken with the "leaders of the five great trades unions in Ireland brutally assaulted in prison." Their leftward lean, he said, was even more pronounced than that of the farmers and producers.[43]

Walsh had combined farmers, producers, and trade unionists and said that Ireland had either to be made free or the Irish would align themselves with Russian communists—exactly what Peter Yorke had said just months earlier. That threat seemed to be becoming something of a theme. About the same time as Yorke's remarks, Walsh, just prior to leaving for Versailles, got a telegram from a close friend reaffirming what Walsh already believed: A "failure to grant [Ireland's] demands will be a blunder that will give Bolshevism its greatest weapon."[44]

In Wilson's mind, for the Irish to link Bolshevism with the Irish Republic and to threaten to "turn to Sovietism" if their national ambitions were unmet was an extension of Yorke's shakedown. There was only one significant difference between Walsh's prediction and Yorke's. Walsh's warning applied only to Ireland and the British Empire; Yorke's involved the Irish and American capitalism. At that, there was also something menacing in Walsh's statement. What Walsh said was bound to provoke Wilson. That may have been Walsh's intent.

If it was, it worked. Grayson's diary entry indicated that Wilson told Walsh that "I know what the Irish situation is and has been." He meant the rebelliousness, not the suffering, "and that it is due to the tactics which you yourselves pursued....—your own speeches in advocacy of the Irish Republic aroused the ire of the British government." Walsh might have told him that arousing the ire of the British government was the whole idea. What else would 1916–19 have been about? The British response to everything the Irish did was always somewhere between annoyance and rage. Soothing British minds was not something the Irish felt morally obliged to try to do. Walsh, however, said none of that. He replied to Wilson's charge only by telling him that "he had simply declared that the Irish of America wanted freedom for Ireland ... under a republican form of government."—under a government, that is, that would remove Ireland from the British Empire.[45]

According to Grayson, Wilson's answer to Walsh was angry and accusatory. Grayson's next sentences were contained within quotation marks; he was quoting Wilson's words: "No one would deny that the freedom which was being endorsed by Mr. Walsh ... was the freedom which only could be secured through *revolutionary* tactics against *the government that was then in power*. Walsh admitted that this was so." Of course Walsh admitted that it was so. There was a revolution in progress. Revolutionaries commonly use revolutionary tactics. The otherworldliness of this exchange is striking. The two men spoke roughly the same language and yet understood nothing of what the other was saying.[46]

During a recess in the negotiations in Versailles, Walsh, Dunne, and Ryan, the Irish "delegation," had made a speaking trip to Ireland. Colonel House said their speeches were "incendiary." He did not elaborate on what he meant by that word. The US ambassador in London, John Davis, wrote to Secretary of State Lansing and said that Ryan "on all occasions [was] violent, and once or twice advocated action similar to that adopted in Easter ... 1916." That was an odd and confusing comment. Odd because Ryan was a conservative Irish nationalist; confusing because Easter 1916 was more than just a violent colonial revolt. It had a social reform side to it.[47]

As for Walsh and Edward Dunne, House said that "although they did not advocate armed rebellion, [they] missed no opportunity of stating that they represented over 20,000,000 American people, all ready to help ... in assisting Ireland to achieve ... an Irish Republic." Wilson told his secretary, the Irish Catholic James Tumulty, that the three Irishmen had "behaved in a way which so inflamed English opinion that the situation has got quite out of hand." All the non-Irish in those exchanges, Wilson certainly, but Grayson and House as well, seemed to know what "the situation" was, and that the Irish were more than just wild colonial girls and boys being their usual rabble-rousing selves, that this republic of theirs had some special and quite non-, when not openly anti-, American features to it. Russia 1917 was as much in play as Ireland 1916. The historian Elizabeth McKillen makes an important and convincing point: Events in Ireland before and immediately after 1916 "produced shockwaves in [the] U.S. . . . as great as those that emanated from the Russian Revolution of 1917. . . . American authorities were profoundly worried about the subversive influence of Irish Sinn Féin revolutionaries on the American labor . . . movements."[48]

• • •

The entirety of the Irish question was distressing to Wilson. Baker recorded in his diary that Wilson said "almost savagely" that "I don't know how long I shall be able to resist telling them what I think of their miserable mischief making." Grayson said the same. Wilson complained to him that the Irish were "absolutely impossible." Then, apparently in one of his playful moods, the president told Grayson that he had the solution: "give [the Irish] Home Rule and reserve the moving picture rights"—Wilson at his wittiest. That was very loose language. The Irish, of course, were asking for a lot more than Home Rule. But what mattered to Wilson was that they had taken a position that jeopardized everything he had tried to do to build a new peaceful and democratic world order.[49]

His response to Walsh and "freedom for Ireland under a republican form of government" cannot be accounted for otherwise. That response was reckless. Grayson said in his diary that Frank Walsh was going to return to the United States and work for Wilson's impeachment. It may be presumed that he told Wilson of that intention; it may also be presumed that Wilson believed him. That does not, however, explain—nor can it or anything else justify—what Wilson responded. He said he feared that the Irish might bring up the League of Nations question in 1920. He was right about that. But he then added that "this would raise a *racial and religious* question which would have far-reaching consequences."[50]

That last clause deserves a very close critical reading. Why would a debate over the League raise racial and religious issues unless Wilson raised them? Wilson returned to the race and religion topic later in June, writing to Tumulty that the Republican Party in the United States might be tempted to use the "Irish agitation" as a political wedge issue. This, Wilson continued, would be a most dangerous course. It would risk "the lining up of the whole country along religious lines." And that, he said, "would be a calamity." A calamity for whom, he did not say.[51]

A possible answer was provided by comments Ray Stannard Baker said Wilson had made a couple of weeks earlier when Wilson's annoyance with Irish meddling in the peace negotiations was at its peak. The source is Baker's diary; the remarks he attributed to Wilson are startling now and would have been then. Baker recorded that he had "asked the President what was done at his meeting with Walsh, Dunne, and Ryan." Wilson told him that "we discussed the Irish question[,] . . . warning me that nothing was to be made public about it. He spoke of these 'mischief makers,' and the trouble they were endeavoring to stir up in America."

It would have been useful had Baker said something about what kind of trouble, but it can be guessed at. Then came this—in my italics: The president said, "I have one weapon I can use against them—*one terrible weapon, which I shall not use unless I am driven to it* . . . unless it appears that the Irish movement has forgotten to be American." That, of course, was the whole idea and always had been. The Irish movement was Irish. Whether it was consonant with being American was less certain. It was also irrelevant.

But what was this "terrible weapon" that Wilson said he might use? The president told Baker that "if necessary," he would "go home and tell the [American] public" of the "indiscretion and unwisdom" of the Irish delegates to Versailles. That, however, was only the start of it. He had a more "terrible weapon" than exposing Walsh, Ryan, and Dunne as tactless and foolhardy. It was an old and well-used one, an American perennial. Wilson told Baker, again with my emphasis, that "*I have only to warn our people of the attempt of the Roman Catholic hierarchy to dominate our public opinion.*"[52]

Later that year, there was a story in the Catholic magazine *America* that Wilson had "warned Mr. Walsh not to try to 'put him in bad with people at home' or he would retaliate." It's hard to know what to make of Wilson's comment and his threat. Words like "demagogic" and "hateful" come close, but even they are inadequate. And did he issue the warning? Did he do as he threatened, invent a popish intrigue and whisper of it? But note this next comment. It is as revealing and as damning as what preceded it. Should Wilson be "driven" to issue the warning, "*there is no doubt about what America will do.*"[53]

Did the Ku Klux Klan hear his whispers? Others who shared Wilson's "descent and education" certainly had some feisty ideas about what to do, as the remainder of the decade would show. Were the "Tribal Twenties" a result? Just before the American declaration of war against Germany, Wilson rather famously predicted that "once lead this people into war and they will forget there ever was such a thing as tolerance." He then proceeded to forget it himself, his prophecy literally self-fulfilled. Intolerance seems to have become habitual. Leading Americans out of war did nothing to improve their memory—or Wilson's own.[54]

Whether Wilson acted on his threat or not, there was an almost immediate increase in KKK and relative anti-Catholic agitation in the summer of 1919. Bruce Nelson points out that, from 1919 on, "powerful forces, including influential Protestant churchmen[,] had mobilized to defend the Anglo-American alliance and to ward off what many perceived as a papist threat to Protestant interests." Those forces were Wilson's allies, the quite powerful cultural hegemons of America. Kerby Miller shared with me some of the research notes he had taken that indicated the same thing—along with this note Miller wrote to himself: "What part did all this play in the growth of the KKK?" There were a lot of Americans who knew as well as Wilson what the well-conditioned response would be if Wilson sounded the nativist alarm signaling that "the papists are coming." They also knew—as did he—that ringing the bell did not require Wilson to offer proof of anything. He could fabricate reasons, literally make them up. Wilson was willing to do that, eager even. He hadn't quite "cried havoc and let slip the dogs of war"—or the dogs of bigotry—but he'd clearly threatened to.[55]

There is a lot of hearsay evidence in the above—Wilson speaking through surrogates, Page, House, Grayson, Baker. But he spoke often enough for himself to make what these others said he'd said seem convincing. It was certainly in character. That's true of this next Wilson proxy as well. William Edward Dodd was a close Wilson associate. He was also one of his more fawning biographers. In early January 1921, Dodd wrote a letter to Sir Alexander Frederick Whyte, an English friend of his. As I have with the others, I assume that Dodd knew what he was talking about and that his remarks describe Wilson's state of mind as well as Dodd's own.

According to Dodd, the defeat of the treaty and the League of Nations had left Wilson a "broken man." The "biggest thing was . . . that the Irish had wrecked his whole programme for adoption of the work at Paris. 'Oh, the foolish Irish . . . would to God they might all have gone back home.' The Irish! What have they not done. . . . The American Irish. . . . set the Irish at home (Ireland?) upon the wrong road in 1914! The Irish queered things at Paris. They defeated the treaty and the League in America."[56]

Dodd's conclusion was sarcastic and bitter, not to mention surpassingly arrogant: "So three or four million Irish in this country govern both Great Britain and America. Is not that logic? . . . Self-determination permits a few people strategically placed to defeat the purposes of the liberals of the world." I am reminded at this point of Orsi's comment about how "deeply Protestant" was modern liberalism. All those liberals, the whole of the supply who counted for anything, lived in Anglo-America, "our civilization," as Wilson had called it. Connolly called them "capitalist Liberals," which made perfect sense of Dodd's final comment: Wilson, he said, was "another Gladstone and he feels it." In other words, another evangelical Protestant Anglo-Saxon Scot liberal done in by shifty Celtic Catholics.[57]

The government's assault on leftists—the Great Red Scare—has been amply documented. So has the nativism that accompanied much of it, the assumption that immigrants were drawn to radicalism. Jews were singled out for particular attention, but so were the Irish. Both were thought to have large "contingents" of "Lenin dreamers." The Green Scare should be added to the Red. There's a fitting example: In 1919, Éamon de Valera asked

Ed Boyce—then retired and rich—whether he would chair the Oregon state association for the "Recognition of the Irish Republic." Boyce wrote back that that was a bad idea. The cause of Ireland, he told de Valera, was commonly thought "tainted with Bolshevism and IWWism" and, given Boyce's radical past, he was not a good choice. For the more nervous in the Wilson administration, including Wilson, the cause of Ireland wasn't just "tainted" with Bolshevism and IWWism; it was indistinguishable from them. That had been the case for some time. Boyce could speak with authority on the subject.[58]

On August 18, 1919, the day before its story about Dunne and his twin heresies, the *New York Call* listed six government departments involved in the surveillance and prosecution of those involved in "seditious" activities. One of the six was the Post Office Department, which compiled a "Censorship Book" with the names of persons suspected of "disloyalty." But disloyalty to what? Wilson's war against Germany was over. Only the "apostles of Lenin in their midst" were left. Those apostles were of two kinds, "agents and sympathizers of the militant labor movement at home, as well as those interested in the freedom of small nations." Ireland was not the only small nation that comes to mind, but it was one of them.

The *Call* went on to say that the list of "disloyalty" in the "Censorship Book" included "Hindus . . . cruelly misgoverned by British Junkers." Even more of the names were of "those who have stood for the political freedom of Ireland from British misrule . . . , and who are "trying to make this country as safe . . . from British rule as Ireland." It was an old Irish habit to give Irish nationalist answers to social-class question. The *Call* did it so unselfconsciously that it appears to have become second nature among non-Irish as well. The *Call* concluded its summary with this final bit of Irish news: "The most startling fact that the 'suspect' list brings out is the manner in which [the Wilson] administration has truckled to the English government."[59]

• • •

"Truckling" to the English is too strong—but not by much. In one account of the issue, the request by Walsh, Dunne, and Ryan that Wilson offer support for a free republic in Ireland made the president "very angry," angry enough that he went to British prime minister David Lloyd George and asked what specifically Lloyd George would like Wilson to do and say about these and all the other bothersome Irish, whether in Ireland or in America. As for England's Irish Problem in general, Wilson didn't need any instructions. The twin rulers of Anglo-America saw the world alike.[60]

The transfer of the colonial spoils of war would not be by a direct British annexation of the territories held by the defeated Germans and Turks. Those spoils would be reassigned under a mandate issued by the League of

Nations, the crown jewel of Wilson's new world order. Baker's description of the mandate system was consistent with the race consciousness of the age: "Weak and backward" people living in the colonies of the nations that had lost the war would be placed under the protection and "tutelage" of the "advanced" nations that had won it. The official language of the League of Nations' charter was only slightly less patronizing than Baker's—and every bit as racially charged: The colonies under mandate were those "not yet able to stand by themselves under the strenuous conditions of the modern world."[61]

The League mandate system incorporated in the Versailles Treaty left Ireland where it had been for at least the last hundred-plus years: a colony under English rule. Wilson was entirely untroubled by this. Drafting a treaty that met the political and financial needs of the British Empire did not threaten any American interests or violate any American principles of governance. On the contrary. It advanced the former and validated the latter. Wilson, writes Richard Drake, was "devot[ed] to the sanctity of the British Empire." *Devoted* is the right word. So is *sanctity*. There was a sacredness to the Anglo-Saxon imperium, the English power to command.[62]

That was the state of affairs in January 1919. The peace talks in Versailles had just been opened, and guerilla warfare involving regular British troops, the Black and Tans, British Auxiliaries, and the Royal Irish Constabulary on the Empire's side and the Irish Republican Army on the other had begun. The Versailles Treaty negotiations took approximately three months. This Irish War of Independence—or Tan War, as the Republicans preferred to call it—would last for almost two years. A truce was declared on July 11, 1921. The London Treaty formally ending hostilities between the United Kingdom and rebel Ireland was signed on December 6 of that same year.[63]

For British prime minister David Lloyd George, the war against Ireland was an extension not just of 1916 but of the Versailles Treaty, a classic postwar war. The "Great War" was over empires. Great Britain won. An independent and left-leaning Irish Republic jeopardized that victory. The British Empire was a system. It had rules. Irish Republicans were attempting to break the most fundamental of them. Imperial governance required oaths to be taken, flags and banners to be saluted, anthems to be sung, "bribed" historians to be commissioned, "crazy" monarchs, "old and jealous" to be knelt down before. Republics, by definition, don't perform those ritualistic acts of obeisance.

In September 1921, Lloyd George reminded Éamon de Valera, now the president of the Provisional Republic of Ireland, that "the whole fabric of the Empire [is] . . . based on . . . the principle of allegiance to the King" and obedience to the king and Parliament's prerogatives and commands. Republics threw out all of that and more. To grant a republic, any republic, would be "fatal" to the British Empire—and hazardous to capitalism, its partner and helpmate. This was not a matter of labeling. The people who lived in republics were citizens; those living in dominions—by whatever name—were subjects. The solution to the Irish problem, said Lloyd George, had to be "set firmly in the British political tradition; there was no room for a republic."[64]

Empires, however, whether being in one or sharing in one, did not suit the Irish. As de Valera told Lloyd George, the whole idea of empires, the care and keeping of them, was "out of harmony with [the Irish] national character ... and ideals and a hindrance to [its] national destiny." To use Pearse and Connolly's language, it was a "moral" issue, not a "material" one. The Irish soul counted for more than the Irish fisc. Late in the negotiations on the treaty that would end the Irish War of Independence, Lloyd George gave the Irish delegation a choice: Ireland could accept the British offer of dominion status and "come within the Empire" as a Free State (*Saor Stát*), swearing an "oath of allegiance" to the British monarch, or it could face renewed "war—and war within three days."[65]

The use of "come within" rather than "stay within" is curious. It was near to saying that Ireland *had* left, that it had seceded from the Empire and was now being forced to come back to it. That sounds like annexation, or reannexation. Either way, "come within" or "remain within," Ireland would be held within by force. In May 1921, Field Marshal Sir Henry Wilson, whose entire military career had been spent protecting that Empire, told the British cabinet that "unless we crush the murder gang," meaning Sinn Féin and the IRA, "we should lose Ireland." But then he added, "and the Empire." Henry Wilson was not given to overstating danger. The English had good reason to fear the Irish threat. After all, they had created it.[66]

The Irish never attempted to quiet the fears of an unforgiving England that as Ireland goes so might go the rest of the British imperial world. In February 1919 the Irish Labour Party said that the "peoples ... of Egypt, India, [and] Indo-China ... [were] suffering under the same imperial yoke as the people of Ireland." They were "sister peoples, ... held in submergence by imperialist and capitalist powers." As such, they were deserving of the "same rights and the application of the same principles as [Ireland] claims for its own people." Sinn Féin agreed. Later that year, the anti–Sinn Féin Dublin-based Unionist Alliance, stalwart opponents of an independent Ireland, after quoting the language the Irish Labour Party had used, warned Lloyd George of "conferences" that had "been held ... between Sinn Fein delegates and those fomenting rebellion in Egypt and India."[67]

Theoretically, De Valera could have assured Lloyd George that if England let Ireland out of the Empire, the Irish would continue to do what they'd been doing for three hundred years and help keep others in it. He never made that promise or anything like it. In fact, he pledged the opposite: "Ours is a common cause. We swear friendship ... and we send our common greetings and our pledges to our brothers in Egypt and in Persia, and tell them also that their cause is our cause." "We are the spear-points of the hosts in political slavery . . . the shafts of dawn for the despairing and the wretched everywhere." That was putting it grandly, but Ireland was leading a grand anti-imperial movement—or trying to.[68]

Two years later, P. S. O'Hegarty, a member of Sinn Féin and former member of the Irish Republican Brotherhood, elaborated on de Valera's sunburstery: "'Ireland's position,'" he wrote, was "'unique.'" It had a "'*special history*'" that allowed it—or compelled it—to "'lead . . . in an anti-Imperial policy against the British Empire. . . .'" Then O'Hegarty turned to the other of Ireland's conjoined causes. A free Irish republic could be "a pivot for Europe and for America as well." Tossing America and Europe into the mix was neither inadvertent nor meaningless. Both were already free; the pivot can only have been toward economic and social democracy, if not socialism. O'Hegarty framed the issue as Connolly might have. As late as December 1921, a British M.P. quoted an Irish paper, *New Ireland*, as having said that "'Ireland has taken the strongest Empire by the throat and has brought it to its knees. . . . And that fact will have a more enduring repercussion on mankind than had either the French Revolution or the Russian Revolution. . . . Henceforward, no small nation will despair, no small people will accept slavery. We have shown the way and others will follow.'"[69]

There was an abstract, if not delusional, quality to Ireland as the great emancipator. On other matters, however, the Irish threat was immediate and quite real. As Lloyd George knew, the *Poblacht na h-Éireann* would be England's enemy on arrival. Not a large or powerful one, to be sure, but a pesky one because a proximate one. "Nits," the English once said of Irish women and children, "make lice." It was easier to deal with nits. A *Poblacht na h-Éireann* next door to the kingdom was a nit. But Ireland's remembered past—even if it be misremembered—its storehouse of "ancestral sorrows," its apparently limitless anglophobia, would contrive to make it a troubling presence.

The British had been of that mind from the very beginning of this latest round of Irish troubles. Two months after the Easter Rising, the British Foreign Office received a field report written by W. Alison Phillips, a fairly obscure English historian, but clearly a "bribed" one. He began with a quite unhistorical description of the people of "southern Ireland," code words for Irish Catholics. Phillips commented on their "unreasonableness, due to slack habits of mind . . . and combativeness." The "practical and unimaginative" English had tried to "impress [their] point of view" on the impractical and imaginative Irish. It hadn't worked; it couldn't work. Ireland "lives on its memories and . . . chews the cud of ancient grievances and grudges." The English had to take into account the fact of how different the Irish were from them. Anglo-Americans were advised to do the same. Clearly, having an aggressively antagonistic Ireland was a domestic security risk.[70]

Racial differences and history were two reasons; geography was another. Ireland was not only too different and defiant to be tolerated as a republic, it was too nearby. As Lloyd George reminded de Valera, Ireland, unlike Canada and Australia, "lies at Britain's side." "Nature" had made Ireland and Britain neighboring islands without making them neighborly, and "no statesmanship can change what geography has "imposed." Ireland was too close for comfort. It was also, at least according to the pro-British Unionist Alliance in Dublin, too formidable. Sometime in early 1919, the alliance tacked up a poster that read that "the Sinn Feiners ... *with truth* ... boast that Ireland would be the Gibraltar of the Atlantic." By "Gibraltar" the Unionist Alliance meant that the Irish would be lords of the sea. Even Sinn Féin never said anything as extravagant as that.[71]

The alliance then went on to explain how Ireland would use its naval power, pointing out that a free Irish republic would be a "hostile country planted right in the heart of the United Kingdom," and in "command of all the sea routes" into and out of Britain. Those routes were England's "lifelines for trade and food supplies." "Lifeline" was intended literally. The clear inference of that last comment was that Ireland's mighty navy could and would cut off England's food. Hibernia would rule the waves. The absurdity of the alliance's comment is evidence of unionist/loyalist fears, not Ireland's capability, or even its ambitions.[72]

That expressed fear would be easy to ignore had Lloyd George not made the same argument in one of his lectures in the form of a letter to de Valera. There was more than a little race-hate in what he said; the nonrational was joined to the calculating. Lloyd George began with geography: "Ireland lies ... across the seaways north and south that link [Britain] with the sister nations of the Empire, the markets of the world and the vital sources of her food supply. ... Britain lives by sea-borne food. ... In recognition of this fact, it is essential that the Royal Navy alone should control the seas around Ireland and Great Britain." It is possible that Lloyd George had read the Irish Dáil's "Democratic Programme" with its insistence that Ireland lived on Irish-borne food, and that that food should first and always be used to feed the people of Ireland. That's the best face that can be put on Lloyd's George's comments.[73]

The worst is closer to the truth: In 1921, seventy years after *an Gorta Mór*, and the British denial of Irish-borne food to millions of starving Irish, the prime minister of Great Britain said publicly that he thought Ireland had to be prevented from depriving the English people of food. There was an element of cheap theatrics in that comment. Lloyd George knew that Ireland would never have the power to blockade the British coast. But there was also something of substance in his remark. It was his indirect way of saying that they *wanted* to. However interpreted, what he said qualifies as among the most obtuse, offensive, and historically illiterate remarks ever made by someone thought to be civilized in charge of a nation said to be civilized. It was also deeply insulting, implying as it did that the Irish were capable of inhumanity on an English scale.

• • •

The work of the Marxist historian C. Desmond Greaves was the sort that Irish revisionist historians either condemn or ignore. His judgment on English rule in Ireland mentions specifically the "opportunism and deviousness, the crudity, brutality and stupidity" of it; the British Empire was the gold standard of piratical imperialism. After World War I, the English would pay a price for their cruelty. A process, inexorable in Greaves's view, had been set in motion: the merger of Red and Green would lead "to the secession of the colonies." But it would also and simultaneously—and as inexorably—lead to "proletarian revolutions." Connolly's nonseverable causes had been dressed up and internationalized. The Russian connection, at least according to Greaves, was giving Ireland a quite outsized influence on the world.[74]

Some of this was communists'—and Greaves's—wishful thinking; they hoped that the fusing of national liberation movements with socialist revolution was the new model for international communism. As the propaganda arm of the Russian People's Commissariat of Nationalities put it, Sinn Féin "would find self-determination impossible under capitalism." The equivalents of Sinn Féin among the nationalists of India, Egypt, Pakistan, Iraq, South Africa, Indo-China, and others inspired by the Irish example, would have found capitalism blocking their paths as well. That being so, "probably no threat to the stability of the British empire is so direct and serious as the Irish movement" of Lenin-dreaming Sinn Féiners.[75]

That the Bolsheviks thought that is less important than that many in the British and American governments thought so too. One side's wishful thinking had become the other side's worst nightmare. For a perfect, and quite possibly highly significant, example, in 1922, Hugh Pollard, a British intelligence agent stationed in Dublin from 1920 to 1924, wrote his *Secret Societies of Ireland*, a short, remarkably bigoted account of Irish resistance to English rule. There are long sections on Irish American organizations and their past and continuing plots against the Anglo-American world—meaning capitalism and empire.

Pollard was like a cartoon character, more Austin Power than James Bond, a landed and well-born Tory adventurer, avid hunter and outdoorsmen, firearms expert, and political intriguer. He was a devout Anglo-American imperialist, a fervent anticommunist, an "extreme right winger" as he called himself. During his time in Ireland, he was involved in what is now called special operations or irregular warfare, including espionage, sabotage, and assorted other political dirty tricks. There is a burlesque quality to his career and to his book. But that book reads like a compilation of reports he may have sent back to the British intelligence service during the Irish War of Independence. Attention must be paid them. There is a chance that they were taken seriously and acted on by the English and the American governments—a possibility damning in its implications.

Pollard described the Catholic Irish as a foul and godless people, "murderous" and "savage." The source of Irish deformity was the same as it had been for Horace Plunkett: The Irish Catholic Church did it. Pollard was himself Catholic; a devout and properly Roman one, he said, exceedingly loyal to the crown. The staunch Irish Republican Ernie O'Malley once wrote of "our countries most persistent enemies, the English Catholics." Pollard fit the description. Roman Catholicism, Pollard insisted, could not be "judged by the Irish rendering of it." That "rendering" was nothing more than "reactionary emotionalism ... superstitious rather than spiritual." Pollard called it "sacramental Satanism." It left the Irish unfit for anything other than service in "murder gangs." As for their avowed love of a republic, "less than five per cent of [the rebels (of which O'Malley was one)] could give any coherent idea" of what republicanism meant. They were not motivated by love of anything. All that drove them was their "intense and vindictive hatred of Great Britain," a hatred that survived "in spite of a century of well-meant British endeavor." Ireland was what, in the racial ordering of affairs, it had to be: "a de jure and de facto British possession."[76]

America should take notice; as surely as England, it was faced with what Pollard essentially viewed as a race war. Irish vindictiveness "would not be aimed [solely] at the British Empire, but will be manifested against Anglo-Saxon thought all over the globe.... America share[d] with the British Commonwealth a joint expression of those ideals which we term Anglo-Saxon." They were "the true American standard." "Briton and other dominant northern races" had a "conception of social order. The Irish people "of the South and West" did not. They suffered from a "pandemic psychosis" arising out of their "fanatical ignorance and their "criminal predisposition." Their "thought processes" were those "of children, some types of criminals, savages, and the lower classes of certain races."[77]

Pollard's final judgment was severe: The leaders of the Irish rebellion were "moral decadents leading a superstitious minority into an epidemic of murder and violent crime.... [T]he Irish problem is a problem of the Irish *race*, and is neither a byproduct of politics nor of environment, but is rooted in the racial characteristics of the people themselves." As noted, the possibility that that sort of lunatic bigotry influenced Lloyd George's policy gives new meaning to John Gaddis's reference to the "ubiquitous spectrum that separates the admirable from the abhorrent."[78]

Their psychotic characteristics also explained for Pollard why the Irish in America were so attracted to communism, a topic that he dealt with extensively in his book and, it may be assumed, his intelligence reports back to London. Pollard had found the Irish to be "easily manipulated by the Bolsheviks." The result was an "identity of interests between Irish-Catholic communities" in the United States "and extremist Labour organizations." "The source of the infection has been . . . the Irish of the United States." They "have been responsible for energizing the Irish of . . . Ireland into active crime." He called it "Sinn Fein Sovietism"—close enough to Celtic communism to be a useful synonym. According to Pollard, symptoms of it could be seen in the 1840s, which pushed the "pandemic psychosis" back to the Great Famine immigration.[79]

Pollard's more direct access to the British government likely gave him greater influence in London than in Washington. In that context, consider the response to Sir Henry Wilson, Britain's chief imperial officer in Ireland from 1918 until his assassination by Irish Republicans in 1922. Pollard was under Wilson's command, as was the British Army and Intelligence Service in Ireland. In late 1918, after the World War had ended, Wilson warned Lloyd George that "a Bolshevik rising was likely" in Ireland. This was before the Comintern had fully entered into its "Irish alliance." A year later, Winston Churchill said that he feared that if the so-called hard men of the Republican movement had their way, "Dublin would fall into the hands of the Industrial Workers of the World." That moved the focus from Moscow to Chicago—or Butte—but it did not allay any concerns.[80]

In early 1919, an unnamed unionist-royalist organization in Dublin elaborated on the theme by issuing a short pamphlet, published by the "University Press" and titled "An Imperial Danger: The Sinn Fein Menace." It said nothing about a Democratic Programme—which may not yet have been passed, but it called specific attention to the December 1918 Irish election, which it interpreted, quite correctly, to mean that the overwhelming majority of the Irish people sought "complete independence" from the Empire. The "Irish problem" was now an "Imperial" problem. The pamphlet then added that the Irish republican movement was solidly aligned with the Irish labor movement, which was "frankly Bolshevik in its character." The "Sinn Fein movement, should it achieve its ends, . . . would mean a hostile state established at [England's] very shores, a jumping-off ground for foreign emissaries of revolution."[81]

Later that year, another pamphlet, likely from the same British unionist source, made clear what was meant by "revolution." Quoting from the *Times*, the pamphlet said that the Russian Bolshevik government's sole purpose was "to bring about world revolution, . . . [and that] Sinn Fein and Bolshevism are hand-in-glove." Together, this most unholy alliance "hopes to obtain what Sinn Fein failed to win in Paris and America . . . and by camouflaging Sinn Fein as a 'labour movement' to seduce loyal labour." Obviously, the "danger ahead is terribly real, terribly urgent." The "blood-stained chronicles of Russia tell us what Bolshevism really means. If the disease gets a firm hold in Ireland, it will not be long before it spreads to Great Britain."[82]

In 1921, the Duke of Northumberland Fund "presented a statement" in the form of a short pamphlet "to a meeting of members of the two houses of Parliament." The title of the pamphlet was "The Conspiracy against the British Empire: Ireland and the Revolution." In addition to that pamphlet, the fund's publications included such titles as "The Conspiracy against Religion," "The Revolutionary Aspects of the Miners' Strike," and the "Plight of Southern Irish Loyalists." Everything was there, ready to be mixed: capitalism, empire, religion, Ireland, revolution. The pamphlet topics were taken straight from the playbook of a High Tory—or the paranoid nonsense of Hugh Pollard.[83]

The pamphlet did not include a name list of the lords and commons in attendance that day, but it is reasonable to assume that the Liberal Lloyd George was among them. It began appropriately with a history lesson. The Irish had been conspiring against the Empire since at least 1792, when the French "'Jacobin Club' sent emissaries to Ireland who formed the United Irishmen." Though openly "founded on the principles of patriotism and nationalism," the "real objects of this and other secret societies . . . were the destruction of the State and property."[84]

That remained the pattern of Irish protest, socialism disguised as nationalism. Labor was leagued with Fenianism; Karl Marx with the Land League; Lenin with Sinn Féin and the Clan na Gael. The Clan, of course, was an entirely American faction. Its inclusion may have been intentional, an effort to extend the "conspiracy" to the United States. It's also possible that the pamphleteer didn't know any better. I prefer to believe the former. It is also worth noting that Pollard had written the same things and that the language of the pamphlet closely matches his own. What came next was conspiracy theory bordering on paranoia. The statement refers to 1903 and the "contemporaneous formation" of Bolshevism and Sinn Féin. This was no coincidence. It "showed the close touch maintained by the Irish movement with the leaders of International Revolution."[85]

The Irish and the Marxists were plotting secretly and had been for years. The members of Parliament were then told what these twin conspirators were up to: "The Irish Movement is seeking independence merely as a means to the establishment of a Workers' Republic on the Russian model and with Russian assistance." As Pollard had also indicated, the "peasants and workers

"A London Charaviri." From *Punch*, January 5, 1921. The two Irishmen, the gangster-looking one on the left, the cartoonish one on the right, are both Sinn Féiners. England had duped them both; they in turn had sold out Irish labor. A charaviri was a kind of theatrical or ritualistic political protest. The Irish played it poorly. Courtesy of *Punch*.

in Ireland are arrayed against British capitalism as peasants and workers in Russia were arrayed against Czardom." "The fight . . . is between Communism and Capitalism."[86]

Which makes it doubly important to be reminded that the fight in question—this semicold war between capitalism and communism—was not between the Soviet Empire and the West. It was between Ireland and Great Britain and Ireland and the United States. The concern seems to have been real that Ireland, the runt of the imperial litter, was a threat to take down the world's most powerful empire, as well as the capitalist system that that empire supplied and looked after. The United States was more than just an interested bystander. But the fear was not just Irish Republicanism; it was Irish Republicans. It was not just the ideology but the ideologues who made Wilson and Lloyd George nervous. If they had to have Irish at all, let them be *shoneens*.

• • •

The Irish, of course, did not get their *Poblacht*. The English would not grant it; the United States refused to recognize it. The Irish guerilla war with England ended with a treaty making Ireland a *Saor Stát*, a Free State, the only such thing in the entire British Empire. The Irish word *saor* not only means free in the political sense; it can mean "without" as in *saor ó chain*, tax-free. It can also mean "cheap" and "budget-priced," not the top of the line, which is exactly what England offered. The *Saor Stát* had its own devolved parliament, also with an Irish name, the *Dáil*, but with limited authority. The island's territorial integrity had been affronted by the partition of northeastern Ulster. Irish men and women were still bowing and curtsying to the British monarch and the British Parliament. The treaty, which formally "disestablished" the Irish Republic, passed the *Dáil* by a vote of 64–57. Even those who voted for it didn't like it. But it seemed better than "war, and war in three days." How much the alleged Sinn Féin–Bolshevik connection had to do with Britain's and America's policy is difficult to judge. From the record, it would appear to be quite a lot.

But even had there been no Fenian-Marxist dalliance, no Irish Republican–Bolshevik "partnership," even had the overthrow of the Tsar and the Bolshevik Revolution never occurred at all, the English and the Americans may not have behaved differently toward a *Poblacht na h-Éireann*. An Irish republic of any sort was anathema to Anglo-America. The Red and Green menace was a part of that, but it was not all that determined Woodrow Wilson's or David Lloyd George's decisions. Irish otherness was established long before Marx or Lenin discovered it. A *Poblacht* was a hazard to Anglo-American interests, with or without alleged Irish racial deformities and communist connections.

In the debate over its ratification, members of the British House of Commons routinely referred to the IRA and Sinn Féin as "murderers, "assassins," and—one that Pollard used as well—"murder gangs." Many of the MPs refused even to call the document they were debating a "treaty"; they called it the "Articles of Agreement." Treaties were negotiated between nations. Ireland wasn't one and never would be. It was a breakaway colony now restored to the imperial fold. As Pollard put it, the partition of northeastern Ulster had "put an end forever to the idea of "Ireland a nation." The articles were approved in the House of Commons by a vote of 401 to 58; in Lords by 166–47.[87]

Irish opponents of the treaty insisted, quite correctly, that a *Saor Stát* did not meet the terms of Patrick Pearse's 1916 Proclamation or of any of the policies adopted by the Irish *Dáil* from 1917 forward. The treaty, they said, was a base violation of a sacred promise, a promise to which those favoring the treaty had also once pledged their lives. Now the Treatyites and the Free State (some called it the "Freak State") were doing Britain's bidding. This wasn't an Irish Civil War; it was an Irish Republicans' Civil War. It lasted for almost two years and was fought with the same ferocity that marks all internecine wars. But with this added element, one far more tragic than ironic: Irish soldiers of the Free State, in every way that counted, were serving as Britain's proxy army. They used artillery supplied them by the British government. And they executed more Irish Republicans in the name of a Free State than the English had in the name of their majesty's Empire.[88]

There is one other point that must be made: The treaty was a kind of winnowing device. Those who favored it were not just loath to continue what they saw as a hopeless war against Britain, they were also of more conservative mind on other aspects of the conflict, including building a leftist Irish republic, the kind proclaimed in 1916 and again in the 1919 Democratic Programme. Poetics were not all that was involved. There was an obvious and crucially important social-class and ideological aspect to both the treaty fight and the Civil War that followed it. The Free State was doing the bidding not just of Lloyd George and the British imperial enterprise; it was a proxy for anticommunists everywhere, including—had he lived to witness it—Woodrow Wilson and the rest of America's Red and Green Scare mongers.

EPILOGUE

The Durability of Culture
The Erratic '20s

> "America . . . the land of the <u>free</u> (?) and the home of the <u>brave</u> (?). . . . Oh, what a farce."
> —Fr. Michael Hannan, Diary, July 4, 1924, Butte, Montana

On Palm Sunday, April 16, 1916, a week and a day before they entered Dublin as part of the Easter Rising, James Connolly was said to have told the soldiers of his Marxist Irish Citizen Army that "the odds against us are a thousand to one." That was too optimistic by half. Connolly then told them that, if the rebels were to beat the odds and "win," they were to "hold on to [their] rifles," and he followed it with an accurate prediction: "the Volunteers may have a different goal." His reference was to the Irish Volunteers (IV) whose nationalism, though hot-blooded enough, was not paired with an equally militant socialism. The goal of the IVs was an independent Ireland. It did not extend much beyond that, and Connolly, anticipating a struggle for the control of the new Ireland, wanted his socialist faction to be prepared and armed.[1]

There is no very good evidence that Connolly ever said the words attributed to him, but he had warned repeatedly over the years that the nationalism of the bourgeois Irish was faithless to the spirit of the Irish people, that is to the cultural and socialist halves of his conjoined causes. Connolly is not usually counted among the most prescient of men, but he got this one right: there were Irish nationalists who did not share his enthusiasm for a workers' republic and some of them were in the IVs. Connolly, of course, did not live to see it, but that those he called recreant nationalists would support the 1921 treaty ending the Irish War of Independence would not have surprised him.[2]

The forces of the *Saor Stát* called into being by the treaty defeated the antitreaty forces in a bloody civil war, the scars of which would last for generations. Ireland was riven. The subtext of that conflict needs again to be noted: There was a powerful social-class aspect to the Civil War: the Left

Republicans, Connolly's "men of no property," lined up against the Free State, led by some with more property than was fitting. The Free State won that war. Diehard Republicans said that the victors were serving as Britain's surrogates—what *shoneens* had always been.

The Ireland that came out of the Civil War bore little resemblance to the Revivalist and Republican dreams. The Irish Free State was very much the Ireland that England had made. Lloyd George had turned over the reins to the Irish bourgeoisie; they would "drive Irish labor" now and corrode the Irish soul as well—the old sow eating her farrow. To say that these views were strongly held is to understate, which is not the same as saying that they were fair or accurate. At that, consider: Ireland was still in the Empire. Its citizens still swore fealty to the British crown, as "old and jealous" as ever. Six Irish counties had been cut out and politically segregated from the other twenty-six. The Irish Left was almost totally excluded from the Free State's governmental apparatus. To the Free State victors went the spoils, such as they were. Ireland's political trajectory was clearly toward compromise, peace, and maybe some palliative care.[3]

The Catholic Church provided the last of those, ably assisted by a suddenly recreant Éamon de Valera. As for Éire as muse, the center of a cultural and artistic reawakening, that too was lost. The "ceremony of innocence," Yeats wrote, "was drowned." R. F. Foster said that the "love affair" of Ireland's "revolutionary generation" was "doomed to disillusionment." The lovers were left to hope and wait for the return of the Ireland they had imagined. Like Godot, Ireland as cultural dreamscape was not coming. Richard Tillinghast changed the analogy: The civil war was Ireland's "national postpartum depression." There was no beauty, not even a terrible one.[4]

The anti-imperialists and anticapitalists had lost their fight for a new old Ireland. So had the writers and the artists and all the others with "vivid faces," all those Irish men and women who were convinced that Ireland could be a kind of cultural lodestar, a workers' republic, creative and tolerant, liberated from the Empire and a full partner in the European world. Most of these, both Revivalists and Republicans, would happily have tolerated a Catholic clergy as providers of spiritual guidance. They would not have separated moral conscience from governance. But what they could not accept was what the clergy became: political credentialing agents and community scolds. The ultimate tragedy might be this last one: the cause of Ireland became the cause of a rigid and reproachful Catholicism. "Faith and fatherland," not poetry and politics or any of the other paired values, were becoming the causes that could not be dissevered. And the first of those, faith, had taken on an admonitory rather than a moral and pastoral role, leaving the second, the fatherland, to play the role of auxiliary to it.[5]

For those with Irish dreams, as well as those who still had Lenin dreams, the Irish Free State that emerged in 1922 was not just unlovely; it was offensive. Rejecting the treaty and continuing the War of Independence might have brought an Irish apocalypse—that's Seamus Deane's word. But accepting the treaty brought boredom—also Deane's word. The fight had been between "two civilizations, one vivacious and wild, the other organized and dull." The Free State, said some, was barely a statelet; those even more disillusioned called it a "Freak State." Ireland's poverty was not the cause of distress; being materially poor was no disgrace. It was, in fact, according to Liam Mellows, the essence of Irishness. Frank O'Connor wanted it understood that people were disillusioned with Ireland "not because the country was poor, but because it was mediocre."[6]

The vision of a new and creative Ireland had been destroyed by narrow-minded Catholic moralists. According to George Russell (Æ), nothing was left of "our spiritual, cultural, and intellectual life." If anything, Ireland "has retrograded. Nothing beautiful in the mind has found freer development." As for the vision of a socialist Ireland, it had been done in by bourgeois capitalists. One radical Irishman even wrote that a "majority of [Irish] working men . . . had a sincere and anxious wish for the return of English rule." Whatever the nature of the betrayal, cultural, social, or both, for these disillusioned dreamers, the Free State was run by "small minded gangsters," as an embittered antitreaty Republican character in John McGahern's *Amongst Women* put it. They had made of Ireland a place of in-house exile.[7]

The antitreaty Republicans had anticipated just such an outcome. Liam Mellows in his 1922 letter from Mountjoy Prison made the point directly. The *"gombeen* men . . . on the side of the Treaty" could be expected to be on the wrong side of everything else: imperialism, capitalism, feminism, the arts, the Church, Ireland's place in the world. Peadar O'Donnell, a leader of the Irish Left, saw the treaty as "a marriage of convenience between British imperialism and the Irish bourgeoisie." O'Donnell once criticized de Valera for policies that were driving far too many Irish to emigrate. De Valera's answer was that a great number of the Irish people would have left the country regardless of which side won the civil war. O'Donnell said that that was true, but "'they would not have been the same people.'" He was right. It was estimated that between 1924 and 1927, upwards of 100,000 of O'Donnell's people left Ireland, sometimes under military escort, and emigrated to the United States. The issue, in other words, was not just the treaty but the Treatyites, the politics of those who supported it and, with their British "allies," won the civil war. It was they who came to govern the semi-nation that the treaty had created.[8]

Among the thousands of Irish who escaped it was James Joyce. It's not likely that Joyce would have stayed in Ireland under any regime, but his comments on the form and structure of the new Ireland are still meaningful. In 1931, Padraic Colum, one of Ireland's great poets both during and after the Revival, wrote a short article for the American magazine the *New Republic*.

He quoted Joyce's famous line from *A Portrait of the Artist as a Young Man* where Stephen Dedalus said that he wished to "forge in the smithy of my soul the uncreated conscience of my race." Colum asked Joyce: what would Dedalus have forged? What sort of nation would the Irish racial conscience have created? Joyce told Colum that "the state for which he had the highest regard was the old Hapsburg Empire." It was "ramshackle"; Joyce liked that about it. As he did its "mellowness of life" and that the "state didn't try to impose . . . upon its own or upon other people. It was not warlike, it was not efficient, and its bureaucracy was not strict; it was the country for a peaceful man." In other words, it was erratic, everything that the Free State was not.[9]

The "conscience of the Irish race" and similarly poetic" topics, were not on Dan Breen's mind; Breen's expatriation bore no resemblance to Joyce's. For Breen, it was the national cause, not the cause of mellow inefficiency that had been betrayed. Breen was an unwavering Republican. He fought against the British in the Irish War for Independence, went then to San Francisco, and, as the treaty fight escalated and civil war was threatened, returned to Ireland to fight against the *Saor Stát*. On his way back, in some haste, he wrote *My Fight for Irish Freedom*. The Free State was a "chimera, . . . was it for [this] that brave Irishmen had fought and died?" So malformed was it that a disgusted East Indian resistance leader turned down Breen's offer to help in expelling the British. The Indian's reasons were instructive. Ireland, his "country," Breen was told, "had abandoned the fight for . . . freedom." The Irish were useless as international knights errant. Rebel India needed stouter friends.[10]

The whole world did. I am aware of no one who spoke more forcibly—and more calmly—on this issue than Ernie O'Malley, one of the acknowledged leaders of the antitreaty IRA who was another of the hundreds of thousands who left Ireland for America. I found no instance when he used the word *shoneen* to describe the leaders of the Free State, but his description of the type is the definition of that strange Irish word and deserves to be cited: O'Malley called them an "outraged bourgeoisie" and said they were "determined to defend this Free State of theirs, which had been handed them on a platter cooked *à l'impériale*."[11]

O'Malley quoted the mid-nineteenth-century Irish dissident James Fintan Lalor, whose sensibilities matched O'Malley's own: "Political rights are but parchment. It is the social constitution that determines the condition of the people.'" A great number of Irish seemed to think that; again, blame history. Frank Walsh had said the same from the perspective of America: "political democracy was an illusion" in the absence of a virile social democracy. O'Malley wanted postcolonial Ireland to get that back. It was, after all, "how Irish history had worked in the sixteenth and seventeenth centuries." O'Malley and the IRA had "fought a civilization which did not suit us"—no revolution has ever been given a gentler expression—to recover "the genius of the race... the old idea of life, the stress on its human values... the personal against the "organized imperialism" of the "impersonal." Lalor was as relevant in 1920 as he had been in 1840. One Irish generation, as Pope Leo had put it, was "remarkably like another."[12]

• • •

The Irish factionalism described by Breen extended to America's Irish as well. "Our countrymen" in the United States, Breen wrote, "are as divided as in Ireland"—a nice if unintentional allusion to transnationalism. Clan na Gael camps, for example, had split, half of the membership favored the treaty, half did not. In Butte, the RELA, by one vote, stayed with Collins and the treaty, the rest formed a new clan, the Sarsfield Social Club. Its leader was Fr. Michael Hannan; the antitreaty clansmen met in his church, as did the women of the equally rebellious Cumann na mBan. As did the Pearse-Connolly Club.[13]

The Irish tendency toward fissiparousness was partly the reason for the split, but so was an understandable confusion. The British and their adopted and allied Anglo-Americans had won the Great War. They claimed victory in the name of the same empire from which the Irish were trying to escape. That great war was followed by two lesser Irish wars, a heroic one with Britain, a heartbreaking one with themselves. Out of it all came the *Saor Stát*; a woefully inadequate return on the commitment and the sacrifice of Irish Republicans. There were some American Irish who understood the moral issue, the fight for psychological as well as political autonomy. James Farrell, for example, called, the post–Civil War years Ireland's singularly offensive Thermidor. Ireland had been hijacked by "the *gombeen* men and the priests"; it was a place of "killing insularity," "wallowing in superstition and ignorance"—something like Studs Lonigan's Chicago, in other words. The poetics of the Irish revolt—the sheer Irishness of it—had been lost.[14]

That did not mean that Ireland had lost its hold on the imaginations—and sensibilities—of some American antimodernists. Yeats had written of the Irish as "born into that ancient sect/ But thrown into the "filthy modern tide." Hannan would have liked that "filthy modern tide" remark, despite knowing little of what Yeats meant by it—or anything else. Yeats then began a hunt for the genuinely Irish in folktales, legends, and myths of the ancient sect. As Yeats put it, they lived lives "that existed before commercialism, and the vulgarity founded upon it." Yeats wasn't the only one who thought that. Gathering the stories of west-country Irish was becoming something of a cottage industry. These were the true Irish, the ones of "uncorrupted values"; perhaps those values, as R. F. Foster put it, would "rub off" on the whole of the world's people.[15]

Notwithstanding the failures of the Free State to realize either the Republican or the poetic dream, for antimodernists the Ireland of the '20s was still something of a theme park, "an escape," said the poet Wallace Stevens, "from an unimaginative modernism," and the hard-hearted capitalism that went with it. Ireland and the Irish were "authentic," simple and unadorned. Ezra Pound joined in the celebration, writing that he was once "drunk with Celticism." He sobered up. So did most of the others. During their binges, however, they confessed to their love of Irish driftiness, and of the almost complete lack of any Irish who claimed—or wanted—mastery. The antimodernists sought alternative landscapes, not to live in but to use as contrasting visions. The poetics of Irishness was the issue; not its collectivist politics.[16]

All of which suggests that most people, English, Irish, and American, didn't know what the *Saor Stát* was. Nor were many Irish Americans fully aware of what had been lost when the home Irish acquiesced in it. The American cousins knew that the singularly not-free Free State was missing six of its parts, but mostly they knew Free State only as the name of the place where Irishmen shot one another. Woodrow Wilson had said that one way to deal with the Irish was to give them a measure of self-government and then give the movie industry the filming rights over what came next. The Irish Civil War came next. The homeland had turned on itself. For America's Irish, that was not just a tragedy; it was an embarrassment. The roaring mass culture of the 1920s brought the Irish a motley list of items. Flappers, washing machines, and radios were among them. So were humiliation, immigration restriction, prohibition, a deformed economy, the Ku Klux Klan, a ginned-up Red and Green Scare, and a bargain-basement Irish statelet.[17]

Examples are in order. Father Michael Hannan, the Irish-born pastor of St. Mary's—Butte's self-proclaimed "Miners' Church," 498 of whose 500 parishioners were Irish—spoke with such force on these issues that I am compelled to return him briefly to the discussion. He "spoke" only to himself in diary entries, but he does not appear to have been one who kept his thoughts to himself. He was a parish priest who gave homilies and administered the sacraments of the Church; he was also the head of Butte's antitreaty Clan na Gael chapter, the Sarsfield Social Club. He knew de Valera and Mellows, among others, of the antitreaty Republicans. It was Hannan whom I quoted earlier, writing in that mordant diary of his that England ruled Ireland as a "stock farm" on which to breed America's "wage slaves."

He began his diary on February 12, 1922, two months after the *Dáil* had approved the treaty and less than a week before the outbreak of the Irish Civil War. I suspect that it was the treaty that made him begin the diary; the Civil War that sustained it. Hannan raged at the treaty. He was one of those who referred to the Free State as the "Freak State"; he knew, because he had counted them by name, how many Protestants there were in its Parliament.

They and the *shoneen* Catholics who were there with them were "Freakers," "traitors," "helots," "murderers," and "England's mercenaries."[18]

Equally noteworthy are the entries in which Hannan expressed his deep hatred of Butte, of America, and of all that passed as modern in the world. Americans were a worthless and sordid people. One diary entry began "God! What a bunch of pagans these Americans are." The United States, he wrote in another entry, "is in every fibre . . . materialistic and sensual." "The withering blasts of atheism and materialism emanate from every region of it." That was something of an Irish trope. It was no trope for Hannan. It was the reality. Came next this final and racialized judgment, the most scornful an Irishman could make: "The full-blooded bulldog at home in England is a far superior class of animal to the Hybrid-breed of this country . . . this fleshpot of Empire."[19]

Among the worst of these hybrids—indeed, the uncrowned heads of all of them—were America's capitalists. They were a "rotten tribe"; "brutes," "vultures," and "rogues," every bit as bad as "the English tyrants." He spoke kindly of the "hobo fraternity" of Butte's miners by which I'm convinced he meant the Industrial Workers of the World, the union home of Butte's "wage slaves." He knew Bill Dunne; in fact, he shared the head table with Dunne and Éamon de Valera during one of the latter's trips to Butte. Hannan lived on the seam as surely as Dunne did.[20]

But what most troubled him was the effect modern American culture was having on Irishness. He feared that the Irish were becoming little more than facsimiles of standard-issue Yankees. He had seen "young Irish girls in their teens going home from . . . noodle parlors and other 'joints' after the filthy picture shows . . . being initiated in vice. . . . And [these], the children of 'the Saints!'" Hannan even arrogated to himself the right to overrule Catholic baptismal names that were not sufficiently Irish and thus offended him. He refused, for example, to baptize "Alana Mona," insisting that her Irish parents should choose from among the "saints' names of their own race." Hannan picked one for them; Alana Mona became "Catherine." Two weeks later, he vetoed an Irish "Leonard" and baptized him as "Francis." In his last will and testament, Hannan insisted that, upon his death, he was to be returned to Ireland for burial, that under no circumstances was the diocesan bishop to put him in American ground. America was to have no part of Michael Hannan.[21]

Frank Walsh's criticism of America was far more retrained and infinitely more informed than Hannan's. Like many in Ireland and among the erratics in the United States, Walsh had hoped for something better than what Ireland got in the treaty ending the Irish war. But he accepted the Free State, as the vast majority of Irish did, as the best that could be had at the time. It was, he said, a "big step forward" toward "the final consummation of Ireland's complete independence." His many discussions with Wilson at Versailles cannot have been forgotten—nor what he considered Wilson's betrayal, forgiven—but the Irish were a patient people. They would have to be.[22]

What had Walsh's full attention was what—following Bruce Nelson's lead—I called Irish nationalist internationalism and the often fierce anti-imperialism that was part of it. Three weeks after he expressed his tepid support for the Free State, he wrote an article on American imperialism in the American journal *The Nation*. His topic was the cruelty and sheer immorality of US involvement in Haiti and Santo Domingo; his comparative model was England's imperial dominance of Ireland. Walsh was unsparing in his criticism of American policy. The "American Foreign Office," he wrote, "is in Wall Street." The moneymen determined policy, not the diplomats, and certainly not Voltaire's citizens of the universe.[23]

Walsh went on. Americans, as he thought then, "were on the eve of the great crusade for democracy, the fight to free small nations" and we were "making a Belgium of Haiti." To Irish Americans "familiar with imperial methods in their own motherland ... the tale of usurpation, terror, and murder in Haiti and in Santo Domingo sounds like an old, old story. ... [O]ur marines act as Black and Tans; ... Padraic Pearse [and] Connolly ... have French and Spanish names; and the [so-called by the English] Irish 'murder gangs' are called Cacos and bandits instead of Sinn Feiners."[24]

Walsh held the British people responsible for "the evil" done the Irish people. They were "morally and legally culpable for the murder and oppression of the Irish," as they were for the entire "fundamental atrocity" of imperialism. So too, and to the same degree, were the American people responsible for "insolent American imperialism." He did not mention Wilson by name, but all who read him knew which insolent American imperialist had sent the marines into Haiti and Santo Domingo. Then came this: the United States was "ousting peasants from their land and making of them itinerant laborers." That is not quite the same as Michael Hannan's charge that English-run Ireland was the labor market for American capitalists, but it's close enough. Walsh's conclusion was harsh—and erratic: "All true Americans and all true Irishmen can now join to bring about ... driving the Imperial US Forces from the republics of Haiti and Santo Domingo."[25]

• • •

Special attention should be paid Walsh's last comment. Note the capitalized reference to "Imperial US Forces" as well as the use of *republic* to describe Haiti and Santo Domingo. "Insolent" Anglo-Americans were behaving like Albion's seed. They were imperialists, running roughshod over republics and making itinerant laborers of peasants. Then came this remarkable and singularly erratic comment: "True" Americans were those who followed the lead of "true" Irish in rejecting and countering this "fundamental atrocity," by which he clearly meant the associated misdeeds of capitalism-imperialism. He essentially equated being a "true American" with being a "true Irishman" and on an issue that defined being Anglo-American. The "true Americans" were ones who thought as the "true Irish" had long thought. Walsh turned the assimilationists, Wilson prominently included, on their collective head. Americanism had been Hibernicized. The failures and deficiencies of the Free State had made the erratics less homesick but it had not brought them any closer to being fully assimilated.

Neither were Anglo-Americans any closer to being Hibernicized. The Ahlstrom thesis was no more historically bounded than IrishCatholic erraticism. Both jumped historical eras with relative ease. IrishCatholic noncompliance—to put it as politely as possible—was as evident in 1920 as it had been in 1850, 1870, and 1890. I am not alone in contending that. Here is a list, partial, selective, and in no particular order, of their nineteenth- and early-twentieth-century contemporaries who—with a cosmopolitan, if not quite global, list to select from—picked Irish Catholics as their case study in contrariness and cultural dissent: Alexis de Tocqueville, George Templeton Strong, Karl Marx, Friedrich Engels, Vladimir Lenin, George Merwin, George Hoar, Harold Frederic, Horace Plunkett, Hugh Pollard, Josiah Strong, Madison Grant, Walter Lippmann, Walter Rauschenbusch, John Commons, Edward Bemis, Max Weber, Werner Sombart, Selig Perlman (by inference), Evelyn Waugh, and Horace Kallen. And those were only the ones who made their feelings on the matter public. IrishCatholics were called a lot of things; add paradigms of cultural divergence to the list. That they also believed themselves to be that—and celebrated the fact—should also be noted.

Here are a few historians, with the same global mélange before them, who used the Catholic Irish as their poster children for cultural noncompliance: Kevin Kenny, Kerby Miller, James Henretta, Ira Berlin, Oliver MacDonagh, Gary Gerstle, E. P. Thompson, Eric Hobsbawm, Herbert Gutman. All of them, for vastly different reasons, were looking for dissonance, behavior and values that separated a racial-ethnic or social-class group from the Anglo-American norm. For each of these historians, Anglo-America's Irish Catholics—white, though of a different color; speakers of a sort of English—were their preferred case in point.

They were also that for another group of Americans, cultural outliers themselves, who saw IrishCatholics as allies in the defense of lost but worthy causes. In the mid-1920s, at the same time that Irish poets and other writers were collecting fairy tales and exalting the peasantry as the most Irish of the Irish, twelve writers from the old southern Confederacy got together and formed a kind of informal writers co-op. The twelve first called themselves the Fugitives. They changed that later to the Agrarians. In 1930, they put together a collection of essays titled *I'll Take My Stand: The South and the Agrarian Tradition*. Change the names and adjust the chronology and the entirety of *I'll Take My Stand* reads like something out of an Irish erratic's instruction manual—a challenge to capitalism with a southern rather than an Irish accent. For three of the Agrarians—I would mention Alan Tate in particular—Irish or Catholics, and by name, were the contrarians of choice; they were better at the role than southerners, in part because more practiced.[26]

Southerners and the Catholic Irish—Faulkner and William Kennedy are my examples here—shared "old-fashioned themes like ... the foreverness of the past." That was not an American theme; Americans believed in the pastness of the past—and in its goneness. What is strongly suggested by this wildly diverse set of contemporaries and historians who chose them as their archetypal erratics is that, despite what history had given them between 1912 and 1923, IrishCatholics were still out of time and out of place. They had not been suddenly transformed by the mass culture of the 1920s.[27]

On this issue, I will borrow the language of Lizabeth Cohen from her book *Making a New Deal: Industrial Workers in Chicago, 1919-1939*. Like many of the others I consulted, Cohen's insightful book is not about the Irish except as they were a component of Chicago's industrial workforce. Martin Dooley and Studs Lonigan don't even make cameo appearances, though John Fitzpatrick, the Irish-born head of the Chicago Federation of Labor and a close friend and ally of Frank Walsh, and William Z. Foster, son of Galway immigrants, are featured players. With those exceptions, however, the Irish, as earlier, are in Cohen's book solely on my assignment.

Like other of Cohen's Chicago "workers," they "were not ... converted to middle-class values." Similarly, like others of her Chicago "ethnics [Irish-Catholics], ... were not Americanized by the commercial triumphs of mass culture." Naming their babies Alana Mona or Leonard did not mean, as Cohen put it later, that they had not been "transformed into more Americanized, middle-class people by the objects they consumed"—or the names they gave their children. The 1920s changed them, but they were erratics going in, and they were the same coming out. As William Allen White wrote of the 1928 presidential campaign of the IrishCatholic Al Smith, "the whole Puritan civilization which has built a sturdy, orderly nation is threatened by Smith." A Methodist minister agreed: Smith's candidacy "signalized the uprise of the unassimilated elements .. against the ideals of our American fathers." Add those two to the list of believers in the ineradicable and subversive differences between IrishCatholics and Protestant Anglo-Americans.[28]

• • •

That is the cultural divergence part of the story. Outside people with outside notions doing Americans mischief has historical importance in itself. In this instance, however, cultural differences affected far more than just the relationship between the people holding them. There was a social-class edge to IrishCatholic dissidence; it had political and social-class repercussions that have not been given the attention they deserve. That applies with particular force to the role they played in American labor and working-class history.

I return briefly to E. P. Thompson and quote from him again: The English working class was made—or made itself—out of stuff having little directly to do with labor. Before they were working class, they were "free-born Englishmen ... as Paine had left [them] or as the Methodists had moulded [them]." They were "the inheritor of Bunyan, of remembered village rights, of notions of equality before the law." They had gone through a "massive religious indoctrination" and had created myriad "new political traditions" long before they ever entered through a factory gate. Their working-class consciousness and ideology cannot be understood without taking all those pre-working-class habits and values into account.

I volunteered a parallel description of IrishCatholics in the American working class. I advert to it again—and add to it. I called them beggar-born Irish; clannish to the point of xenophobic; semianarchic colonials with a colonial's bad disposition and a streak of banditry in them. They were a people out of time and out of place; the inheritors of ancestral sorrows; molded and indoctrinated by a devotional Catholicism that was doctrinally rigid and backward-looking—and intensely, at times ferociously, anglophobiac. That's a partial list. I also argued for their "good-heartedness"; their sense of reciprocity; their instinct, bordering on an imperative, to share and be shared with.

Add to that what to modern Anglo-Americans was their bizarre association of grievances, their insistence that the Irish were a subject people, Ireland a subject nation, workers a subject class—and that the causes went together, were in fact the same cause. They deserve no special praise for the best of these cultural traits; no condemnation for the worst of them. There were times in their history, both as British colonials and as American workers, when those cultural values and practices, particularly semianarchy and clannishness, were all that kept them sane—and alive. In either case, as Haines explained to Dedalus; it was all history's doing.

These IrishCatholic cultural sensibilities were as relevant to the making of an Irish American working class as Methodism and the memory of "village rights" had been to the making of an English one. Irish and Catholic values profoundly affected the response of IrishCatholic workers to modern American capitalism, and to the ways they would contest capitalism's principles and power. I assume that some of them had read widely in the literature of working-class resistance. I grant freely that their work experience in American industries was often brutal; American capitalism did, in fact, press hard on them. In the final analysis, however, most of the IrishCatholic workers' challenge to the ideology of American capitalism, including their embrace of the idea of industrial unionism, was inherited rather than acquired. It came out of their storeroom of erratic notions. The Irish Catholic role in the transformation of the underlying principles of modern American capitalism had its origins in cultural divergence. Their dissent from American capitalism arose from that.

This is giving a lot of political power to cultural values that were hidden from view, even from that of the people who held them. They were part of a "social unconscious." The iron law of wages under laissez-faire capitalism and what one historian called the "savageries" of labor markets ruled by that law, called them back to consciousness. The Great Depression then called them to their political duties. "Culture," as Terry Eagleton put it, "is an indispensable medium of political power.... Interests and affections are the seedbed of politics." And this, also from Eagleton: "Culture and tradition can ... be disruptive forces as well as preservative ones." They were that and more in the case of erratic IrishCatholics in the American working class.[29]

In January 1919, culture and tradition were on display in the Sinn Féin Party's *Clár Oibre Poblacánaighe*, the program passed by the Irish Dáil, by which the workers' Republic of Ireland would be governed. The *Clár* was written first in Irish—attesting to the fact that these were the principles of a *Gaelic* Ireland—then in English—that those voting could read them. In every paragraph, the proclamation emphasized the difference between these "native" Irish principles of self-governance and the "foreign" principles by which Ireland as a subject colony had been governed. The program—with my emphasis added—was "based on our unbroken *tradition* of nationhood, *on a unity in a national name* which has never been challenged, on our possession of a *distinctive national culture and social order*, on the moral courage and dignity of our people in the face of *alien* aggression."[30]

That tradition applied to every part of the program: Irish children were to be fed; elderly and infirm Irish cared for. Those were the native values that would replace the foreign and alien values under which the Irish had been forced to live. But why the use of two words, *foreign* and *alien*, when either one alone would seem to serve? *Foreign* did not mean by government not located in Ireland—England and the English were never mentioned. *Alien* meant of another and different world, one whose principles violated native Irish beliefs. Those alien values were also described variously as *odious*, *unjust*, and *cruel*, but those moral failings were secondary to—and a function of—their being not-Irish.

In that context, consider what this program of a democratic, *workers'* republic had to say on matters affecting the working class. First, this Gaelic

Ireland was to establish "a standard of Social and Industrial Legislation with a view to a general and lasting improvement in the conditions under which the working classes live and labour." That was appropriately vague, but this followed it: The new "nation's sovereignty extends . . . to all . . . the wealth and all the wealth-producing processes within" its borders. And this: "The nation reaffirms that all right to private property [was to be] subordinated to the public . . . welfare." I would draw special attention to the use of "*reaffirm.*" Sinn Féin was restating an old truth. Finally, and in the same context, the Republic was to encourage native industries; but it was also to "ensure" that they were "developed on the most beneficial and progressive cooperative and *industria*l lines.[31]

That last is a strange construction, but I believe that by "industrial lines" was meant "industrial democracy" precisely as Frank Walsh, among the many, intended it. And I'm certain that it meant the right of labor to organize collectively by industry. Whether the proposition was radical depends on one's definition of radicalism. That it was contrary to the spirit and mentality of free market capitalism is self-evident. Affixed to the copy of the Programme that I read was this comment from "Liam Lynch, "We have declared for an Irish Republic. We will live by no other law." Lynch was identified as "General, IRA." For those who insist on distinguishing between the two, I would note that it was his nationalist credentials that were put on display, not his labor ones.

I acknowledge again that the Democratic Programme might have been, as some called it, "poetry," Sinn Féin's insincere thank-you note to the Irish Labor Party and the entire Irish Left for not contesting the 1918 parliamentary elections and allowing Sinn Féin nationalists to dominate the field. Even if meaningless poetry is all it was, it was poetry expressive of a political culture and put to political and cultural purposes. It reflected the values and policies of the Irish Left; it borrowed from IrishCatholic erratics in America, especially those who championed the cause of industrial democracy and industrial unions; and it established as few other single documents have just how culturally different the Irish "natives"—at their most erratic Irish selves—were from Anglo-American "foreigners."

I think parts of the Frank Walsh report on industrial conditions in America found their way into the Democratic Programme. I think the American bishops' *Plan of Reconstruction* might also have. If they did, then *Rerum Novarum* is also represented. And so, return the favor; transnationalize the Programme as well as the 1916 Proclamation of the Irish Republic and make them relevant to the making of the Irish American working-class and, to the extent that the Irish influenced it, the challenge the American labor movement posed to the "new ideology" of English and American capitalism and colonialism.

My focus has been on what IrishCatholics contributed to the "preventive countermovement tending toward" capitalism's "restriction" that preceded the New Deal and of which the New Deal became a part. "Preventive countermovement" is Polanyi-speak. It's from his *The Great Transformation*, where he argued that the emergence of market capitalism in the late eighteenth century was accompanied by the simultaneous emergence of anticapitalism—or, at the least, noncapitalism. The great transformation was played out in the context of the conflict between these two antithetical ideas, the yin and yang of what Polanyi called a "double movement," one forward-looking and toward capitalism, one an often backward-looking countermovement away from it.

Ideologies, at least at the outset, had little to do with the countermovement. As Polanyi framed the issue, a system of unchecked free-market capitalism would have been "disastrous," a "calamity." It would have "annihilated ... human ... society." That being so—and the consequences of the British policy of letting free markets rule policy during the Great Irish Famine was nothing if not annihilative—basic survival instincts were all that was required to trigger a countermovement "tending toward [the] restriction" of free-market economies.[32]

For Polanyi, trade unions and working-class movements generally were "a key part of" such countermovements. He mentions the Chartists specifically; but "all groups in society ... participated" in what Polanyi called "the project." The one thing that held that project together was that all its participants believed in collectivism. That's a word with at least two meaning and Polanyi uses both: "From the point of view of the community as a whole ... collectivism is merely the continuation of that endeavor ... always associated with Christian tradition ... to make society a distinctively human relationship of persons." Let me Hibernicize that: In Ireland, collectivism "never stood for much more than a fundamental goodness of heart." "From the point of view of the economic system," on the other hand, it was a "radical departure from the immediate [and capitalist] past." Either way, collectivism equaled anti-laissez-faire capitalism.[33]

The first, or social, definition is a cultural matter. In addition to Christian tradition and old Irish "truisms, Polanyi could have taken it from Pope Pius XI's encyclical *Quadragesimo Anno*, in which the pope defined collectivism-socialism, in its more innocent and nonviolent form, as "inclin[ing] toward the truths which Christian "tradition has always held sacred." The second, economic, definition, with radicalism as a part of it, is a political matter. Polanyi could have taken it from countless sources. At first glance, the economic-political definition would seem to pose the more threatening challenge to the ideology of capitalism. The social-cultural definition would appear to be the opposite, a drifty premodern curiosity, little more than a constant annoyance.[34]

But consider again Terry Eagleton: "Not everything in a culture is ideological, though anything in it might become so." And when it does, culture becomes "an indispensable medium of political power." "Culture and tradition," once politicized, "can . . . be disruptive forces," indeed, transformative forces. Challenging traditions, sacred or profane—or, as with Irish Catholics, mixtures of both—figures to provoke countermovements, collective rebellions of a sort. Eagleton goes further: "large numbers of men and women will slaughter or be martyred, for culture in the sense of an ethnic, religious, or national identity." In the case of IrishCatholics, most of that rebelliousness was subterranean; it was expressed in the simple, daily acts of living IrishCatholic lives. Every now and again, it surfaced, and the disruptive erraticism of it was put on display. At both times and in both guises, erratic IrishCatholic workers in America constituted a countermovement.[35]

By 1930, with the collapse of the free-market economy, it had become one of considerable and growing power. IrishCatholic workers had come "to recognize their common fate with other ethnicities" and move toward their proper place in an interethnic working class—where Irish Catholics from Ed Boyce to the Irish Progressive League had always wanted them to be. Their countermovement had been made more democratic and inclusive. Tom, Dick, and Harry had joined Pat, Mike, and Tim in an increasingly cosmopolitan American working class.

On the other side of the Ahlstrom thesis, by 1930, the anti-Irish, anti-Catholic movement that *was* the United States had been measurably weakened by the same forces that moved Irish Catholics out of ethnic hiding and into a multiethnic—though not multiracial—working-class countermovement. The mostly Irish clerics "who ran the U.S. Roman Catholic Church" had replaced Protestant Social Gospelers as prophets of Christian reform. America, according to one historian, "had awakened from the long dream of Anglo-Saxon dominance." Franklin Delano Roosevelt frequently read from Pope Pius's *Quadragesimo Anno*; it's unimaginable that Theodore Roosevelt had ever read, not to mention read from, Leo's *Rerum Novarum*.[36]

By Polanyi's reckoning, modern capitalism had reached its "maximum extent around 1914." Which means that for well over a century, the Anglo-American society was based in part on the belief that labor was to "be dealt with as that which it [is], a commodity which must find its price in the market," and that if "the market [were] "given charge of the poor . . . things [would] look after themselves." Those were the "laws of nature" that made them the "laws of God." By IrishCatholic standards, it was a strange god indeed who would countenance such foolishness and cruelty. It is the case that those Irish standards smacked of medievalism, but the collapse of modern capitalism—and modernism generally—made medievalism seem less irrational and infinitely more humane than the new ideology. A certain driftiness had become a new form of mastery.[37]

The New Deal, Polanyi's "model" countermovement, was awash in it. Listen to just a couple of FDR's promises, with my emphasis: "We may now restore [the] temple to the *ancient truths*." Whose ancient truths, he didn't say, but that was a distinctly erratic comment regardless of whose temple Roosevelt had in mind. He followed by telling the American people that the iron law of wages had been repealed, that they had to be high enough to provide "something to live for" not just live by. He then took the twain subject of politics and economics out of their separate spheres and reintroduced them to one another: "The political equality we once had won has been rendered meaningless in the face of *economic inequality*." Obviously, there were not uniquely IrishCatholic ideas. Many of Polanyi's collectivist double movers, in "labor . . . and other groups," were of the same mind. But I must add that James Fintan Lalor, Ernie O'Malley, Frank Walsh, James Connolly, and many thousands more of my erratics were among them.[38]

And had been for many generations. The New Deal was not entirely a response to the Depression; one could imagine something like it emerging out of what I'll call a naturally occurring double movement. I earlier quoted the Irish Catholic laborite Ed Keating, who insisted that the "Catholic Church did not suddenly become 'liberal' in 1931." It only—and suddenly—became relevant about then. Premodern values were made if not modern at least part of the response to modern capitalism's failure. But, as Evelyn Waugh was to put it in 1947, Irish Catholic antimodernists and non- if not anticapitalists, drawing from their "hard, ancient wisdom," derived from "ancient grudges" and the "melancholy of the bogs," had been resisting modern capitalism and its "multifarious frauds" for countless generations.[39]

There's a delusional quality to Waugh's remark. At the same time, there is no reason to think that it required initiation into the ranks of the modern for premodern American workers to understand the language, policies, and ideological mentality of the New Deal. Social security in old age, for example, was known to them; they didn't need the Social Security Act to awaken them to the idea of it. I would say the same of other New Deal initiatives: The historian Lizabeth Cohen says that the New Deal was an effort to bring about "moral capitalism," which sounds like what Terry Eagleton called the "moral economy of the Irish countryside, in which custom, tradition, and sentiment could accrue the force of legal right."[40]

Another historian, Jefferson Cowie, describes much of the New Deal as an effort to secure "collective economic rights." Nonmarket, premodern, organic, tribal societies knew nothing else. As for the New Deal's insistence that "labor practices" should be "fair," that to erratic IrishCatholics was a moral given. An American recognition of it was long past due. There can have been little that the New Dealers did that was new or—the word from the Democratic Programme—"foreign" to them. That, of course, has been my argument from the beginning.[41]

The New Deal, writes Cowie, was the "great exception" to American politics in the century after the Civil War. The United States, according to one overly excited observer, was "gradually shifting from a capitalistic community to a laboristic one." Union memberships went up more than 500 percent during FDR's presidency. Laboring people were becoming the nation's "strongest single influence." In a wonderful turn of phrase, Cowie calls these years a "working-class interregnum"; the economist Paul Krugman, quoted by Cowie, called them "an interregnum between two gilded ages." (The "restoration" of the capitalist "regnum" would take place in 1980 with Ronald Reagan and the Republican Party in the roles of Charles II and the Stuart monarchs.) I will make that a continuing metaphor and say that the counter movers within the double movement were regicides of a sort—an advance on Robert Orsi's "subversives."[42]

It is in that context that I address an implied question posed by Lizabeth Cohen in *Making a New Deal*. Her book is quintessential new labor history, labor history full of laborers, including their "subversive ethnic subcultures." Toward the end of it, however, she admits that it is "extremely difficult to know just where workers' orientation to moral capitalism came from." How is it that "working people's world view[s]," largely formed, Cohen argues, by what they encountered in modern capitalist America, came to make room for Polanyi's "radical departure from the immediate past"? I have attempted to provide a partial answer for one important segment of those working people. IrishCatholics had a culture and a "world view shaped" by their history, before they became America's out-of-time and out-of-place diggers and scrubbers. Work in modern capitalist Anglo-America was a chapter in that history, but there were chapters that preceded it that need also to be taken into account.[43]

It was on labor matters, particularly what Cohen calls the "culture of unity" that was central to industrial unionism and the Committee, later the Congress, of Industrial Organizations (CIO), that the IrishCatholic world view was on fullest display and had its greatest influence. As had the Industrial Workers of the World—though to altogether different purpose—the CIO-affiliated unions brought together men and women, Black and white (in theory, at least) workers of different skill levels, and different ethnic cultures. Irish Catholics were a major part of that. Which raises a question not unlike that posed by Cohen: how is it that IrishCatholic workers, the inheritors of rural townland habits and culture, keenly attentive to traditions and the dead generations who guarded them, could come to embrace the idea of a union organized on industries.[44]

Raymond Williams and E. P. Thompson said there was a working-class "structure of feeling" to working-class neighborhoods. One could "sense" it. I am here arguing for a certain IrishCatholic structure of feeling to the CIO. I sensed it in Butte when the Butte Miners' Union, under mostly Irish leadership, reformed in 1934, merged with the smelter worker unions in Anaconda and Great Falls, immediately went on and won a major strike and became a founding member of the CIO. This was Butte, however; an Irish structure of feeling was built in.[45]

• • •

So was it in the case of another CIO-affiliated union, the New York City Transit Workers Union (TWU), led from 1934 until his death in 1966 by Irish-born Michael Quill. The TWU was not the largest local in the CIO, but it may have been its most important, in part because of its dalliance with the Communist Party of the United States (CPUSA), in greater part because it revealed the CIO's culture of unity more clearly than any other CIO affiliated industrial union. All of that, of course, came after 1930, the concluding date of this book. There is a full accounting of its history—and Quill's role in it—in Joshua Freeman's splendid *In Transit*. My focus is different. I'm more interested in what preceded Quill's career; what explains, in Cohen's words again, his "orientation to moral capitalism" and to a "culture of unity" within the TWU and the CIO?[46]

In his book, Freeman provides an "Irish" answer. But, as was true also with Cohen, Freeman's answer needs to be shoved back in time. More than half of the TWU rank-and-file were Irishmen, many of them Irish-born, many more of them former or current members of the militant Irish Republican Clan na Gael, the America version of the Irish Republican Brotherhood, later Republican Army. The TWU took its name from James Connolly and Jim Larkin's Irish Transit and General Workers Union. In 1938, less than a year after it had begun publication, the *CIO News* carried a banner headline that Connolly could have written—which Connolly, in fact, had written. It read "The interests of the people are the interests of labor, ... the interests of labor are the interests of the people." I'll extend the headline: and they "could not be dissevered."[47]

I think Mike Quill and the other erratics in the TWU-CIO had a lot to do with that headline and with the cultural values behind it; indeed, with the cultural values that gave life to the TWU and the CIO generally. Quill was born in 1905, the son of Irish-speaking middling farmers from Gortloughera, in the townland of Kilgarvan, County Kerry, in far western Ireland. It is not necessary to go into detail, but consider: Between 1845 and 1850, the death and emigration rate in Kenmare, ten miles from Kilgarvan, reduced the population by almost one-third. It is altogether safe to assume that sixty years later, the Irish Catholics of Gortloughera, as Seamus Heaney wrote, were still genuflecting to the "famine god." And still cashing the remittances sent back by the thousands of their friends "exiled" from the neighborhood.

God and the gods were still present among the people of Gortloughera. The dead still had a vote in their counsels. In this connection, it's worth mentioning that Kilgarvan was less than twenty miles from the "townland of Garrynapeaka, in the district of Inchivgeela, in the parish of Iveleary, in the barony of West Muskerry, in the [neighboring] county of Cork," the address, as he gave it, of [Tim Buckley,] the tailor, a man "prodigal of time," and his wife, Anastasia, (Ansty), with their wound and unset clock. Mike Quill came from the traditional, "countermovement," world of the *Tailor and Ansty*.[48]

And from this one, equally dissident: He was eleven at the time of the Easter Rising and the execution of Connolly and the others who planned and led it. While in his teens, he served as an IRA dispatch rider and scout for the No. 2 Kerry Brigade in the War of Independence, and then, still in his teens, joined the antitreaty IRA during its civil war with the Free State. In 1926, Quill left Ireland for New York City and a job in the city's subway system. Quill took his politics—both its Irish nationalist component and its laborite one—from James Connolly, but the Irish component came first. He didn't begin to read Connolly seriously until he got to New York. Freeman writes that the "left republicans" of the TWU—Quill predominate among them—"saw themselves as the heirs of James Connolly and the combination of Irish nationalism, international socialism, and militant industrial unions that he had preached"—the leftist version of seamed causes. In other words, Freeman implies that it was the felt realities of life in America that made Quill a labor radical.[49]

As Freeman put it, the "idea of unionism and especially industrial unionism, was "familiar and attractive to many of the transit workers, *in spite of their own rural, non-union backgrounds.*" That raises a question: if their backgrounds cannot have prepared them for the "idea... of industrial unionism," how is it that so many were "familiar" with and "attracted" to it? It is in that context that I would offer a couple of important amendments to Freeman's singularly important comments. First, even at sixteen Quill would have known something of the social-class as well as the republican and nationalist aspects of the Civil War. The Free State was not only not the independent national state the rebels of 1916 and the IRA after them had fought for, it was a counterfeit "*shoneen* state." That was the reason he fought against it in Ireland and against anything that looked remotely *shoneen* in America.[50]

Dating it back ever further, Mike Quill and thousands like him would have been familiar with and liked the idea of industrial unionism not despite their rural Irish backgrounds but because of them. They were well on their way to industrial unionism long before they got to America. Freeman acknowledges, indeed highlights, the sheer Irishness of the TWU and, by clear inference, the CIO. This Irish collectivist Left, however, was older than Connolly. It was older than Marx or Lenin. Ironically, no one knew that better or repeated it more often than Connolly; a collectivist ethic, he said, arose from the "genius of the Irish race." So did the idea behind industrial unionism.

To be an "heir of Connolly" was, by Connolly's own reckoning, to be an heir of Irish history, Asquith's "hovering malignant genius." Reading Connolly introduced Quill to Karl Marx and V. I. Lenin and assorted other leftist notables. He may have later read them in the original, but he met them first through the gloss that Connolly had put on them. Assuming Quill read Connolly carefully—and I do so assume—he would have encountered passages like the following: In 1896 and again in 1908 Connolly wrote that collectivism, of whatever sort, was inspired "by the Brehon laws of our ancient forefathers," what Connolly called "tribal Communism." He allowed that those ancient laws would have to be made to fit new conditions, but that was a simple task and the Irish were equal to it.[51]

In a later article, Connolly wrote of "the sagacity of his Celtic forefathers, who foreshadowed in the democratic organization of the Irish clan the more perfect organization of the free society of the future," concluding that the Irish system was entirely consistent with the "conceptions of social rights and duties which we find the ruling classes today denouncing so fiercely as 'Socialistic.'" And this: The Irish were as "Socialistic as the industrial development of their time required." They had only to renew it. The English civilization against which they fought," on the other hand, "was ... thoroughly individualistic." So was the Anglo-American civilization against which Quill and the TWU-CIO fought.[52]

Irish values infused the TWU and the entire CIO with Irish "truisms," goodness of heart among them, but including reciprocity, distributive justice, social and economic democracy, and other cultural leftovers from "Ireland before the conquest," before, that is, English Protestants overran and transformed the place. I find it striking that John Ryan and the American bishops' "Plan of Reconstruction," as well as Karl Polanyi, said the same—and applied their Irish lesson globally.

With the TWU and Mike Quill as examples, the CIO's culture of unity, its inclusiveness, its militancy, even its association with the Communist Party came out of the Irish bogs via James Connolly and—though to a lesser extent—*Rerum Novarum*. The TWU wasn't the Irish club the Butte Miners' Union had once been. It was less clannish and insular, more militant, and far less willing to sacrifice labor to the cause of Ireland. The members of the Irish Progressive League—not to mention Ed Boyce and Frank Walsh—would have loved it. If I had to choose a totemic model of the "personality as ecology" of the IrishCatholic working-class erratic, I would be hard pressed to decide between Francis Patrick Walsh and Michael Joseph Quill. Fr. Hannan would happily have baptized both. I happily acknowledge the good-hearted erraticism of both.

The irony here is huge and inescapable: The United States during the "working-class interregnum" in which Mike Quill was a key player, was closer to a workers' republic than was the Irish Free State. It's worth asking: Was it the working-class interregnum that made the American republic a proper model for the Irish? And the reverse of it: Was the Irish Left always a proper model for an American countermovement?

I said earlier that small acts can reveal matters of consequence; the apparently trivial can say a very great deal about the weighty. IrishCatholics' ontological fault lines come to mind. That is the methodological assumption behind the two accounts that follow: the trivial as explicative. The first is from the time in 1939 when Mike Quill invited a "labor priest," Father Charles Owen Rice, to address a TWU convention. Rice was the son of Irish immigrants and a close friend of Philip Murray, the founder of the Steel Workers Organizing Committee and later the head of the CIO. Murray was born in Scotland and so was accounted a Scottish immigrant. I am all but required to add, however, that—like James Connolly, also born in Scotland, and Jim Larkin, born in England—Philip Murray was the son of an Irish-born Catholic industrial laborer, one of Ireland's many thousands of *spailpíní*.

The room in which Fr. Rice was to talk was filled with a great many men who, Rice said, wore "the badge of Catholicism over [their] hearts." That carried responsibilities with it. They had to be people "of tolerance and charity." The badge, however, also gave them more ideological freedom than they might have known they had. Both Quill and Austin Hogan, another Irish American TWU officer, had been accused of being communists. "Celtic" was not appended. Rice disputed the charge, in language that the professed and defiantly Catholic Jim Larkin might have used: Rice said, "I think I am much more radical than the two of them." Let Quill and Hogan catch up with him. The "only quarrel" Rice had with the CIO was that it was not leftist enough. Then came this: "The Pope's encyclicals are ... far more radical than the CIO." I think he meant "popes," plural, *Rerum Novarum* as well as *Quadragesimo Anno*, but he certainly meant the former.[53]

Freeman quoted Rice, who quoted Leo, who quoted Aquinas, who relied on Aristotle. That's what Brad Gregory meant when he said that the "distant past" should not be "left behind" by historians of American labor in the twentieth century. The radical industrial unionism of Freeman's analysis of the TWU, its embrace of the CIO's culture of unity, its inclusiveness, its Irishness, and—however unofficial—its Catholicism, is fully revealed in his discussion of the remarks of Fr. Rice. Historians of American labor routinely tells us of the great number of Irish Catholics in the American industrial labor force. If Quill and Rice were at all representative—and I think they were—it's past time for those historians to add that they were not a drag on American labor radicalism; they were not so benighted by dogma and hocus-pocus—nor were a great number of the priests who specialized in it—as to be anything other than mindless reactionaries. That is a myth and it should be put to rest.[54]

My second small act is Mike Quill's funeral. Quill died on January 28, 1966, two weeks after the strike of New York City's transit workers that immobilized the city had ended. It ended with the Quill-led TWU workers getting a 15 percent wage hike. During the work stoppage, Quill said of Mayor John Lindsay that he was "strictly silk stocking and Yale"—in short, a *shoneen*. "We (the TWU) don't like him." During the strike, Quill and five other TWU officers—four of them with indisputably Irish surnames—were jailed for contempt of court. Quill, it seems, had told the judge "to drop dead in his black robes."

Three days later, Quill was dead. His funeral mass was held at the fortress church of American Catholics, St. Patrick's Cathedral. His casket was brought from St. Patrick's to the Gate of Heaven Cemetery, where, as it happened, the cemetery workers were on strike. They "dropped their picket lines so that he could be buried." Most revealing of all, the casket was draped in the flag of the IRA. I would not have expected the American flag. Quill had been in the United States for the last forty years of life, unassimilated and unassimilable. The Soviet flag was unimaginable and never considered. The TWU, however, must have had at least a banner or a sash. The Catholic Church had an abundance of both. Quill chose—or perhaps someone chose for him—the flag of militant Irish republicanism, the flag of Irish dreamers, including the dreamers of Gortloughera.

The eulogy was delivered by Fr. Rice. His remarks were apparently unrecorded, so Freeman cited what Rice had said about Quill in an earlier address, on the altogether safe assumption that he would have said something similar at Quill's requiem. "Michael, you are a real prince, you are a prince of the working man.... You came from the peasantry of Ireland and rose to the leadership of the industrial peasantry of the United States." There was another eulogist: Reverend Martin Luther King Jr., in a letter written soon after Quill's death, wrote of Quill that "he spent his life ripping the chains of bondage off his fellow man." Voltaire would have called him a citizen of the universe.[55]

Reembedding the economy in society, subordinating the economic to the social, was not the way Quill or any of the other IrishCatholic erratics would have put it, but it is what they were about. Quill once said that "most of my life I've been called a lunatic because I believe that I am my brother's keeper," not out of a sense of service, but out of solidarity. For lunatic, read erratic. The ideology of laissez-faire capitalism had no place for such. The importance of reciprocity, of sharing, of sociability, of friendships and kinships, and neighborliness, of good-heartedness, all were thoroughly in the rural Irish Catholic grain. Quill and Connolly—not to mention generations of Irish before them—were of one mind on those cultural values. The TWU and the CIO were built on them.[56]

Aileen Kraditor said that the Irish should have put their ideas about nationalism, culture, and history in a sphere separate from their ideas on economics and the role and rights of labor. I realize that she ended her book in 1917 when Mike Quill was twelve. But there were a lot of others before Quill whose ideas Kraditor could have consulted. Quill himself was a product of an older Irish and Catholic world; he could have told Kraditor that nationalism, culture, and history were central to the politics of labor—were, in fact, the source of those politics. That was true for all the years between 1870 and 1930. It was true after 1930 as well. The failures and deformities of the Free State had left the seam tattered, but intact.

I am left with an abiding curiosity: Would historians of American labor find it less difficult to know where the countermovement politics of labor came from if they were to jump over Orsi's "ultimate limit," take a "culture turn" toward "Presence," and let it be part of their analysis? Similarly, would Polanyi have been less oblique had he studied Arensberg's Irish peasants with the same care that he brought to his analysis of Melanesians and Berbers? Polanyi used the term "market mentality" (adding that by the mid-1920s it was "obsolete")—in much the same way that Max Weber had used "the spirit of capitalism." I will follow Polanyi's lead: the New Deal countermovement was based on the nonmarket mentality that preceded it—by a decade in Freeman's, Kazin's and Cohen's case, by centuries in my Irish version of it.

The consequences for American labor were enormous. It pushed American politics as far toward collectivism as Americans' embrace of capitalism would permit. It domesticated capitalism, softened and humanized it—as in made it more human and humane. The spirit, the nonmarket mentality, behind New Deal policies, made the state a moral as well as a narrowly legal arbiter of a variety of new deals—an ecclesia of a sort, outward and visible, where always the twain—the economy and morality—met and were joined.

• • •

In his wonderful book on the Famine era, *The End of Hidden Ireland*, Robert Scally said he had long wondered what the "Irish ingredients [were] in the stew that formed the antebellum [American] republic on the eve of its bloodiest trial." A few years earlier, another fine historian, Laurence Moore, in his book *Religious Outsiders,* had raised the same question and then answered it: He said he was "inclined to agree with those who argue that the most important cause of the Civil War was the Irish potato famine." Scally's question and Moore's answer had very little to do with the percentage of the Irish Catholic vote that went to the Democratic Party or with the nativist origins of the Republican Party. The two were not acting out a political science quiz. Scally's "Irish ingredients" in the "American stew" would be found in the culture of hidden Ireland; Moore's "inclination" arose from the religious outsideness of the Catholic Irish.[57]

I'm making the same point regarding American labor and its challenge to and eventual domestication and transformation of American capitalism. What was the "Irish ingredient" in that stew? Was it the "most important" cause of the idea of moral capitalism, the reembedding of the economy and ideas of social and distributive justice? I'm not quite ready to answer as Moore did Scally's implied question and say "the Irish did it," but I'm assuredly inclined to place IrishCatholic worker culture high on the list of causes. There is a biography of Father John Ryan titled "Right Reverend New Dealer." It's an apt title—to which should be appended a subtitle indicating the medieval origins of Ryan's new deals. The nonmarket mentality behind Roosevelt's New Deal cannot be similarly predated. At that, I'm struck by the image of FDR reading from Pius's *Quadragesimo Anno* during a fireside chat.

With the obvious and crucially important exception that the federal government rather than some collective moral reawakening would be the agent of transformation, literally everything the New Deal tried to do can be found in the political playbook of IrishCatholic erratics. To borrow Moore's words, I'm also "inclined to think" that that playbook had a very substantial role in pushing policy toward what Cowie's subtitle calls the "limits of American politics" reached in the New Deal. John Ryan and Frank Walsh, in fact, often tried to push them further than did the Roosevelt administration. And Ed Boyce and Bill Dunne certainly did.[58]

The laborite challenge to American capitalism is an American story. So is the transformation of capitalism by labor and all the others in countermovements. But there were parts of both stories that originated in Ireland. Other parts, as Brad Gregory makes clear, began in the Reformation. Those who would tell that story should read—at Orsi's urging, "intersubjectively"—accounts of the Irish's ancestral sorrows and the cultural values, that "vast repository of instincts, prejudices, pieties, sentiments, half-formed opinions and spontaneous assumptions," that arose from them.

I would include among the sorrows those that arose from the Ahlstrom thesis as well as from the IrishCatholic experiences working for their "American masters." I would add to this the "ultimate line" crossing, a close reading of *Rerum Novarum*, with its subtitle, *On the Condition of Labor* and its phantom working-class "authorship" constantly in mind and all preconceptions about what's in it set aside. That could be followed by selections from James Connolly, both in the cause of Ireland and the cause of labor; along with the position papers of Sinn Féin, especially the 1919 Democratic Programme of *Dáil Éireann*.

Finally, read *The Tailor and Ansty* and sing along with Tim and Anastasia Buckley, "Come day, go day, let's have another day." Join that paean to mindlessness of the clock with friendliness and sociability and a preference for people over stumps and add them to the transnational package of traditional cultural sensibilities that Irish Catholics brought to modern, corporate, and capitalist Anglo-America. Calculate the erraticism quotient, the breadth and depth of the cultural divergence between IrishCatholics in the American working class and the capitalist Anglo-American masters for whom they worked. Those were the ingredients in the stew from 1870 to 1930 and the eve of America's "workers' interregnum," the labor-led double movement that transformed American capitalism.

Notes

Introduction

1. Alexis de Tocqueville wrote in 1835 that "I see the whole destiny of America contained in the first Puritan who landed on its shores," *Democracy in America* (Chicago: University of Chicago Press, [1835] 2000), 267. See Maura Farrelly, *Anti-Catholicism in America, 1620–1860* (Cambridge: Cambridge University Press, 2018).

2. Luke Gibbons, *Gaelic Gothic: Race, Colonization, and Irish Culture* (Galway City, Ire.: Arlen House, 2004), 10, 13; Oliver MacDonagh, "The Irish Famine Emigration to the United States," *Perspectives in American History* 10 (1976): 357–447, 445 (quote).

3. John Lewis Gaddis, *The Landscape of History: How Historians Map the Past* (New York: Oxford University Press, 2002), 128.

4. For Irish Catholics as overwhelmingly in the working class, see Kerby Miller, *Emigrants and Exiles: Ireland and the Irish Exodus to North America* (New York: Oxford University Press, 1985), 161–64, 266–70, 311–21, 501–6; and Eric Foner, "Class, Ethnicity, and Radicalism in the Gilded Age: The Land League and Irish-America," in *Politics and Ideology in the Age of the Civil War* (New York: Oxford University Press, 1980), 150–61.

5. Declan Kiberd, *Inventing Ireland: The Literature of the Modern Nation* (Cambridge, MA: Harvard University Press, 1995), 223.

6. Raymond Williams, *Keywords: A Vocabulary of Culture and Society* (New York: Oxford University Press, 2015), 49; Williams, *Culture and Society, 1780–1950* (New York: Columbia University Press, 1983), xvi, 282; Terry Eagleton, *Culture* (New Haven, CT: Yale University Press, 2016), xvi–ix,

7. Eagleton, *Culture*, 49–50.

8. Eagleton, *Culture*, 1–3, 49–50 (quotes), 95 (quote).

9. Eagleton, *Culture*, 53–54 (quote), 95, 6 (quote; my emphasis), 50.

10. Eagleton, *Culture*, 13 (first quote), 15 (second quote).

11. Eagleton, *Culture*, 66, 12, 161, 6 (page numbers in order of quotations).

12. Kevin Kenny, "Diaspora and Comparison: The Irish as a Case Study," *Journal of American History* 90 (June 2003): 134–62.

13. Eagleton, *Culture*, 59; Tawney quoted in Williams, *Culture and Society*, 225; *The Century Dictionary: An Encyclopedic Lexicon of the English Language* (New York: Century, 1913), 5494.

14. Karl Polanyi, *The Great Transformation: The Political and Economic Origins of Our Time* (Boston: Beacon, 2001), 124.

15. Greg Dening, *The Death of William Gooch: A History's Anthropology* (Honolulu: University of Hawaii Press, 1995), 13–14; Williams, *Culture and Society*, xii, my emphasis; Arensberg, "Anthropology as History," in *Trade and Market in the Early Empires*, edited by Karl Polanyi, Conrad Arensberg, and Harry Pearson (Glencoe, IL: Free Press, 1957), 97–113, 101–2; Eagleton, *Culture*, 93, 38, 27, 72, 80 (page numbers in order of quotations).

16. On Americans' inheritance from the English, see David Hackett Fischer, *Albion's Seed: Four British Folkways in America* (New York: Oxford University Press, 1989).

17. "Race patriots" from Paul Kramer, "Empires, Exceptions, and Anglo-Saxons: Race and Rule between the British and United States Empires, 1880–1910," *Journal of American History* 88 (Mar. 2002): 1315–53. See also Eagleton, *Culture*.

18. Philip Bagenal, *The American Irish and Their Influence on Irish Politics* (London: Kegan, Paul, Trench, 1882), 41, 59.

19. Sean Connolly, *On Every Tide: The Making and Remaking of the Irish World* (New York: Basic Books, 2022), 3; Fischer, *Albion's Seed*, 605–31, 870–98. See also Eagleton, *Culture*, 105.

20. Strong from *Diary*, edited by Alan Nevins and M. H. Thomas, 4 vols. (New York: Macmillan, 1953), 1: 348 (July 1857).

21. E. P. Thompson, *The Making of the English Working Class* (New York: Vintage, 1966), 13; Williams, *Culture and Society*, 295.

22. Seamus Deane, *Strange Country: Modernity and Nationhood in Irish Writing since 1790* (Oxford: Oxford University Press, 1997), 149.

23. Deane, *Strange Country*, 4; Jackson Lears, *No Place of Grace: Antimodernism and the Transformation of American Culture, 1880–1920* (New York: Pantheon, 1981), xiii–xviii. See also Brad Gregory, *The Unintended Reformation: How a Religious Revolution Secularized Society* (Cambridge, MA: Harvard University Press, 2012), 365–88.

24. Gaddis, *Landscape*, 148; Eagleton, *Culture*, 38.

25. Gaddis, *Landscape*, 148; Engels quoted in Williams, *Culture and Society*, 267 (my emphasis). See also Arensberg, "Anthropology," 102.

26. See, in particular, Herbert Gutman, *Work, Culture, and Society in Industrializing America: Essays in American Working-Class and Social History* (New York: Vintage, 1977).

27. Polanyi, *Great Transformation*, 52.

28. Conrad Arensberg, *The Irish Countryman: An Anthropological Study* (Garden City, NY: Natural History Press, 1968); Arensberg, *Family and Community in Ireland* (Cambridge, MA: Harvard University Press, 1968).

29. Polanyi, *Great Transformation*, 53, 67; Polanyi, "The Economy as Instituted Process," 246, and Polanyi, "Aristotle Discovers the Economy," 64–96, both in *Trade and Market*.

30. Polanyi, *Great Transformation*, 46, 71, 103, 222–23, 253–55, 293, 299, 302, 309, 335 (page numbers in order of quotations). Polanyi was not a Marxist.

31. Fred Block, Introduction to Polanyi, *Great Transformation*, xix, xxv; Polanyi, *Great Transformation*, 31–32; Polanyi, "Aristotle," 66.

32. Block, Introduction, to Polanyi, *Great Transformation*, xxv–xxvi; Eagleton, *Culture*, 6–10, 15, 101; Gregory, *Unintended*, 244–47.

33. Friedrich Engels, "The Origin of the Family, Private Property and the State," in Karl Marx and Friedrich Engels, *Ireland and the Irish Question* (1853–70; Moscow: Progress, 1971), 341.

34. Polanyi, *Great Transformation*, 52–57, 301 (my emphasis); Arensberg, "Anthropology."

35. Robert Orsi, *History and Presence* (Cambridge, MA: Harvard University Press, 2016), 3. See also Gibbons, *Gaelic Gothic*, 10, 13, 88.

36. Orsi, *History and Presence*, 57–58, 216.

37. Orsi, *History and Presence*, 25.

38. Orsi, *History and Presence*, 5, 15, 38. Orsi doesn't tell us whether he would write the same sentence in the present tense.

39. Orsi, *History and Presence*, 4, 5, 37–38, 15, 9, 64, 258n7 (page numbers in order of quotations; my emphasis in each case). "Inherently subversive" from 5.

40. Eamon Duffy, *Faith of Our Fathers: Reflections on Catholic Tradition* (London: Continuum 2004), 129; G. K. Chesterton, *Orthodoxy* (San Francisco: Ignatius Press, [1908] 1995), chap. 4, "The Ethics of Elfland."

41. Orsi, "U.S. Catholics between Memory and Modernity," in *Catholics in the American Century: Recasting Narratives of U.S. History*, edited by R. Scott Appleby and Kathleen Cummings (Ithaca, NY: Cornell University Press, 2012), 16. Orsi did, however, refer to the United States as a "Protestant land" in *History*, 16, 154, 156.

42. Orsi, *History*, 37–42, 46.

43. *Rerum Novarum*, the 1891 encyclical of Pope Leo XIII, "On the Condition of Labor," in *The Church and Labor*, edited by John A. Ryan and Joseph Husslein (New York: Macmillan, 1924), 58, 67.

44. Virgin and Dynamo from Henry Adams, *The Education of Henry Adams* (New York: Modern Library, [1907] 1999), 379–90. On the transfer of sovereignty, see Jean Bethke Elshtain, *Sovereignty: God, State, and Self* (New York: Basic Books, 2008), esp. 78–79, 127–33.

45. For my argument for articulation, see *Beyond the American Pale: The Irish in the West, 1845–1910* (Norman: University of Oklahoma Press, 2010, 334–35; *Selected Writings of John V. Kelleher on Ireland and Irish America*, edited by Charles Fanning (Carbondale: Southern Illinois University Press, 2002), 153.

46. Yorke quoted in Emmons, *Beyond the American Pale*, 269.

47. Polanyi, *Great Transformation*, 279.
48. Gregory, *Unintended*, 9.

Chapter One. "Ancestral Sorrows"

1. Toynbee quoted in C. Vann Woodward, *The Origins of the New South, 1877–1913* (Baton Rouge: Louisiana State University Press, 1951), facing ix. Asquith offered his remark during the debate in Parliament over the treaty ending the Irish War of Independence (*Hansard's Parliamentary Debates*, vol. 149, Dec. 19, 1921, cc 144).

2. "Ancestral sorrows" from "The Dedication to a Book of Stories Selected from the Irish Novelists," in William Butler Yeats, *The Poems*, edited by Richard Finneran (New York: Macmillan, 1983), 45; history as nightmare from James Joyce, *Ulysses*, edited by Hans Gabler (New York: Vintage, [1921] 1986), 28; Haines from Joyce, *Ulysses*, 17.

3. "To Ireland in the Coming Times," in Yeats, *Poems*, 73.

4. Anglophobia as hegemonic device from Kerby Miller, "Emigration as Exile: Cultural Hegemony in Post-Famine Ireland," in Miller, *Ireland and Irish America: Culture, Class, and Transatlantic Migration*, 79–99 (Dublin: Field Day, 2008).

5. Renan quoted in Linda Colley, *Britons: Forging the Nation, 1707–1837* (New Haven, CT: Yale University Press, 1992), 20. See also Thomas O'Flaherty, *Cliffmen of the West* (London: Gollancz, 1935), 244, 261.

6. Deane, *Strange Country*, 190. On revisionism, see D. George Boyce and Alan O'Day, eds., *The Making of Modern Irish History: Revisionism and the Revisionist Controversy* (London: Routledge, 1996); and Ciaran Brady, ed., *Interpreting Irish History: The Debate on Historical Revisionism* (Dublin: Irish Academic Press, 1994). See also Seamus Deane, "Wherever Green Is Read," in Brady, *Interpreting*, 234–45; and Kiberd, *Inventing Ireland*, 15.

7. "Eschewing blame casting" from Donald Akenson, *The Irish Diaspora: A Primer* (Toronto: P. D. Meaney, 1996), 19. Liam Kennedy cites Akenson using the term "famine porn" in Liam Kennedy, *Unhappy Land* (Dublin: Irish Academic Press, 2016), 104. See also Lears, *No Place*, xviii, xix; Deane, *Strange Country*, 187; Gaddis, *Landscape*, 122.

8. Healy quoted in Max Aitken, *The Decline and Fall of Lloyd George* (London: Collins, 1963).

9. Emmet Larkin, "The Devotional Revolution in Ireland, 1850–1875," *American Historical Review* 77 (June 1972): 648. Eagleton quoted in *Mapping the Great Irish Famine: An Atlas of the Famine Years*, edited by Liam Kennedy, Paul S. Ell, E. M. Crawford, and L. A. Clarkson (Dublin: Four Courts, 2000), 15; Heaney from "At a Potato Digging," *Poems, 1965–1975* (New York: Noonday, 1980), 21. Orsi quoted from *History*, 64–65; see also 231–32.

10. Gilad Hirschberger, "Collective Trauma and the Social Construction of Meaning," *Frontiers in Psychology* 9 (Aug. 2018), https://www.frontiersin.org/articles/10.3389/fpsyg.2018.01441/full (my emphasis).

11. Robin Cohen, *Global Diasporas: An Introduction* (New York: Routledge,

2008); Christine Kinealy, *This Great Calamity: The Irish Famine, 1845–52* (Dublin: Gill and Macmillan, 1994). For Mitchel's verdict, see, among many sources, Edna Delaney, *The Curse of Reason: The Great Irish Famine* (Dublin: Gill and Macmillan, 2012), 93–94, 107–8, 177–81, 184–89.

12. Edmund Spenser, *A View of the Present State of Ireland* (London: Perfect Library, [1596] 2013).

13. Brian Friel, *Translations*, in *Selected Plays* (Washington, DC: Catholic University of America Press, 1986), 444 (my emphasis).

14. Friel, *Translations*, 418, 448, 399, 420. Davis quoted in Eagleton, *Culture*, 84.

15. "English child" from Kiberd, *Inventing Ireland*, 268. See also Deane, *Strange Country*, 4, 8–9, 55, 96.

16. Larkin, "Devotional Revolution," 639.

17. Larkin, "Devotional Revolution," 638–45, 650; Deane, *Strange Country*, 96; Thomas Burke, *Lectures on Faith and Fatherland* (Glasgow: R. and T. Washbourne, 1872), 79, 117.

18. Larkin, "Devotional Revolution," 646.

19. Hirschberger, "Collective Trauma."

20. Miller, *Emigrants and Exiles*, 107, 358–59; Kelleher, *Selected Writings*.

21. Colley, *Britons*, 8. Colley's context was British, not American, but her words apply to both.

22. George Hoar, *Autobiography of Seventy Years*, 2 vols. (New York: Scribner, 1903), 2: 285.

23. Hoar, *Autobiography of Seventy Years*, 1: 178, 188–89; 2: 278–93.

24. Harold Frederic, *The Damnation of Theron Ware, or Illuminations* (New York: Penguin, [1896] 1986), 48–50, 280.

25. Frederic, *The Damnation of Theron Ware*, 48–49.

26. Frederic, *The Damnation of Theron Ware*, 48-49 (my emphasis).

27. Frederic, *The Damnation of Theron Ware*, 234–35 (my emphasis).

28. Henry Childs Merwin, "The Irish in American Life," *Atlantic Monthly*, Mar. 1896, 289–301, 289, 296. See also Merwin, "Recent Impressions of the English," *Harper's Magazine*, May 1903, 929–32.

29. Merwin, "Irish," 294–95.

30. Merwin, "Irish," 291.

31. Merwin, "Recent Impressions," 931 (my emphasis); Barbara Solomon, *Ancestors and Immigrants: A Changing New England Tradition* (Chicago: University of Chicago Press, 1972), 118, 184.

32. Merwin, "Irish," 289, 290, 295, 296.

33. Merwin, "Recent Impressions," 930.

34. Madison Grant, *The Passing of the Great Race, or The Racial Basis of European History* (New York: Scribner, [1916] 1936), 75–76; see also 136 (my emphasis).

35. US Congress, *Reports of the Immigration Commission*, 41 vols.; vol. 5, *Dictionary of Races or Peoples* (Washington, DC: Government Printing Office, 1911), 54–55, 79, 124.

36. James Turner, *Language, Religion, Knowledge: Past and Present* (Notre Dame, IN: University of Notre Dame Press, 2003), 35–38, 49; Gibbons, *Gaelic Gothic*, 10, 13, 88.

37. Eagleton, *Culture*, 8. To some of the race patriots, Anglo-Americans were being purposefully outbred, a different form of subversion.

38. Williams, *Culture and Society*, 332–34.

39. Josiah Strong, *The New Era*; or, *The Coming Kingdom* (New York: Baker and Taylor, 1893), 175, 332.

40. Strong's other book was the better known *Our Country: Its Possible Future and Its Present Crisis* (New York: Baker and Taylor, 1890).

41. Leo Ward, *Holding Up the Hills: The Biography of a Neighborhood* (New York: Sheed and Ward, 1941), 57–58. For sabbatarianism, see Roy Rosenzweig, *Eight Hours for What We Will: Workers and Leisure in an Industrial City, 1870–1921* (Cambridge: Cambridge University Press, 1983.

42. Eagleton, *Culture*, 119.

43. Fischer, *Albion's Seed*.

44. Miller, *Emigrants and Exiles*, 4, 107.

45. Kenny, "Diaspora," 135–36; Akenson, *Irish Diaspora*, 237–38.

46. Miller, *Emigrants and Exiles*, 493.

47. Finley Peter Dunne, "On Gold Seeking," in *Mr. Dooley in Peace and War* (Boston: Small, Maynard, 1898), 100–101, 103–4. See also Miller, *Emigrants and Exiles*, 108.

48. Mary Doyle Curran, *The Parish and the Hill* (New York: Feminist Press, 2002), 78, 105. My sincere thanks to Beth O'Leary Anish for bringing this important book to my attention.

49. Curran, *The Parish and the Hill*, 30–31.

50. Curran, *The Parish and the Hill*, 30–31.

51. I could, of course, have chosen F. Scott Fitzgerald, Eugene O'Neill, John O'Hara, or James Farrell, better known and more celebrated Irish American writers who also wrote about what distinguished them from the rest of the Americans.

52. Polanyi, *Great Transformation*, 48–52, 301. See also Polanyi, "Aristotle Discovers the Economy," in 64–96; and Polanyi, "The Economy as Instituted Process," in *Trade and Market*, 243–306.

53. James Tully, *Shanty Irish* (New York: Albert and Charles Boni, 1928), 58. See also Ron Ebest, *Private Histories: The Writings of Irish Americans, 1900–1935* (Notre Dame, IN: Notre Dame University Press, 2005), 23.

54. Kennedy quoted in Ebest, *Private Histories*, 238.

55. James Henretta, "The Study of Social Mobility: Ideological Assumptions and Conceptual Bias," in *The Labor History Reader*, edited by Daniel Leab (Urbana: University of Illinois Press, 1985), 35, 37 (Henretta's emphasis).

56. Henretta, "Study of Social Mobility," 37 (my emphasis); Gregory, *Unintended Reformation*, 261 (his emphasis).

57. Henretta, "Study of Social Mobility," 40, 37.

58. Williams, *Culture and Society*, 331–32; Henretta, "Study of Social Mobility," 39.

59. Henretta, "Study of Social Mobility," 39, 37. See also Foner, "Class, Ethnicity, and Radicalism," 152, 188.

60. Kenny, "Diaspora," 146, 154 (my emphasis).

61. Herbert Gutman, "Joseph P. McDonnell and the Workers' Struggle in Paterson, New Jersey," in *Power and Culture: Essays in the American Working Class*, edited by Ira Berlin (New York: New Press, 1987), 93–116. For another account of the American "Dark Ages" and the Irish response, see Foner, "Class, Ethnicity, and Radicalism."

62. Gutman, "Joseph P. McDonnell"; Gompers, *Seventy Years of Life and Labor: An Autobiography*, 2 vols. (New York: E. P. Dutton, 1925), 1: 103.

63. Gompers, *Seventy Years*, 1: 88, 102–6, 128–49; Marx, "Position of the IWA in Germany and England," Sept. 22, 1871, in Marx and Engels, *Ireland*, 301–4. See also Cormac Ó Gráda, "Fenianism and Socialism: The Career of Joseph Patrick McDonnell," *Saothar* 1 (May Day, 1975): 31–41. Gutman's admission of his neglect of the Catholic question is from *Power and Culture*, 332.

64. Orsi, *History*, 22.

65. Dorothy Thompson, *Outsiders: Class, Gender and Nation* (London: Verso, 1993), 122. Eric Foner writes that the relationship between "class-conscious unionism and Irish national consciousness" was "symbiotic" ("Class, Ethnicity, and Radicalism"), 176.

66. Elshtain, *Sovereignty*, 77–80, 129.

67. Orsi, *History*, 39–40.

68. Elshtain, *Sovereignty*, 79, 128. Brad Gregory makes a similar argument in *Unintended Reformation*. Consider only the titles of three of his chapters: "Excluding God," "Subjectivizing Morality," and "Against Nostalgia."

69. Elshtain, *Sovereignty*, 128.

70. De Tocqueville, *Democracy in America*, 275.

71. De Tocqueville, *Democracy in America*, 267.

72. Elshtain, *Sovereignty*, 129–30, 79. See also Brad Gregory's superb "'No Room for God'? History, Science, Metaphysics, and the Study of Religion," *History and Theory* 47 (2008): 495–519. See also Polanyi, "Economy as Instituted Process," 233.

73. Deane, *Strange Country*, 4, 151.

74. Polanyi, "Economy as Instituted Process," 224, 227, 233.

75. Gregory, *Unintended Reformation*, 270.

76. *Hansard's Debates*, vol. 85, Apr. 24, 1846, col. 1027; Wilfred King, *The Wealth and Income of the People of the United States* (New York: Macmillan, 1915), 231–32. In 2023, the wealthiest 1 percent had more than five times the wealth of the bottom 50 percent combined (*New York Times*, Mar. 7, 2023).

77. See Polanyi, *Great Transformation*, 141–57.

78. Polanyi, *Great Transformation*, 232–33.

79. Tawney quoted in Williams, *Culture and Society*, 223–24.

80. Elshtain, *Sovereignty*, 130. See also Williams, *Culture and Society*, 326, 329.

81. Robert Schmuhl, *Ireland's Exiled Children: America and the Easter Rising* (New York: Oxford University Press, 2013), 5–10. See also Foner, "Class, Ethnicity, and Radicalism," 160. Brian Friel used the term "East American" in his play *Philadelphia, Here I Come* (in *Selected Plays*).

82. Miller, *Emigrants and Exiles*, 358–59.

Chapter Two. "And a Fourth There Is Who Wants Me to Dig"

1. Shakespeare, *The Tempest* (1610–11; New York: Folger Shakespeare Library, 2023), Act I, Scene II; Leo Marx, *The Machine in the Garden: Technology and the Pastoral Ideal in America* (New York: Oxford University Press, 1964), 34–74; Ronald Takaki, "The Tempest in the Wilderness: The Racialization of Savagery," in *A Different Mirror: A History of Multicultural America* (Boston: Little, Brown, 1993), 24–45 (my emphasis).

2. John Tenniel. *Punch*, Mar. 19, 1870; from Punch Magazine Archive.

3. James Joyce, *Ulysses*, 168, 6; Shakespeare, *The Tempest*, Act I, Scene II.

4. Joyce, *Ulysses*, 17. "Old sow": Joyce, *A Portrait of the Artist as a Young Man* (New York: Viking, [1916] 1968), 203).

5. Miller, "Emigration as Exile, 79–99; Miller, *Emigrants and Exiles*, 427–91.

6. Quoted in Thomas Brown, *Irish-American Nationalism, 1870–1890* (Philadelphia: Lippincott, 1966), 64.

7. Hannan Diary, Apr. 12, 1923, Butte/Silver Bow Archives, Butte, Montana. See also David Emmons, "'A Tower of Strength to the Movement': Father Michael Hannan and the Irish Republic," *American Journal of Irish Studies* 12 (2015): 77–116.

8. Kelleher, *Selected Writings*, 150, 152. See also Foner, "Class, Ethnicity, and Radicalism," 151.

9. Elshtain, *Sovereignty*, 31–32.

10. Polanyi, "Economy as Process," 244–45.

11. "Anti-slave theory" quoted in Christopher Lasch, *The Revolt of the Elites and the Betrayal of Democracy* (New York: W. W. Norton, 1995), 63; David Montgomery, *Beyond Equality: Labor and the Radical Republicans* (New York: Alfred Knopf, 1967), 251. See also Mark Lause's excellent *Free Labor: The Civil War and the Making of an American Working Class* (Urbana: University of Illinois Press, 2015).

12. Harrington, Foreword to Werner Sombart, *Why Is There No Socialism in the United States?* (White Plains, NY: M. E. Sharpe, [1906] 1976), ix.

13. Robert Penn Warren, *The Legacy of the Civil War: Meditations on the Centennial* (New York: Random House, 1961), 28–29, 69.

14. Eric Foner, *Free Soil, Free Labor, Free Men: The Ideology of the Republican Party before the Civil War* (New York: Oxford University Press, 1970), 14, 63–64; Lasch, *Revolt*, 62.

15. Garrison quoted in Lasch, *Revolt*, 62, 63n.

16. Phillips from Lasch, *Revolt*. Eric Foner argues that Phillips, James Redpath, and Patrick Ford were on the side of both abolitionism and free labor reform; they were, but only intermittently and temporarily (Foner, "Class, Ethnicity, and Radicalism").

17. Lasch, *Revolt*, 62–64. See also Montgomery, *Beyond Equality*, 123–24.

18. On being of "English blood," see *Life and Letters of Edwin Lawrence Godkin*, 2 vols., edited by Rollo Ogden, 1: 1 (New York: Macmillan, 1907).

19. Godkin's remark on the eight-hour day is from Montgomery, *Beyond Equality*, 248.

20. Edwin Godkin, "American Opinion on the Irish Question," *Nineteenth Century*, July–Dec. 1887, 285–92. Description of Irish workers is from Godkin, *Life and Letters of Edwin*, 2: 182–83.

21. Godkin, "The Week," *The Nation*, Apr. 27, 1871, 281; see also Godkin, *Life and Letters* 1, 181–84. Matthew Frye Jacobson deals with Godkin in his *Whiteness of a Different Color: European Immigrants and the Alchemy of Race* (Cambridge, MA: Harvard University Press, 1998), esp. 167, 183.

22. Orsi, "U.S. Catholics," 16, 18–19, 15, 32, 41.

23. Three out of every four workers in American industries in 1917 were either foreign-born (58%), or native-born of a foreign father (17%). It is safe to say that the majority of industrial workers were Catholic. (Statistics from W. Jett Lauck and Edgar Sydenstricker, *Conditions of Labor in American Industries* [New York: Funk and Wagnalls, 1917], 1–2.)

24. Gerstle, "Liberty, Coercion, and the Making of Americans," *Journal of American History* 84 (Sept. 1997): 524–58, 558; Orsi, *History*; Elshtain, *Sovereignty*; Gregory, *Unintended Reformation*.

25. *Irish World*, Apr. 5, 1879; Orsi, "U.S. Catholics," 31. See also Foner, "Class, Ethnicity, and Radicalism."

26. For the effect of Italian immigration on the Irish, see Solomon, *Ancestors and Immigrants*, 182.

27. Emmons, *Beyond the American Pale*, 52–60.

28. Thomas Leonard, *Illiberal Reformers: Race, Eugenics, and American Economics in the Progressive Era* (Princeton, NJ: Princeton University Press, 2016).

29. Sydney Ahlstrom, *A Religious History of the American People* (New Haven, CT: Yale University Press, 1972), 798; Josiah Strong, *Our Country* (New York: Baker and Taylor, 1890). The quoted material is from his chapter titles.

30. Strong, *Our Country*, 89–91, 75, 82.

31. Strong, *New Era*, 35–36, 12.

32. Walter Rauschenbusch, *Christianity and the Social Crisis* (New York: Hodder and Stoughton, 1907), 221, 323.

33. Rauschenbusch, *Christianity and the Social Crisis*, 176–78, 192.

34. Rauschenbusch, *Christianity and the Social Crisis*, 1–93.

35. Hell's Kitchen from Ronald Bayor and Timothy Meagher, *The New York Irish* (Baltimore, MD: Johns Hopkins University Press, 1996), 6, 217–18, 625n17.

36. On this issue, see Ahlstrom, *Religious History*, 801.

37. For copies sold, see Robert Wiebe, *The Search for Order, 1877–1920* (New York: Hill and Wang, 1967), 44.

38. E. A. Ross, *Changing America: Studies in Contemporary Society* (New York: Century, 1919), 45; Ross, *The Old World in the New* (New York: Century, 1914), 34, 40.

39. Thomas Leonard, *Illiberal Reformers: Race, Eugenics, and American Economics in the Progressive Era* (Princeton, NJ: Princeton University Press, 2016), 114 (my emphasis).

40. Leonard, *Illiberal Reformers*, 144. For Commons, see 35–41, 53, 61–70, 100–104, 134–37; for Bemis, 139–44.

41. Bemis, "Restriction of Immigration," *Andover Review*, Mar. 1888, 251–64, 251 (my emphasis).

42. Bemis, "Restriction," 252.

43. Statistics from Miller, *Emigrants and Exiles*, 569.

44. James Barrett and David Roediger, "The Irish and the 'Americanization' of the 'New Immigrants' in the Streets and in the Churches of the Urban United States, 1900–1930," *Journal of American Ethnic History* 24 (Summer 2005): 3–34; Barrett, *The Irish Way: Becoming American in the Multiethnic City* (New York: Penguin, 2012), 5–6.

45. Bemis, "Restriction," 256.

46. On Irish literacy, see Miller, *Emigrants and Exiles*, 351, and Bemis, "Restriction," 256, 263 (my emphasis).

47. Leonard, *Illiberal Reformers*, 143, 149.

48. Bemis, "Restriction," 259, 260.

49. Bemis, "Restriction," 259, 260.

50. John R. Commons, *Myself: The Autobiography of John R. Commons* (Madison: University of Wisconsin Press, [1934] 1964), 51, 59–63, 150.

51. Paul Kellogg, *Wage-Earning Pittsburgh* (New York: Russell Sage Foundation, 1914; facsimile repr., New York: Arno, 1974), 117.

52. Quoted in Solomon, *Ancestors and Immigrants*, 141, 143.

53. John R. Commons, *Races and Immigrants in America* (New York: Macmillan, 1907), 28, 35–40, 115. See also Commons, *Social Reform and the Church* (New York: Thomas Crowell, 1894).

54. Commons, *Myself*, 8, 53, 115–16, 150.

55. Commons, *Myself*, 8, 53, 115–16, 150; Commons, *Races and Immigrants*, 115–18, 121.

56. Commons, *Races and Immigrants*, ch. 1, "Race and Democracy."

57. Commons, *Races and Immigrants*, ch. 1, "Race and Democracy." US Commission on Industrial Relations, *Final Report* (Washington, DC: Government Printing Office, 1915), 337.

58. Commons, *Myself*, 140; Commons, *Races and Immigrants*, 117, 153, 183; ch. 3, "The Negro."

59. Commons, *Races and Immigrants*, ch. 4, "Nineteenth Century Additions."

60. Commons, *Races and Immigrants*, ch. 9, "Amalgamation and Assimilation"; ch. 8, "Politics."

61. Nick Salvatore, *Eugene V. Debs: Citizen and Socialist* (Urbana: University of Illinois Press, 1982), 62–68, 151–52, 229–31, 311–12; Jacob Dorn, "'In Spiritual Communion': Eugene V. Debs and the Socialist Christians," *Journal of the Gilded Age and Progressive Era* 2 (2003): 303–25, 303.

62. Dorn, "In Spiritual Communion," 309–10.

63. Eugene V. Debs, "The Rights of Working Women," *Melting Pot* (St. Louis), 1, no. 3 (Mar. 1913), 12–13. Letter to Warren cited in Dorn, "In Spiritual Communion," 309; Salvatore, *Debs*, 60, 153–54, 192, 229, 274, 295, quote on 309.

64. Debs, "Rights of Working Women," 12–13. Salvatore makes no references in his biography of Debs to Debs's anti-Catholicism.

65. Debs, "Rights of Working Women," 12–13. Boyce described the trip in his diary (Boyce Papers, Eastern Washington Historical Society, Spokane).

66. William Leuchtenberg, Introduction to Lippmann, *Drift and Mastery* (Englewood Cliffs, NJ: Prentice-Hall, [1914] 1961), 7; Lippmann, *Drift and Mastery*, 146, 162.

67. Lippmann, *Drift and Mastery*, 158, 117, 118, 144–46. Scott quoted in Gaddis, *Landscape*, 143–44.

68. Lasch, *Revolt*, 168–70; Lasch, *The New Radicalism in America, 1889–1963: The Intellectual as a Social Type* (New York: Knopf, 1965), 253–54, 220, 78, 112–113; Lippmann, *Drift and Mastery*, 16.

69. Leuchtenberg, Introduction, 5; Lippmann, *Drift and Mastery*, 115, 204.

70. Lippmann, *Drift and Mastery*, 116.

71. For an example, likely only partially fictionalized, of overwrought and lurid Catholic language, and this at a Jesuit-run school, see Joyce, *Portrait*, 107–38.

72. Robert Darnton, *The Great Cat Massacre and Other Episodes in French Cultural History* (New York: Basic Books, 1984), 5.

73. Lippmann, *Drift and Mastery*, 142, 151, 148, 153–55, 151, 163–64, 147, 118–20.

74. Lippmann, *Drift and Mastery*, 143. Orsi, "U.S. Catholics," 40.

75. Flynn, *The Rebel Girl: An Autobiography* (New York: International, [1951] 1973), 23.

76. Leo XIII, Pope, *Rerum Novarum*, 58.

77. Leo XIII, *Rerum Novarum*, 84.

78. Gary Gerstle, "Historical and Contemporary Perspectives on Immigrant Political Incorporation: The American Experience," *International Labor and Working-Class History* 78 (Sept. 2010): 110–17, 110, 112.

79. Gerstle, "The Protean Character of American Liberalism," *American Historical Review* 99 (Oct. 1994): 1043–73, 1064–65.

Chapter 3. A Transnational "Freemasonry of the Disinherited"

1. Peter Rachleff, "Two Decades of the 'New' Labor History," *American Quarterly* 41, no. 1 (Mar. 1989): 184–89: David Brody, "Reconciling the Old Labor History and the New," *Pacific Historical Review* 62, no. 1 (Feb. 1993): 1–18.

2. Rachleff, "Two Decades," 186.

3. Rachleff, "Two Decades," 188.

4. Orsi, *History*, 51, 68–69, 252. See also Daniel Rodgers, *Atlantic Crossing: Social Politics in a Progressive Age* (Cambridge, MA: Harvard University Press, 1998), 524n67, where Rodgers argues that historians ignored *Rerum Novarum* because of a latent anti-Catholicism.

5. Orsi, *History*, 252.

6. On this point, see Dening, *Death of William Gooch*, 54, 64.

7. Selig Perlman, *A History of Trade Unionism in the United States* (New York: Macmillan, 1922), ch. 3, "The Beginning of the Knights of Labor and of the American Federation of Labor."

8. Perlman, *A Theory of the Labor Movement* (New York: Macmillan, 1928), 8–10, 28; Sombart, *Why No Socialism?* 13.

9. Perlman, *Theory*, 168–69.

10. For the Irish Catholics in the Chartist Movement, see Dorothy Thompson, *Outsiders*.

11. On the Molly Maguires, see Perlman, *Theory*, 168–69. See also Kiberd, *Inventing Ireland*, 223.

12. Connolly quoted in James Farrell, "Portrait of James Connolly," in *On Irish Themes*, edited by Dennis Flynn (Philadelphia: University of Pennsylvania Press, 1982), 31, 119, 205.

13. For a different and slightly opposing view, see Foner, "Class, Ethnicity, and Radicalism," esp. 158–76.

14. Bertram Wolfe, *Strange Communists I Have Known* (New York: Stein and Day, 1982), 52–71; Emmet Larkin, *James Larkin: Irish Labor Leader, 1876–1947* (Cambridge, MA: MIT Press, 1965), 194–95.

15. One of the unintended consequences in Brad Gregory's *Unintended Reformation* was that capitalism devoured the Protestantism that created it. It did that by "disembedding [Polanyi's term] . . . economics from public morality." Gregory writes, "As things turned out, Catholics, Lutherans, Reformed Protestants, and Western Christianity in general all lost" (160, 243).

16. Max Weber, *The Protestant Ethic and the Spirit of Capitalism*, translated by Talcott Parsons (1930; London: Routledge 2005), 18, 4, 8, 6, 8. For cites to Franklin, see 18–22; 28–29; 35–37 (my emphasis). Weber's "disenchantment" is Polanyi's "disembededness." Declan Kiberd has a fascinating discussion of Weber in the context of Irishness in *Inventing Ireland*, 447–48.

17. Weber, *Protestant Ethic*, 21, 8, 10, 6, 104; Farrell, "Portrait," 161, 171.

18. Leo Ward, *All Over God's Irish Heaven* (Chicago: Henry Regnery, 1964), 193, 231. See also Miller, *Emigrants and Exiles*, 470, 504, and Gutman, *Work, Culture*, 28, 23–24.

19. Eric Cross, *The Tailor and Ansty* (Dublin: Mercier, [1942] 1999), 20; Lippmann, *Drift and Mastery*, 163.

20. E. P. Thompson, *The Making of the English Working Class* (New York: Vintage, 1966), 8–11, 189–212 (my emphases). Thompson deals with Weber and Tawney; see ibid., 355–58.

21. David Emmons, "Homecoming: Finding a Catholic Hermeneutic," in

Faith and the Historian: Catholic Perspectives, edited by Nick Salvatore, 49–81 (Urbana: University of Illinois Press, 2007). See also Bruce Laurie, *Artisans into Workers: Labor in Nineteenth Century America* (New York: Noonday, 1989), 6. 5–9; E. P. Thompson, *Making*, 251; Ira Berlin, "Class Composition and the Development of the American Working Class, 1840–1890," in Gutman, *Power and Culture*, 380.

22. E. P. Thompson, *Making*, 10–11, 194. See also Ira Berlin, "The Workers' Search for Power," in Gutman, *Power and Culture*, 15, 20; Berlin, "Class Composition," 331, 336.

23. E. P. Thompson, *Making*, 10.

24. Thompson, *Making*, 10, 194. Jackson Lears makes the same point about the use of "bourgeoisie" in *No Place*, xix.

25. E. P. Thompson, *Making*, 194 (my emphasis),

26. Strong, *New Era*, 195; Perlman, *Theory*, 168. Debs, "The United Front: Shall We Have Solidarity or Be Slaughtered?" *New Age*, June 22, 1922.

27. Gramsci, "Americanism and Fordism," in *The Antonio Gramsci Reader*, edited by David Forgacs (New York: New York University Press, 2000), 279; Berlin, "Workers' Search," in Gutman, *Power and Culture*, 25, 37–39.

28. Brody, "Reconciling the Old Labor History and the New: In Search of the American Working Class," *Pacific Historical Review* 62 (Feb. 1993): 15; David Montgomery, *Citizen Worker: The Experience of Workers in the United States with Democracy and the Free Market during the 19th Century* (Cambridge: Cambridge University Press, 1993).

29. Thompson, *Making*, 9, 429.

30. Sombart, *Why Is There No Socialism?* 28.

31. Thompson, *Making*, 13.

32. Thompson, *Making*, 430, 194.

33. Thompson, *Making*, 434. Dorothy Thompson, E. P. Thompson's wife, wrote two books on the British Chartists movement, *Outsiders*, and *The Chartists* (New York: Pantheon, 1984). She discusses in some detail the many Irish Catholics who were involved as Chartists; some were quite radical. Her husband agreed and wrote of it. Thompson, *Making*, 440–45. Chartism, however, began in the late 1830s; as E. P. Thompson put it, by the time of Chartism, the English working class was "no longer in the making . . . but [was] already made" (E. P. Thompson, *Making*, 801).

34. E. P. Thompson, *Making*, 439.

35. Thompson, *Making*, 434.

36. Thompson, *Making*, 34, 37, 435, 437; Weber, *Protestant Ethic*.

37. Thompson, *Making*, 439.

38. Sean O'Faolain, *King of the Beggars: A Life of Daniel O'Connell* (New York: Viking, 1938).

39. Thompson, *Making*, 194, 354, 436–37, 439. See also "Politics and Culture," in *The Essential E. P. Thompson*, edited by Dorothy Thompson (New York: New Press, 2001), 6.

40. Thompson, *Making*, 432–37.

41. Thompson, *Making*, 442.

42. Thompson, *Making*, 442.

43. Marx letter to Sigfrid Meyer and August Vogt, Apr. 9, 1870, in Marx and Engels, *Ireland*, 293. Engels, "Letters from London," in ibid., 33. See also 34 and 41–42.

44. Hobsbawm, *Workers: Worlds of Labor* (New York: Pantheon, 1984), 53, 59–63, 222.

45. Thompson, *Making*, 11.

46. D. Thompson, *The Essential*, 445–80.

47. Lears, *No Place*, 10–12; Gramsci, "Americanism," 281.

48. Fischer, *Albion's Seed*.

49. Thompson, "Time, Work-Discipline, and Industrial Capitalism," *Past and Present* 38 (1967): 56–97, 90–91.

50. *J. M. Synge's Guide to the Aran Islands*, edited by Ruth Wills Shaw (Old Greenwich, CT: Devin-Adair, 1975), 42, 59, 94–95.

51. E. P. Thompson, "Time," 61. Polanyi used the phrase "satanic mill" (*Great Transformation*, 35).

52. James Bryce, *The American Commonwealth*, 2 vols. (New York: Macmillan, 1897), 2: 299–300; Thompson, "Time," 91. See also Thompson, *Making*, 435–37.

53. On Irish folk beliefs, see Estyn Evans, *The Personality of Ireland: Habitat, Heritage and History* (Dublin: Lilliput, 1992) . The possession by fairies story is from Angela Bourke's splendid *The Burning of Bridget Cleary: A True Story* (New York: Viking, 2000).

54. Benedict Anderson, *Long-Distance Nationalism: World Capitalism and the Rise of Identity Politics* (Amsterdam: Center for Asian Studies, 1992). See also Thompson, *Making*, 9.

55. Berlin, Introduction to Gutman, *Power and Culture*, 3.

56. Chesterton cited in E. J. Dionne, "We're All Liberals Now," *Commonweal*, Nov. 19, 1999.

57. Evelyn Waugh, "The American Epoch in the Catholic Church," *Life*, Sept. 19, 1949, 135–46, 135, 137; Lears, *No Place*, 7.

58. Waugh, "American Epoch," 138, 146. 3–6.

59. Alan Tate, "Remarks on the Southern Religion," in *I'll Take My Stand: The South and the Agrarian Tradition by Twelve Southerners* (New York: Harpers, [1930] 1962): 155–75, 162.

60. Orsi, *History*, 162–200.

61. Lippmann, *Drift and Mastery*, 118, 158–62.

62. Arensberg, *Irish Countryman*, and *Family and Community in Ireland* (Cambridge, MA: Harvard University Press, 1968). See also Evans, *Personality*, esp. 18–41, 68–88.

63. I treat this issue in *Beyond*, 122–24.

64. Berlin, "Workers' Search," in Gutman, *Power and Culture*, 37.

65. Lears, *No Place*, 12. See also Elshtain, *Sovereignty*, 78–80, 127–30.

66. Engels, "The Family," in Marx and Engels, *Ireland*, 341.

Chapter 4. An Irish Catholic Working Class

1. Connolly, "The Irish Flag," *Workers' Republic*, Apr. 8, 1916. In James Connolly Internet Archive [hereafter, JCIA].

2. Connolly, "The Irish Flag"; Sean Cronin, *Irish Nationalism: A History of Its Roots and Ideology* (New York: Continuum, 1981), 3–4; P. Beresford Ellis, "Celtic Communism," in *A History of the Irish Working Class* (London: Pluto, 1972), 11.

3. James Connolly, "Recruiting the ICA," *Workers' Republic*, Nov. 6, 1915. See also Cronin, *Irish Nationalism*, 114. JCIA.

4. Connolly, *The Re-conquest of Ireland* (New York: Nu Vision, [1915] 2007), 10; Kiberd, *Inventing Ireland*, 223; Polanyi, *Great Transformation*, 46.

5. Connolly quoted in Erhard Rumpf and A. C. Hepburn, *Nationalism and Socialism in Twentieth Century Ireland* (New York: Harper and Row, 1977), 19.

6. For a slightly different view, see Matthew Frye Jacobson, *Special Sorrows: The Diasporic Imaginations of Irish, Polish, and Jewish Immigrants in the United States* (Cambridge, MA: Harvard University Press, 1995).

7. "Prudential" from Laurie, *Artisans*, 277.

8. Laurie, *Artisans*, 277. See also Perlman, *Theory*, 165–70; Gutman, *Work, Culture, and Society*, 3–78.

9. Perlman, *Theory*. See also Commons, *Myself*, 73, 81, 87.

10. Perlman, *Theory*, 192, 239, 242. Italics in original.

11. Perlman, *Theory*, 242, 289.

12. Connolly, "British Labour and Irish Politicians" (1913); Connolly, "Irish Flag."

13. David Emmons, *The Butte Irish: Class and Ethnicity in an American Mining Town, 1875–1925* (Urbana: University of Illinois Press, 1989); Emmons, *Beyond the American Pale*, 15–29, 30–36, 225–27, 243–46, 268–79, 302–6. The BMU came back to life as a charter member of the Committee for Industrial Organizations (later Congress of Industrial Organizations) in 1934.

14. Emmons, *Butte Irish*, 55, 270, 316, 344.

15. Hobsbawm, *Workers*, 234; Perlman, *Theory*, 243.

16. Emmons, *Butte Irish*, 200. The song is from Wayland Hand, "The Folklore, Customs, and Traditions of the Butte Miner," *California Folklore Quarterly* 5 (1946): 1–25, 153–78.

17. James Connolly, "A Continental Revolution," *Forward*, Aug. 15, 1914. JCIA.

18. Boyce deserves far more attention than he's had from historians. Edward Boyce Papers at the Eastern Washington Historical Society in Spokane are a rich source. [Cited hereafter as Boyce Papers.]

19. "Constitution and By-laws of the Western Federation of Miners," Mining Department, Industrial Workers of the World, [4], Western Federation of Miners Papers, University of Colorado, Boulder. See also *Butte Bystander*, May 15, 1897.

20. Boyce's comments are from Robert Emmet Literary Association, Minutes Books, Oct. 5, 1899, Irish Collection, Butte/Silver Bow Archives, Butte, Montana.

21. All the transcriptions are in the Boyce Papers. See also Emmons, *Butte Irish*, 298, 231–35, 306, and Melvyn Dubofsky, *We Shall Be All: A History of the Industrial Workers of the World* (Chicago: Quadrangle, 1969), 29, 59–67. See also *Miners' Magazine* (Denver), June 1901.

22. Connolly, "Let Us Free Ireland," *Workers' Republic*, 1899; Connolly, "Erin's Hope," pamphlet, 1897; Connolly, "Socialism and Nationalism," *Shan Van Vocht*," Jan. 1897—all in JCIA. See also the 1896 "Irish Socialist Republican Party Manifesto" and articles from the *Workers' Republic*, 1898-1902, in *The Words of James Connolly*, edited by James Connolly Heron (Cork City, Ire.: Mercier, 1986).

23. Daly from Emmons, *Butte Irish*, 19–21. Boyce's attacks are from *Miners' Magazine*, Dec. 1900 and Mar. 1901; "green sunburst of Erin" is from Connolly, *Forward*, Mar. 11, 1911, in Heron, *Words*, 115.

24. *Miners' Magazine*, Dec. 1900.

25. *Miners' Magazine*, Mar. 1901.

26. Examples of Boyce's radicalism can be found in his open letter to "the Members of the Unions of the W. F. of M., wherever found," Sept. 6, 1897, WFM Collection. Univ. of Colorado Archives; "Miners' Union Day at Butte, Montana," speech delivered by Edward Boyce on June 15, 1899, in the *Miners' Magazine*, Mar. 1900, 37–38 (my emphasis). See also Boyce's comments from the *Miners' Magazine* (Denver), Dec. 1900 and Mar. 1901. William Haywood said that Boyce was his "mentor" in radicalism (William Haywood, *The Autobiography of Bill Haywood* [New York: International, (1929) 1966]), 62–65, 71–73, 79–00). See also *Miners' Magazine*, Jan. 1902.

27. Boyce's comments from WFM, "Proceedings, Ninth Annual Convention, 1901 (Pueblo, CO: Courier Print, 1901), 10 (my emphasis).

28. Job Harriman, "Western Federation of Miners." Copy in Boyce Papers. See also Boyce's "Miners' Union Day Speech" of June 15, 1899, *Miners' Magazine*.

29. Boyce's remarks are from WFM, *Proceedings, Fifth Annual Convention*, Salt Lake City, 1897, WFM Collection, University of Colorado, Boulder. See also the convention coverage in the *Butte Bystander*, July 15, 1897, and the reaction of the Mine Owners' Association of Colorado to Boyce's threat to arm miner's union locals in "Criminal Record of the WFM from Coeur D'Alene to Cripple Creek, 1894–1904" (Colorado Springs: Mine Owners' Association of Colorado, 1904), 7.

30. Gompers to Boyce, Mar. 9, 1897; Boyce to Gompers, Mar. 16, 1897. See also Gompers, "Address to the WFM in Convention Assembled," 1897, *Salt Lake Tribune*, May 16, 1898, also covered in the *New York Daily News*, Nov 15, 1898, copies in Boyce Papers. Army numbers are from Dept. of Defense, *Selected Manpower Statistics—Fiscal Year 1897*. Gompers's comment on Boyce's "treason" cited in J. Anthony Lukas, *Big Trouble: A Murder in a Small Western Town Sets Off a Struggle for the Soul of America* (New York: Simon and Schuster, 2007), 213.

31. Boyce, Travel Diaries, June 1, 7, 11, 1897; *Miners' Magazine*, Dec. 1902. Two years after his move to Denver, workers in the Hercules Mine, an Idaho silver mine owned by Boyce's wife, struck a rich vein of silver-bearing ore. Ed

Boyce was suddenly a millionaire. In 1903, he bought a luxury hotel in Portland, Oregon, and retired. See also Lukas, *Big Trouble*, 215–17.

32. The reference to union members on the ACM payroll is from W. F. Dunne, "Speech to the Founding Convention of the Workers Party of America," New York City, Dec. 26, 1921, in William Francis Dunne Papers, Tamiment Institute, New York University (microfilm copy) [cited hereafter as Dunne Papers]. See also Emmons, *Butte Irish*, 264, 272–75.

33. Emmons, *Butte Irish*, 277–82.

34. Emmons, *Butte Irish*, 282, 285.

35. *Montana Socialist*, July 22, 1916.

36. *Butte Independent*, Sept. 25, Oct. 23, 1915. For an example of another Irish American newspaper critical of Larkin, see almost any issue of the *Irish Standard* (Minneapolis) from 1913 to 1917. Larkin was called a "blathering, self-appointed . . . professional agitator" who was "sapping energy . . . from Home Rule" (Jan. 17, 1914).

37. *Butte Independent*, Mar. 1, 1913; May 2 and Feb. 14, 1914; Sept. 25, 1915.

38. *Butte Independent*, Oct. 31, 1914. On wages, see *Butte Independent*, Jan. 3, 1914. Mulcahy's lavish praise of ACM began immediately after he bought the *Butte Independent*. See June 18, 1910. Occasionally, Mulcahy would add the BMU to the ACM as one of the Irish organizations. See the entire run of issues from June to Nov. 1914. On socialists and anti-Irishism, see *Butte Socialist*, Mar. 29, 1913, and Nov. 7, 1914. On the fear of conservative Irish Americans that Irish nationalism was moving toward socialism, see David Brundage, *Irish Nationalists in America: The Politics of Exile, 1798–1998* (New York: Oxford University Press, 2016), 136.

39. *Butte Independent*, Oct. 31, 1914. "*Genius*" was Connolly's word too; never had it led in such different directions.

40. *Butte Independent*, Sept. 25, 1915. The *Butte Socialist* said the *Independent* was the "pet organ" of ACM, Mar. 7, 1914. See also *Butte Independent*, Sept. 20, 27, 1913, Oct. 24, 1914, Sept. 25, 1915, Jan. 20, and May 19, 1917. That ACM brought Mulcahy to Butte and set him up in the newspaper business is very likely.

41. Fr. English's remarks are in the *Anaconda Standard*, Mar. 18, 1915. See also Emmons, *Butte Irish*, 345–49, 356. On pro-German sentiment among Irish Americans generally, see *Butte Irish*, 85–87, 149, and Brundage, *Irish Nationalists in America*, 145. See also Connolly, "The War upon the German Nation," *Irish Worker*, Aug. 29, 1914, JCIA. For James Larkin's feelings about Germany and the war, see Emmet Larkin, *James Larkin: Irish Labour Leader* (London: Routledge, 1977), 192–95.

42. It is difficult to explain the reference to "gallant [German] allies in Europe" except as a purposeful provocation. See also Roger Casement, "Ireland, Germany, and Freedom of the Seas: A Possible Outcome of the War of 1914" (New York: Irish Press Bureau, 1914), and the two accounts by John McGuire, ex-mayor of Syracuse: *The King, the Kaiser and Irish Freedom* (New York: Devin-Adair, 1915), and *What Could Germany Do for Ireland?* (New York: Wolfe Tone, 1916).

43. Schmuhl, *Ireland's Exiled Children*, 95. Many Irish in the labor movement in particular were still antiwar even after the US entry (Barrett, *Irish Way*, 244, 257–61).

44. R. F. Foster, *Modern Ireland* (New York: Viking, 1989), 479. See also Foster, *Vivid Faces: The Revolutionary Generation in Ireland* (New York: W. W. Norton, 2014), 226, 302; Emmet O'Connor, *Reds and the Green: Ireland, Russia and the Communist Internationals, 1919–1943* (Dublin: University College Dublin Press, 2004), 16; Cronin, *Irish Nationalism*, 4, 110; Connolly, "Irish Flag"; and "Socialism and Nationalism," *Shan Van Vocht*, Jan. 1897, JCIA.

45. Farrell, "Portrait," 119. See also V. I. Lenin, "Imperialism: The Highest Stage of Capitalism," in *Collected Works*, 19: 160, 176, Lenin Internet Archive [hereafter LIA]. "The British Liberals and Ireland," *Put Pravdy*, Mar. 12, 1914, and Mar. 20, 148–51; LIA Connolly, "Erin's Hope"; Marx and Engels, *Ireland*, 30–31, 8. See also Nicholas Mansergh, *The Irish Question, 1840–1921* (Toronto: University of Toronto Press, 1975), 103–32.

46. Trotsky quoted in Ellis, *History*, 231.

47. Cronin, *Irish Nationalism*, 115. See also Foster, *Vivid Faces*, 181; Ellis, *History*, 212; David Krause, "*The Plough and the Stars*: Socialism (1913) and Nationalism (1916)," *New Hibernia Review* 1 (Winter 1997): 29; Krause, "Connolly and Pearse: The Triumph of Failure?" *New Hibernia Review* 3 (Winter 1999), 58; "Means to an end" from Connolly, "Socialism and Political Reformers," *Workers' Republic*, July 8, 1899. Propaganda of the deed implied in Connolly, "Physical Force in Irish Politics," *Workers' Republic*, July 22, 1899, and Connolly, "Courts-Martial and Revolution," *Irish Work*, Dec. 19, 1914. JCIA.

48. Lenin, "Class War in Dublin," *Collected Works*, 19: 299–300. See also Mansergh, *Irish Question*, 103–32, and C. and A. B. Reeve, *James Connolly in the United States* (Atlantic Highlands, NJ: Humanities, 1978), 289–91.

49. Lenin, "Class War in Ireland," *Pravda*, Aug. 29, 1913, in *Collected Works*, vol. 19, LIA; Pearse, "The Sovereign People" (Dublin: Whelan and Son, 1916). "Startlingly radical" from Cronin, *Irish Nationalism*, 109. See also Ellis, *History*, 117.

50. Pearse, "Sovereign People."

51. Desmond Ryan, *James Connolly, His Life and Work* (London: Labour, 1924); Cronin, *Irish Nationalism*, 4, 100–103. See also Emmet O'Connor, *James Larkin* (Cork City, Ire.: Cork University Press, 2003), 52–53. On the Pearse-Connolly "partnership," see J. J. Lee, *Ireland, 1912–1985: Politics and Society* (Cambridge: Cambridge University Press, 1990) 38; Ruth Edwards, *Patrick Pearse: The Triumph of Failure* (London: Gollancz, 1977), 257; Ellis, *History*, 223; and Kieran Allen, *1916: Ireland's Revolutionary Tradition* (London: Pluto, 2016), 46.

52. Emmons, *Butte Irish*, 350–51.

53. Emmons, *Butte Irish*, 358–59, 384, 389. For Connolly's association with Lehane, see Phil Quinlan to Lehane, Sept. 1, 1914. There is also a letter from Larkin to Lehane, dated July 1, 1914. Both are in the Lehane File, Dept. of War, Military Intelligence Division, National Archives, College Park, MD (microfilm copy), reel 8. See also O'Connor, *James Larkin*, 60.

54. Pearse cited in Krause, "Connolly and Pearse," 66–67; Emmons, *Butte Irish*, 358–62.

55. Emmons, *Butte Irish*, 362–65.

56. Emmons, *Butte Irish*, 362–65. See the account of the protest in the *Anaconda Standard*, June 4, 1917, and Burton Wheeler, *Yankee from the West* (New York: Doubleday, 1962), 135–37.

57. "Strike Call," first number of the *Butte/Anaconda Joint Strike Bulletin*, June 5, 1917 (microfilm), Butte/Silver Bow Archives.

58. Emmons, *Butte Irish*, 363–64.

59. On Dunne's Irishness, see Joseph Freeman, *An American Testament* (New York: Farrar and Rinehart, 1936), 293–94. See also "Lehane File," Dept. of War, Military Intelligence Division ("microfilm"), reel 8.

60. "Women and the Labor Movement," n.d., in Dunne Papers, box 2, folder 25.

61. Emmons, *Butte Irish*, 268–72.

62. Emmons, *Butte Irish*, 364.

63. Report of H. G. Claybaugh, quoting from the letter of a representative of the Thiel Detection Service in Duluth, July 7, 1917, Dept. of War, Military Intelligence Division, Record Group 60 (microfilm), reel 2. See also Emmons, *Butte Irish*, 365; *Anaconda Standard*, June 5, 1917; Report of Agent E. W. Byrn, Butte, Sept. 14, 1917, in Dept. of War, Military Intelligence Division, National Archives (microfilm), reel 2; and Spalpeen,

64. On the strike, see William Francis Dunne, "The Communist Party and the AFL," n.d., reel 4, box 3, folder 12, Dunne Papers; letter to the editors of "Partisan Review and Anvil," Mar. 23, 1936, reel 1, box 2, folder 1, Dunne Papers. See also Charles Merz, "The Issue in Butte," *New Republic*, Aug. 1917, 217.

65. See also Report of Agent E. W. Byrn, Butte, July 24, 1917, in Dept. of War, Military Intelligence Division, National Archives (microfilm copy), reel 2.

66. William Dunne, letter to "Partisan Review and Anvil," 1936, Dunne Papers. Quote re. "Irish group" from Emmons, *Butte Irish*, 365. See also Joseph Freeman, *American Testament*, 292–94. Both Dunne and Michael Grace—an Irish-born Butte miner—testified that the strike was called before the Speculator fire ("U.S. v. William Haywood," July 12 and 15, 1918), IWW Collection, Wayne State University. The *Butte Daily Post*, June 10, 1917, also had a story indicating the strike was over the "draft registration issue" and was called before the disaster.

67. Barrett, *Irish Way*, 111.

68. William Dunne, "The Communist Party and the AFL," series 5: MSs (1936–48), folder 7, Dunne Papers.

Chapter Five. Celtic Communists

1. Aileeen Kraditor, *The Radical Persuasion: Aspects of the Intellectual History and the Historiography of Three American Radical Organizations* (Baton Rouge: Louisiana State University Press, 1981), 12, 22.

2. Kraditor, *Radical Persuasion*, 318.

3. Kraditor, *Radical Persuasion*, 12.

4. For the IPL, see Bruce Nelson, *Irish Nationalists and the Making of the Irish Race* (Princeton, NJ: Princeton University Press, 2013), 19–224, 232, 236; Joseph Doyle, "Striking for Ireland on the New York Docks," in Bayor and Meagher, *New York Irish*, 357–73; Francis Carroll, *American Opinion and the Irish Question, 1910–1923* (New York: Gill and Macmillan, 1978), 106–14, 122, 127; Brundage, *Irish Nationalists in America*, 146–62; Brundage, "The Easter Rising and New York's Anticolonial Nationalists," in *Ireland's Allies: America and the 1916 Easter Rising*, edited by Miriam Nyhan Grey, 347–60 (Dublin: University College Dublin Press, 2016).

5. Kraditor, *Radical Persuasion*, 22.

6. Wolfe, *Strange Communists*, 52–71, 55.

7. Luke Gibbons, "American Reactions to the 1916 Rising," unpublished paper, Nov. 11–12, 2016, Irish Centre for the Histories of Labour and Class, National University of Ireland, Galway (conference recordings), ichic.wordppress.com.

8. Gibbons, "American Reactions."

9. Kenny, "Diaspora," 154.

10. Kenny, "Diaspora," 154, 135. Larkin's Catholicism is acknowledged in Wolfe, *Strange Communists*, 55–71. See also Larkin, *James Larkin*, xvi, 183–84, 194–95, 290–91. For Connolly as a lapsed Catholic, see Heron (ed.), *Words*, 122. For Carney, see [Donal Nevin] "Larkin and Connolly," in *James Larkin: Lion of the Fold*, edited by Donal Nevin (Dublin: Gill and Macmillan, 1998), 400, 528; for Farrell, see Farrell, "Portrait," 113–16, 131–35, 141–42. R. F. Foster also argues that Connolly had left the Church. See *Vivid Faces*, 248.

11. Lenin, "The Significance of the Right to Self-Determination and Its Relation to Federation," *Collected Works*, 19: 302–3, LIA; E. O'Connor, *Reds and the Green*, 43 (my emphasis).

12. Lenin, "The Significance of the Right to Self-Determination and Its Relation to Federation," *Collected Works* (Moscow: Progress, 1964), 9: 302–3.

13. Connolly cited in Cronin, *Irish Nationalism*, 116.

14. Connolly cited in Cronin, *Irish Nationalism*, 116. C. Desmond Greaves, *Liam Mellows and the Irish Revolution* (London: Lawrence and Wishart, 1971), 142; E. O'Connor, *Reds and the Green*, 5.

15. Lenin, "Socialism and the Self-Determination of Nations," *Collected Works* 19: 407–14, 430; Lenin, "The Irish Rebellion of 1916," *Collected Works* 19: 50–51. See also Irish Labour Party and Trade Union Congress, *Ireland at Berne . . . Reports and Memoranda Presented to the International Labour and Socialist Conference . . . Feb. 1919* (Dublin: Talbot, 1919), 28–29. See also Greaves, *Liam Mellows*, 149; Greaves, "October and the British Empire," *Labour Monthly*, Nov. 1967; R. F. Foster, *Vivid Faces*, 69; Ellis, *History*, 247. Russia, of course, did not keep its pledge, but Germany would never have made such a pledge. Neither would the United States.

16. Marx and Engels, *Ireland*, 143–51, 162–63, 210–59, 272–300 (emphasis in original), Engels quote from 146; Mansergh, *Irish Question*, 127; Colm Bryce, "Ireland and the Russian Revolution," *Irish Marxist Review* 6 (2017): 42; Cronin,

Irish Nationalism, 152; Lenin, "The Meaning of the Right to Self-Determination and Its Relation to Federation," *Collected Works* 19: 299–303, and "The Irish Rebellion," *Collected Works* 19: 50–51; E. O'Connor, *Reds and the Green*, 13–15.

17. Mansergh, *Irish Question*, 129–30, 248 (my emphasis); Lenin, "Irish Rebellion," *Collected Works* 19: 51.

18. Marx and Engels, *Ireland*, 242, 250; Mansergh, *Irish Question*, 127–29 (emphasis on "oppressing" mine; on "immense practical" in original).

19. Larkin from E. Larkin, *James Larkin*, 276–77. See also Mansergh, *Irish Question* 263–64.

20. Leslie was an Anglo-Irish writer, diplomat and convert to Catholicism (quoted in Schmuhl, *Ireland's Exiled Children*, 3).

21. Irish Labour Party and TUC, *Ireland at Berne*, 28–29, 40–41.

22. Spalpeen, "Sinn Fein," 4.

23. Spalpeen, "Sinn Fein," 10–12.

24. Spalpeen, "Sinn Fein," 14, 7–8. A great number of women were spalpeens and a small contingent of other women were among the eight hundred who fought on April 24. Some of that contingent may once have been transient spalpeens. That the self-identified Spalpeen was male is only an assumption based on the ratio of women to men among the Easter rebels.

25. Spalpeen, "Sinn Fein," 12, 17, 20, 22–23, 8 (my emphasis).

26. On the perennial issue of how the international communist movement has handled nationalism and national idiosyncrasies: as it relates to the United States, see Jacob Zumoff, *The Communist International and U.S. Communism* (Chicago: Haymarket, 2015), 15, 72–75, 139–40. As it relates to Ireland, E. O'Connor, *Reds and the Green*.

27. Nelson, *Irish Nationalists*, 9–10, 16, 66–67, 212, 234, 237–41, quotes from 234.

28. Arthur Mitchell and Pádraig Ó Snodaigh, eds., *Irish Political Documents, 1916–1949* (Dublin: Irish Academic, 1985), 41–42, 48–49.

29. *Workers' Republic*, Dec. 4, 1915, in Heron (ed.), *Words*, 111; Irish Labour Party and TUC, *Ireland at Berne*, 19, 30–31; *Butte Independent*, Nov. 28, 1914.

30. E. O'Connor, *Reds and the Green*, 23–24.

31. Mitchell and Ó Snodaigh (eds.), *Irish Political Documents*, 51.

32. For the 1918 election, see, among many sources, Jason Knirck, *Imagining Ireland's Independence: The Debate over the Anglo-Irish Treaty of 1921* (Lanham, MD: Rowman and Littlefield, 2006), 45.

33. The Democratic Programme is copied in Knirck, *Imagining Ireland's Independence*, 59–61, and in Ellis, *History*, 240. Cronin, *Irish Nationalism*, 123; Foster, *Vivid Faces*, 269; and Kiberd, *Inventing Ireland*, 223, cite from it. See also E. O'Connor, *Reds and the Green*, 26.

34. Mitchell and Ó Snodaigh (eds.), *Irish Political Documents*, 59.

35. Mitchell and Ó Snodaigh (eds.), *Irish Political Documents*, 59–60 (my emphasis).

36. Irish Labour Party and TUC, *Ireland at Berne*, [3], 52, 4–22, 25–30.

37. Irish Labour Party and TUC, *Ireland at Berne*, 51.

38. Irish Labour Party and TUC, *Ireland at Berne*, 17, 21, 25, 26–30, 43. For praise of Lenin and Trotsky, see ibid., 33. See also Leo XIII, *Rerum Novarum*, 69–70.

39. Bagenal, *American Irish*, 174–75 (my emphasis).

40. Hugh Pollard, *The Secret Societies of Ireland: Their Rise and Progress* (Kilkenny, Ire.: Irish Historical Press, [1922] 1998), 185.

41. Irish Labour Party and TUC, *Ireland at Berne*, 27, 7, 10.

42. Irish Labour Party and TUC, *Ireland at Berne*. The first edition of "Erin's Hope" came out in 1897; the American edition in 1909 (Pollard, *Irish Secret Societies*, 81).

43. Pollard, *Irish Secret Societies*, 183; Andrew Russell (comp.), *The Behan Quotation Book* (London: Somerville, 2015), 27, 50; Michael Gold, "Ode to Walt Whitman," in *Walt Whitman: The Measure of His Song*, edited by Jim Perlman, Ed Folsom, and Dan Campion (Duluth, MN: Holy Cow, 1998), 168–71, 171.

44. Foster quoted in Arthur Zipser, *Working-Class Giant: The Life of William Z. Foster* (New York: International, 1981), 9–10.

45. William Foster, *Pages from a Worker's Life* (New York: International, 1939), 271–72.

46. Benjamin Gitlow, *The Whole of Their Lives* (New York: Scribner, 1948), 37. Gitlow later recanted his communism and became an anticommunist. See also Ralph Chapin, "The Picket Line of Blood," *One Big Union Monthly*, June 20, 1920, 9–13.

47. Gitlow, *Whole*.

48. Goldman, Bryant, and Mencken quoted in Tara Stubbs, *American Literature and Irish Culture, 1910–1955* (Manchester, UK: Manchester University Press, 2013), 142.

49. Gitlow, *Whole*, 37, 38, 42–43 (my emphasis). See also Gitlow, *I Confess: The Truth about American Communism* (New York: E. P. Dutton, 1940), 42.

50. Gitlow's comments are from *I Confess*, 143, and *Whole*, 156; Freeman is quoted from *American Testament*, 293–94. The best biography of Dunne is the short one in the William Francis Dunne Papers, Tamiment Collection, no. 145, box 1, folder 1, Bobst Library, New York University (microfilm). The *Butte Bulletin* of Oct. 12, 1918, and Apr. 9, 1920, also had biographical details.

51. Gitlow, *I Confess*, 143; Freeman, *American Testament*.

52. Flynn, *Rebel Girl*, 190, 175; Foster, *Pages*, 272; E. Larkin, *James Larkin*, 234, 236; Emmet O'Connor, *James Larkin*, (Cork City: Cork University Press, 2003), 60; Connolly, *The Socialist* (1904) in Heron (ed.), *The Words*, 116. See also Wolfe, *Strange Communists*, 32–36, 64–65.

53. Gitlow, *Whole*, 106, 156; Gitlow, *I Confess*, 419. See also Zumoff, *Communist International*, 98, 125, 211, 283n36; and William Dunne, *The Struggle against Opportunism in the Labor Movement—for a Socialist United States* (New York: New York Communications Committee, 1947), v–vii.

54. *Butte Bulletin*, Dec. 27, 1918, Jan. 8, 1919, Apr. 16, 1920, Oct. 16, 1920; Maj. A. A. Peake to Director Military Intelligence, Apr. 28, 1920, Record Group 60 (microfilm), reel 19, Dept. of War, Military Intelligence Division, National Archives.

55. W. Dunne, *Struggle against Opportunism*, v. He also praised Lenin and the Bolsheviks for "publicly declar[ing] that the treatment of Ireland by England would warrant a declaration of war by Soviet Russia on England" (*Butte Bulletin*, Apr. 9, 1921). See also Jan. 22 and 23, 1919; Dunne, "Speech to the Founding Convention of the Workers Party of America," New York City, Dec. 26, 1921, cited in "Liberty Lovers 'Need Watching': Mossback Democrats Fear Activity of Mind of the Forward-Looking," *New York Call*, Aug. 19, 1919. See further Zumoff, *Communist International*, 34. During World War II, Dunne had a job with a private company that contracted with the US Army to provide food for the troops stationed in the Aleutian Islands in Alaska. There are broad hints in the Dunne Papers that he was also looking out for Japanese activities in the north Pacific and sending what he'd learned to the Soviets. In 1946, he was expelled from the Communist Party USA for "ultra-leftism" and alcoholism. Six years later, he was back in Butte, where he formed a "James Connolly Association"—this time without Pearse's name. It was short-lived ("Biography," box 3, folder 10, Dunne Papers).

56. *Butte Bulletin*, Feb. 2 and 9, Oct. 20, Mar. 24 and 30, 1920.

57. *Butte Bulletin*, Mar. 17, 1919; Apr. 9, 1920; Mar. 26, Feb. 3, 1921.

58. *Butte Bulletin*, Sept. 11, 1919; Feb. 3, 1921; Dec. 23, June 16, Feb. 25, 1919; June 2, 1920. There were banner headlines about Ireland in the issues of Aug. 30 and 31 and Nov. 20, 1918; and Mar. 11 and 12 and Apr. 15, 1919.

59. For Gellert, see Freeman, *American Testament*, 256, 288, 309–10, 339, 372–73, 378.

60. *Butte Bulletin*, Feb. 17, 1922. Dunne may well have taken the "sleeve of green" reference directly from a Connolly article in the *Workers' Republic*, June 10, 1899, JCIA.

61. *Butte Bulletin*, Sept. 7, 1918; Aug. 13, Dec. 15, 1920; Shane Leslie, *The Irish Issue in Its American Aspect* (New York: Scribner, 1917), 187.

62. Con Kelley was the son of Jeremiah Kelley, an Irish immigrant and close friend of Marcus Daly. Both Kelleys had worked as underground hard-rock miners; Con walked with a limp from falling rock breaking his leg. (The second "e" in Kelley is a mystery.)

63. *Butte Bulletin*, Feb. 16 and 17, Mar. 3, 1921; *Engineering and Mining Journal*, Feb. 26, 1921. On O'Rourke: *Butte Bulletin*, Apr. 27 and 28, Oct. 18, 1920; on Mulcahy: Feb. 10, 1919; May 15 and 18, July 31, 1920.

64. *The Truth* (Duluth, MN), May 9, 1919.

65. *Butte Bulletin*, July 9, 1919; Nov. 20, 1920; Mar. 26, 1921.

66. Richard Dawson, an Englishman who worried excessively about Irish ties to Bolsheviks, wrote in 1920 of a "story . . . going the round . . . that the Soviet Republic was subsidizing Sinn Féin to the tune of some millions of rubles," *Red Terror and Green: The Sinn Fein–Bolshevik Movement* (New York: E. P. Dutton, 1920), 214). Kelley's comments and "rumors" are from *Butte Bulletin.*, Feb. 14 and Nov. 16, 1919, Aug. 18, 1922.

67. See also "The Progress of Radicalism in the U.S. and Abroad," Conference Report (Special Supplement), Dec. 8, 1919, Record Group 60, Dept. of War, Military Intelligence Division, National Archives; and Harvey Klehr, John Haynes,

Fridrikh Igorevich Firsov, *The Secret World of American Communism* (New Haven, CT: Yale University Press, 1995), 21–24.

68. See also Richard Hudelson, "Jack Carney and the *Truth* in Duluth," *Saothar* 19 (1994): 129–39. "Feisty" from *The Truth*, Mar. 26, 1922.

69. *Butte Bulletin*, Dec. 28, 1920; see also Jan. 16, 1921. Carney's career is from E. Larkin, *James Larkin*, viii–ix, 215–16, 236, 245–49, 283, 290–92, 298, 303–6; E. O'Connor, *James Larkin*, 32, 53–55, 58–60, 67–75, 90–92, 95–97; Donal Nevin, "Forming the Irish Citizen Army," 293–95; "The Larkin Affidavit," 340–42; "Larkin and Connolly," 405, 410–16, in Nevin (ed.), *Lion*; E. O'Connor, *Reds and the Green*, 11, 82, 111–14, 122–27, 131–32, 135–41.

70. *The Truth*, Feb. 1, 8, and 15, 1918. See also May 5, 1918, Jan. 31, 1919, Nov. 7, 1919, Jan. 23, 1920, and Mar. 12, 1920; US Dept. of Justice, "Weekly Bulletin of Radical Activities," Jan. 1–6, 1920, reel 16, Dept. of Justice Files, US National Archives (microfilm); Dept. of War, Military Intelligence Division, Special Supplement "on the Progress of Radicalism in the United States and Abroad," Dec. 8, 1919, reel 24, US National Archives (microfilm); *Irish Felon* from Minnesota Historical Society, St. Paul (microfilm).

71. Duluth is in the center of the Mesabi Iron Range; there were eighteen thousand Finnish-born residents of St. Louis County (Duluth) in 1920 and four thousand Irish-born (Hudelson, "Jack Carney," 133); Frith to director of Military Intelligence, *The Truth*, July 23, 1920, Record Group 60.

72. *The Truth*, May 5 and 19, 1918.

73. *The Truth*, May 19, 1918 (my emphasis). See also *The Truth*, June 16, 1920, Nov. 1, Dec. 27, 1918, June 27, 1919, and June 11, 1920. See further Carney's 1919 pamphlet, "Mary Marcy" (Chicago: Charles Kerr, 1922)—copy in Minnesota Historical Society.

74. *The Truth*, Nov. 7, 1919, Apr. 23, 1920, and Feb. 20, 1923. This last appeared after Carney had returned to Ireland.

75. *Butte Bulletin*, Apr. 22, 1919. Carney was in Butte to speak before the Trades and Labor Council and the "Irish societies." For Carney's attacks on the United States, see *The Truth*, Feb. 20, 1920, and Apr. 21, 1920, and *Butte Bulletin*, Sept. 5, 1920. In 1921, Carney made another trip to Butte, speaking at Finnish Workers Hall near Hibbing, MN, on "The Case of Jim Larkin" (*Butte Bulletin*, Jan. 15, 1921).

76. *The Truth*, June 27, 1919.

77. A complete run of the *Producers' News* is available on microfilm at the Montana Historical Society Library in Helena. On the Nonpartisan League, see Michael Lansing, *Insurgent Democracy: The Nonpartisan League in North American Politics* (Chicago: University of Chicago Press, 2015). Taylor's comment about communist financing and control was made to Charles Vindex, "Radical Rule in Montana," *Montana, The Magazine of Western History* 18 (Winter 1968): 2–18.

78. For Wallace's rebelliousness, see *Producers' News*, Oct. 15, 1926, and Sept. 27, 1929. Verlaine McDonald discusses Wallace in *Red Corner: The Rise and Fall of Communism in Northeastern Montana* (Helena: Montana Historical Society Press, 2010), 97–99. Dunne strongly supported farm-labor coalitions (*Butte Bulletin*, Aug. 20, 1918, Oct. 8, 1918, Jan. 27, 1919, June 24, 1920, and July 30, 1920). Wallace's praise of Scandinavians is from *Producers' News*, Feb. 25, 1926.

79. *Producers' News*, June 26, 1925; *Daily Worker* as quoted in ibid., July 17, 1925. Wallace and O'Flaherty were both Connachtmen, born within twenty miles of one another.

80. *Producers' News*, May 27, 1927. See also Oct. 2, 1925, Apr. 13, 1928, July 19, 1929.

81. Thomas O'Flaherty, *Aranmen All* (London: Golancz, 1930), 161; *Producers' News*, May 20, 1927, had a piece on O'Flaherty's life: O'Flaherty, "A Radical Irish Magazine," *The Worker* (New York), June 2, 1923. Like Dunne, whom he knew well, O'Flaherty had a reputation for drinking (E. O'Connor, *Reds and the Green*, 103).

Chapter Six. A "People Very Unlike Any Other People"

1. Quote in R. F. Foster, *Vivid Faces*, 27. See also Nelson, *Irish Nationalists*.

2. Foster, *Vivid Faces*, 85.

3. On American antimodernists, see Lears, *No Place*.

4. Declan Kiberd and P. J. Mathews, eds., *Handbook of the Irish Revival: An Anthology of Irish Cultural and Political Writings, 1891–1922* (Notre Dame, IN: University of Notre Dame Press, 2015), 271. See also B. Anderson, *Imagined Communities*, 195–96; Thomas Garvin, *Nationalist Revolutionaries in Ireland, 1858–1928* (Dublin: Gill and Macmillan, 2005); Garvin, "Priests and Patriots: Irish Separatism and Fear of the Modern, 1890–1914," *Irish Historical Studies* 25 (May 1986): 67–81; and Richard Tillinghast, *Finding Ireland: A Poet's Exploration of Irish Literature and Culture* (Notre Dame. IN: University of Notre Dame Press, 2008).

5. Lady Gregory, "'Ireland Real, and Ideal'" (1898); O'Farrelly, "Smaointe ar Árainn" (1902); Hyde, "The Necessity for De-anglicising Ireland" (1892)—all three in Kiberd and Matthews, *Handbook*.

6. Constance Markiewicz, "Women, Ideals and the Nation," (1909), in Kiberd and Matthews, *Handbook*, 78.

7. Nelson, *Irish Nationalists*, 230–32.

8. Nelson, *Irish Nationalists*, 47.

9. Mellows's dislike of the United States is in David Fitzpatrick, *Harry Boland's Irish Revolution* (Cork City, Ire.: Cork University Press, 2003), 206. See also Nelson, *Irish Nationalists*, 230, 232, 244. Jim Herlihy, *Peter Golden: The Voice of Ireland* (Cork City, Ire.: Commemoration Committee, 1994); George William Russell (Æ), "Ireland and the Empire at the Court of Conscience" (Dublin: Talbot, 1921); Tim Pat Coogan, *The Man Who Made Ireland: The Life and Death of Michael Collins* (New York: Roberts Rinehart, 1992), 22, 54 (my emphasis).

10. Lady Gregory, "Ireland Real," in Kiberd and Mathews, *Handbook*, 51–52. Markiewicz, "Women," in ibid., 76–78. See also Cumann na mBan, in ibid., 103.

11. B. Anderson, *Imagined Communities*, 144. He did not make specific reference to Ireland, but he lived there when he wrote that.

12. Mellows is from Nelson, *Irish Nationalists*, 218–28, 230–37, 247–257; Gavin Foster, *The Irish Civil War and Society: Politics, Class and Conflict* (London:

Basingstoke, 2015); and Greaves, *Liam Mellows*. See also Lears, *No Place*, xviii; Christopher Lasch, *The True and Only Heaven: Progress and Its Critics* (New York: W. W. Norton, 1991).

13. Voltaire, "Patrie" (1764), cited in Scott Horton, "Voltaire Defines Patriotism," *Harper's Magazine*, Oct. 10, 2009.

14. Weber, *Protestant Ethic*, 38.

15. Spalpeen, *Sinn Fein and Labour*.

16. B. Anderson, *Imagined Communities*, 195; Nelson, *Irish Nationalists*, 54, 195–96.

17. Kenny, "Diaspora," 146; Lady Gregory, "Ireland Real," 51; Nelson, *Irish Nationalists*, 44; Merwin "The Irish," 298; Benedict Anderson, "Exodus," *Critical Inquiry* 20 (Winter 1994): 314–27; Ebest, *Private Histories*, 70.

18. American Celticism from Ebest, *Private Histories*, 89. See also B. Anderson, *Imagined Communities*, 80.

19. MacManus, "Sinn Fein," *North American Review* 185 (Aug. 16, 1907): 825–36.

20. MacManus, *The Story of the Irish Race* (New York: Devin-Adair, [1921] 1977), 432; MacManus, "Sinn Fein," 827–28, 831–33. See also Nelson, *Irish Nationalists*, 242.

21. MacManus, *Story of the Irish Race*, 288.

22. MacManus, "Reminiscence," n.d. (but post-1950) in catholicauthors.com (my emphasis).

23. Sir Horace Plunkett, *Ireland in the New Century* (New York: E. P. Dutton, 1904). Co-ops in ch. 8. See also Plunkett, *The Rural Life Problem of the United States: Notes of an Irish Observer* (New York: Macmillan, 1911).

24. Plunkett, *Ireland in the New Century*, 6.

25. Plunkett, *Ireland in the New Century*, 54, 110. "Simple people" is from *Rural Life*, 131; "tribal relic" is from 21–22.

26. Plunkett, *Ireland in the New Century*, 7, 37–42; 71–76, 98, 143.

27. Plunkett, *Ireland in the New Century*, 38–40.

28. Plunkett, *Ireland in the New Century*, 38–40.

29. Plunkett, *Ireland in the New Century*, 212–14.

30. Plunkett, *Ireland in the New Century*, 214.

31. Plunkett, *Ireland in the New Century*, 101–2, 107. That it was the same misreading that Marx and Lenin were guilty of is further proof of Irish Catholic erraticism.

32. Plunkett, *Ireland in the New Century*, 151–52.

33. Plunkett, *Ireland in the New Century*, 93–120, esp. 101–3.

34. Plunkett, *Ireland in the New Century*, 107–10.

35. Plunkett, *Ireland in the New Century*, 74.

36. Plunkett, *Ireland in the New Century*, 74.

37. Plunkett, *Ireland in the New Century*, 54–55, 57.

38. Plunkett, *Ireland in the New Century*, 80–81.

39. Plunkett, *Ireland in the New Century*, 54–55, 59 (my emphasis).

40. Plunkett, *Ireland in the New Century*, 160–63.

41. Plunkett, *Ireland in the New Century*, 160–63.

42. Gibbons, *Gaelic Gothic*, 88.

43. Michael O'Riordan, *Catholicity and Progress in Ireland* (London: Kegan Paul Trench, 1906; St. Louis: B. Herder, 1906), 224–29, 253, 421, 126, 123.

44. O'Riordan, *Catholicity*, 89, 59, 83, 76.

45. Leo XIII, *Rerum Novarum*, 67, 74, 69; O'Riordan, *Catholicity*, 84.

46. Nelson, *Irish Nationalists*, 16.

47. Connolly, *The Irish Worker*, Aug. 5, 1899; Farrell, "A Portrait of James Connolly," in *Irish Themes*, 119; Mellows cited on 216–17 and in Nelson, *Irish Nationalists*.

48. Nelson, *Irish Nationalists*, 16. See also Joseph McCartin's "Working-Class Catholicism: A Call for a New Investigation, Dialogue, and Reappraisal," *Labor* 4 (2007): 99–110.

49. Orsi, *History*; Plunkett, *Ireland in the New Century*, 212–14; Elshtain, *Sovereignty*.

50. Plunkett, *Ireland in the New Century*, 61; Lady Gregory from frontispiece.

51. See the discussion of the IPL in Greaves, *Liam Mellows*, 149–65. See also the excellent collection of articles in Patrick Mannion and Fearghal McGarry, eds., *The Irish Revolution: A Global History*. New York: New York University Press, 2022.

52. Yeats, *The King's Threshold and On Baile's Strand* (London: A. H. Bullen, 1904).

53. Nelson, *Irish Nationalists*, 16, 368–69; Joe Doyle, "Striking for Ireland on the New York Docks," in Bayor and Meagher, *New York Irish*," 357, 359–73; see also Elizabeth McKillen, "Divided Loyalties: Irish American Women Labor Leaders and the Irish Revolution," *Éire-Ireland* 51 (Fall/Winter 2016): 165–88. Brundage, *Irish Nationalists in America*, 156–60; Miriam Grey, "Dr. Gertrude B. Kelly and the Founding of New York's Cumann na mBan," in Grey, *Ireland's Allies*, 75–90; and Patricia Keefe Durso, "The Other Narrative of 'Sisterhood' in 1916: Irish and Irish-American Suffragists," in Grey, *Ireland's Allies*, 329–46.

54. John A. Ryan, *Social Reconstruction* (New York: Macmillan, 1920); Leo XIII, *Rerum Novarum*, 84.

55. Connolly, *Re-conquest*, 29, JCIA; Farrell, "Portrait," 139; Weber, *Protestant Ethic*, 42, 166–67.

56. For the Catholic Welfare Council, see Michael Williams, *American Catholics in the War* (New York: Macmillan, 1921); John A. Ryan and Joseph Husslein, eds., *The Church and Labor* (New York: Macmillan, 1924), 145, 182, 194–95. "So-called" is from Bishop O'Connell in Ryan and Husslein, *Church and Labor*, 182; John Ryan, *Social Reconstruction*. The English translation of Weber had not appeared, but there were American bishops who could read German.

57. Ryan and Husslein, *Church and Labor*, viii, xii, xv. See also J. Ryan, *Social Reconstruction*, 201, 209, 238.

58. Leo XIII, *Rerum Novarum*, 91, 73; Nelson, *Irish Nationalists*, 230; Barrett, *Irish Way*, 93.

59. Keating, "The Encyclicals of Pope Leo XIII and Pope Pius XI: An Address

before the Students of . . . Catholic University," May 16, 1932, in Keating Papers, Western Historical Collections, University of Colorado, Boulder.

60. Barrett, *Irish Way*, 93.

61. J. Ryan, *Social Reconstruction*, 18; Ryan and Husslein, *Church and Labor*, 237.

62. Statistics from David Montgomery, *Fall of the House of Labor* (Cambridge: Cambridge University Press, 1987), 407; and his *Workers' Control in America* Cambridge: Cambridge University Press, 1979, 97, 24–25; Commission on Industrial Relations, *Final Report* (Chicago: Barnard and Miller, 1915), 28.

63. Frank Walsh, "Supplemental Statement of CIR," in *Final Report*, 299; Lippmann from Joseph McCartin, *Labor's Great War: The Struggle for Industrial Democracy and the Origins of Modern American Labor Relations, 1912–1921* (Chapel Hill: University of North Carolina Press, 1997), 27. See also the articles in the excellent collection of Nelson Lichtenstein and John Harris Howell, *Industrial Democracy in America: The Ambiguous Promise* (Cambridge: Cambridge University Press, 1993). See also John A. Ryan, *Industrial Democracy from a Catholic Viewpoint* (Washington, DC: Rossi-Bryn, 1925); and David Brundage, "American Labour and the Irish Question," *Saothar* 24 (1999): 59–66.

64. Nelson, *Irish Nationalists*, 230.

65. Nelson, *Irish Nationalists*, 216. The Irish Democratic Programme is on pp. 59–60 of Mitchell and Ó Snodaigh, eds., *Irish Political Documents*; Connolly from "The Irish Flag," *Workers' Republic*, Apr. 8, 1916; Collins quoted in L L Lee, *Ireland*, 64.

66. Ryan and Husslein, eds., *Church and Labor*, xvi–xvii, 234–35, 272–73; J. Ryan, *Social Reconstruction*, 232.

67. McCartin, *Labor's Great War*, 4–7; Ryan, *Distributive Justice* (New York: Macmillan, 1906), 210–33. Ryan cited P. W. Joyce's 1903 study, *A Social History of Ancient Ireland*, on 11.

68. Leo XIII, *Rerum Novarum*, 72; Ryan, *A Living Wage: Its Ethical and Economic Aspects* (New York: Macmillan, 1912), 433; Ryan, *Social Reconstruction*, 179.

69. Ryan and Husslein, eds., *Church and Labor*, xvi. See also Gregory, *Unintended Reformation*.

70. John Ryan did write that Walsh was "more radical" on the labor question "than most Catholics," *Social Reconstruction*, 12. He may have been that on the Irish question as well. On this, see Julie Manning. *Frank P. Walsh and the Irish Question* (Washington, DC: Georgetown University Press, 1989).

71. Timothy Shanley, "Mister Frank Walsh's Career," *America*, July 5, 1918, 329–31, 330; Dante Barton, "Frank P. Walsh," *Harper's Weekly*, Sept. 27, 1913, 24; "Unnecessary evil" from Shelton Stromquist, *Re-inventing "the People": The Progressive Movement, the Class Problem, and the Origins of Modern Liberalism* (Urbana: University of Illinois Press, 2006), 174, 196.

72. McCartin, *Labor's Great War*, 21–24, 87. Among those he stood in for was John Fitzpatrick, Irish-born head of the Chicago Federation of Labor, a close

Walsh ally on both labor and Irish issues (McCartin, *Labor's Great War*, 18, 33, 55, 82–83, 119, 160–161, 176, 197).

73. McCartin, *Labor's Great War*, 12; Melvyn Dubofsky, "Abortive Reform: The Wilson Administration and Organized Labor, 1913–1920," in *Work, Community, and Power: The Experience of Labor in Europe and America, 1900–1925*, edited by James Cronin and Carmen Sirianni (Philadelphia: Temple University Press, 1983): 197–220. See also Graham Adams, *Age of Industrial Violence, 1910–1915: The Activities and Findings of the United States Commission on Industrial Relations* (New York: Columbia University Press, 1971).

74. CIR, *Final Report*, 184–85.

75. Walsh, "Ireland Today," June 11, 1920, speech given in Windsor Hall, Montreal, 8. Facsimile reprint, www.ForgottenBooks.com. n.d, n.p.

76. Ryan, *Social Reconstruction*, 143–44.

77. CIR, *Final Report*, 383, 384, 326, 403; Record of Testimony (1915), 7916, 7926; Stromquist, *Re-inventing*, 185, 189, 177. See also Walsh, "A Message of Peace to All the World," n.d., 1921 (copy in box 32; MSS Collection 3211, Frank P. Walsh Papers, 1896–1939, New York Public Library); CIR, *Final Report*, 301. See also J. Ryan, *Social Reconstruction*, 11–12, 142–44.

78. Ryan, *Social Reconstruction*, 12, 36.

79. Walsh, "Ireland Today," 5, 14–15; Nelson, *Irish Nationalists*, 369; McCartin, *Labor's Great War*, 152–56.

80. Walsh, "Ireland Today," 2–5.

81. Walsh was a counsel for the American Commission on Conditions in Ireland. He led much of the examination of witnesses. There was considerable testimony, much of it from native Irish witnesses on the close association of Irish labor and Irish nationalism and on the British understanding of that association (American Commission on Conditions in Ireland, "Evidence on Conditions in Ireland" [Washington, DC: Bliss Building, 1921]).

82. Sacred fire is from Walsh, "Windows Alight in Connaught," *America*, June 7, 1919, 226. Walsh's references to Irish labor are from his "Irish Labor Movement," n.d., [1921], box 32, Mss Collection 3211, Walsh Papers, 1896–1936. "Kinship" reference is also from Walsh, "Irish Labor Movement."

83. Walsh, "Windows Alight."

84. John Hays Hammond, *The Autobiography of John Hays Hammond*, 2 vols. (New York: Farrar and Rinehart, 1935); Charles Van Onselen, *The Cowboy Capitalist: John Hays Hammond, the American West, and the Jameson Raid in South Africa* (Charlottesville: University of Virginia Press, 2018).

85. CIR, *Record of Testimony*, 7465, 7513–16, 7988, 7992–95. It's worth noting that Hammond's remarks were in direct rebuttal to testimony given earlier by Lewis Brandeis, an American Jew, who strongly supported industrial democracy. "Greenbaum" and "Kelley" were still on the same political side. (John Hays Hammond and Jeremiah Jenks, *Great American Issues: Political, Social, Economic* [New York: Scribner, 1923], 10).

86. CIR, *Record of Testimony*, 7992, 8002.

87. Hammond and Jenks, *Great American Issues*, 100, 97.

88. Stromquist, *Re-inventing*, 181.

89. Walsh cited in Stromquist, *Re-inventing*, 188; Commons is from CIR, *Final Report*, 326, 337, 338, 383, 384, 403; *Record of Testimony*, 7678, 7916, 7926; Commons, *Myself*, 106, 169, 143; Stromquist, *Re-inventing*, 185, 189, 177.

90. Walsh is from Stromquist, *Re-inventing*, 185.

91. Stromquist, *Re-inventing*, 8–9, 26, 132; CIR, *Final Report*, 396, 397 (my emphasis).

92. Commons, *Myself*, 106, 169.

93. Commons, *Myself*, 42, 168, 181 (my emphasis).

94. A. James Fuller, *Chaplain to the Confederacy: Basil Manly and Baptist Life in the Old South* (Baton Rouge: Louisiana State University Press, 2000). See also Basil Manly, "Labor's Share of the Social Product," *Annals of the American Academy of Political and Social Science* 69 (Jan. 1917): 128–32.

95. Walsh on capitalists is from CIR, *Final Report*, 301.

96. CIR, *Final Report*, 56.

97. Walsh is from CIR, *Final Report*, 297–301; Manly is from ibid., 12. The Commons dissenting Report is on pp. 307–401.

98. CIR, *Final Report*, 302, 78–79, 189.

99. Walsh, "Ireland Today." American Commission, "Evidence of Conditions," discussions beginning on 92, 182, and 636. The two civilizations quote is from 944. Basil Manly also played a major role as a lead questioner of witnesses before the commission. His sympathies for the suffering of the Irish people, and for labor and anti-imperialism, were on full display ("Evidence of Conditions," esp. 979–1052).

Chapter Seven. "The Irish Movement Has Forgotten to Be American"

1. Eric Hobsbawm, *The Age of Capital: 1848–1875* (New York: Vintage, 1996); Hobsbawm, *The Age of Empire: 1875–1914* (New York: Vintage, 1989).

2. Thomas Brown, *Irish-American Nationalism*.

3. *New York Call*, Aug. 19, 1919.

4. Lloyd Ambrosius, *Woodrow Wilson and American Internationalism* (Cambridge: Cambridge University Press, 2017); Cara Lea Burnidge, *A Peaceful Conquest: Woodrow Wilson, Religion, and the New World Order* (Chicago: University of Chicago Press, 2016); A. Scott Berg, *Wilson* (New York: Berkley, 2013).

5. Berg, *Wilson*, 11–12, 269, 761n49, 244–46, 269–70, 307–12, 345–50, 481–87.

6. Berg, *Wilson*, 347–50; Ambrosius, *Woodrow Wilson*, 19–20, 22, 63–93.

7. Burnidge, *Peaceful Conquest*, 19, 30; Ambrosius, *Woodrow Wilson*, 72.

8. Dillingham Commission, *Dictionary*, 5, 54–55, 79–80, 125. Spring Rice quoted in Schmuhl, *Exiled Children*, 94. Schmuhl's inclusion of Wilson among Ireland's "exiles" is nothing short of bizarre.

9. Wilson believed along with John Fiske, another Anglo-Saxon supremacist, that Americans were members of the "English race" (Fiske cited in Solomon,

Ancestors and Immigrants, 68). See also US Congress, *Reports of the Immigration Commission*, 41 vols.; vol. 5, *Dictionary of Races or Peoples* (Washington, DC: Government Printing Office, 1911), 55; Berg, *Wilson*, 28, 221–22, 761; Wilson, "The Ideals of America," *Atlantic Monthly*, Dec. 1902, 721–34, 723; Cary Grayson, Diary, June 11, 1919, in *The Papers of Woodrow Wilson*, 68 vols., edited by Arthur Link (Princeton, NJ: Princeton University Press, 1966–83), 60: 381. See further Wilson, *A History of the American People*, 5 vols. (New York: Harper and Brothers, 1902), 1: 58.

10. Kramer, "Emigrants, Exceptions, and Anglo-Saxons," 1334. Matthew Frye Jacobson calls it "Patriotism of race" (*Whiteness of a Different Color: European Immigrants and the Alchemy of Race* [Cambridge, MA: Harvard University Press, 1999]), 209.

11. On Wilson's appreciation of IrishCatholic clownishness, including the quoted remarks, see Schmuhl, *Ireland's Exiled Children*, 99; Ambrosius, *Woodrow Wilson*, 75; Berg, *Wilson*, 221–22; Leonard, *Illiberal Reformers*, 157; Burnidge, *Peaceful Conquest*, 16, 26, 65, 74, 79, 99. See also John Mulder, *Woodrow Wilson: The Years of Preparation* (Princeton, NJ: Princeton University Press, 1978), 33. Grayson, Diary, Mar. 5, 1919, in Link, ed., *Papers of Woodrow Wilson*, 55: 443.

12. Jacobson, *Whiteness of a Different Color*, 208–9; Stuart Anderson, *Race and Rapprochement: Anglo-Saxonism and Anglo-American Relations, 1895–1904* (New York: Rutherford, 1981), 98; Wilson, "Ideals," 727; Ambrosius, *Woodrow Wilson*, 74; John Seeley, *The Expansion of England* (1883; New York: Little, Brown, 1922).

13. Wilson, "Ideals"; Wilson, "Address of President Wilson at the Unveiling of the Statue to the Memory of Commodore John Barry, Washington, DC, May 16, 1914," in Link, ed., *Papers of Woodrow Wilson*, 30: 34–36; Hans Vought, "Division and Reunion: Woodrow Wilson, Immigration, and the Myth of American Unity," *Journal of American Ethnic History* 13 (Spring 1994): 24–50, 4.

14. Wilson, "Address," 34; Wilson, *History of the American People*, 4: 159–62, 164.

15. Vought, "Division and Reunion," 26, 33.

16. On the Reconstruction Era and the KKK, see *History of the American People*, 4: 159–64.

17. Burton J. Hendrick, *The Life and Letters of Walter H. Page, 1855–1918*, 2 vols. (Garden City, NY: Garden City Publishing, 1927) 1: 257–59.

18. Hendrick, *The Life and Letters of Walter H. Page*, 1: 258.

19. Hendrick, *The Life and Letters of Walter H. Page*, 2: 254.

20. Hendrick, *The Life and Letters of Walter H. Page*, 2: 254 (my emphasis.)

21. See Wilson to Lansing, Apr. 10, 1917, in Link, ed., *Papers*, 42: 24. For an Irish perspective on Wilson's pro-Allies position, see Greaves, *Liam Mellows*, 158; Richard Drake, *The Education of an Anti-imperialist: Robert La Follette and U.S. Expansion* (Madison: University of Wisconsin Press, 2013), 279.

22. "Policy of the V.C." (Clan na Gael), in Pollard, *Secret Societies*, 257.

23. *New York Times*, Apr. 20, 1920; Frank Walsh, chair of the American Committee on Irish Independence, "Treaty of Peace with Germany," in US Senate, *Hearings before the Committee on Foreign Relations*, June 3, 1919, 332–33.

24. Link, ed. *Papers*, 21: 439; 37: 115. Bernadette Whelan, "The Wilson Administration and the 1916 Rising," in *The Impact of the 1916 Rising: Among the Nations*, edited by Ruan O'Donnell (Dublin: Irish Academic Press, 2008), 289.

25. In *Documents of American History*, edited by Henry Steele Commager (New York: Appleton-Century-Crofts, 1958), 2: 317–19. See also O'Connor, *Reds and the Green*, 13, 44–45.

26. Commager, ed., *Documents*, 2: 317–19.

27. Robert Lansing, *The Peace Negotiations: A Personal Narrative* (Boston: Houghton Mifflin, 1921), 97–98.

28. "American Interpretation in Commager," ed., *Documents*, 2: 320. See also Berg, *Wilson*, 468–72, 503–4. See also Connolly's article, written while he was in the United States: "The Harp" (1909), in Heron, *Words*, 22.

29. On Russia and Ireland, the indispensable source is O'Connor, *Reds and the Green*, 13–54.

30. Gibbons's comment from cypher by Colville Barclay, a British embassy official, Nov. 10, 1918, in the British Foreign Office Files, 115/2398, London, from notes taken by Professor Kerby Miller and made available to me. See also Bagenal, *American Irish*, 73–75, 111, 174–75. Hugh Pollard repeated the point in 1922 in his *Secret Societies*, 35, 185, 187, 197.

31. Yorke, *America and Ireland*, Apr. 10, 1918 (Lexington, KY: Leopold Classic Library, 2010), 41.

32. Yorke, *America and Ireland*, 46–47.

33. Yorke, *America and Ireland*, 17. See also John Duff, "The Versailles Treaty and the Irish-Americans," *Journal of American History* 55 (Dec. 1968): 582–98.

34. Lansing to Wilson, May 19, 1918, in Link, ed., *Papers*, 4: 64. See also Pat McCartan, *With de Valera in America* (Dublin: Fitzpatrick, 1932), 2–4, and Edward Cuddy, "Are the Bolsheviks Any Worse than the Irish?" *Éire-Ireland* 11 (Fall 1976): 13–32.

35. Mitchell and Ó Snodaigh, eds., *Irish Political Documents*, 58–59.

36. Mitchell and Ó Snodaigh, eds., *Irish Political Documents*, 58–59; Irish Labour Party and TUC, *Ireland at Berne*.

37. Mitchell and O' Snodaigh, eds., *Irish Political Documents*, 61–63.

38. Terence Phelan, "Woodrow Wilson and Bolshevism," *Fourth International*, 4, no. 4 (Apr. 1943): 106–11.

39. Phelan, "Wilson and Bolshevism," 108. Phelan's citation was to Baker's *Woodrow Wilson and World Settlement* (Garden City, NY: Doubleday, Page, 1922), 64, as cited in Louis Fischer, *The Soviets in World Affairs: A History of the Soviet Union and the Rest of the World, 1917–1929* (New York: Random House, 1960), 174. See also Baker, *What Wilson Did at Paris* (Garden City, NY: Doubleday, Page, 1919), 52.

40. Wilson quoted in David Fogelsong, *America's Secret War against Bolshevism: US Intervention in the Russian Civil War, 1917–1920* (Chapel Hill: University of North Carolina Press, 1995), 226. See also Phelan, *Woodrow Wilson*.

41. Phelan, "Wilson and Bolshevism," 111.

42. On Wilson and Walsh, see McCartin, *Labor's Great War*, 19–20, 34–36, 196–98, and Stromquist, *Re-inventing*, 180–98.

43. Walsh often warned that a "wave of ultraradicalism was sweeping through the world" (McCartin, *Labor's Great War*, 176). Cardinals James Gibbons of Baltimore and William O'Connell of Boston also warned that the Irish, including those in America, might turn to Bolshevism if Ireland's just demands were not met.

44. Brennan to Walsh, Mar. 31, 1919, box 28, "Irish Independence," MSS Collection 3211, Frank P. Walsh Papers, New York Public Library.

45. Diary of Dr. Cary Grayson, June 11, 1919, in Link, ed., *Papers*, 60: 385–86.

46. Link, ed., *Papers*, 60: 385–86 (my emphasis).

47. Carroll, *American Opinion*, 132–36; Charles Tansill, *America and the Fight for Irish Freedom* (New York: Devin-Adair, 1957), 307–40.

48. Tansill, *America and the Fight*, 314. Wilson to Tumulty, June 8, 1919, in Link, ed., *Papers*, 61: 291; McKillen, "The Irish Sinn Féin Movement and Radical Labor and Feminist Dissent in America, 1916–1921," *Labor* 60 (Sept. 2019): 11–37.

49. Diary of Ray Stannard Baker, May 29, 1919, in Link, ed., *Papers*, 59: 604. See also Grayson diary, Mar. 31, 1919, in Link, ed., *Papers*, 56: 438. Another of Wilson's advisers wrote that the president became angry merely at the suggestion that Ireland be made free ("Diary of David Hunter Miller," Mar. 18, 1919, in Link, ed., *Papers*, 56: 79). For an excellent general discussion, see Elizabeth McKillen, "Ethnicity, Class, and Wilsonian Internationalism Reconsidered: The Mexican-American and Irish-American Immigrant Left and U.S. Foreign Relations, 1914–1922." *Diplomatic History* 25 (Fall 2001): 576–80.

50. Grayson and impeachment from Grayson's diary, June 11, 1919, in Link, ed., *Papers*, 60: 383 (my emphasis).

51. Wilson to Tumulty, June 27, 1919, in Link, ed., *Papers*, 61: 291.

52. My three paragraphs are all from Baker, Diary, in Link, ed., *Papers*, 59: 646 (my emphasis). Robert Schmuhl (*Ireland's Exiled Children*, 109) also cites Baker's comments, without criticism of them.

53. *America*, June 28, 1919, 294; Baker, Diary, Sept. 13, 1919, in Link, ed., *Papers*, 59: 560.

54. Wilson's "tolerance" remark from John Heaton, ed., *Cobb of "the World": A Leader in Liberalism* (Freeport: Books for Libraries, 1971), 270. See also Berg, *Wilson*, 550–52, 665–72, 686–97.

55. Nelson, *Irish Nationalists*, 231. See also B. Pelly, British consul in Seattle, to C. R. Lindsay, Chargé d'Affaires, British Embassy, Washington, DC, Aug. 4, 1919, British Foreign Office Files 115/2514 and 115/2599, from Miller notes; also British Foreign Office 115/2671. Miller also wrote to himself: "files [that] contain a lot of pro-British, hysterically anti-Catholic letters from Americans seeing the whole thing (the Irish agitation) as a Papal plot."

56. In Link, ed., *Papers*, 67: 44–45. Ray Stannard Baker and Dodd coedited Wilson's *New Democracy*. 2 vols. (New York: Harper and Brothers, 1927).

57. Link, ed., *Papers*, 67: 44–45; Connolly, "Socialism and Political Reformers."

58. For the Boyce story, see de Valera to Boyce, Sept. 20, 1919; Boyce to de Valera, Sept. 23, 1919 (Boyce Papers). See also Emmons, *Butte Irish*, 374.

59. *New York Call*, Aug. 18, 1919. Sean Cronin argues that the British "tried to link Sinn Féin with the Bolsheviks, but to no avail" (*Irish Nationalism*, 130). I would contend that they had their avail with Wilson.

60. Ray Stannard Baker, *What Wilson Did at Paris* (Garden City, NY: Doubleday, 1919), 45, 61.

61. Baker, *What Wilson Did*, 30, 34. The system of League mandates is from Article 22 of the League's Charter.

62. Baker, *What Wilson Did*, 62; Drake, *Education*, 279.

63. R. F. Foster, *Vivid Faces*, 280–84, and *Modern Ireland*, 431–515; J. J. Lee, *Ireland*, 1–68.

64. Lloyd George to de Valera, Sept. 17, 1921, in Tim Coates, ed., *The Irish Uprising, 1914–1921: Papers from the British Parliamentary Archive* (London: Stationery Office, 2000), 199.

65. Lloyd George's threat of "war within three days" is noted in all accounts. See, for a moving example, Ernie O'Malley, *The Singing Flame* (1978: London: Anchor, 1992), 41. For a more detached assessment, see Frank Pakenhham, *Peace by Ordeal* (London: Jonathan Cape, 1935), 115–16; de Valera to Lloyd George, Aug. 10, 1921 (while the War of Independence was still being fought), in Coates, ed., *Irish Uprising*, 164–65. See further Brundage, *Irish Nationalists in America*, 165.

66. Sean Cronin, "Liam Mellows," *The Starry Plough*, n.d. http://www.oocities.org/starry.plough/mellows.html; Brundage, *Irish Nationalists in America*, 165.

67. Irish Labour Party and Trade Union Congress, *Ireland at Berne*, 46–47.

68. De Valera quoted in Nelson, *Irish Nationalists*, 231. De Valera did tell Lloyd George that Ireland would never let itself be used as a staging ground for an invasion of Britain (Sept. 17, 1921, in Coates, ed., *Irish Uprising*, 199.

69. Nelson, *Irish Nationalists*, 231–32. See also Jason Knirck, "The Dominion of Ireland: The Anglo-Irish Treaty in an Imperial Context," *Éire-Ireland* 42 (Spring–Summer 2007): 250 (my emphasis); *Hansard's Parliamentary Debate*, Dec. 18, 1921, vol. 149, cc 158.

70. Walter Alison Philips, "Report on the State of Ireland," July 16, 1916, copy in British Foreign Office Files, 115/2244. 250 (my emphasis). See also D. M. Leeson, "British Conspiracy Theories and the Irish War of Independence," *Éire-Ireland* 56 (Spring–Summer 2021): 176–208.

71. Lloyd George to de Valera, Sept. 17, 1921, in Coates, ed., *Irish Uprising*, 198–99 (my emphasis). See also Jason Knirck, "The Dominion of Ireland: The Anglo-Irish Treaty in an Imperial Context," *Éire-Ireland* 42 (Spring–Summer 2007): 229–37.

72. "The Irish Unionist Alliance on Sinn Fein and Bolshevism," in Mitchell and Ó Snodaigh, eds., *Political Documents*, 63–64; Irish Labour Party and Trade Union Congress, *Ireland at Berne*, 42.

73. Lloyd George to de Valera, July 20, 1921, in Coates, ed., *Irish Uprising*, 158.

74. Coates, ed., *Irish Uprising*, 158; Greaves, *Liam Mellows*, 167.

75. Greaves, *Liam Mellows*, 167; O'Connor, *Reds and the Green*, 41, 43, 46, 238–39.

76. Pollard, *Secret Societies*, 130–31, 180, 186, 189, 192, 193, 209–11; Ernie O'Malley, *The Singing Flame* (Dublin: Anvil, 1992), 154.

77. Pollard, *Secret Societies*, 186, 189, 199, 209. Some of Pollard's material on Irish Catholic defects was taken directly from and attributed to the American nativist and anti-Catholic publication, "The Rail Splitter." For the paper, see National Endowment for the Humanities, "About the Rail-Splitter," Milan, IL, 1915–193? in *Chronicling America*. chronoclingamerica.loc.gov.

78. Pollard, *Secret Societies*, 193.

79. Pollard, *Secret Societies*, 180.

80. Cronin, *Irish Nationalism*, 152. Churchill's comment came during the British Parliamentary debate over the ratification of the treaty (*Hansard's Parliamentary Debates*, vol. 149, Dec. 18, 1921, cc182).

81. "An Imperial Danger: The Sinn Fein Menace," (Dublin: The University Press, 1919). Copies in Irish Pamphlet Collection. Mansfield Library. University of Montana.

82. "Imperial Danger."

83. Duke of Northumberland Fund, "The Conspiracy against the British Empire: Ireland and the Revolution," May 11, 1921 (London: Boswell, 1921). Copy in Irish Pamphlet Collection. Mansfield Library. University of Montana .

84. Duke of Northumberland Fund, "Conspiracy."

85. Duke of Northumberland Fund, "Conspiracy."

86. Pollard, *Secret Societies*, 5–7, 66–67, 120.

87. Pollard, *Secret Societies*.

88. For the Free State as Britain's proxy, see Brundage, *Irish Nationalists in America*, 152.

Epilogue

1. The Connolly quote is from C. Desmond Greaves, *The Life and Times of James Connolly*, 403.

2. John Newsinger found no evidence that Connolly ever said that about the IVs to the ICA (*Rebel City: Larkin, Connolly and the Dublin Labour Movement* [London: Merlin, 2004], 131–32). See also Gavin Foster, "Class Dismissed: The Debate over a Social Basis to the Treaty Split and Irish Civil War," *Saothar* 33 (2008): 73–86.

3. For a somewhat contradictory view, see Jason Knirck, *Afterimage of the Revolution: Cumann na nGaedheal and Irish Politics, 1922–1932* (Madison: University of Wisconsin Press, 2021).

4. W. B. Yeats, "The Second Coming," in Yeats, *The Poems*, edited by Richard Finneran, 187. See also Foster, *Vivid Faces*, 73; Tillinghast, *Finding Ireland*, 13, 16, 42–43, 57, 125, 140, 194, 243–44. "Post-partum depression" from 152.

5. Krause, "Plough and Stars," 28–30. See also Allen, *1916*, 28–41.

6. "Boredom and Apocalypse" from Deane, *Strange Country*, 145–97. See also Frank O'Connor, *An Only Child* (London: Macmillan, 1961), 210.

7. Æ cited in R. F. Foster, *Vivid Faces*, 299. The quote about working men came from Thomas Cashman, "Daily Journal of Observation during Trip to Ireland, 1925," copy in Kerby Miller's collection in Miller's possession, Columbia, MO. "Gangsters" is from John McGahern, *Amongst Women* (London: Penguin, 1991), 66.

8. Cronin, *Irish Nationalism*, 153–54; Gavin Foster, "Class Dismissed," 76. One of those "escapees" was Mike Quill, who became the head of the New York Transit Workers Union. See also Joshua Freeman, *In Transit: The Transport Workers Union in New York City, 1933–1955* (New York: Oxford University Press, 1989).

9. *New Republic*, May 12, 1931.

10. Dan Breen, *My Fight for Irish Freedom* (Dublin: Anvil, [1924] 1989), 167.

11. O'Malley, *Singing Flame*, 154, 279.

12. Lalor quote from O'Malley, *On Another Man's Wound* (Boulder, CO: Roberts Rinehart, [1936] 1999), 62. Pope Leo, *Rerum Novarum*, in Ryan and Husslein, *Church and Labor*, 91.

13. Emmons, "A Tower," 77–116; 97–99. That the Pearse-Connolly's met there is noted in the *Anaconda Standard*, Apr. 9, 1917.

14. Tansill, *Irish Freedom*, 369–442; Carroll, *American Opinion*, 159–60, 180–85. See also Farrell, *Irish Themes*, 162, 164, 179–80, 189; Farrell, "Appreciation: Farrell in Ireland," *Éire-Ireland*, 18 (Spring 1983): 109–31, 110.

15. Yeats, "The Statues," in Yeats, *The Poems*, edited by Richard Finneran, 337; Yeats, ed., *Fairy and Folk Tales of Ireland* (New York: Macmillan, [1892] 1983). "Rub off" is from R. F. Foster, *Vivid Faces*, 19. Yeats and the "vulgarity" of modernity cited in Kiberd, *Inventing Ireland*, 132; on the cult of the peasant generally, see 133–90; and Terence Brown, *Ireland: A Social and Cultural History, 1922–2002* (New York: Harper, 2011), ch. 2, "An Irish Ireland," 52–55.

16. Stevens and Pound from Stubbs, *American Literature*, 84, 142.

17. Michael Kazin writes that after World War I there was a "new Republic of Eire." That's a careless error in an otherwise superb book, *The Populist Persuasion: An American History*, rev. ed. (Ithaca, NY: Cornell University Press, 1998), 111.

18. The original copy of the Hannan diary is in the Butte/Silver Bow Archives, Butte, Montana. Material for the section at hand is taken from Emmons, "Tower," which is fully drawn from the Diary.

19. Emmons, "Tower," 100–101.

20. Emmons, "Tower," 103–6. Hannan's ideas—minus Coughlin's overt anti-Semitism—were similar to those of Father Charles Coughlin. On this point, see Kazin, *Populist Persuasion*, 109–37; and Alan Brinkley, *Voices of Protest: Huey Long, Father Coughlin, and the Great Depression* (New York: Vintage, 1982).

21. Emmons, "Tower," 103–4. In John McGahern's novel, *Amongst Women*, one of the daughters of the staunchly antitreaty Republican Michael Moran is

named Mona. "The Last Will and Testament of Reverend M. J. Hannan," May 12, 1928, in Diocese of Helena Office, Helena, Montana.

22. Carroll, *American Opinion*, 180; Walsh to Clemens J. France, Jan. 5, 1922, box 112, Frank P. Walsh Papers, New York Public Library.

23. Frank Walsh, "American Imperialism," *The Nation*, Feb. 1, 1922, 115–116. Of note is Bill Dunne's assertion that John Ryan, the head of ACM, and "other Wall Street barons (as this writer [Dunne] can prove) ordered the invasion of Mexico under General Pershing as a prelude to the crusade 'to make the world safe for democracy'" ("The Long War," draft MS, box 3, folder 15, William Francis Dunne Papers, Tamiment Institute, New York University (microfilm copy).

24. Walsh, "American Imperialism," 116.

25. Walsh, "American Imperialism," 116.

26. Twelve Southerners, *I'll Take My Stand*.

27. The Kennedy-Faulkner connection is from Thomas Flanagan, "O Albany! Review of William Kennedy, *Roscoe* in *New York Review of Books*, Apr. 25, 2002.

28. Lizebeth Cohen, *Making a New Deal: Industrial Workers in Chicago, 1919–1939* (Cambridge: Cambridge University Press, 1990), 97, 119. White's and the Methodist minister's comments about Smith from Barrett, *Irish Way*, 226.

29. "Savageries" from Jefferson Cowie, *The Great Exception: The New Deal and the Limits of American Politics* (Princeton, NJ: Princeton University Press, 2017), 15. See also Eagleton, *Culture*, 70, 74, 125.

30. Sinn Féin, "Clár Oibre Poblacánaighe," in Mitchell and Ó Snodaigh, eds., *Irish Political Documents* (my emphasis).

31. Mitchell and Ó Snodaigh, eds., *Irish Political Documents*.

32. *Great Transformation*, 151, 242. See also Fred Block, introduction to Polanyi, *Great Transformation*, xxviii. As for my presumed, if not presumptuous, Irish connection to Polanyi's dual meanings and double movements, I'm counting, as before, on his close association with Conrad Arensberg to help make it for me.

33. Polanyi, *Great Transformation*, 242.

34. Pius XI, Pope, *Quadragesimo Anno*, para. 14. Polanyi, *Great Transformation*, 242.

35. Eagleton, *Culture*, 53, 54, 128; Pius XI, *Quadragesimo Anno*, para. 14.

36. Kazin, *Populist Persuasion*, 109–11; L. Cohen, *Making a New Deal*, 238; Cowie, *Great Exception*, 20, 24. The question of industrial unionism and Black rights is a tricky one. Racial tolerance was the CIO's promise, but the union, more often than not, did not live up to it (Bruce Nelson, "Class, Race and Democracy in the CIO: The 'New' Labor History Meets the 'Wages of Whiteness,'" *International Review of Social History* 41 [1996]: 351–74).

37. Polanyi, *Great Transformation*, 122.

38. Quoted in Cowie, *Great Exception*, 3, 7, 9.

39. Keating, "The Encyclicals" (1931); Waugh, "American Epoch," 36–37.

40. Cohen, *Making a New Deal*, 315; Eagleton, *Culture*, 69.

41. Cowie, *Great Exception*, 9.

42. Cowie, *Great Exception*, 9–10. See also Kazin, *Populist Persuasion*, 136.

43. L. Cohen, *Making a New Deal*, 315. See also Cowie, *Great Exception*; Eagleton, *Culture*, 69.

44. L. Cohen, *Making a New Deal*, 333–49.

45. I should also mention that, in 1942, the Butte Miners' Union was officially rebuked by the CIO for refusing to allow Blacks to work underground (Matt Basso, *Meet Joe Copper: Masculinity and Race on Montana's World War II Home Front* [Chicago: University of Chicago Press, 2013], ch. 6).

46. Joshua Freeman, *In Transit*. On the CIO in general, see, among many sources, Robert Zieger, *The CIO, 1935–1955* (Chapel Hill: University of North Carolina Press, 1995).

47. Headline quote is from Kazin, *Populist Persuasion*, 137.

48. Great Famine figures from Kennedy, Ell, Crawford, and Clarkson, eds., *Mapping*. See also Joshua Freeman, *In Transit*, 45; Cross, *The Tailor*, 13, 14, 119.

49. Quill's Irish years are recounted in his wife, Shirley Quill's, *Mike Quill—Himself: A Memoir* (New York: Devin-Adair, 1985). See also Manus O'Riordan, "Mike Quill—Kerry Founder of the TWU of America," address to the Ancient Order of Hibernians, Killarney, Oct. 11, 2002; aoh61.com; Joshua Freeman, *In Transit*, 47, 52–53.

50. Joshua Freeman, *In Transit*, 47 (my emphasis).

51. J. Connolly, "Irish Socialist Republican Party" (1896), reissued in *The Harp*, Mar. 1908.

52. J. Connolly, "Erin's Hope," 1909.

53. Joshua Freeman, *In Transit*, 149.

54. Joshua Freeman, *In Transit*, 149.

55. Joshua Freeman, *In Transit*, 335. Quill also opposed the anti-Semitism of Fr. Charles Coughlin and the Christian Front (Joshua Freeman, *In Transit*, 143–46). John Ryan also denounced Coughlin in a 1936 letter to the lay Catholic journal *Commonweal*, in Ryan, *Seven Troubled Years* (Washington, DC: Catholic University Press, 1937), 300–301.

56. O'Riordan, "Mike Quill."

57. Robert Scally, *The End of Hidden Ireland: Rebellion, Famine, and Emigration* (New York: Oxford University Press, 1995), 227; Laurence Moore, *Religious Outsiders and the Making of America* (New York: Oxford University Press, 1987), 70. I wonder whether Joyce was perhaps making a typically oblique allusion to "Irish ingredients" when he wrote of his "our American cousin, Patsy Caliban." *Our American Cousin* was the name of the play the Lincolns were watching the evening the president was assassinated.

58. Cowie, *Great Exception and the Limits of American Politics*.

Bibliography

Archival Collections

Butte/Silver Bow Archives, Butte, Montana
    Diary of Father Michael Hannan
    Irish Collection
Diocese of Helena Office, Helena, Montana
    Bishop John Carroll Papers
    Michael Hannan File
Edward Boyce Papers, Eastern Washington State Historical Society, Spokane
Edward Keating Papers, Western History Collection, University of Colorado, Boulder
Frank Walsh Papers, New York Public Library
Irish Pamphlet Collection, University of Montana Archives, Mansfield Library, Missoula
IWW Collection, Walter P. Reuther Library of Labor and Urban Affairs, Wayne State University, Detroit
K. Ross Toole Archives, University of Montana, Missoula
    D. J. Glasser File
    Irish Collection
    James E. Murray Papers
Marxists' Internet Archives Library, https://www.marxists.org/archive/index.htm
    James Connolly Internet Archive, https//www.marxists.org/archive/connolly
    V. I. Lenin Internet Archive, https//www.marxists.org/archive/lenin
Minnesota Historical Society, St. Paul
Montana Historical Society Library, Helena
William Francis Dunne Papers, 1914–1951, Tamiment Institute, New York University (cited in Primary Sources as Dunne Papers)

Government Records and Publications

GREAT BRITAIN

British Foreign Office Files. From notes taken by Professor Kerby Miller.
Hansard's Parliamentary Debates (London) 1846, 1921.

UNITED STATES

US Commission on Industrial Relations. *Final Report and Testimony*. Sixty-Fourth Congress, first session. vol. 4. Washington, DC: Government Printing Office, 1915.
US Congress. *Reports of the Immigration Commission*. 41 vols. Vol. 5, *Dictionary of Races or Peoples*. Washington, DC: Government Printing Office, 1911.
US Congressional Record.
US Department of Defense. "Selected Manpower Statistics—Fiscal Year 1897." Washington, DC: Government Printing Office, 1898.
US v. Haywood et al. Transcripts in IWW Collection. Walter Reuther Library of Labor and Urban Affairs, Wayne State University, Detroit.

Primary Sources: Books and Articles

Adams, Henry. *The Education of Henry Adams*. New York: Modern Library, [1907] 1999.
American Commission on Conditions in Ireland. *Evidence of Conditions in Ireland*. Washington, DC: American Commission on Conditions in Ireland, 1921.
Bagenal, Philip, *The American Irish and Their Influence on Irish Politics*. London: Kegan, Paul, Trench, 1882.
Baker, Ray Stannard. *What Wilson Did at Paris*. Garden City, NY: Doubleday, 1919.
Baker, Ray Stannard. *Woodrow Wilson and World Settlement*. Garden City, NY: Doubleday, Page, 1922.
Barton, Dante. "Frank P. Walsh." *Harper's Weekly*, Sept. 27, 1913.
Bemis, Edward. "Restriction of Immigration." *Andover Review*, Mar. 1888, 251–64.
Breen, Dan. *My Fight for Irish Freedom*. Dublin: Anvil, [1924] 1989.
Bryce, James. *The American Commonwealth*. 2 vols. New York: Macmillan, 1897.
Burke, Thomas. *Lectures on Faith and Fatherland*. Glasgow: R. and T. Washbourne, 1872.
Carney, Jack. "Larkin and Connolly." In *James Larkin: Lion of the Fold*. Edited by Donal Nevin. Dublin: Gill, 2014.
Carney, Jack. "Mary Marcy." Chicago: Charles Kerr, 1922. Copy in Minnesota Historical Society, St. Paul.
Casement, Roger. "Ireland, Germany, and Freedom of the Seas: A Possible Outcome of the War of 1914." New York: Irish Press Bureau, 1914.
Chapin, Ralph. "The Picket Line of Blood." *One Big Union Monthly*, June 1920.
Chesterton, G. K. *Orthodoxy*. San Francisco: Ignatian Press, [1908] 1995.

Coates, Tim, ed. *The Irish Uprising, 1914–1921: Papers from the British Parliamentary Archive*. London: Stationery Office, 2000.
Colum, Padraic. "James Joyce's Birthday Party." *New Republic*. May 12, 1931.
Commager, Henry Steele, ed. *Documents of American History*. 2 vols. in one. New York: Appleton-Century-Crofts, 1958.
Commons, John R. *Myself: The Autobiography of John R. Commons*. Madison: University of Wisconsin Press, [1934] 1964.
Commons, John R. *Races and Immigrants in America*. New York: Macmillan, 1907.
Commons, John R. *Social Reform and the Church*. New York: Thomas Crowell, 1894.
Connolly, James. "British Labour and Irish Politicians." *Forward*, May 3, 1913.
Connolly, James. "A Continental Revolution." *Forward*, Aug. 15, 1914.
Connolly, James. "Courts Martial and Revolution." *Irish Work*, Dec. 19, 1914.
Connolly, James. "Erin's Hope." Pamphlet, 1897; rev. ed., 1909. James Connolly Online Archive.
Connolly, James. "The Irish Flag." *Workers' Republic*, Apr. 8, 1916.
Connolly, James. "Irish Socialist Republican Party" (1896), republished in *The Harp*, Mar., 1908.
Connolly, James. "Physical Force in Irish Politics." *Workers' Republic*, July 22, 1899.
Connolly, James. "The Re-conquest of Ireland." New York: Nu Vision, [1915] 2007.
Connolly, James. "Recruiting the ICA." *Workers' Republic*, Nov. 6, 1915.
Connolly, James. *Socialism and the Irish Rebellion: Writings from James Connolly*. St. Petersburg, FL: Red and Black, 2007.
Connolly, James. "Socialism and Nationalism." *Shan Van Vocht*, Jan. 1897.
Connolly, James. "Socialism and Political Reformers." *Workers' Republic*, July 8, 1899.
Connolly, James. "Socialism in Ireland." *The Harp*, Mar., 1908.
Connolly, James. "The War upon the German Nation." *Irish Worker*, Aug. 29, 1914.
Dawson, Richard. *Red Terror and Green: The Sinn Fein–Bolshevik Movement*. New York: E. P. Dutton, 1920.
Debs, Eugene V. "The Rights of Working Women." *Melting Pot*, Mar. 1913, 12–13.
Debs, Eugene V. "The United Front: Shall We Have Solidarity or Be Slaughtered?" *New Age*, June 1922.
Duke of Northumberland Fund. "The Conspiracy against the British Empire: Ireland and the Revolution." May 11, 1921. London: Boswell, 1921. Irish Pamphlet Collection, University of Montana Archives.
Dunne, Finley Peter. *Mr. Dooley in Peace and War*. Boston: Small, Maynard, 1898.
Dunne, William F. "The Brit General Strike" (copy). Dunne Papers.
Dunne, William F. "Gastonia—the Class Struggle in the South" (copy). Dunne Papers.
Dunne, William F. *The Struggle against Opportunism in the Labor Movement—for a Socialist United States*. New York: New York Communications Committee, 1947.

Dunne, William F. "The Threat to the Labor Movement" (copy). Dunne Papers.
Dunne, William F. "The Trotskyite Permanent Counter Revolution." (copy). Dunne Papers.
Dunne, William F. "Why Hearst Lies about Capitalism" (copy). Dunne Papers.
Dunne, William F. "Workers Correspondence" (copy). Dunne Papers.
Flynn, Elizabeth Gurley. *The Rebel Girl: An Autobiography*. New York: International, [1951] 1973.
Foster, William. *Pages from a Worker's Life*. New York: International, 1939.
Frederic, Harold. *The Damnation of Theron Ware; or, Illuminations*. New York: Penguin, [1896] 1986.
Freeman, Joseph. *An American Testament*. New York: Farrar and Rinehart, 1936.
Gitlow, Benjamin. *I Confess: The Truth about American Communism*. New York: E. P. Dutton, 1940.
Gitlow, Benjamin. *The Whole of Their Lives*. New York: Scribner, 1948.
Godkin, Edwin. "American Opinion on the Irish Question." *Nineteenth Century*, July–Dec. 1887, 285–92.
Godkin, Edwin. *Life and Letters of Edwin Lawrence Godkin*. 2 vols. Edited by Rollo Ogden. New York: Macmillan, 1907.
Gold, Michael. "Ode to Walt Whitman (1935)." In *Walt Whitman: The Measure of His Song*, 168–72. Edited by Jim Perlman, Ed Folsom, and Dan Campion. Duluth, MN: Holy Cow Press, 1998.
Gompers, Samuel. *Seventy Years of Life and Labor: An Autobiography*. 2 vols. New York: E. P. Dutton, 1925.
Grant, Madison. *The Passing of the Great Race; or, The Racial Basis of European History*. New York: Scribner, [1916] 1936.
Hammond, John Hays. *The Autobiography of John Hays Hammond*. 2 vols. New York: Farrar and Rinehart, 1935.
Hammond, John Hays, and Jeremiah Jenks. *Great American Issues: Political, Social, Economic*. New York: Scribner, 1923.
Hand, Wayland. "The Folklore, Customs, and Traditions of the Butte Miner." *California Folklore Quarterly* 5 (1946): 1–25, 153–78.
Haywood, William. *The Autobiography of Bill Haywood*. New York: International, [1929] 1966.
Hendrick, Burton. *The Life and Letters of Walter H. Page, 1835–1918*. 2 vols. Garden City, NY: Garden City Publishing, 1927.
Heron, James Connolly, ed. *The Words of James Connolly*. Cork City, Ire.: Mercier, 1986.
Hoar, George. *Autobiography of Seventy Years*. 2 vols. New York: Scribner, 1903.
Irish Labour Party and Trade Union Congress. *Ireland at Berne: . . . Reports and Memoranda Presented to the International Labour and Socialist Conference . . . Feb. 1919*. Dublin: Talbot, 1919.
Joyce, James. *A Portrait of the Artist as a Young Man*. New York: Viking, [1916] 1968.
Joyce, James. *Ulysses*. Edited by Hans Gabler. New York: Vintage, [1921] 1986.

Kellogg, Paul. *Wage-Earning Pittsburgh*. New York: Russell Sage Foundation, 1914. Repr., New York: Arno, 1974.
Kiberd, Declan, and P. J. Mathews, eds. *Handbook of the Irish Revival: An Anthology of Irish Cultural and Political Writings, 1891–1922*. Notre Dame, IN: University of Notre Dame Press, 2015.
King, Wilfred. *The Wealth and Income of the People of the United States*. New York: Macmillan, 1915.
Lansing, Robert. *The Peace Negotiations: A Personal Narrative*. Boston: Houghton Mifflin, 1921.
Lauck, W. Jett, and Edgar Sydenstricker. *Conditions of Labor in American Industries*. New York: Funk and Wagnalls, 1917.
Lenin, V. I. *Collected Works, 1893–1923*. 45 vols. Vols. 19 (1913) and 22 (Dec. 1915–July 1916). Moscow: Progress, 1964. Also in Lenin Internet Archive.
Leo XIII, Pope. *Rerum Novarum: On the Condition of Labor*. In *The Church and Labor*. Edited by John A. Ryan and Joseph Husslein, 57–94. New York: Macmillan, 1924.
Leslie, Shane. *The Irish Issue in Its American Aspect*. New York: Scribner, 1917.
Link, Arthur, ed. *The Papers of Woodrow Wilson*. 68 vols. Princeton, NJ: Princeton University Press, 1966–83.
Lippmann, Walter. *Drift and Mastery*. Englewood Cliffs, NJ: Prentice Hall, [1914] 1961.
MacManus, Seumas. "Sinn Fein." *North American Review* 185 (Aug. 1907): 825–36.
MacManus, Seumas. *The Story of the Irish Race*. New York: Devin-Adair, [1921] 1977.
Manly, Basil. "Labor's Share in the Social Product." *Annals of the American Academy of Political and Social Science* 69 (Jan. 1917): 128–32.
Marx, Karl, and Friedrich Engels. *Ireland and the Irish Question [1853–70]*. Moscow: Progress, 1971.
McCartan, Patrick. *With de Valera in America*. Dublin: Fitzpatrick, 1932.
McCarthy, Conor, ed. *The Revolutionary and Anti-imperialist Writing of James Connolly, 1891–1916*. Edinburgh: Edinburgh University Press, 2016.
McGuire, John. *The King, the Kaiser and Irish Freedom*. New York: Devin-Adair, 1915.
McGuire, John. *What Could Germany Do for Ireland?* New York: Wolfe Tone, 1916.
Merwin, Henry Childs. "The Irish in American Life." *Atlantic Monthly*, Mar. 1896, 289–301.
Merwin, Henry Childs. "Recent Impressions of the English." *Harper's Magazine*, May 1903, 929–32.
Merz, Charles. "The Issue in Butte." *New Republic*, Aug. 1917.
Mine Owners' Association of Colorado. "Criminal Record of the WFM from Coeur D'Alene to Cripple Creek, 1894–1904." Colorado Springs, CO: Mine Owners' Association of Colorado, 1904.
Mitchell, Arthur, and Pádraig Ó Snodaigh, eds. *Irish Political Documents, 1916–1949*. Dublin: Irish Academic, 1985.

O'Brien, William, and Desmond Ryan, eds. *Devoy's Post Bag, 1871–1928*. 2 vols. Dublin: Academic Press, 1948, 1953.
O'Flaherty, Thomas. *Aranmen All*. London: Gollacz, 1930.
O'Flaherty, Thomas. *Cliffmen of the West*. London: Gollancz, 1935.
O'Flaherty, Thomas. "A Radical Montana Magazine." *The Worker* (New York), June 2, 1923.
O'Malley, Ernie. *On Another Man's Wound*. Boulder, CO: Roberts Rinehart, [1936] 1999).
O'Malley, Ernie. *The Singing Flame*. Dublin: Anvil, 1992.
O'Riordan, Michael. *Catholicity and Progress in Ireland*. London: Kegan Paul Trench, 1906. US edition, St. Louis: B. Herder, 1906.
Pearse, Patrick. "The Sovereign People." Dublin: Whelan and Son, 1916.
Phelan, Terence. "Woodrow Wilson and Bolshevism." Article presented to *Fourth Communist International*. Vol. 4, no. 4. (Apr. 1943). Marxists' Internet Archives.
Plunkett, Horace. *Ireland in the New Century*. New York: E. P. Dutton, 1904.
Plunkett, Horace. *The Rural Life Problem of the United States: Notes of an Irish Observer*. New York: Macmillan, 1911.
Pollard, Hugh. *The Secret Societies of Ireland: Their Rise and Progress*. Kilkenny, Ire.: Irish Historical Press, [1922] 1998.
Rauschenbusch, Walter. *Christianity and the Social Crisis*. New York: Hodder and Stoughton, 1907.
Ross, E. A. *Changing America: Studies In Contemporary Society*. New York: Century, 1919.
Ross, E. A. *The Old World in the New*. New York: Century, 1914.
Russell, Andrew, comp. *The Behan Quotation Book*. London: Sommerville, 2015.
Russell, George William (Æ). "Ireland and the Empire at the Court of Conscience." Dublin: Talbot, 1921.
Ryan, John A. *Distributive Justice*. New York: Macmillan, 1906.
Ryan, John A. *A Living Wage: Its Ethical and Economic Aspects*. New York: Macmillan, 1912.
Ryan, John A. *Seven Troubled Years*. Washington, DC: Catholic University Press, 1937.
Ryan, John A. *Social Reconstruction*. New York: Macmillan, 1920.
Seeley, John. *The Expansion of England*. New York: Little, Brown, [1883] 1922.
Shanley, Timothy. "Mister Frank Walsh's Career." *America*, July 5, 1918, 329–31.
Sheehy-Skeffington, Hanna. "Impressions of Sinn Féin in America: An Account of Eighteen Months' Irish Propaganda in the United States." Dublin: Davis, 1919.
Sombart, Werner. *Why Is There No Socialism in the United States?* White Plains, NY: M. E. Sharpe, [1906] 1976.
Spalpeen. "Sinn Féin and the Labour Movement." Dublin: Patrick Mahon, 1917. Copy in Irish Pamphlet Files, University of Montana Archives, Missoula.
Spenser, Edmund. *A View of the Present State of Ireland*. London: Perfect Library, [1596] 2013.

Strong, George T. *The New Era; or, The Coming Kingdom*. New York: Baker and Taylor, 1893.
Strong, George Templeton. *Our Country*. New York: Baker and Taylor, 1890.
Strong, Josiah. *Diary*. Edited by Alan Nevins and M. H. Thomas. 4 vols. New York: Macmillan, 1953.
Synge, John M. *John M. Synge's Guide to the Aran Islands*. Edited by Ruth Willis Shaw. Old Greenwich, CT: Devin-Adair, [1897] 1975.
Tocqueville, Alexis de. *Democracy in America*. Chicago: University of Chicago Press, [1835] 2000.
Tully, James, *Shanty Irish*. New York: Albert and Charles Boni, 1928.
Walsh, Frank. "American Imperialism." *The Nation*, Feb. 1, 1921.
Walsh, Frank. "Ireland Today." Windsor Hall, Montreal, June 11, 1920, forgottenbooks.com (facsimile reprint).
Walsh, Frank. "The Irish Labor Movement." 1921. Walsh Papers. New York Public Library.
Walsh, Frank. "A Message of Peace to All the World." n.d., [1921]. Box 32, Mss Collection 3211, Walsh Papers. New York Public Library.
Walsh, Frank. "Windows Alight in Connaught." *America*, June 7, 1919, 224–27.
Ward, Leo. *Holding Up the Hills: The Biography of a Neighborhood*. New York: Sheed and Ward, 1941.
Weber, Max. *The Protestant Ethic and the Spirit of Capitalism*. Translated by Talcott Parsons. London: Routledge, [1904] 2005.
Wheeler, Burton. *Yankee from the West*. New York: Doubleday, 1962.
Wilson, Woodrow. *A History of the American People*. 5 vols. New York: Harper and Brothers, 1902.
Wilson, Woodrow. "The Ideals of America." *Atlantic Monthly*, Dec. 1902, 721–34.
Wilson, Woodrow. *The New Democracy*. 2 vols. Edited by Ray Stannard Baker and William Dodd. New York: Harper and Brothers, 1926.
Yeats, W. B. *The King's Threshold and On Baile's Strand*. London: A. H. Bullen, 1904.
Yeats, W. B. *The Poems*. Edited by Richard Finneran. New York: Macmillan, 1983.
Yorke, Peter. "America and Ireland." Lexington, KY: Leopold Classic Library, [1918] 2010.

Secondary Sources

Abell, Aaron. *American Catholicism and Social Action: A Search for Social Justice*. Notre Dame, IN: University of Notre Dame Press, 1967.
Adams, Graham. *Age of Industrial Violence, 1910–1915: The Activities and Findings of the United States Commission on Industrial Relations*. New York: Columbia University Press, 1971.
Ahlstrom, Sydney. *A Religious History of the American People*. New Haven, CT: Yale University Press, 1972.
Aitken, Max. *The Decline and Fall of Lloyd George*. London: Collins, 1963.
Akenson, Donald. *The Irish Diaspora: A Primer*. Toronto: P. D. Meaney, 1996.

Akenson, Donald. *Small Differences: Irish Catholics and Irish Protestants*. Kingston, ON: McGill-Queens University Press, 1988.

Allen, Kieran. *1916: Ireland's Revolutionary Tradition*. London: Pluto, 2016.

Ambrosius, Lloyd. *Woodrow Wilson and American Internationalism*. Cambridge: Cambridge University Press, 2017.

Anderson, Benedict. "Exodus." *Critical Inquiry* 20 (Winter 1994): 314–27.

Anderson, Benedict. *Imagined Communities: Reflections on the Origins and Spread of Nationalism*. London: Verso, 1991.

Anderson, Benedict. *Long-Distance Nationalism: World Capitalism and the Rise of Identity Politics*, Amsterdam: Center for Asian Studies, 1992.

Anderson, Stuart. *Race and Rapprochement: Anglo-Saxonism and Anglo-American Relations, 1895–1904*. New York: Rutherford, 1981.

Arensberg, Conrad. "Anthropology as History." In *Trade and Market in the Early Empires*. Edited by Karl Polanyi, Conrad Arensberg, and Harry Pearson, 97–113. Glencoe, IL: Free Press, 1957.

Arensberg, Conrad. *Family and Community in Ireland*. Cambridge, MA: Harvard University Press, 1968.

Arensberg, Conrad. *The Irish Countryman: An Anthropological Study*. Garden City, NY: Natural History Press, 1968.

Barrett, James. *The Irish Way: Becoming American in the Multiethnic City*. New York: Penguin, 2012.

Barrett, James, and David Roediger. "The Irish and the 'Americanization' of the 'New Immigrants' in the Streets and in the Churches of the Urban United States, 1900–1930." *Journal of American Ethnic History* 24 (Summer 2005): 3–34.

Basso, Matt. *Meet Joe Copper: Masculinity and Race on Montana's World War II Home Front*. Chicago: University of Chicago Press, 2013.

Bayor, Ronald, and Timothy Meagher, eds. *The New York Irish*. Baltimore, MD: Johns Hopkins University Press, 1996.

Bell, Geoffrey. *Hesitant Comrades: The Irish Revolution and the British Labour Movement*. London: Pluto, 2016.

Berg, A. Scott. *Wilson*. New York: Berkley, 2013.

Berlin, Ira. "Class Composition and the Development of the American Working Class." In Herbert Gutman, *Power and Culture: Essays in the American Working Class*. Edited by Ira Berlin. New York: New Press, 1987.

Bourke, Angela. *The Burning of Bridget Cleary: A True Story*. New York: Viking, 2000.

Boyce, D. George, and Alan O'Day, eds. *The Making of Modern Irish History: Revisionism and the Revisionist Controversy*. London: Routledge, 1996.

Brady, Ciaran, ed. *Interpreting Irish History: The Debate on Historical Revisionism*. Dublin: Irish Academic Press, 1994.

Brinkley, Alan. *Voices of Protest: Huey Long, Father Coughlin, and the Great Depression*. New York: Vintage, 1982.

Brody, David. "Reconciling the Old Labor History and the New." *Pacific Historical Review* 62 (Feb. 1993): 1–18.

Brown, Terence. *Ireland: A Social and Cultural History, 1922–2002*. New York: Harper, 2011.
Brown, Thomas. *Irish-American Nationalism, 1870–1890*. Philadelphia: Lippincott, 1966.
Brundage, David. *Irish Nationalists in America: The Politics of Exile, 1798–1968*. New York: Oxford University Press, 2016.
Brundage, David. "1 February 1922: Frank Walsh's 'American Imperialism.'" In *Ireland 1922*. Edited by Darragh Gannon and Feargal McGarry. Dublin: Royal Irish Academy, 2022, 43–47.
Bryce, Colm. "Ireland and the Russian Revolution." *Irish Marxist Review* 6 (2017): 42–54.
Burnidge, Cara Lee. *A Peaceful Conquest: Woodrow Wilson, Religion, and the New World Order*. Chicago: University of Chicago Press, 2016.
Carroll, Francis. *American Opinion and the Irish Question, 1910–1923* New York: Gill and Macmillan, 1978.
Cohen, Lizabeth. *Making a New Deal: Industrial Workers in Chicago, 1919–1939*. Cambridge: Cambridge University Press, 1990.
Cohen, Robin. *Global Diasporas: An Introduction*. New York: Routledge, 2008.
Colley, Linda. *Britons: Forging the Nation, 1707–1837*. New Haven, CT: Yale University Press, 1992.
Connolly, Sean. *On Every Tide: The Making and Remaking of the Irish World*. New York: Basic Books, 2022.
Coogan, Tim Oat. *The Man Who Made Ireland: The Life and Death of Michael Collins*. New York: Roberts Rinehart, 1992.
Cowie, Jefferson. *The Great Exception: The New Deal and the Limits of American Politics*. Princeton, NJ: Princeton University Press, 2017.
Cronin, Sean. *Irish Nationalism: A History of Its Roots and Ideology*. New York: Continuum, 1981.
Cronin, Sean. "Liam Mellows." *The Starry Plough*, n.d., http://www.oocities.org/starry.plough/mellows.html.
Cross, Eric. *The Tailor and Ansty*. Dublin: Mercier, [1942] 1999.
Cuddy, Edward, "Are the Bolsheviks Any Worse than the Irish?" *Éire-Ireland* 11 (Fall 1976): 13–32.
Curran, Mary Doyle. *The Parish and the Hill*. New York: Feminist Press, 2002.
Darnton, Robert. *The Great Cat Massacre and Other Episodes in French Cultural History*. New York: Basic Books, 1984.
Deane, Seamus. *Strange Country: Modernity and Nationhood in Irish Writing since 1790*. Oxford: Oxford University Press, 1997.
Delaney, Edna. *The Curse of Reason: The Great Irish Famine*. Dublin: Gill and Macmillan, 2012.
Dening, Greg. *The Death of William Gooch: A History's Anthropology*. Honolulu: University of Hawaii Press, 1995.
Dione, E. J. "We're All Liberals Now." *Commonweal*, Nov. 19, 1999, 44–45.

Dorn, Jacob. "'In Spiritual Communion': Eugene V. Debs and the Socialist Christian." *Journal of the Gilded Age and Progressive Era* 2 (2003): 303–25.

Drake, Richard. *The Education of an Anti-imperialist: Robert La Follette and U.S. Expansion*. Madison: University of Wisconsin Press, 2013.

Dubofsky, Melvyn. "Abortive Reform: The Wilson Administration and Organized Labor, 1913–1920." In *Work, Community, and Power: The Experience of Labor in Europe and America, 1900–1925*. Edited by James Cronin and Carmen Siriani, 197–220. Philadelphia: Temple University Press, 1983.

Dubofsky, Melvyn. *We Shall Be All: A History of the Industrial Workers of the World*. Chicago: Quadrangle, 1969,

Duff, John. "The Versailles Treaty and the Irish-Americans." *Journal of American History* 55 (Dec. 1968): 582–98.

Duffy, Eamon. *Faith of Our Fathers: Reflections on Catholic Traditions*. London: Continuum, 2004.

Eagleton, Terry. *Culture*. New Haven, CT: Yale University Press, 2016.

Ebest, Ron. *Private Histories: The Writings of Irish Americans, 1900–1935*. Notre Dame, IN: University of Notre Dame Press, 2005.

Edwards, Ruth. *Patrick Pearse: The Triumph of Failure*. London: Gallancz, 1977.

Ellis, P. Beresford. *A History of the Irish Working Class*. London: Pluto, 1972.

Elshtain, Jean Bethke. "Augustine and Diversity." In *A Catholic Modernity?* Edited by James Heft, 95–104. New York: Oxford University Press, 1999.

Elshtain, Jean Bethke. *Sovereignty: God, State, and Self*. New York: Basic Books, 2008.

Emmons, David. *Beyond the American Pale: The Irish in the West, 1845–1910*. Norman: University of Oklahoma Press, 2010.

Emmons, David. *The Butte Irish: Class and Ethnicity in an American Mining Town, 1875–1925*. Urbana: University of Illinois Press, 1989.

Emmons, David. "Homecoming: Finding a Catholic Hermeneutic." In *Faith and the Historian: Catholic Perspectives*. Edited by Nick Salvatore, 49–81. Urbana: University of Illinois Press, 2007.

Emmons, David. "'A Tower of Strength to the Movement': Father Michael Hannan and the Irish Republic." *American Journal of Irish Studies* 12 (2015): 77–116.

Evans, Estyn. *The Personality of Ireland: Habitat, Heritage, and History*. Dublin: Liliput, 1992.

Farrell, James. "A Portrait of James Connolly." In *On Irish Themes*. Edited by Dennis Flynn, 109–42. Philadelphia: University of Pennsylvania Press, 1982.

Fischer, David H. *Albion's Seed: Four British Folkways in America*. New York: Oxford University Press, 1989.

Fitzpatrick, David. *Harry Boland's Irish Revolution*. Cork City, Ire.: Cork University Press, 2003.

Flanagan, Thomas. "O Albany!" Review of *Roscoe*, by William Kennedy. *New York Review of Books*, Apr. 25, 2002.

Flynn, Dennis, ed. *On Irish Themes*. Philadelphia: University of Pennsylvania Press, 1982.

Fogelsong, David. *America's Secret War against Bolshevism: US Intervention in the Russian Civil War, 1917–1920*. Chapel Hill: University of North Carolina Press, 1995.

Foner, Eric. "Class, Ethnicity, and Radicalism in the Gilded Age: The Land League and Irish-America." In *Politics and Ideology in the Age of the Civil War*, 150–200. New York: Oxford University Press, 1980).

Foner, Eric. *Free Soil, Free Labor, Free Men: The Making of the Republican Party before the Civil War*. New York: Oxford University Press, 1970.

Foster, Gavin. "Class Dismissed: The Debate over a Social Basis to the Treaty Split and the Irish Civil War." *Saothar* 33 (2008): 73–86.

Foster, Gavin. *The Irish Civil War and Society: Politics, Class and Conflict*. London: Basingstoke, 2015.

Foster, Gavin. "No 'Wild Geese' This Time? IRA Emigration after the Irish Civil War." *Eire-Ireland* 47 (Spring/Summer 2012): 94–122.

Foster, Gavin. "*Res Publica na hÉireann*? Republican Liberty and the Irish Civil War." *New Hibernia Review* 16 (Autumn 2011): 20–42.

Foster, R. F. *Modern Ireland*. New York: Viking, 1989.

Foster, R. F. *Vivid Faces: The Revolutionary Generation in Ireland*. New York: W. W. Norton, 2014.

Freeman, Joshua. *In Transit: The Transport Workers Union in New York City, 1933–1966*. New York: Oxford University Press, 1989.

Friel, Brian. *Translations*. In *Selected Plays*. Introduction by Seamus Deane. Washington, DC: Catholic University Press, 1986.

Fuller, A. James. *Chaplain to the Confederacy: Basic Manly and Baptist Life in the Old South*. Baton Rouge: Louisiana State University Press, 2000.

Gaddis, John Lewis. *The Landscape of History: How Historians Map the Past*. New York: Oxford University Press, 2002.

Gannon, Darragh, and Feargal McGarry, eds. *Ireland 1922*. Dublin: Royal Irish Academy, 2022.

Garvin, Thomas. *Nationalist Revolutionaries in Ireland, 1858–1928*. Dublin: Gill and Macmillan, 2005.

Garvin, Thomas. "Priests and Patriots: Irish Separation and Fear of the Modern, 1890–1914." *Irish Historical Studies* 25 (May 1986): 67–81.

Gerstle, Gary. "Historical and Contemporary Perspectives on Immigrant Political Incorporation: The American Experience." *International Labor and Working-Class History* 78 (Sept. 2010): 110–17.

Gerstle, Gary. "Liberty, Coercion, and the Making of Americans." *Journal of American History* 84 (Sept. 1997): 524–58.

Gerstle, Gary. "The Protean Character of American Liberalism." *American Historical Review* 99 (Oct. 1994): 1043–73.

Gibbons, Luke. "American Reactions to the 1916 Rising." Paper delivered Nov. 12, 2016, to the conference *Ireland and the Wobbly World*. Irish Centre for the Histories of Labour and Class, National University of Ireland. Galway. ichlc.wordpress.com.

Gibbons, Luke. *Gaelic Gothic: Race, Colonization, and Irish Culture.* Galway city, Ire.: Arlen House, 2004.

Gramsci, Antonio. "Americanism Fordism." In *The Antonio Gramsci Reader.* Edited by David Forgacs. New York: New York University Press, 2000.

Greaves, C. Desmond. *Liam Mellows and the Irish Revolution.* London: Lawrence and Wishart, 1971.

Greaves, C. Desmond. *The Life and Times of James Connolly.* London: Lawrence and Wishart, 1961.

Greaves, C. Desmond. "October and the British Empire." *Labour Monthly,* Nov. 1967.

Gregory, Brad. "'No Room for God'? History, Science, Metaphysics and the Study of Religion." *History and Theory* 47 (2008): 495–519.

Gregory, Brad. *The Unintended Reformation: How a Religious Revolution Secularized Society.* Cambridge, MA: Harvard University Press, 2012.

Grey, Miriam Nyhan, ed. *Ireland's Allies: America and the 1916 Easter Rising.* Dublin: University College Dublin Press, 2016.

Griffin, Patrick. *The People with No Name: Ireland's Ulster Scots, America's Scots Irish, and the Creation of a British Atlantic World.* Princeton, NJ: Princeton University Press, 2001.

Gutman, Herbert. *Power and Culture: Essays on the American Working Class.* Edited by Ira Berlin. New York: New Press, 1987.

Gutman, Herbert. *Work, Culture, and Society in Industrializing America: Essays in American Working-Class and Social History.* New York: Vintage, 1977.

Heaney, Seamus. *Poems, 1965–1975* New York: Noonday, 1980.

Heaton, John, ed. *Cobb of "the World": A Leader in Liberalism.* Freeport, ME: Books for Libraries, 1971.

Henretta, James. "The Study of Social Mobility: Ideological Assumptions and Conceptual Bias." In *The Labor History Reader.* Edited by Daniel Leab, 28–41. Urbana: University of Illinois Press, 1985.

Herlihy, Jim. *Peter Golden: The Voice of Ireland.* Cork City, Ire.: Cork Commemoration Committee, 1994.

Hirschberger, Gilad. "Collective Trauma and the Social Construction of Meaning." *Frontiers in Psychology* 9 (Aug. 2018), https://www.frontiersin.org/articles/10.3389/fpsyg.2018.01441/full.

Hobsbawm, Eric. *The Age of Capital, 1848–1875.* New York: Vintage, 1996.

Hobsbawm, Eric. *The Age of Empire, 1875–1914.* New York: Vintage, 1989.

Hobsbawm, Eric. *Workers: Worlds of Labor.* New York: Pantheon, 1984.

Horton, Scott. "Voltaire Defines Patriotism." *Harper's Magazine,* Oct. 10, 2009.

Hudelson, Richard. "Jack Carney and the *Truth* in Duluth." *Saothar* 19 (1994): 129–39.

Jacobson, Matthew Frye. *Special Sorrows: The Diasporic Imagination of Irish, Polish and Jewish Immigrants in the United States.* Cambridge, MA: Harvard University Press, 1995.

Jacobson, Matthew Frye. *Whiteness of a Different Color: European Immigrants and the Alchemy of Race.* Cambridge, MA: Harvard University Press, 1999.

Kazin, Michael. *The Populist Persuasion: An American History*. Rev. ed. Ithaca, NY: Cornell University Press, 1998.
Kelleher, John. *Selected Writings of John V. Kelleher on Ireland and Irish America*. Edited by Charles Fanning. Carbondale: Southern Illinois University Press, 2002.
Kennedy, Liam. *Unhappy Land*. Dublin: Irish Academic Press, 2016.
Kennedy, Liam, Paul S. Ell, E. M. Crawford, and L. A. Clarkson, eds. *Mapping the Great Irish Famine: An Atlas of the Famine Years* Dublin: Four Courts, 2000.
Kenny, Kevin. "Diaspora and Comparison: The Irish as a Case Study." *Journal of American History* 90 (June 2003): 134–62.
Kiberd, Declan. *Inventing Ireland: The Literature of the Modern Nation*. Cambridge, MA: Harvard University Press, 1995.
Kinealy, Christine. *This Great Calamity: The Irish Famine, 1845–1852*. Dublin: Gill and Macmillan, 1994.
Klehr, Harvey, John Haynes, and Fridrikh Igorevich Firsov, eds. *The Secret World of American Communism*. New Haven, CT: Yale University Press, 1995.
Knirck, Jason. *Afterimage of the Revolution: Cumann na nGaedheal and Irish Politics, 1922–1932*. Madison: University of Wisconsin Press, 2021.
Knirck, Jason. "The Dominion of Ireland: The Anglo-Irish Treaty in an Imperial Context." *Éire-Ireland* 42 (Spring–Summer 2007): 229–55.
Knirck, Jason. *Imagining Ireland's Independence: The Debate over the Anglo-Irish Treaty of 1921*. Lanham, MD: Rowman and Littlefield, 2006.
Kraditor, Aileeen. *The Radical Persuasion: Aspects of the Intellectual History and the Historiography of Three American Radical Organizations*. Baton Rouge: Louisiana State University Press, 1981.
Kramer, Paul. "Emigrants, Exceptionalism, and Anglo-Saxons: Race and Rule between the British and United States Empires, 1880–1910." *Journal of American History* 88 (Mar. 2002): 1315–53.
Krause, David. "Connolly and Pearse: The Triumph of Failure?," *New Hibernia Review* 3 (Winter 1997: 47–61.
Krause, David. "*The Plough and the Stars*: Socialism (1913) and Nationalism (1916)." *New Hibernia Review* 1 (Winter 1997): 10–34.
Kuzni, Hari. "Socialists on the Knife-Edge." *New York Review of Books*, Aug. 18, 2022, 46–49.
Lansing, Michael. *Insurgent Democracy: The Nonpartisan League in North American Politics*. Chicago: University of Chicago Press, 2015.
Larkin, Emmet. "The Devotional Revolution in Ireland, 1850–1875." *American Historical Review* 77 (June 1972): 642–60.
Larkin, Emmet. *James Larkin: Irish Labor Leader, 1876–1947*. Cambridge, MA: MIT Press, 1965.
Lasch, Christopher. *The New Radicalism in America, 1889–1963: The Intellectual as a Social Type*. New York: Knopf, 1965.
Lasch, Christopher. *The Revolt of the Elites and the Betrayal of Democracy*. New York; W. W. Norton, 1995.

Lasch, Christopher. *The True and Only Heaven: Progress and Its Critics*. New York: W. W. Norton, 1991.

Laurie, Bruce. *Artisans into Workers: Labor in Nineteenth Century America*. New York: Noonday, 1989.

Lause, Mark. *Free Labor: The Civil War and the Making of an American Working Class*. Urbana: University of Illinois Press, 2015.

Lears, Jackson. *No Place of Grace: Antimodernism and the Transformation of American Culture, 1880–1920*. New York: Pantheon, 1981.

Leary, William. "Woodrow Wilson, Irish Americans and the Election of 1916." *Journal of American History* 54 (June 1967): 57–72.

Lee, J. J. *Ireland, 1912–1985: Politics and Society*. Cambridge: Cambridge University Press, 1990.

Leeson, D. M. "British Conspiracy Theories and the Irish War of Independence." *Éire-Ireland*. 56 (Spring–Summer 2021): 176–208.

Leonard, Thomas. *Illiberal Reformers: Race, Eugenics, and American Economics in the Progressive Era*. Princeton, NJ: Princeton University Press, 2016.

Lichtenstein, Nelson, and Howell John Harris, eds. *Industrial Democracy in America: The Ambiguous Promise*. Cambridge: Cambridge University Press, 1993.

Link, Arthur, ed. *The Papers of Woodrow Wilson*. 68 vols. Princeton, NJ: Princeton University Press, 1966–83.

Lukas, J. Anthony. *Big Trouble: A Murder in a Small Western Town Sets Off a Struggle for the Soul of America*. New York: Simon and Schuster, 2007.

MacDonagh, Oliver. "The Irish Famine Emigration to the United States." *Perspectives in American History* 10 (1976): 357–446.

Manning, Julie. *Frank P. Walsh and the Irish Question*. Washington, DC: Georgetown University Press, 1989.

Mannion, Patrick, and Fearghal McGarry, eds. *The Irish Revolution: A Global History*. New York: New York University Press, 2022.

Mansergh, Nicholas. *The Irish Question, 1840–1921*. Toronto: University of Toronto Press, 1975.

Marx, Leo. *The Machine in the Garden: Technology and the Pastoral Ideal in America*. New York: Oxford University Press, 1964.

McCartin, Joseph. *Labor's Great War: The Struggle for Industrial Democracy and the Origins of Modern American Labor Relations, 1912–1921*. Chapel Hill: University of North Carolina Press, 1997.

McCartin, Joseph. "Working-Class Catholicism: A Call for a New Investigation, Dialogue, and Reappraisal." *Labor* 4 (2007): 99–110.

McDonald, Verlaine. *Red Corner: The Rise and Fall of Communism in Northeastern Montana*. Helena: Montana Historical Society Press, 2010.

McGahern, John. *Amongst Women*. London: Penguin, 1991.

McKillen, Elizabeth. "Divided Loyalties: Irish American Women Labor Leaders and the Irish Revolution." *Éire-Ireland* 51 (Fall/Winter 2016): 165–88.

McKillen, Elizabeth. "Ethnicity, Class, and Wilsonian Internationalism Reconsidered: The Mexican-American and Irish-American Immigrant Left and U.S. Foreign Relations, 1914–1922." *Diplomatic History* 25 (Fall 2001): 576–80.

McKillen, Elizabeth. "The Irish Sinn Féin Movement and Radical Labor and Feminist Dissent in America, 1916–1921." *Labor* 60 (Sept. 2019): 11–37.

Miller, Kerby. *Emigrants and Exiles: Ireland and the Irish Exodus to North America*. New York: Oxford University Press, 1985.

Miller, Kerby. "Emigration as Exile: Cultural Hegemony in Post-Famine Ireland." In *Ireland and Irish America: Culture, Class, and Transatlantic Migration*, 79–99. Dublin: Field Day, 2008.

Montgomery, David. *Beyond Equality: Labor and the Radical Republicans*. New York: Alfred Knopf, 1967.

Montgomery, David. *Citizen Worker: The Experience of Workers in the U.S. with Democracy and the Free Market during the 19th Century*. Cambridge: Cambridge University Press, 1993.

Montgomery, David. *Fall of the House of Labor*. Cambridge: Cambridge University Press, 1987.

Montgomery, David. *Workers' Control in America*. Cambridge: Cambridge University Press, 1979.

Mulder, John. *Woodrow Wilson: The Years of Preparation*. Princeton, NJ: Princeton University Press, 1978.

Nelson, Bruce. "Class, Race and Democracy in the CIO: The 'New' Labor History Meets the 'Wages of Whiteness.'" *International Review of Social History* 41 (1996): 351–74.

Nelson, Bruce. *Irish Nationalists and the Making of the Irish Race*. Princeton, NJ: Princeton University Press, 2013.

Nevin, Donal, ed. *James Larkin: Lion of the Fold*. Dublin: Gill and Macmillan, 1998.

Newsinger, John. *Rebel City: Larkin, Connolly and the Dublin Labour Movement*. London: Merlin, 2004.

O'Connor, Emmet. *Reds and the Green: Ireland, Russia and the Communist Internationals, 1919–1943*. Dublin: University College Dublin, 2004.

O'Connor, Emmet. *James Larkin*. Cork City, Ire.: Cork University Press, 2003.

O'Connor, Frank. *An Only Child*. London: Macmillan, 1961.

O'Faolain, Sean. *King of the Beggars: A Life of Daniel O'Connell*. New York: Viking, 1938.

O'Faolain, Sean. *The Story of the Irish Race*. New York: Random House, 1983.

Ó Gráda, Cormac. "Fenianism and Socialism: The Career of Joseph Patrick McDonnell." *Saothar* 1 (May Day 1975): 31–41.

O'Riordan, Manus. "Mike Quill—Kerry Founder of the TWU of America." Address to the Ancient Order of Hibernians, Killarney, Oct. 11, 2002, aoh61.com.

Orsi, Robert. *History and Presence*. Cambridge, MA: Harvard University Press, 2016.

Orsi, Robert. "U.S. Catholics between Memory and Modernity." In *Catholics in the American Century: Recasting Narratives of U.S. History*. Edited by R. Scott Appleby and Kathleen Cummings, 11–43. Ithaca, NY: Cornell University Press, 2012.

Perlman, Selig. *A History of Trade Unionism in the United States*. New York: Macmillan, 1922.

Perlman, Selig. *A Theory of the Labor Movement*. New York: Macmillan, 1928.

Polanyi, Karl. "Aristotle Discovers the Economy." In *Trade and Market in the Early Empires*. Edited by Karl Polanyi, Conrad Arensberg, and Harry Pearson, 64–96. Glencoe, IL: Free Press, 1957.

Polanyi, Karl. "The Economy as Instituted Process." In *Trade and Market in the Early Empires*. Edited by Karl Polanyi, Conrad Arensberg, and Harry Pearson, 243–306. Glencoe, IL: Free Press, 1957.

Polanyi, Karl. *The Great Transformation: The Political and Economic Origins of Our Time*. Boston: Beacon, 2001.

Quill, Shirley. *Mike Quill—Himself*. New York: Devin-Adair, 1985.

Rachleff, Peter. "Two Decades of the 'New' Labor History." *American Quarterly* 41, no. 1 (Mar. 1989): 184–89.

Reeve, C., and A. B. *James Connolly in the United States*. Atlantic Highlands, NJ: Humanities, 1978.

Rodgers, Daniel. *Atlantic Crossing: Social Politics in a Progressive Age*. Cambridge, MA: Harvard University Press, 1996.

Rosenzweig, Roy. *Eight Hours for What We Will: Workers and Leisure in an Industrial City, 1870–1921*. Cambridge: Cambridge University Press, 1983.

Rowland, Thomas. "Irish-American Catholics and the Quest for Respectability in the Coming of the Great War." *Journal of American Ethnic History* 15 (Winter 1996): 3–31.

Rumpf, Erhard, and A. C. Hepburn. *Nationalism and Socialism in Twentieth Century Ireland*. New York: Harper and Row, 1977.

Ryan, Desmond. *James Connolly, His Life and Work*. London: Labour Publishing, 1924.

Ryan, John A., and Joseph Husslein, eds., *The Church and Labor*. New York: Macmillan, 1924.

Salvatore, Nick. *Eugene V. Debs: Citizen and Socialist*. Urbana: University of Illinois Press, 1982.

Schmuhl, Robert. *Ireland's Exiled Children: America and the Easter Rising*. New York: Oxford University Press, 2013.

Shakespeare, William. *The Tempest* (1610–11). New York: Folger Shakespeare Library, 1923.

Solomon, Barbara. *Ancestors and Immigrants: A Changing New England Tradition*. Chicago: University of Chicago Press, 1972.

Spragens, Thomas. *Capitalism and Democracy: Prosperity, Justice, and the Good Society*. Notre Dame, IN: University of Notre Dame Press, 2021.

Stromquist, Shelton. *Re-inventing "the People": The Progressive Movement, the Class Problem, and the Origins of Modern Liberalism*. Urbana: University of Illinois Press, 2006.

Stubbs, Tara. *American Literature and Irish Culture, 1910–1955*. Manchester, UK: Manchester University Press, 2017.

Takaki, Ronald. "The Tempest in the Wilderness: The Racialization of Savagery."

In *A Different Mirror: A History of Multicultural America*, 24–45. Boston: Little, Brown, 1993.
Tansil, Charles. *America and the Fight for Irish Freedom*. New York: Devin-Adair, 1957.
Tate, Alan. "Remarks on Southern Religion." In *I'll Take My Stand: The South and the Agrarian Tradition*. Edited by Twelve Southerners, 155–75. New York: Harper, [1930] 1962.
Thompson, Dorothy. *The Chartists*. New York: Pantheon, 1984.
Thompson, Dorothy. *Outsiders: Class, Gender and Nation*. London: Verso, 1993.
Thompson, Dorothy, ed. *The Essential E. P. Thompson*. New York: New Press, 2001.
Thompson, E. P. *The Making of the English Working Class*. New York: Vintage, 1966.
Thompson, E. P. "Politics and Culture." In *The Essential E. P. Thompson*, 3–184. Edited by Dorothy Thompson. New York: Free Press, 2006.
Thompson, E. P. "Time, Work-Discipline, and Industrial Capitalism." *Past and Present* 38 (1967): 56–97.
Tillinghast, Richard. *Finding Ireland: A Poet's Exploration of Irish Literature and Culture*. Notre Dame, IN: University of Notre Dame Press, 2008.
Townend, Paul. *The Road to Home Rule: Anti-imperialism and the Irish National Movement*. Madison: University of Wisconsin Press, 2016.
Turner, James. *Language, Religion, Knowledge: Past and Present*. Notre Dame, IN: University of Notre Dame Press, 2003.
Twelve Southerners. *I'll Take My Stand*. New York: Harper, [1930] 1962.
Van Onselen, Charles. *The Cowboy Capitalist: John Hays Hammond, the American West, and the Jameson Raid in South Africa*. Charlottesville: University of Virginia Press, 2018.
Vindex, Carl. "Radical Rule in Montana." *Montana Magazine of Western History* 18 (Winter 1968): 2–18.
Vought, Hans. "Division and Reunion: Woodrow Wilson, Immigration, and the Myth of American Unity." *Journal of American Ethnic History* 13 (Spring 1994): 24–50.
Ward, Leo. *All over God's Irish Heaven*. Chicago: Henry Regnery, 1964.
Warren, Robert Penn. *The Legacy of the Civil War: Meditations on the Centennial*. New York: Random House, 1961.
Waugh, Evelyn. "The American Epoch in the Catholic Church." *Life*, Sept. 19, 1949.
Whelan, Bernadette. "The Wilson Administration and the 1916 Rising." In *The Impact of the 1916 Rising: Among the Nations*. Edited by Ruan O'Donnell. Dublin: Irish Academic Press, 2008.
Wiebe, Robert. *The Search for Order, 1877–1920*. New York: Hill and Wang, 1967.
Williams, Michael. *American Catholics in the War*. New York: Macmillan, 1921.
Williams, Raymond. *Culture and Society, 1780–1950*. New York: Columbia University Press, 1983.
Williams, Raymond. *Keywords: A Vocabulary of Culture and Society*. New York: Oxford University Press, 2015.

Wolfe, Bertram. *Strange Communists I Have Known*. New York: Stein and Day, 1982.
Woodward, C. Vann. *The Origins of the New South, 1877–1913*. Baton Rouge: Louisiana State University Press, 1951.
Yeats, W. B., ed. *Fairy and Folk Tales of Ireland*. New York: Macmillan, [1892] 1983.
Zieger, Robert. *The CIO, 1935–1955*. Chapel Hill: University of North Carolina Press, 1995.
Zipser, Arthur. *Working-Class Giant: The Life of William Z. Foster*. New York: International, 1981.
Zumoff, Jacob. *The Communist International and U.S. Communism*. New York: Haymarket, 2015.

Index

Page references in *italics* refer to illustrations.

abolitionists, use of gospel, 65
absence, God's: American, 112; among American socialists, 91and God's presence, 17, 18, 35, 41, 46–47, 273n38; in modernity, 17, 18, 35; Protestant, 20, 38, 46, 49, 89, 92, 112
Agrarians (Southern writers group), 253–54
Ahlstrom, Sydney: anti-Catholicism thesis, 17, 47, 63–64, 110, 253, 259, 268; on Josiah Strong, 66
Akenson, Donald Harmon, 39
Ambrosius, Lloyd, 213
American Commission on Conditions in Ireland (1921): on British atrocities, 210; Walsh's service with, 299n81
American Federation of Labor (AFL), 126, 169; Catholic majority in, 91
American Institute of Christian Sociology, 73
American Socialist Party, Irish Left in, 161
Anaconda Copper Mining Company (ACM): agreement with BMU, 120–21, 127–28, 131; arming of miners, 165; hiring preferences, 121, 128; Irish Catholic management of, 120, 131–32; Neversweat Mine (Butte), 164; sham nationalists of, 124–25; union employees, 287n31. *See also* Butte Miners' Union
Ancient Order of Hibernians (AOH), 124, 127, 140; following Easter Rising, 137
Anderson, Benedict, 194; on national communities, 161; residence in Ireland, 295n11
Anglo-Americans: antitraditional, 13; beliefs and culture of, 1, 3, 12, 30; celebration of money, 110; collective beliefs of, 9; foundational myths of, 8; historical success of, 21; Irish threat to, 236; liberal reformers, 62–64; on Marxist Ireland, 175; meddlesomeness of, 38; outbred, 276n37; separation of politics and economy, 116; on social justice, 111; socioeconomic mobility of, 42; spiritual poverty of, 194; TWU-CIO opponents of, 264; view of Enlightenment, 199; in World War I, 217–18. *See also* Protestants; race patriots; Yankees
the Anglo-Irish: Lady Gregory on, 178; Protestant Ascendancy of, 183–84
Anglophobia, Irish, 86, 90, 255; hegemonic, 274n4; in Irish Catholic culture, 22; kinship with English in, 37; in nationalism, 102

Anglo-Saxons: Irish view of, 22, 238; race patriotism of, 213–14, 218, 231; sacrifice to immigrants, 74; supremacists, 213; Woodrow Wilson's belief in, 213–14

anti-Catholicism, 1–2, 17–18, 47; following World War I, 230; free labor and, 65; individualism in, 110; Lippmann's, 78–81; nativism and, 3; racialized, 187; weakening of, 259

anticolonialism, Irish, 115, 180; Irish nationalism and, 167, 191, 193

anti-imperialism, Bolshevik, 152

anti-imperialism, Irish, 134, 156–57, 190, 214–15; in Anglo-American century, 215; assault on all imperialism, 215; of ILPTUC, 159; of Irish Republic, 234–35; of Irish Workers' Republic, 194

antimodernism, American, 178, 209, 249

antimodernism, Irish, 184–85, 260; erraticism of, 13; Revival, 182

antimodernists, on Irish Free State, 250

antisocialism, Catholic, 89–91, 117

The Appeal to Reason (nativist journal), 77

ard ríthe (high kings), corporate owners as, 124

Arensberg, Conrad, 8, 35, 38, 57, 307n32; on land, 113; study of Irish peasants, 13–14, 15, 267

Aristotle, 14

Asquith, Herbert, 264; on English imperialism, 21

assimilation, Irish American: versus adaptation, 19–20; as colonization, 182; and Free State failures, 253; possibility of, 39; power of, 30; Wilson on, 215

Austro-Hungarian Empire, immigrants from, 137

authors, Irish American, 276n51

The Awful Disclosures of Maria Monk, 29, 48

Bagenal, Philip, 160

Baker, Ray Stannard: on mandate system, 233; work with Wilson, 225, 226, 229–30

Balfour, Arthur, 177, 182; on Anglicized Ireland, 178, 187

"Ballaghaslane Beara," letter to *The Irish World*, 55

Barrett, James: *The Irish Way*, 133, 197; on labor reform, 144

Behan, Brendan, 161

Bellamy, Edward: on Woodrow Wilson, 213

Bemis, Edward, 76–77; on immigration restriction, 70–73

Berlin, Ira, 85, 98, 99, 113

Berne labor conference (1919), Irish labor radicals at, 224

The Birth of a Nation (film), cultural background of, 213

bishops, American: Program of Reconstruction, 194–97, 199–200, 264

Black and Tans, 233

Block, Fred, 15

Boer War, Hammond's role in, 205

Bolshevism: attraction for alienated Americans, 175; Easter Rising and, 149–51; recognition of Irish Republic, 212, 216; relationship with the Irish, 152, 172–73, 221–22, 232; Sinn Féin and, 239–40, 242; in Versailles Peace Talks, 225; Woodrow Wilson's response to, 220

Boston Daily Advertiser, on working class, 60

bourgeoisie, Irish: economic interests of, 55, 56; in Irish Free State, 246. *See also* shoneens

Bourne, Randolph, 79

Boyce, Ed, 205, 259, 285nn18,20; advocacy of militias, 126–27; on capital/labor relations, 125–26; early life of, 123; enemies of, 127; on Irish Republic, 232; leadership of WFM, 123, 126, 127, 209; and Marcus Daly, 125, 168; nationalism of, 124; pushing of political limits, 268; radicalism of, 286n26; retirement of, 132; on sham nationalists, 124–25; silver fortune of, 287n31; tour of mines, 78

Brandeis, Lewis, 299n85

Breen, Dan: on Irish Americans, 249; *My Fight for Irish Freedom*, 248

Bridget (Irish stereotype), 54

Brody, David, 85; on working class diversity, 98
Brossat, Alain: *Revolutionary Yiddishland*, 11
Bryant, Louise, 162
Bryce, Viscount James: on Irish working class, 108
Buckley, Tim and Ansty, 93–94, 263, 269
Bunyan, John, 100
Burke, Edmund: on love of country, 6
Burke, M. J.: BMU presidency, 127
Burke, Thomas: *Lectures on Faith and Fatherland*, 28
Burnidge, Cara Lea, 213
Butte (Montana): alien registry list of, 138–39; antiwar demonstration in, 138–40; copper strike (1917), 141–44; erratic Irish of, 137; Finnish socialists of, 137, 138–39, 140; following Easter Rising, 137; ICA in, 142; Irish government of, 119–20; Irish Left of, 160; Miners' Union Day, 121–22, 128, 141; Neversweat Mine, 164; Pearse-Connolly Irish Independence Club, 137–38; St. Patrick's Day parade, 132; working-class character of, 10, 11
Butte Daily Bulletin, 164; coverage of Ireland, 166, 293n58; Dunne's editorship of, 140, 164, 165; radicalism of, 165–66
Butte Independent (newspaper), 128–30, 132
Butte Miners' Union (BMU), 168, 222, 262; anti-strike position, 140; CIO and, 285n13, 308n45; factionalism in, 119; Hiberno-centricism of, 119–20, 264; insurgents within, 139–40; insurgent violence against, 128–29, *129*, 132; Irish nationalism of, 121–23, 128; IWW and, 128; prudential unionism of, 120; relationship with Anaconda Company, 120–21, 127–28, 131; self-destruction of, 120, 128; theft of money from, 128, 129; Union Hall dynamiting (1914), 128, *129*, 131, 138; WFM and, 123, 127
Butte "Rising" (1917), 138–40, 226; and Easter Rising, 145. *See also* copper strike; Speculator Mine (Butte, Montana), mining disaster

Butte Socialist (newspaper), 132

Caliban (*The Tempest*), imperialistic aspects of, 54
Caliban, Patsy (American labor figure), 37, 54–55, 60, 165, 175; blood traditions of, 63; and cultural divergence, 56; as hooligan, 62; as liar, 103; place in labor pool, 61, 106; in *Ulysses*, 54, 308n57. *See also* labor; working class, Irish Catholic
Calvinism, influence on capitalism, 93
capitalism: acquisition in, 92; antisocial, 41; of British Empire, 151; Calvinist diaspora and, 93; Catholic beliefs affecting, 88; collectivism versus, 258; of Cromwellian settlement, 195; as economic discontentment, 181; English working class and, 105; failure of, 260; following the Reformation, 196, 197, 199–200, 268; imperialism and, 44, 124; industrial ideologies of, 95, 107; Irish erraticism and, 11, 13, 44; during Irish Famine, 258; Irish reinforcement of, 108; Jewish radicals on, 125; Leo XIII's encyclical on, 18–19; maximum extent of, 259–60; moral principles of, 4, 260, 261, 268; Protestant values in, 43, 185, 196, 282n15; socialist challenge to, 5; time discipline in, 107; translation of working class into, 96; vices following, 178; working-class resistance to, 86, 255. *See also* economies, market; laissez faire
capitalism, American: domestication of, 268; Hannan on, 251; IPL challenge to, 193; Irish Catholic challenge to, 4, 38–44, 227, 255–56, 268; Irish labor for, 252; master-slave relationship in, 58–69; post-Civil War, 59; in Protestant nation-state, 198; "workers' interregnum" and, 269
Carbery, Ethna, 182
Carney, Jack, 150; association with W. F. Dunne, 171; in Communist Labor Party, 170; in Duluth, 171; editorship of *The Truth*, 170–72; "Memory of

Carney, Jack (*continued*)
the Irish Rebellion," 171–72; jailing of, 171; Larkin and, 170; return to Ireland, 294n74; visits to Butte, 294n75

Catholic Church, Roman: effect on self-reliance, 187; in Irish Free State, 246; nationalism of, 89, 101–2, 109; semifeudalism of, 108; threat to individual freedom, 66. *See also* Leo XIII, Pope: *Rerum Novarum*

Catholicism: affecting capitalist beliefs, 88, 187; Anglo-American prejudice concerning, 8; anti-economic, 187; anti-materialism of, 82, 197; as anti-socialist, 89–91, 117; charges of illiteracy in, 75; cultural identity under, 27–28; the dead in, 17; effect on self-sufficiency, 80; as enchantment, 102; under English colonialism, 27; English converts to, 110; global evangelization of, 55; hierarchy of, 48; as inauthentic, 8, 47; inward/outwardness of, 47; labor historians on, 87; labor's resistance to, 88; mixing with politics, 150; opposition to laissez faire, 196; *qua* slavery, 65; race patriots on, 34–35, 75; real presence in, 16–17, 18, 87; saving of Irish Catholic from, 84; Social Gospel reformers on, 65; threat from, 63, 65, 66. *See also* Irish Catholics

Catholic Welfare Council (CWC): Ryan's work in, 196. *See also* National Catholic War Council

Celticism, 22, 115–16, 137, 160; American, 182; Connolly on, 264; otherwordliness of, 194; Renaissance of, 180–81; xenophobic, 178

Celts: communist, 115–16, 137; Yankee characterization of, 32, 33. *See also* communism, Celtic; Gaels

Charles II (king of England), 261

Chartist Movement, 89; Irish Catholics in, 282n10, 283n33

Chesterton, G. K.: on Catholic traditionalism, 17, 78; on apostate papists, 110

Chicago Federation of Labor, 254, 298n72

children, Irish Catholic, 35

Christian Brothers, parochial schools of, 182

Christian Socialism, 73, 77

Churchill, Winston: on Irish Republicanism, 239, 305n80

civil rights, Black, 208–9

Civil War, American: American-English reconciliation following, 214; cultural divergence following, 58–59; Irish Famine and, 268; scarcity following, 118; social order following, 59

Civil War, Irish: following creation of *Saor Stát*, 243, 245; *gombeen* men of, 249; republican/nationalist aspects of, 263; social/class aspect of, 245–46

Clan na Gael, 137, 240, 262; on Free State Treaty, 249, 250; nationalism of, 170; radicalism of, 124; on US wartime intervention, 219

clannishness, Irish, 32, 33; and American opportunity, 189; democratic organization of, 264; Woodrow Wilson on, 216, 224; xenophobic, 35

Clár Oibre Poblacánaighe. See "Democratic Programme of Dáil Éireann" (1919)

class consciousness: Catholicism in, 90; community in, 36; of English working class, 95–96; ethnic cultures of, 86

class warfare, 96, 113; in England, 152; in Irish literature, 164; Lehane on, 137; union solutions to, 126

clock time, 263; American workers', 107–8; Synge on, 107–8. *See also* timekeeping

coal stokers, Irish: strike (1920), 194

Cobb, Frank, 221

Coeur d'Alenes, strike (1892), 126

Cohen, Lizabeth: *Making a New Deal*, 254, 260, 261, 262

Cohen, Robin: *Global Diasporas*, 25–26

collectivism: in American politics, 267; capitalism versus, 258; economic-political definition of, 258–59; goodness of heart as, 258; of Irish Left, 264

Colley, Linda, 29
Collins, Michael, 179, 198, 249
colonialism: break from, 22–23; following World War I, 233; mandate system, 233; resistance to law and, 38; working classes under, 122
colonialism, British, 23–28, 30, 53; atrocities of, 219, 252; Irish American victims of, 212; Irish bourgeoisie in, 55; Irish resistance to, 24; Lenin on, 134; modernity in, 27; National School system, 27; suppression of language, 26–27; translation of Ireland, 26–28, 55, 96; turn to Catholicism under, 27; as ventriloquism for Ireland, 177. See also imperialism, British
Colum, Padraic: interview with Joyce, 247–48
Commissariat of Nationalities, Russian: on Sinn Féin, 237
Commission on Industrial Relations (CIR), US: Commons's service on, 206–7, 209; final report, 198, 209; Hammond's appearance before, 205–6, 299n85; minority report of, 206–7, 209; Walsh Plan of, 201–2, 205; Walsh's appointment to, 201; witnesses before, 205
Commons, John Rogers, 70, 73–76; anti-Catholicism of, 88; belief in capitalism, 207; Calvinism of, 73, 74; CIR service, 206–7, 209; on Irish Catholics, 76; nativism of, 207; in Pittsburgh Survey, 73–74; on race, 74–75, 207–8; on self-government, 208; theory of capitalism, 206; upbringing of, 73; on wage-conscious labor, 118; Walsh Plan disagreements, 206–9
commonwealth, Irish conception of, 47
communalism, Irish, 116; versus American individualism, 39; Celtic, 137, 166; communism and, 172; Irish nationalism and, 148; socialism and, 90, 91; Woodrow Wilson on, 216
communism, Celtic, 115–16, 137, 239, 264; among Irish Americans, 160, 163, 170; Irish version of, 163; transnational, 226. See also Celts

communism, international: nationalism and, 291n26
communism, Irish, 23, 163; labor and, 115–16
Communist International (Comintern): Irish nationalism and, 170; "Reports of the Fourth Communist International," 225; W. F. Dunne and, 169–70
Communist International, Third: on aid to Ireland, 152
Communist Labor Party (CLP), 170
Communist Party of the United States (CPUSA): alliance with TWU, 262; Irish spokesmen of, 174–75
Communists, Americans: dilettantes, 164
communities, national, 22, 161. See also neighborhoods
Congress of Industrial Organizations (CIO): Catholicism of, 265–66; culture of unity, 261, 264, 265; erraticism of, 267; on racial tolerance, 307n36; rebuke to Butte Miners' Union, 308n45; structure of feeling in, 262
Congress of Nations, Irish representation at, 224
Connolly, James, 44, 46, 143, 155, 199; address to Irish Citizen Army, 245; American experiences, 160; American readership of, 124; on arming strikers, 165; at Butte, 130; on capitalism, 133, 195, 231; Catholicism of, 150, 290n10; on Catholic rights and duties, 90; Celticism and, 163, 264; on collectivism, 264; on communalism, 115–16, 122; on Conscription Bill, 156; on cooperative commonwealths, 196; on democracy, 196; during Easter Rising, 133, 136; on English imperialism, 151; "Erin's Hope," 160; execution of, 137, 151, 263; "heirs of," 264; internationalism of, 191; Irish Citizen Army of, 150, 159 165; Irish Marxism of, 163; on Irish race, 119, 179; on Irish Republic, 124, 133–34; on labor, 115–16; Lehane and, 137, 288n53; nationalism of, 133–35; nonserverable causes of, 162, 166, 237; protest against industry,

Connolly, James (*continued*) 179; radicalism of, 136, 148; as revolutionist, 163, 174; "The Re-conquest of Ireland," 195, 197; Union Square speech, *163*; WFM organizing by, 130; Workers' Republic of, 178, 198

Connolly, Nora: May Day address (1919), 172–73

Connolly, Sean: *On Every Tide,* 9

consciousness, false, 10

Conscription Bill (Great Britain), Irish response to, 156–57

"The Conspiracy against the British Empire" (Duke of Northumberland Fund publication), 240, 242

copper strike (Butte, Montana, 1917), 141–44; class/ethnicity in, 142; effect on war effort, 142–43; racial identities in, 144; violence in, 143. *See also* Butte "Rising"; Metal Mine Workers' Union

Corkery, Daniel, 49

Coughlin, Fr. Charles, 306n20

counterculture, American: Irish in, 110

Cowie, Jefferson: on "limits of American politics," 268; on New Deal, 260–61

criminality, Irish history and, 37–38

Cromwell, Oliver, 24, 47, 134; capitalist settlements of, 195; Puritan army of, 67, 68

Cronin, Sean, 115; on Connolly, 134, 148; on Democratic Programme, 158; on Sinn Féin and Bolshevism, 304n59

Cross, Eric: *The Tailor and Ansty,* 263, 269

Cullen, Archbishop Paul, 27

cultural divergence: from capitalism, 256, 269; following Civil War, 58–59; following Reformation, 17; historians' study of, 253; Irish Catholic/Protestant, 1–3, 10, 17–18, 56, 86, 92, 145; papist, 65

culture: common language for, 111–12; Eagleton's discussion of, 5–7; entrenched values of, 6; filtering of experience, 113; in identification of groups, 6; intellectual, 5; martyrdom for, 259; as medium of power, 6, 259; perceptions of reality in, 113; social reality of, 6; and spiritual development, 5–6; symbolic practices of, 6; unconscious, 8; untotalizable, 8

culture, Irish American: defiance in, 39–40; economics within, 49; estrangement from American culture, 28–29; individualism and, 43, 184, 189; otherness in, 7; persistence of, 101, 107; Protestant damage to, 83; real presence in, 87; semi-inchoate forms of, 8; transgenerational, 28; the trivial in, 39–40; of working class, 10. *See also* communalism, Irish; goodness of heart; worldview, Irish Catholic

culture, Irish Catholic, 5; composite, 11; dissent in, 253; erraticism in, 42, 49, 94; immigrant, 7; non-racial, 7–8; "untotalizable," 22

Cumann na mBan, on Free State Treaty, 249

Curren, Mary Doyle, 42; *The Parish and the Hill,* 40–41

Dáil Éireann (Irish Parliament), 157, 191, 242; approval of Free State treaty, 250; "Message to the Free Nationals of the World," 223–24; passing of "Democratic Programme," 158, 256; on Poor Laws, 158. *See also* "Democratic Programme of Dáil Éireann"; Sinn Féin

Daly, Marcus: Boyce and, 127, 131; sham nationalism of, 125; as shoneen, 125

Darnton, Robert, 80–81

Davis, John, 228

Davis, Thomas: on Irish language, 26–27

Dawson, Richard, 6

Deane, Seamus, 48, 247; on exile, 27; on Irish history, 23–24; *Strange Country,* 11

Debs, Eugene V.: on American working class, 97; illiberal liberalism of, 77–78; nativism of, 78; on Roman Catholic Church, 77–78

democracy: economic inequality and, 50; Irish sense of, 200; "mastery test" for, 79; personal traits for, 75

democracy, industrial: American, 198,

200; Brandeis's support for, 299n85; *Clár Oibre Poblacánaighe* on, 257; Hammond on, 205; Irish Left on, 199; labor/politics connection in, 208; labor's struggle for, 198–99; racial aspects of, 207–8; self-government and, 208; Walsh on, 202, 210
"Democratic Programme of Dáil Éireann" (1919), 202, 256–57, 261, 269, 291n33; American industrial democracy and, 200; as blueprint of the Irish Republic, 158; culture/tradition in, 256; Gaelic language of, 256; Irish-borne food in, 236; mining proposal of, 210; passage of, 158, 224, 256; poetic aspects of, 158, 257; on property, 257; Sinn Féin's adoption of, 198; Walsh Report and, 257–58; on working class, 256. See also *Dáil Éireann*
Dening, Greg, 8
determinism, zoological/racial, 7
de Tocqueville, Alexis: *Democracy in America*, 48; on the Irish, 47–48; on Puritans, 271n1
de Valera, Éamon, 231–32; American tour of, 179, 251; on emigration, 247; on empires, 234; in Irish Free State, 246; Lloyd George and, 233–35, 236, 304n68; on new Ireland, 179
Devotional Revolution, 28
Dillingham Commission, *Reports of the Immigration Commission* (1911), 34, 71
dissidence, Irish Catholic, 3, 4, 17–18; in American labor, 255; socio-class elements in, 255
Dixon, Thomas: *The Leopard's Spots*, 213
Dodd, William Edward, 231
Dorn, Jacob, 77
Drake, Richard, 218, 233
drift, societal, 79, 81; mastery and, 94, 106
Dubofsky, Melvyn, 201; on Walsh Plan, 202
Duffy, Eamon, 17
Duke of Northumberland Fund, Tory pamphlets of, 240
Duluth (Minnesota), Finnish-born residents of, 171, 294n71

Dunne, Edward, 227, 228
Dunne, Finley Peter, 42; Mr. Dooley stories, 40, 41, 48, 254
Dunne, William Francis, 139, 164–70; appearance of, 164; on arming strikers, 165; association with Carney, 171; on Butte copper strike, 141, 143–44, 289n66; Catholicism of, 164; communism of, 165, 170; on Con Kelley, 168; editorship of *Butte Daily Bulletin*, 140, 164, 165; erraticism of, 212; expulsion from Communist Party, 293n55; on farm-labor coalitions, 294n78; Hannan and, 251; on Irish communalism, 166; Irish nationalism of, 165–66; Irishness of, 164, 289n59; on Lenin, 293n55; *New York Call* on, 165, 212; pushing of political limits, 268; relationship with Comintern, 169–70; on shoneens, 169; and Stalin, 165; support for Irish republic, 212; during World War II, 293n55

Eagleton, Terry, 14; on cultural response to trauma, 25; *Culture*, 5–7; on culture and tradition, 256; on ideology, 44, 259; on Irish Catholic children, 35; on Irish moral economy, 260; on obligations, 7; on traditional societies, 15; on the unconscious, 8; on universalism, 11; on violation of norms, 38
Easter Rising (1916), 116, 119, 132–33; "alliance" with Germany, 212; American Revolution and, 156; anarchist propaganda for, 135; anti-imperialism of, 159; Bolshevism and, 149–51, 153, 172; and Butte Rising, 145; commemoration of, 171; effect on Irish Americans, 136; executions following, 137; impact on US, 228–29; long-term effects of, 149; Pearse-Connolly Club in, 142; Russian Revolution and, 150–51, 172–73; scholarly aspects of, 162; as socialist revolt, 162; trade unionists in, 159
ecology: cultural, 12; personality as, 12, 24, 28, 45
economics: formal and substantive, 158; versus politics, 49, 192–93;

economics (*continued*)
  separation from nationalism, 267; subordination of the social to, 266
economies, market: American, 57–58; autonomy of, 48; British, 158; emergence of, 13; ideological jurisdictions of, 46–47; laissez-faire, 50; laws governing, 50; versus nonmarket, 38; rise of, 57–58; self-regulating, 57; separation of the political from, 49; social ecology of, 14; social fairness for, 69. *See also* capitalism; laissez faire
economies, nonmarket, 15; as archaic, 41; communistic psychology of, 116; embedded in society, 94; Irish Catholics' separation from, 16; versus market economies, 38; New Deal and, 267; in post-Civil War era, 58; prior to Reformation, 199–200; social ties in, 41
economy, American: group psychology of, 118; Irish American culture and, 49; Irish erratics on, 89; Irish labor supply for, 55–56; market society of, 57–58; re-embedding in society, 198; scarcity-based, 118–19; separation from politics, 116
Elshtain, Jean Bethke, 46–47, 48, 192; on modernity, 193
emancipation: from British imperialism, 62; Enlightenment on, 63
emancipation from slavery: American mythology of, 64; effect on Irish Catholics, 63; free labor following, 58–69
Emmons, David M.: *The Butte Irish*, 119
Engels, Friedrich, 15, 114; on Ireland, 152
English, Fr. James, 132, 287n40; on "gallant" Germany, 216
the English (*Sassenach*): as commercial people, 183; suppression of Irish soul, 180. *See also* working class, English
Enlightenment, Anglo-Americans view of, 199; on emancipation, 63
erraticism: economics of, 49, 191;

etymology of, 3; social ecology of, 20; in Weber's work, 92
erraticism, Irish Catholic, 296n31; in American working class, 256; Anglo-American unawareness of, 35; antimodernism of, 13; assimilation and, 20; capitalism and, 11, 13, 36, 44; on commodities, 112; culture of, 42, 49, 94; "distant past" in, 20; economics in, 49; and Free State failures, 253; as "ill-balanced refinement," 189; Irish identity and, 190; of Irish Left, 210; in Irish Literary Revival, 179; of neighborhoods, 41; of New Deal, 268; out of time and place, 178; outward expressions of, 38; skepticism of premodernity, 87; sociocultural recidivism of, 12; subordination of the economic to the social, 266; Woodrow Wilson and, 212
erratics, glacial (petrology), 2–3
erratics, Irish Catholic: on American economy, 89; attitude toward law, 37–38; belief in fair labor, 260–61; of Butte, 137; as cultural fifth columnists, 197; on economic inequality, 260; on labor supply, 56; on moral issues, 192; post-1870, 28; premodernist, 20, 56; resistance to fraud, 111, 114; social mobility and, 44; sorrowing ancestors of, 52; subversive, 39; as useful misfits, 175; use of history, 23; visitors to America, 46, 52; worldview of, 50
ethnicity: in Butte copper strike, 142; class consciousness and, 86; social class and, 4–5, 10, 11. *See also* Irishness
eugenics, 76; in immigration restriction, 70
exiles: the Irish as, 27, 37, 160, 212, 222, 247; voluntary, 37

fairness, detachment from governance, 50, 52
Famine, Irish, 24–25; and American Civil War, 268; American labor supply following, 56; British

response to, 25, 178, 236, 258; collective trauma following, 25–26, 28; creation of cultural immigrants, 28; English response to, 58; ethnic annihilation in, 26; exiles from, 37; immigration following, 239; lasting results of, 263; "paupers" following, 76; sharing in, 49
farmers, coalitions with industrial workers, 173–74, 294n78
Farrell, James: on Connolly, 150, 191; on post-Civil War years, 249
Faulkner, William, 254
Fenians, 62, 104, 124, 160; ignoring of clergy, 89; Marxist, 115
Finns: radical, 147; socialists, 137, 138–39, 140
Fischer, David Hackett: *Albion's Seed*, 9, 38; on folkways, 93; on time ways, 106
Fiske, John, 300n8
Fitzpatrick, John, 254, 298n72
folk beliefs, Irish: collection of, 253; persistence of, 108; in Yeats's work, 249
folkways, 93; culturally determinative, 38; persistence of, 109
Foner, Eric, 277n65, 279n16
Ford, Patrick, 55, 64
Foreign Relations of the United States (1918), 221
Foster, R. F., 167, 249; on Irish revolution, 246
Foster, William Z., 254; *Pages of a Worker's Life*, 161
Fourteenth Amendment, US, 208; opponents of, 209
Foxe, John: *Book of Martyrs*, 30, 73
Franco-Belgians, radical, 147
Franklin, Benjamin, 93; Poor Richard aphorisms, 92
Frederic, Harold: *The Damnation of Theron Ware*, 30–32, 35, 42, 71, 189; on the Irish race, 189–90
freedom, individual: Roman Catholic threat to, 66
Freeman, Joseph, 164
Freeman, Joshua, 263; on Fr. Rice, 266; *In Transit*, 262–64

Friel, Brian, 96; *Translations*, 26, 215
Fugitives (Southern writers group), 253

Gaddis, John Lewis, 24; *The Landscape of History*, 2; on use of metaphor, 11–12; on variables, 39
Gaelic American (newspaper), Revivalism of, 182
Gaelic Athletic Association, 182
Gaelic League, American, 182
Gaels: Engels on, 104; "Hebrews" and, 161; the Irish as new, 179; lost causes of, 180. *See also* Celts
Garrison, William Lloyd: on free labor, 60
Gellert, Hugo: "John Bull to the Irish Bourgeois," 167–68, *168*
Gerstle, Gary, 64, 79; on incorporation of immigrants, 83
Gibbons, Cardinal James, 78, 222, 223, 303n43
Gibbons, Luke, 2; on Irish anti-imperialism, 150, 151; on Irishness, 4, 190
Gilded Age, American: "Catholic question" in, 45–46; crises of, 65; moral purpose in, 45
Giovannetti, Arturo, 128
Gitlow, Benjamin: on Irish revolutionists, 162–64; recanting of communism, 292n46; on W.F. Dunne, 164, 165, 169
God: sovereignty of, 19, 273n44; trinitarian, 16
Godkin, E. L., 61–62, 65, 279n21; on eight-hour day, 279n19; on Irish American militants, 160; on Workingman's Party, 127
Gold, Michael: "Ode to Walt Whitman," 161
Golden, Peter, 179; in IPL, 193
gombeen men: Irish American, 124; support for Irish Free State treaty, 247; traitors to heritage, 125
Gompers, Samuel, 126, 127, 286n30
goodness of heart, Irish, 5, 11, 117, 133; in American working class, 255; collectivism as, 258; omnipresent gods of, 46; socialism as, 90, 116; in TWU/CIO, 264

Gore-Booth, Constance (Countess Markievicz), 204; on the English, 178–79
An Gorta Mór (Great Irish Hunger). See Famine, Irish
Gortloughera (Ireland), ancestors of, 263
Grace, Michael, 289n59
Gramsci, Antonio, 97; on ultramodernity, 106
Grant, Madison: *The Passing of the Great Race*, 34, 71
Grayson, Cary, 214, 221; on Irish Republic, 227; at Versailles Peace talks, 226, 227–28
Great Britain: Anglo-Saxon inheritance from, 8, 272n16; election of 1918, 157–58, 239, 257, 291n32; execution of Irish Republicans, 243; Poor Laws, 158. See also colonialism, British; imperialism, British; working class, English
Great Depression, 256
Great Red Scare: "Green" merger with, 237, 242, 243; nativism in, 231; of 1919, 225–29
Greaves, C. Desmond: on English colonialism, 237
Gregory, Brad, 268, 277n68; on distant past, 265; on market economies, 49; *Unintended Reformation*, 20, 282n15
Gregory, Lady Augusta: on Anglo-Irish, 178; on English-based stereotypes, 182; on the Gaels, 180; on Irish lost causes, 203; on religion and politics, 193; revivalism of, 204
Gutman, Herbert, 12, 48, 85, 106; on Gilded Age, 45–46; and modern divergence, 56; on oppositional working-class culture, 109; on pre-industrial societies, 13; regard for worker culture, 113; on working classes, 97, 99, 103

Hammond, John Hays, 124; appearance before CIR, 205–6, 299n85; capitalism/imperialism of, 205; on capitalist management, 206; on industrial democracy, 205; on industrial wages, 206; mining operations of, 205
Hannan, Fr. Michael, 306n20; Butte parishioners of, 250; diary of, 55–56, 250; on Free State treaty, 250–51; hatred of modernity, 251; leadership of Sarsfield Social Club, 249
Harriman, Job, 126
Harrington, Denis, 140
Harrington, Michael, 59
Healy, Tim, 24
Heaney, Seamus, 25, 263
Hell's Kitchen (New York City), 68
Henretta, James, 42–44, 59
Hercules Mine (Idaho), silver ore of, 286n31
Hillquit, Morris: New York mayoral candidacy of, 148
Hirschberger, Gilad, 25, 28
history: capitalist account of, 23; as interpretation of interpretation, 87; as past transformed, 8; revisionist, 23–24; variables in, 39
history, Irish: cartographic representation of, 21–23; colonial, 23, 24, 26; criminality and, 37–38; cultural, 38; disasters in, 100; in Irish Catholic behavior, 41; psychological, 38; role in Irish nationalism, 153; sorrowful, 8, 21–22, 24, 35; transformation of, 8, 13, 41. See also Ireland
Hoar, George, 30, 32, 253
Hobsbawm, Eric, 110; on labor market, 120–21
Hogan, Austin, 265
Home Rule, Irish, 62, 136, 137, 186
House, Edward, 221, 228
hunger strikes, Irish Catholic, 109, 171, 193–94

ICA. See Irish Citizen Army
identity, American: Irish Catholics and, 1–2; pluralism of, 83
identity, Irish Catholic: community in, 36, 39, 44; effect of colonialism on, 28; erraticism in, 190; hybridized, 7; interdependent variables of, 45; rising from community, 114;

transgenerational collective, 28. *See also* Irishness

Ignatius of Loyola, *Spiritual Exercises of*, 80

I'll Take My Stand: The South and the Agrarian Tradition (Agrarian essays), 254

immigrants: Asian, 70; from Austro-Hungarian Empire, 137; citizenship rights of, 83; desirable, 71; effect on democracy, 75; Finnish, 147, 160; Franco-Belgian, 147, 160; German, 215; incorporation into society, 83; Italian, 64; Jewish, 25, 147, 160, 162; literacy tests for, 209; motives of, 55; new, 70–71, 75; from preindustrial cultures, 12; radical, 147, 160, 162, 231; social mobility of, 43; southern European, 70; translation into Americans, 215; transnationalist, 182; Ulster Protestant, 9

immigrants, Irish Catholic: assimilation of, 20; conflict with economic institutions, 15–16; as conservative, 192; cultural, 28; diasporic sensibilities of, 7, 28, 105, 106; hard labor by, 22; influence on later immigrants, 71; from Irish Free State, 247; Irish identity of, 188; letters home, 51; literacy rates, 71; numbers of, 64–65, 71, 108; post-Civil War, 58; of post-Famine generation, 14, 24, 28; reduction of Irish population, 263; remittances to Ireland, 263; wakes, 108; as white colonials, 155–56. *See also* Irish Catholics, American

immigration: Dillingham Commission report on, 34; as European "safety valve," 73; following Irish Famine, 239; in "old labor history," 86; quotas for, 71–72; racial bias in, 70–71, 74–75; restriction of, 70–75, 207, 209, 250; Social Gospel Reform movement on, 67; threats from, 66

Immigration Restriction League, 74

"An Imperial Danger: The Sinn Fein Menace" (Unionist pamphlet, 1919), 239

imperialism: Anglo-American, 215; capitalism and, 44, 124; lawfulness and, 38; Reformation influence on, 200; in World War I, 233

imperialism, American: in Caribbean, 252

imperialism, British: break from, 51; capitalism and, 151; following world War I, 249; Irish threat to, 135, 234–35, 242; Irish under, 5, 6, 23, 24, 62; piratical, 237; in South Africa, 124; in *The Tempest*, 54; in *Ulysses*, 54. *See also* colonialism, British

individualism, American: anti-Catholicism in, 110; versus Irish Catholic communalism, 39; Irish Catholic culture and, 43, 184, 189; Irish Catholic view of, 114

individualism, Protestant, 196

industrialism: class divide in, 202, 207; despotism in, 202; social world of, 96; time discipline in, 107

industrialization, American: market economy in, 57–58; post-Civil War response to, 59; of the South, 208

Industrial Revolution, class divide in, 202

industrial workers, coalitions with farmers, 173–74, 294n78

Industrial Workers of the World (IWW), 128, 141, 261; and BMU, 128; and Butte strike, 144; name of, 86; nativism of, 131; religious views of, 147–48

International Labour and Socialist Conference (Berne, Germany), ILPTUC delegates to, 159

International Union of Mine, Mill, and Smelter Workers, 141. *See also* Western Federation of Miners

International Working Man's Association (IWMA), Marxist, 45

Ireland: "actual people" of, 135, 137; Anglo-Irish Ascendancy class, 216; "Black '47," 28; British National Schools in, 27; as Catholic theocracy, 129; copper mines of, 55; as creative muse, 180, 204; as cultural

Ireland (*continued*)
dreamscape, 246; cultural versus political aspects, 177–78; de-Anglicization of, 178; English translation of, 26–28, 55, 96; ethnic cleansing of, 26, 123; as example for anticolonialists, 180; fantasists versus realists of, 192; Free, 51, 210; Gaelic principles of, 256–57; Home Rule for, 62, 136, 137, 186; imagined community of, 180; May Day celebration (1919), 172; as miniature America, 51; moral beauty of, 179; as "not-England," 23; opportunity in English distress, 216–17; partition of, 242, 243, 246; place names, 26, 27; reawakening of, 161, 178–80; rebellion of 1798, 100; rejection of British culture, 179; removal of capitalists from, 153; Revivalist, 178–81, 182; as *sacra insula*, 192; self-government for, 81, 154, 256; severing of Catholicism from, 116; socialism in, 90; socioeconomic justice for, 117; spirituality of, 179; as subject nation, 23, 40, 149; threat to British imperialism, 135, 234–35, 242; two-nation theory of, 185; under Versailles Treaty, 233. *See also* colonialism; history, Irish; Irish Free State; Irish Republic

the Irish: American intrusion on, 183; ancestral sorrows of, 8, 21–22, 35, 41, 117, 216, 235, 268–69; Anglophobia of, 22, 37, 86, 90, 102; Bolshevik relationship with, 152, 172–73, 221–22, 232; bourgeoisie, 55; under British imperialism, 5, 6; British propaganda on, 166; as British puppets, 177; civilization based on, 179; collective memory of, 113; as conquered people, 33; disaffected working classes of, 211; driftiness of, 108, 194, 250, 260; English translation of, 26, 27, 55; in English working class, 98–104, 108; genius of, 116; historical sensibilities of, 21–22; imagined community of, 180; incompatibility with Anglo-Americans, 183; interclass nature of, 155; as internal exiles, 27, 247; as made by the English, 177; Marx on, 104, 124; national consciousness of, 277n65; nonrational sensibilities of, 192; nostalgia of, 180; outlawry of, 103–4; poetic qualities of, 178–80; "posing as Americans," 20; Protestants, 9, 100, 185, 214; psychological autonomy for, 115, 154, 178; rebelliousness of, 104; reciprocity among, 15, 255; sacred obligations of, 14; secret societies of, 103–4; as semifeudal, 101–2, 104, 108, 112, 114; sense of place, 26; survival in twentieth century, 184, 185–86; timelessness of, 93–94, 263; view of Russian Revolution, 151; Woodrow Wilson on, 212, 214–16, 219, 221, 224, 226–32, 302n11; Yankee depictions of, 32–33

the Irish, west-country: Arensberg's study of, 13–14, 15, 267; emigrants from, 32; folk stories of, 249; noneconomic institutions of, 14

Irish Agricultural Organization Society (IAOS), 184

Irish Catholics: as adversarial, 3; Anglo-Protestant ideas about, 184; antisocialism of, 117; breeding habits, 66; capitalism and, 4, 38–44; in cartoons, 29, 57; charges of racial inferiority against, 7, 33, 70, 74–76; in Chartist Movement, 282n10, 283n33; contradiction of democracy, 4; cultural contrariness of, 183, 253; cultural ecology of, 12; as disinherited, 104, 108–9, 110; dissident, 3, 4, 17–18, 255; divergence from Protestant governance, 51; drunkenness of, 103; effect of emancipation from imperialism, 62; ethnically privileged, 120; ethnic/social class congruency among, 4–5; as impractical, 235; inherited contempt for, 9; loyalty to the pope, 64; master-servants relationships of, 109; modernity and, 11; mutual aid among, 104; nationalists, 89, 101–2, 109; as neighbor-reliant, 36; nostalgia among, 12, 113; outside dominant culture, 111; outsideness of, 33, 42, 205, 268; premodernity of, 12–16, 32, 46, 64, 87, 101; pride in origins, 111; racial characterizations of, 1, 2, 10, 16, 30–34; as racial threat, 66, 70; "reactionary emotionalism" of, 238; reformist politics of, 44; siege mentality of, 36; sociability of, 93; social unconscious of, 46; sociocultural formation of, 105, 245; as subject class, 5, 46; subjugation to Protestantism, 7; subversiveness of, 39, 254; transatlantic networks of, 44; transnational, 7, 249; view of America, 3, 39; view of World War I, 132; Woodrow Wilson on, 214

Irish Catholics, American: adaptations to American life, 39; American identity and, 1–2; American opportunity and, 189; Anglo-American masters of, 54–55, 58; anticolonialism of, 188; attraction of communism for, 239; capitalists, 172; in cartoons, 30; Celtic communism among, 160, 163, 170; challenge to capitalism, 4, 38–44, 227, 255–56, 259; changing of America, 3; citizenship of, 2; colonial issues among, 191; contribution to modernity, 20; countercultural, 110; deportation of, 109; dominant identity of, 19; as exiles, 37, 160, 212, 222; factionalism among, 249; fashioning by Natives, 182; on Free State Treaty, 249; government surveillance of, 232; as impure citizens, 82; influence in antebellum America, 267–68; internationalism among, 188, 191–92; Irish nationalism of, 62, 165–66, 188; Italian immigrants and, 279n26; in labor unions, 76, 117; "lace curtain," 40; landlessness of, 32–33; majority among American Catholics, 66; militancy of, 160; as "New Ireland," 159; as non-American, 218; non-assimilated, 3; otherness of, 2; pro-German sentiments, 132, 133, 141, 142, 216, 287n41, 287nn41–42; radicals, 45, 128, 159–62; relevance of Democratic Programme for, 257; as semifeudal, 188; social consciousness of, 256; social estrangement of, 175; as Strangers, 2–4, 19, 82; threat to institutions, 63; transactional relationship with America, 19–20; as visitors, 188; the west and, 113; women activists, 194, 195; Woodrow Wilson and, 217–20, 226; during World War I, 132, 218, 219; Yankee prejudice against, 29–35. *See also* immigrants, Irish Catholic; working class, Irish Catholic

Irish Citizen Army (ICA), 150, 159, 165; in Butte, 142; Connolly's address to, 245; Marxism of, 115

Irish Felon, 171

Irish Free State (*Saor Stát*), 173; antitreaty Republicans in, 247; as Britain's proxy, 305n88; in British Empire, 246; Catholic Church in, 246; Civil War following, 243, 245–46, 249, 263; creation of, 184, 242; disillusionment with, 247, 263; emigration from, 247; failures of, 253, 267; Left opposition to, 245–46; shoneens of, 246, 248, 251, 263; treaty establishing, 243, 305n80

Irish Homestead (Revivalist newspaper), 184

Irish Labour Party: in elections of 1918, 157–58, 239, 257; on imperialism, 234; on Irish independence, 203; on Irish nationality, 154; on Irish unity, 157; protest of Queen Victoria's Jubilee, 159; Sinn Féin and, 181

Irish Labour Party and Trade Union Congress (ILPTUC), 158; on Connolly, 160; internationalism of, 154; praise for Lenin, 159; report to International Labour and Socialist Conference, 159; in strike of 1918, 157

Irish language: sensibilities of, 27; suppression of, 26–28

Irishness: antiquity of, 196; effect of American culture on, 251; English suppression of, 178; internal conflicts of, 11; Irish American education in, 182; paired with Catholicism, 109; poetics of, 154, 178–80, 200, 243, 250; poverty in, 247; social justice in, 181; tribal, 117, 193, 199

Irish Parliamentary Party, dominionists in, 157–58
Irish Progressive League (IPL), 259, 264; Catholicism of, 148; nationalism of, 193; on national questions, 154; radicalism of, 148; women leaders of, 193, 194
Irish question: in America, 188; as racial problem, 238; Ulster's exemption from, 185; Walsh on, 298n70; Wilson and, 218, 226–32
Irish race, 119; charges of inferiority against, 7, 33, 70, 74–76; collectivist ethic of, 264; conscience of, 248; genius of, 116, 167, 172; interclass nature of, 155; versus Irish nation, 177; manifest destiny of, 184; as morally decadent, 238; perceptions of inferiority, 7. See also race
Irish Race Convention (1919), 227
Irish Republic, provisional, 133–34; anti-capitalism of, 155; anti-imperialism of, 234–35; blockade threat by, 236; Bolshevik recognition of, 213, 216; British Empire and, 233–34; British reaction to, 135; Butte miners' sympathy with, 144; English working class and, 218; Irish American working class and, 218; in London Treaty, 233–34; naval power of, 236; ownership of resources, 136; refusals to recognize, 242; Soviet aid to, 152; struggle for control of, 245; threat to Anglo-American interests, 242; threat to Great Britain, 233–36; Woodrow Wilson on, 227; as Workers' Republic, 135, 157, 158, 221, 223, 240, 246, 256–57. See also *Dáil Éireann* (Irish Parliament)
Irish Republican Army, 233; antitreaty, 263
Irish Republican Brotherhood, 235, 262
Irish Transit and General Workers Union (ITGWU), 262; Larkin's leadership of, 130
Irish Volunteers (IV), 154, 159; nationalism of, 245
Irish Worker (newspaper), American, 170

Irish World (newspaper), Revivalism of, 182
The Irish World and American Industrial Liberator, 55, 64
irrationality, Irish: accusations of, 8, 193; foreignness and, 186; of hunger strikes, 193–94; of IrishCatholic neighborhoods, 41

Jacobins, French: emissaries to Ireland, 240
Jacobson, Matthew Frye, 279n21
Jefferson, Thomas, 3, 64
Jews: immigrant, 25, 147, 160, 162; radical, 147
job opportunities, fair distribution of, 118–19
Joyce, James: expatriatism of, 247–48; on Ireland's sorrows, 21; on Patsy Caliban, 53, 308n57
justice, distributive, 205, 206, 268; Irish Catholic assumptions concerning, 192, 196, 264

Kallen, Horace, 83
Kazin, Michael, 306n17
Keating, Edward, 196; on Catholic "liberalism," 260
Kelleher, John V., 56
Kelley, Cornelius, 131, 132, 293n62; on Butte unions, 168–69
Kelley, Jeremiah, 293n62
Kellogg, Paul, 74
Kennedy, William, 42, 254
Kenny, Kevin, 39; on assimilation, 19; "Diaspora and Comparison," 44, 45; on diasporic sentiment, 7, 105, 106; on transnationalism, 150
Kepler, J.: "Uncle Sam's Lodging-House," 57
Kiberd, Declan, 116, 282n16; *Inventing Ireland*, 4–5
Kickham, Charles, 53
Kilvargan (Ireland), 263
Kinealy, Christine: *The Great Calamity*, 26
King, Martin Luther, Jr., 266
Knights of Labor, 89
Know-Nothings, 29, 216

Kraditor, Aileen, 175, 215; on nationalism/economic separation, 267; *The Radical Persuasion*, 147–48, 149, 160, 161

Krugman, Paul, 261

Ku Klux Klan, 230, 250

labor: class issues in, 62; commodification of, 106, 259; equality in, 58–59; moral arguments concerning, 15; non-commodified, 14; timekeeping in, 93, 106–7, 112

labor, American: "apostles of Lenin" and, 232; aristocracy of, 120–21; of Chicago, 254; collective opportunity in, 118; countermovement politics of, 267; economic revolution and, 222–23; group psychology of, 118; Irish Catholic dissidence in, 255; for Irish Catholic prosperity, 22, 55–56; Irish dimension in, 117–18, 222–23; Irish tutoring of, 169; laws governing, 201; liberalism in, 62–64; nationalism in, 267; during New Deal, 261; as nonseverable from Irish cause, 192; oppositions in, 105; presence in, 267; role of state in, 201; social crises in, 197. *See also* Caliban, Patsy; strikes; working class

labor, free, 50, 58–62, 279n15; biblical imagery for, 61; growth of Catholicism and, 65; wage slavery and, 60–63

labor, Irish: alliance with Fenianism, 240; for American capitalism, 252; and cause of Ireland, 200; Communist Russian support for, 221; Connolly on, 115–16; English policy on, 55–56; internationalism of, 203–4; militants, 89; moral cause of, 117; nationalism and, 44, 46, 55–56, 121–22, 128–29, 140, 144, 166, 191, 203, 299n81; Sinn Féin on, 198; strike of 1918, 156–57; support for Russian Revolution, 154, 159; worker control of, 199. *See also* working class, Irish Catholic

labor history: Catholic presence in, 87, 100–101; on Irish Catholicism, 109; Irish problem in, 145; the past in, 265; prerevolution, 86; social, 85–86; transformations to, 85; without laborers in, 95

labor history, new, 46, 86, 92, 261; Thompson's work in, 94–98; working-class homogeneity in, 97

labor market, American: scarcity in, 118, 120–21

labor movements: Catholic dimension of, 91; "fissiparous," 11; Irish Americans in, 45, 288n43. *See also* unionism

labor movements, Irish, 115; Sinn Féin and, 155

labor reform, 50, 59–65, 279n16; American liberalism in, 62–64; eight-hour day, 62, 279n19; Irish nationalism and, 144–45, 166, 192; Protestant, 69

laissez faire, 118, 256; Catholic opposition to, 19, 196; Irish obedience to, 50. *See also* capitalism

laity, Catholic: antisocialism of, 90; "Labor Manifesto" of, 89

Lalor, James Fintan, 248–29, 260

land: Irish view of, 32–33, 113; quantification of, 112–13

Land League, Marxism of, 240

land reform, Irish, 26, 150

Lansing, Robert, 149, 220, 223, 228

Larkin, Emmet, 27, 161; on Catholic identity, 28; on Great Famine, 24–25

Larkin, Jim, 44, 139; American experiences, 160; anti-war production efforts, 141; Catholicism of, 149, 150, 163, 290n10; as Celtic revolutionist, 163; communism of, 91, 149, 163; conflict with Mulcahy, 130, 131–32; on Easter Rising, 153; ICA of, 127; Irish American newspapers on, 287n36; Irish experiences of, 164; ITGWU leadership, 130; Left nationalism of, 130; on race solidarity, 130; visits to Butte, 130–32, 137; Walsh's defense of, 210

Lasch, Christopher, 61, 79

League of Nations: colonial territories under, 232–33; Irish in defeat of, 231; Irish view of, 229; mandate system, 233; propaganda against, 226

Lears, Jackson, 11, 42; on American modernists, 57, 111; on antimodernists, 110; on "bourgeoisie," 283n24; on capitalism, 50–51; on historiography, 23; on timekeeping, 106
Lee, J. J.: on Pearse, 136
Left, American: as dilettantes, 164; Irish in, 160, 161; newspapers, 169; opposition to Free State, 245–46; Protestant, 82; reading of Marx, 124; on Walsh Plan, 202
Left, Irish: in American Socialist Party, 161; as Catholic Left, 149; collectivist, 264; erraticism of, 210; Irish Americans among, 160; labor and, 155, 199; as model for American countermovement, 265; in 1918 election, 257; noncommunist, 180; radical social change agenda, 211; Russian Revolution and, 151–53, 159; warning to Woodrow Wilson, 224; working class liberation under, 211
Lehane, Con, 139, 141; association with Connolly, 137, 288n53; class warfare advocacy, 137
Lenin, Vladimir, 296n31; on Easter Rising, 135, 150–51; on English colonialism, 134; ILPTUC praise for, 159; on Irish nationalism, 151, 152–53, 160, 167, 169, 218; self-determination under, 152
Leonard, Thomas: *Illiberal Reformers*, 65–66, 70, 206
Leo XIII, Pope: *Rerum Novarum*, 264; antimaterialism of, 197; assault on socialism, 82–83; belief in the past, 196, 204; capitalism in, 18–19; Catholic workers and, 89; CWC's use of, 196–97; historians' ignoring of, 282n4; on labor, 88–89, 194, 197, 202, 268; National Catholic War Council on, 89; on property, 159; sources for, 265; Walsh's interpretation of, 203; working-class "authorship," 269
Leslie, Shane, 291n20; on anti-British sentiment, 153; on Irish nationalism, 221; on John D. Ryan, 168
liberalism, American: Anglo-American, 62–63; hostility to tradition, 84;
illiberal, 68–71, 77–78, 210; in labor reform, 62–65; post–Civil War, 62; Protestantism of, 231; un-Irish, 51
liberty: antislave theory of, 61; Irish Catholic ideology of, 64
Lincoln, Abraham, 308n57; Gettysburg Address, 3
Lindsay, John, 266
Lippmann, Walter, 78–82, 182, 221; anti-Catholicism of, 78–81; on drift, 94, 106; *Drift and Mastery*, 79; on industrial democracy, 198; as public intellectual, 77; on time, 112; on traditionalism, 112
Literary Revival, Irish, 178, 193. See also Revival, Irish
Little, Frank, 141
Lloyd George, David, 240, 242; caricature of, 167, *168*; de Valera and, 233–35, 236, 304n68; on Irish blockade threat, 236; Irish conscription policy, 156; and Irish Free State, 243; and Irish War of Independence, 233; racial bigotry influencing, 238–39; threat to Ireland, 234, 304n65; Woodrow Wilson's request to, 232
Locke, John: commonwealth of, 47, 48
"A London Charaviri" (*Punch*, 1921), *241*
London Treaty (1912), 233–34
longshoremen strike (Manhattan, 1929), 194
Lonigan, Studs (Fictitious character), 249
Lynch, Liam, 257

MacDonagh, Oliver, 2
MacManus, Seumas: on Irish Revival, 182–83; *Story of the Irish Race*, 183
MacSwiney, Terrence: American strikes supporting, 194; hunger strike of, 171, 193–94
Mangan, John Sherry, 225
Manly, Basil: authorship of Walsh Report, 206, 208–9; and Fourteenth Amendment, 209; questioning of CIR witnesses, 300n99
Mannix, Daniel, 194
Mansergh, Nicholas, 153, 160

Mansion House rally (Dublin), 153, 154
Marx, Karl, 151, 296n31; on the Irish, 104, 124, 218
Marx, Leo, 53, 54
mastery, 80; amnesia in, 82; cultural sensibilities of, 106; drift and, 94, 106; of human understanding, 79
materialism: American, 91, 251; British, 124; Irish struggle against, 179; moralist opposition to, 192
McCartin, Joseph: on CIR, 201; *Labor's Great War*, 198; on Walsh, 201
McDonnell, Joseph, 45–46, 99, 106
McGahern, John: *Amongst Women*, 247
McKillen, Elizabeth, 228
Mellows, Liam, 56; on Celtic Renaissance, 180–81; dislike of US, 295n9; internationalism of, 191, 204; in IPL, 193; on Irish Free State, 247; on Irish soul, 179
Melrose (Iowa), Irish farm community of, 37
Menace (newspaper), 78
Mencken, H. L.: on Irish radicals, 162
Merwin, Henry Childs: essays on Irish Americans, 32–34, 36, 37, 188; on Irish clannishness, 189
Mesabi Iron Range, Finnish residents of, 294n71
Metal Miner Workers' Union (MMWU), demand for six-hour day, 142–43. *See also* copper strike (Butte, Montana, 1917)
metaphor, historians' use of, 2–3, 11–12, 16
Methodism, in English working class, 103, 105
Michaels, Tony: *Jewish Radicals*, 11
Miller, Kerby, 51, 230–31, 303n55; *Emigrants and Exiles*, 28–29, 37, 38–39; on Irish worldview, 38–39
miners, Irish Catholic (Butte), 251; alliance with Finns, 140; antiwar protest, 138–40; cause of Ireland and, 143–44; coalition with farmers, 173; practicality of, 85, 119, 120; strikes, 141–44, 145, 165. *See also* Butte Miners' Union; Western Federation of Miners

mining, nationalization proposals for, 209
Mitchel, John, 25
mobility, social: desire for, 43; Irish working class and, 43–44; personal worth and, 42
modernism: banality of, 31; high, 79
modernity: absence and presence in, 17, 18, 35; American frauds of, 111–12, 114; commodification of time, 106; compartmentalization in, 50; culture codes of, 111; dissentient, 19; inwardness of, 48; Irish American contribution to, 20; Irish disregard for, 180; mastery in, 106; privatization of religion, 48; of Protestantism, 17; self-regulating market of, 57; timekeeping in, 106. *See also* premodernity
Molly Maguires, 89, 282n11
Monk, Maria: *Awful Disclosures of,* 29, 48
Montgomery, David, 59
Mooney, Tom, 144, 210
Moore, Laurence: *Religious Outsiders*, 267–68
morality: in capitalism, 4; Gilded Age, 45; of Irish erratics, 192; in Irish labor, 117; materialism and, 192; relationship to politics, 46, 200
Mormonism, 66
Mulcahy, James B., 128, 169; attacks on Connolly, 130; conflict with Larkin, 130, 131–32; Irish nationalism of, 129–31; praise of ACM, 287n38

Nast, Thomas, 29
The Nation (reform journal), 63
National Catholic War Council, 89; Program of Reconstruction, 194–97, 199–200, 264. *See also* Catholic Welfare Council
National Civic Federation: on bishops' Program of Reconstruction, 197; Hammond's membership on, 205
National Defense Act (1916), 132
nationalism: commercial/military aspects of, 181; of labor reform, 192, 203; Voltaire on, 181

nationalism, Irish, 23, 44, 89; American involvement in, 62, 165–66, 188; anticapitalism of, 151; anticolonialism and, 167, 191, 193; versus British efficiency, 186; of Butte Miners' Union (BMU), 121–23, 128; Catholic, 89, 101–2, 109; as Catholic theocracy, 129; Comintern and, 170; cultural, 178, 179; internationalism of, 191–93; of IPL, 193; Irish communalism and, 148; Irish radicalism and, 147, 157, 175, 211; of Irish Volunteers, 245; labor and, 44, 46, 55–56, 121–22, 128–29, 140, 144, 166, 191, 203, 299n81; Lenin on, 151, 152–53, 160, 167, 169, 218; physical-force, 133; poetic approach to, 53, 224; practical importance of, 153; racialized, 183; restoration of moral resources, 154; role of Irish history in, 153; sham, 124–25; of Sinn Féin, 181; social class divisions in, 130, 232; socialism and, 133–34, 136, 162, 211, 245; threat to England, 151; Woodrow Wilson's distrust of, 231; during World War I, 133

nation-state, Protestantism of, 75, 198

Natives: American Protestants as, 1, 3, 19; fashioning of Irish Americans, 182; gulf between Strangers and, 82; paranoia among, 29

nativism: Commons's, 207; in Great Red Scare, 231; socialist, 131; Woodrow Wilson's, 226

nativism, anti-Catholic, 3, 30, 32, 106, 216; on Catholic inwardness, 47; Debs's, 78; illiberal reformism of, 68–70; lawlessness and, 38; of Social Gospel movement, 67

neighborhoods: institutions of, 95; mobility from, 42; working-class, 35–36. *See also* communities

neighborhoods, Irish Catholic: attachment to, 33; children of, 35; class/ethnic relationships of, 10; cultural boundaries of, 191; erraticism of, 41; ethnic closure of, 35; Hell's Kitchen, 68; institutions of, 109; structure of feeling in, 262; tribal character of, 117

Nelson, Bruce, 210; on anti-Catholicism, 230; on industrial democracy, 198; on Irish Democratic Programme, 200; *Irish Nationalists and the Making of the Irish Race*, 191–92

New Deal, 258; as double movement, 260; fair labor practices in, 260–61; ideological mentality of, 260; Irish-Catholic erraticism of, 268; as limit of American politics, 268; nonmarket mentality preceding, 267; union membership under, 261

newspapers, American: Irish nationalism and, 170–74, 175

New York Call: on government surveillance, 232; on W.F. Dunne, 165, 212

New York City Transit Workers Union (TWU): Communist Party alliance, 262; erraticism of, 262, 267; Irish members of, 262; left republicans of, 263; radical industrial unionism of, 265–66

Nonpartisan League, 173, 294n77

the nonrational, American view of, 8

O'Callaghan, Eugene: on immigrant experience, 51
O'Connell, Daniel, 102, 104
O'Connell, John, 49
O'Connell, William, 303n43
O'Connor, Emmet, 151; on Irish conscription, 157
O'Connor, Frank, 247
O'Donnell, Peadar, 247
O'Faolain, Sean, 38
O'Farrelly, Agnes, 178
O'Flaherty, Liam, 23
O'Flaherty, Thomas, 25; in American communist movement, 173; *Aranmen All*, 174; on Irish history, 23, 37; *Producers' News* contributions, 173
O'Hegarty, P. S., 235
O'Malley, Ernie, 238, 260; on shoneen, 248
O'Riordan, Michael: on American capitalism, 190–91; *Catholicism and Irish Progress*, 190–91
O'Rourke, John K., 169
Orsi, Robert, 58, 267, 273n38; on

freedom of religion, 47; on historical catastrophes, 25; *History and Presence*, 16–18, 20; on intersubjectivity, 86; on loyalty to the pope, 64; on modernity, 82, 87, 111, 112; on modern liberalism, 231; on presence and absence, 17, 35, 41, 46, 47, 192, 273n38; on subversiveness, 261, 273n39

otherness: Irish Catholic, 2, 7; racialized, 53

Page, Walter Hines: on aid to England, 217; Anglo-Americanism of, 217–18; on Irish American identity, 220; on "non-American people," 218

Paine, Thomas, 100, 105, 255

Parliament, British: Sinn Féin candidates for, 157

the Past: in American labor history, 265; American Southerners on, 254; belief in, 25; as imposter, 112; invented, 8; Irish attachment to, 113; in Irish Catholic erraticism, 20; in Irish Republic, 134. *See also* premodernity

patriotism, Irish: in America, 109. *See also* nationalism, Irish

Peake, A. S., 165

Pearse, Patrick, 81; Easter Rising proclamation, 133, 135, 136, 158, 243; execution of, 137; on national sovereignty, 224; on property, 159; "The Sovereign People," 135–36Pearse-Connolly Irish Independence Club (Butte, Montana), 137, 141, 170; antiwar pamphlet, 138–39, 143; "Butte Strike Bulletin," 140; on Free State Treaty, 249; strike activism, 139–44

peasantry, Irish: American changes to, 111; ancestral sorrows of, 41; in British working class, 114; Connolly's ideal of, 196; ethnography of, 13–14; migration to England, 100; and modern idea of property, 15; moral economy of, 260; non-economic institutions of, 14; outnumbering of working class, 211; sociability of, 93

Perlman, Selig, 88–92, 140; on American labor movement, 91, 117–18; on antisocialism, 90; *History of the Labor Movement*, 92; on labor market, 120–21; *Theory of the Labor Movement*, 88, 92; on working class heterogeneity, 97

Pershing, General John, 307n32

personality, ecology as, 12, 24, 28, 45

petrology, metaphors from, 2–3

Phelan, Terence. *See* Mangan, John Sherry

Phillips, W. Alison, 235

Phillips, Wendell, 61; on wage slavery, 60

Pittsburgh Survey, Commons's work in, 73–74

Pius IX, Pope: Syllabus of Errors (1864), 3

Pius XI, Pope: *Quadragesimo Anno* (1931), 258, 259, 268

place names, Irish: translation of, 26, 27

Plentywood (Montana), *Producers' News* of, 173–74

Plunkett, Horace, 238; American ranch of, 184, 193; association with Harold Frederic, 189–90; on Home Rule, 186; *Ireland in the New Century*, 183–90; on Irish American allegiance, 221; on Irish antimodernism, 184–85; on Irish Catholic Church, 187; on Irish nationalism, 186; on politics versus business, 192–93; race patriotism of, 184, 187; two-nation theory of, 185

an Poblacht na h-Éireann. *See* Irish Republic

Polanyi, Karl: on archaic societies, 41, 49; association with Arensberg, 307n32; on disembeddedness, 14, 15, 193, 196, 282n16; "double movement of, 15, 69, 94, 158, 200, 202, 258, 259, 269, 307n32; on free labor, 50; *The Great Transformation*, 13–17, 51, 57–58, 258; on market mentality, 267; New Left use of, 13; on nonmarket economies, 20, 35, 38; on nonmarket psychology, 116; on working-class movements, 258; on zoological determinism, 7–8

politics: versus economics, 192–93; separation from market economies, 49; separation of conscience from, 50
Pollard, Hugh, 240; on Catholic Irish, 238; on Celtic socialists, 160–61; imperialism of, 237–38; intelligence reports of, 238, 239; on Irish Americans, 239; on partition of Ireland, 243; *Secret Societies of Ireland*, 237–39; sources of, 305n77
postcolonialism, imagining of nations, 182
Post Office Department, Censorship Book of, 232
poststructuralism, on experience, 97
Pound, Ezra: on Irish Free State, 250
Powderly, Terence, 89
precapitalism, 87, 92
preindustrial societies, 13; American, 199; immigrants from, 12; Irish Catholic, 101, 117–18; race and, 96
prejudice, anti-Irish: Anglo-American, 8, 29–36
premodernity: erratic, 20, 56; as function of chronology, 16; and preindustrialism, 56; traditionalist, 13. *See also* modernity; the Past
premodernity, Irish Catholic, 12–16, 32, 46, 87; preindustrialism and, 101; social improvement and, 64
presence, God's: and God's absence, 16–17, 18, 35, 38, 41, 46–47, 87, 192, 273n38; in American labor, 267; erratic nature of, 47; in modernity, 17
the present, as essence of time, 112
priests, labor, 265, 266
The Producers' News (Nonpartisan League organ), 173–74; editors of, 173; on O'Flaherty, 295n81; O'Flaherty's contributions to, 174
production, for use/gain, 15
Progressives, on political corruption, 76
propaganda, Irish: in Comintern budget, 170; during World War I, 222
Protestantism: God's absence in, 20, 38, 46, 49, 89, 92, 112; in American Gilded Age, 45; Anglo-Saxon, 213–14; capitalism and, 43, 185, 196, 282n15; Cromwellian, 195; cultural hegemony of, 114; individualism of, 196; modernity of, 17; of nation-state, 75; of northern Ireland, 9, 38, 100, 185
Protestants, American: creation story of, 4; cultural divergence from Irish Catholics, 1–3, 10, 17–18, 56, 86, 92, 145; fear of Irish Strangers, 3; as "Natives," 1, 3, 19
Puritanism: in foundation of capitalism, 74; Irish weakening of, 103; Social Gospel movement and, 67, 68

Quill, Michael: erraticism of, 267; experience of Civil War, 263; funeral of, 266; industrial unionism of, 263–64; in IRA, 263; labor radicalism of, 263, 266; opposition to anti-Semitism, 308n55; reading of Connolly, 264; traditional upbringing of, 262–63, 267; unassimilated life of, 266; in "working-class interregnum," 265

race: conflation with religion, 66–67, 72, 75–76; as determination of national borders, 220; Woodrow Wilson's beliefs on, 212–14, 226. *See also* Irish race
race patriots, Anglo Saxon, 9, 10, 30, 272n17; Anglo-American imperialism of, 215; on the English, 33–34; on immigration restriction, 74–75; Plunkett, 184, 187; on religion, 34; Woodrow Wilson, 213–14, 218, 231; in World War I, 218
Rachleff, Peter, 85, 86
racism: pseudo-scientific, 213; scientific, 69
Radek, Karl, 135
radicalism, global, 147
radicalism, American: Catholicism and, 148; class structure of, 149
radicalism, Irish: Irish nationalism and, 147, 157, 175, 211; link with Irish history, 147; as racial calling, 175; traditionalism in, 149
radicals: Finns, 147, 160, 175; Franco-Belgian, 147, 160, 175; Jewish, 125, 147, 160, 175

radicals, Irish Catholic, 44–45, 159–62; labor, 45, 88, 128–29, 224
"The Rail Splitter" (nativist publication), 305n77
Rauschenbusch, Walter, 73, 78; *Christianity and the Social Crisis*, 67–68; Christian socialism of, 77; pastoral work of, 67–68
Reagan, Ronald, 261
reciprocity: among the Irish, 15, 255; social benefits of, 181; in traditional societies, 15
Red October (1917), 150
Reed, John, 162, 170
Reformation: Anglo-American view of, 199; capitalism following, 196, 197, 199–200, 268; cultural divergence following, 17; influence on imperialism, 200; "nation-states" of, 47; in origin of American state, 110; political liberty and, 75; Social Gospel movement on, 67
reformers: exclusionist, 77; gulf between Irish Catholics and, 82; on Irish Catholic defectiveness, 83–84. *See also* Social Gospel movement
religion: conflation with race, 66–67, 72, 75–76; in English working class, 100; segregation by, 101. *See also* Catholicism; Protestantism
religious freedom, in U.S., 47
Renan, Ernst, 23
republicanism, "artisanal," 199
republicanism, Irish: of Clan na Gael, 137; English working class and, 218; social radicalism and, 181. *See also* Irish Republic
Republican Party, US: and "Irish agitation," 229; of 1980s, 261
Rerum Novarum. See Leo XIII, Pope: *Rerum Novarum*
Revival, Irish, 178–81, 182, 204; agricultural cooperatives in, 184; in America, 182–83; American Celticism and, 182; in American newspapers, 182; antimodernism of, 182; IAOS in, 184; racial regeneration in, 183
Rhodes, Cecil, 124, 205

Rice, Charles Owen, Fr., 265–66; eulogy for Quill, 266
Robert Emmet Literary Association (RELA), 144; endorsement of Free State treaty, 249; following Easter Rising, 137; during World War I, 138
Rogers, W. A.: "Poor House from Galway," 29
Roosevelt, Franklin Delano: on ancient truths, 260; reading of *Quadragesimo Anno*, 259, 268; on wage labor, 260
Ross, E. A.: Protestant Christian reform of, 69
Royal Irish Constabulary, 233
Royal Navy, British: control around Ireland, 236
Russell, George (Æ): on Irish Free State, 247
Russian Revolution: Easter Rising and, 150–51, 172–73; Irish Left and, 151–53, 159. *See also* Bolshevism
Ryan, John, Fr., 131, 168, 264; *The Church and Labor*, 196; conservative nationalism of, 228; on industrial classes, 202; Irish speaking trip, 228; on living wage, 202; new deals of, 268; on ownership of production, 199; on the Reformation, 199–200; *Social Reconstruction*, 197, 202; on Walsh, 298n70
Ryan, Michael, 227

Sabbatarianism, Irish Catholic view of, 37
Sallau, Ernest: carbide lamp of, 141, 143
Salvatore, Nick, 77
Sarsfield Social Club (Butte, Montana), 249, 250
Scally, Robert: *The End of Hidden Ireland*, 267, 268
Schmuhl, Robert, 133, 300n8
science: racial, 70; social gospel and, 69, 79
Scotch-Irish, separation from the Irish, 34. *See also* Ulster
Scott, James, 79
Second Amendment, in arming of unions, 209
Seeley, John, 215

self-determination: under Lenin, 152; racial depictions of, 75, 81, 208; Woodrow Wilson on, 219, 220, 227, 250
sensibilities, Irish Catholic: anticlerical, 90; in Butte strike, 144; diasporic, 7, 28, 105, 106; filtering of experience, 95; historical differences forming, 9; of Irish language, 27; transnational, 269
Shakespeare, William: *The Tempest*, 53–54
shoneens (*seoíníní*), 20, 23, 124; versus "actual people" of Ireland, 137; capitalist, 172; caused by the English, 178; influence of, 169; of Irish Free State, 246, 248, 251, 263; Larkin's condemnation of, 130; mine owners, 122; ostracism of, 41; stage, 167. *See also* bourgeoisie, Irish
Sinn Féin, 154; anticonscription movement, 221; Bolshevism and, 239–40, 242; candidates for Parliament (1918), 157–58; conferences with colonial peoples, 224; on Conscription Bill, 156; influence on American labor, 229; Irish labor movements and, 155; Irish Revival and, 183; "Message to the Free Nationals of the World," 223–24; nationalism of, 181; position papers of, 269; *Punch* cartoon of, *241*; Soviet ties of, 239–40, 293n66; strike (1918), 156–57. See also *Dáil Éireann*; "Democratic Programme of Dáil Éireann"; Irish Republic, provisional
slaves, emancipated: free labor of, 58–69
Smith, Al: presidential campaign of, 254
social class, ethnicity and, 4–5, 10, 11
Social Gospel movement, 64–69, 76–77, 206, 259; on Catholicism, 65; conflation of race and religion, 66–67; Debs and, 77; in emergence of social science, 69; on immigration restriction, 72; Puritanism and, 67, 68; xenophobia of, 69
socialism, 5; absence in, 91; Catholic resistance to, 89–91; goodness of heart as, 90, 116; Irish American, 161; Irish communalism and, 90, 91; Leo XIII's encyclical on, 18–19, 82; working class resistance to, 88
socialism, radical: Irish nationalism and, 133–34, 136, 162, 211, 245
Socialist Labor Party, religious views of, 148
Socialist Party, American: intolerance of Irish in, 91; religious views of, 147–48
social justice: Catholic teaching on, 149, 191; and slavery, 59; in Walsh's program, 208
social justice, Irish, 181; cultural hegemony and, 110–11; IPL on, 148; political freedom and, 117; real presence and, 87–88
social science, Commons's work in, 73–74
Social Security Act, US, 260
Sombart, Werner, 91; *Why Is There No Socialism in the United States?*, 88, 99
South Africa, British imperialism in, 124
sovereignty, God's: transfer to state, 19, 273n44
Soviet Revolution, 119
Spalpeen ("Spailpín"), 157, 168; "Sinn Féin and the Labour Movement," 154–55, 181
spalpeens (*spailpíní*, itinerant laborers), 154, 265; women, 291n24
Speculator Mine (Butte, Montana), 289n66; Irish in, 143; mining disaster, 140–41, 143, 145. *See also* Butte "Rising"
Spenser, Edmund: on Irish speech, 27; *View of the Present State of Ireland*, 26, 27
Spring-Rice, Cecil, 213
Stalin, Josef: on W. F. Dunne, 165
Stevens, Wallace: on Irish Free State, 250
strikes, American: Coeur d'Alenes (1892), 126; of early twentieth century, 197–98; longshoremen (Manhattan, 1929), 194; violence in, 126, 165, 209. *See also* copper strike (Butte, Montana, 1917)

Stromquist, Shelton, 206; *Re-inventing the People*, 207
Strong, George Templeton, 2, 3; race patriotism of, 10
Strong, Josiah: anti-Catholicism of, 66–67; on English working class, 97; on individuality, 80; *The New Era*, 36; *Our Country*, 66–67, 276n40
sunburstery (nationalist oratory), 22, 69, 168; Carney's, 171
supremacy: Anglo-Saxon, 163, 213, 217, 300n8; Protestant, 7, 22; white, 204
Synge, John Millington: on clock time, 107–8; recording of folkways, 109

Taft, William: on F. Walsh, 201
Takaki, Ronald, 53, 54
Tate, Allen, 254; on tradition, 111
Tawney, R. H., 7, 50
Taylor, Charles (Red Flag), 173
Tenniel, John: "Patsy O'Caliban," 53
Thiel Detective Agency, 141
Thomas Aquinas, 199
Thompson, Dorothy, 46; on Chartists, 283n33
Thompson, E. P., 156, 157, 185; on culture bearers, 106; on English working class, 255; on the Irish, 99–105, 114; on Irish Catholic nationalism, 109; *The Making of the English Working Class*, 10, 94–107; on religion, 100, 102–3; on "Romanism," 102; "Time, Work-Discipline, and Industrial Capitalism," 106–7; on time, 106–8; on working-class neighborhoods, 262
Tillinghast, Richard, 246
time, commodification of, 112
timekeeping: Catholic attitudes toward, 35, 93, 107–8, 263; in labor, 93, 106–7, 112; in modernity, 106; orderly, 93; and work discipline, 106. *See also* clock time
time ways, 38, 106; Irish, 93, 107
Toynbee, Arnold: on Anglo-Americans, 21
Trade and Market in the Early Empires (Polanyi and Arensberg), 13–14
traditionalism, economic: Protestant emancipation from, 93
traditionalism, Irish Catholic, 13, 20, 63, 80–81; erraticism of, 50; intolerance of, 82; loyalty to dead in, 111; modernity and, 27; nostalgic, 112; reformers' hostility toward, 84; of working class, 261–62
transcendence, in American religions, 16
transformation: inwardness/outwardness in, 48; of Irish history, 8; socioeconomic, 13, 14, 16–17, 41, 46, 51
translation: of colonial Irish, 26–28, 55, 96; as cultural appropriation, 215; of immigrants, 215; of Irish place names, 26, 27
transnationalism: of Celtic communism, 226; Irish American, 7, 249; temporal aspects of, 28; working class, 150
"Tribal Twenties," US, 230
Trotsky, Leon: on Irish working class, 134
The Truth (Workers' Socialist Publishing Company), 170–72; on communism, 172; on World War I armistice, 171
Tully, James, 41–42
Tumulty, James, 228, 229
Turner, James, 34

Ulster: partitioning of, 242, 243, 246; Protestants of, 9, 100, 185
Uncle Sams (*Uncailiní Somhair*), 20
unionism, American: Black rights and, 307n36; industrial, 126, 261, 263–64, 307n36; Irish in, 117; under New Deal, 261; prudential, 117, 118–20, 127; trade versus industrial, 126. *See also* labor movements
Unionist Alliance (Ireland), opposition to independence, 234
Unionists, Irish: in Easter Rising, 159; in election of 1918, 157; pamphlets of, 239–40
unions: arming of, 165, 209; Irish Catholic organizers of, 76. *See also* Butte Miners' Union (BMU); strikes

United Irish League, 137
United States: as British achievement, 217; as civilizing agency, 73; compartmentalization of, 48; Cromwellian, 214; détente with England, 159; political/economic separation in, 49; as promised land, 189; as Protestant land, 273n41; as "safety valve," 73; during "working-class interregnum," 265, 269

Versailles Peace talks: Irish issues at, 226–30; Walsh at, 226–30, 252; Wilson at, 223–30
Versailles Treaty: communism in, 225; Ireland under, 233; mandate system in, 233
Voltaire, 252; on nationalism, 181

Wallace, Patrick J.: on coalition building, 173–74; editorship of *Producers' News*, 173; rebelliousness of, 294n78
Walsh, Francis Patrick, 200–205, *204*; advocacy for poetic Ireland, 201; anti-imperialism of, 203, 252; on assimilation, 253; on British culpability, 252; as Catholic Irish contrarian, 210; CIR service, 201, 202, 227; on class divisions, 206; condemnation of white supremacy, 204; criticism of America, 251–52; defense of Mooney, 210; disagreement with Commons, 206–9; discussions with Woodrow Wilson, 227–30, 252; on distributive justice, 205; early life of, 200, 210; erraticism of, 203; on free Ireland, 210; on illusionary democracy, 248–29; on industrial democracy, 257; on industrial despotism, 202; internationalism of, 203–4; interpretation of *Rerum Novarum*, 203; Irish Catholic sensibilities of, 207; on Irish Free State, 251–52; in Irish Left, 200; on Irish question, 298n70; on Irish soul, 203, 204; service with American Commission on Conditions in Ireland, 210, 299n81; on ultraradicalism, 303n43; at Versailles Peace talks, 226–30, 252; on wage slavery, 202, 203; on War Labor Board, 201
Walsh Plan (CIR report), 205; Democratic Programme and, 257–58; on democratized industry, 201; human rights in, 208–9; on industrial unrest, 201–2; Manly's authorship of, 206, 208–9, 300n99; omission of Black civil rights, 208; radicalism of, 201–2
Ward, Leo: on eternal present, 93; *Holding Up the Hills*, 37
War of Independence, Irish: British atrocities during, 210; British intelligence service during, 238; declaration of, 227; duration of, 233; London Treaty ending, 233–34; participants in, 233; as race war, 238. *See also* Easter Rising
Warren, Fred, 77–78
Warren, Robert Penn, 59
Waugh, Evelyn: on American Irish Catholics, 110–11; on Irish Catholic antimodernists, 260; on Irish nostalgia, 113
Wayland, J. A., 78
wealth, American: unequal distribution of, 49–50, 201, 277n76
Weber, Max, 94, 181, 182; on acquisition, 92; on disenchantment, 92, 282n16; on erraticism, 92; on Irish Catholicism, 92–93, 101; new labor history and, 92; *The Protestant Ethic and the Spirit of Capitalism*, 92, 185, 297n56
The West, American future in, 113
Western Federation of Miners (WFM): BMU and, 123, 127; Boyce's leadership of, 123, 126, 127, 209; membership of, 123–24. *See also* International Union of Mine, Mill, and Smelter Workers
White, William Allen, 254
Whyte, Alexander Frederick, 231
Williams, Raymond, 8; *Culture and Society*, 5; on social mobility, 43; on working-class neighborhoods, 35–36, 262
Wilson, Henry, 234; on Irish Bolshevism, 239

Wilson, Woodrow, 132, 201, 242; American imperialism of, 215; on American Revolution, 214; Anglo-Saxon race patriotism of, 213–14, 218, 231; animosity toward Irish America, 226; anticolonialism of, 219–20; on Bolshevism, 226; declaration of war, 217, 218–19; expansionism of, 215; "Final Address in Support of the League of Nations," 226; Fourteen Points of, 219–21; *A History of the American People*, 213, 215–16; on immigrants, 215–16; on the Irish, 212, 214–16, 219, 221, 224, 226–32, 302n11; Irish American belief in, 219–20; on Irish American disloyalty, 226; on Irish anti-Imperialism, 215; on Irish/Bolshevist link, 227; and Irish erraticism, 212; Irish Protestantism of, 213, 214; and League of Nations defeat, 231; and Lloyd George, 232; nativism of, 226; as Orangeman, 213; Protestant allies of, 230; racial beliefs of, 212–14, 226; response to Bolsheviks, 220; and sanctity of British Empire, 233; scare mongering by, 243; Scottish ancestry of, 213, 214; on self-determination, 219, 220, 227, 250; tour of 1919, 226; at Versailles Peace talks, 223–30; Walsh's discussions with, 227–30, 252; war against radicals, 212

Wolfe, Bertram, 91, 149

Women Pickets for the Enforcement of America's War Aims, boycott of British goods, 194

Woods, Robert A., 74

working class: chrono-illiteracy in, 106; under colonialism, 122; community patterns of, 95; control of production, 199; hereditary, 118; recognized members of, 118; self-awareness of, 118; transnational, 150

working class, American: "alien citizens," 97; complaints among, 60; diversity of, 97–98; versus employing class, 46; escape from, 42; eugenicist views on, 69; foreign-born, 279n23; heterogeneous, 86, 87; Irish dominance in, 223; in labor history, 85; links to Irish liberation, 150; multiculturalism of, 97, 259; native-born, 64; neighborhoods, 35–36; Northern, 58, 60; opportunities for, 60; participation in management, 198; permanent, 62; religious makeup of, 18; resistance to capitalism, 86, 255; resistance to socialism, 88; social class and, 60, 88, 97; Social Gospel reform movement and, 66–67; traditions of, 86, 261–62; understanding of Neal Deal, 260; wages, 198; as wage slaves, 60–63; "working-class interregnum" of, 265, 269

working class, English, 74, 94–101; Catholic Irish in, 98–104, 108; class consciousness in, 95–96; communities of, 95, 98; cultural superstructure of, 96–97; divide from employers, 97; under factory system, 96; Irish republicanism and, 218; life experiences of, 94; Methodism in, 103, 105; native-born, 97; notions of equality, 255; opposition to capitalism, 105; Protestant, 97, 100; revolutionary element in, 104–5; translation into capitalism, 96; village rights of, 255

working class, Irish Catholic: American radicals and, 161–62; among Northern workers, 58, 60; of Butte, 119–23; 125, 128, 132–33; clannishness of, 255; contrarian, 107; counterhegemonic, 112; cultural divergence from Protestants, 1–3, 10, 17–18, 56, 86, 92, 145; Debs's championing of, 78; disaffection from American system, 51; Easter Rising and, 133; effect on American capitalism, 268; free-spiritedness of, 89–90; insurgent elements in, 128; in interethnic working class, 259; Irish nationalism of, 121; job consciousness of, 119; learned identity of, 4; left-leaning, 133; in makeup of American working class, 99, 101; numbers of, 211; oppositional, 109–10; "personality as ecology" among, 265; reciprocity

working class, Irish Catholic (*continued*)
among, 255; regard for Marcus Daly, 125; on World War I, 123; rejection of American class structure, 149; social mobility and, 43–44; traditionalism of, 261–62; as victims of colonialism, 212; xenophobia of, 255. *See also* Irish Catholics

Workingman's Party, 62, 127

worldview, Irish Catholic: as disabling, 39; erraticism of, 50. *See also* culture, Irish American; Irishness

World War I: Anglo-Americanism in, 217–18; anti-Catholic agitation following, 230; armistice, 171; colonial annexations following, 232–33; copper production during, 141–42; imperialism following, 249; Irish Americans during, 132, 218, 219; Irish pro-German sentiment in, 132, 133, 141, 142, 287nn41–42; Irish propaganda during, 222; Irish rebellion and, 217; racial entente cordiale of, 219; registration of immigrants for, 137; Russia in, 220; US entry into, 128, 133, 138, 212, 217, 218–19; as war over empires, 233. *See also* Versailles Peace talks

Yankees: Irish becoming, 251; Irish Catholic, 20, 40, 41; prejudice against Irish Catholics, 29–36; social unconscious of, 30. *See also* Anglo Americans; Protestants

Yeats, William Butler, 246; on ancestral sorrows, 8, 21–22; on hunger striking, 109; on modernity, 249; on psychological autonomy, 178; on "work of Ireland," 179

Yorke, Fr. Peter, 20, 106, 227; on Irish Americans in wartime, 222–23; thanks to Bolsheviks, 222

DAVID M. EMMONS is a professor emeritus of history at the University of Montana. His books include *The Butte Irish: Class and Ethnicity in an American Mining Town, 1875–1925* and *Beyond the American Pale: The Irish in the West, 1845–1910.*

The University of Illinois Press
is a founding member of the
Association of University Presses.

University of Illinois Press
1325 South Oak Street
Champaign, IL 61820-6903
www.press.uillinois.edu